THE EDGE OF MOSBY'S SWORD

THE EDGE OF MOSBY'S SWORD

The Life of Confederate Colonel William Henry Chapman

Gordon B. Bonan

Southern Illinois University Press • Carbondale

Printed in the United States of America

First printed September 2009.

Library of Congress Cataloging-in-Publication Data
Bonan, Gordon B.
The edge of Mosby's sword : the life of Confederate Colonel William Henry Chapman / Gordon B. Bonan.
p. cm.
Includes bibliographical references and index.
ISBN-13: 978-0-8093-2932-8 (alk. paper)
ISBN-10: 0-8093-2932-8 (alk. paper)
1. Chapman, William Henry, 1840–1929. 2. Soldiers—Confederate States of America—Biography. 3. Guerrillas—Confederate States of America—Biography. 4. United States—History—Civil War, 1861–1865—Biography. 5. Mosby, John Singleton, 1833–1916. 6. United States. Internal Revenue Service—Officials and employees—Biography. I. Title.
E467.1.C48B66 2009
973.7092—dc22
[B] 2009002582

Printed on recycled paper ♲

SIU
Southern Illinois University System

To Alice Sampson Bonan (1929–2002)
and Frederic Paul Bonan Jr. (1928–2008)
for giving me a love of history

Contents

Illustrations

ACKNOWLEDGMENTS

My first memory of the Civil War was between the ages of nine and eleven while living in Wallingford, Connecticut. The rolling hills, meadows, and forests of the Choate School, where my family lived at the time, were my Virginia, which I tenaciously defended against Northern aggression with my sword, pistol, and battle flag. It was a memory born of my mother and her family—children, grandchildren, and great-grandchildren of Lt. Col. William Henry Chapman of Mosby's Rangers. The tales of his life that I heard as a youth shaped my own life. Some years later, when the time came to go to college, there was but one choice—Charlottesville, the University of Virginia. I was a New England Yankee and needed to experience the South for myself, to learn its customs and history directly. I eventually spent eight years in Charlottesville.

This story of William Chapman is written a generation too late. My mother, her sisters and brother, and her cousins grew up surrounded by the Chapman children and grandchildren. Her mother, Josephine Brooking Sampson (1892–1959), and grandmother, Esther Foote "Hettie" Chapman Brooking (1867–1947), were her link to the past. My mother heard the stories of Mosby's Rangers directly. I never had the chance to meet these two women. And now, my mother, her brother and sisters, and others of her generation from whom I learned of Chapman and Mosby's Rangers have passed away and cannot partake in reading of the man they had so admired.

Chapman's story could not have been completed without the support, efforts, and contribution of several family members. Archer Ellis Hansen, my mother's cousin, and her nephew Ned Fanfani graciously supplied Chapman family letters written over the period 1875–1919. Archer also provided numerous photographs, personal memorabilia, and oral histories. Carolyn Russell and her husband, Chris Russell (whose father was a cousin of my mother), provided wartime letters, photographs, and postwar correspondence, including Chapman's ledger book for the period 1886–1905. Max Roha and his wife, Mary Chapman Roha (Chapman's granddaughter), reconstructed the Chapman and Jeffries families; Max kindly gave me that genealogy. This led to the published genealogies upon which their research was based and also to census records. Ritchie Sampson, my mother's brother, too, provided family photographs and correspondence.

The story of William Chapman could not be told without the effort of many others. I am indebted to Jeffry Wert, Hugh Keen and Horace Mewborn, and James Ramage for their prior histories of Mosby's Rangers. James Ramage encouraged me at a critical point to tell Chapman's story. Horace Mewborn kindly read the material on Mosby's Rangers and offered his insights to ranger history. A biography of William Chapman would not be complete without a biography of his brother Sam Chapman. For that, I am indebted to Peter Brown. His book, given to me by my uncle Ritchie Sampson on a cold, wintry day in 2002 at Gordonsville, Virginia, following my mother's funeral, reminded me of family history, eased my grief, and impelled me to write this biography of William Chapman. Most important, though, are Sylvia Frank Rodrigue and her colleagues at Southern Illinois University Press, for seeing something in this story worth telling, encouraging and nurturing me with my writing, and diligently working to improve the manuscript. I am also indebted to John Wilson, for his meticulous copyediting.

I could not have written this book without the help of Amie, who supported me as I explored my past, read every page of the manuscript, and endured the sufferings of being married to a would-be historian. Thomas, Alice, and David, as they studied the Civil War in elementary school, reminded me of our shared past. Their interest allowed me to find the words to tell the story of William Chapman. It is a story more complex and richer than the simple war hero of my youth.

THE EDGE OF MOSBY'S SWORD

1 | A Man's Courage

The 43rd Battalion Virginia Cavalry was one of the famed Southern cavalry units of the Civil War. Its commander, Col. John Singleton Mosby, was an astute military tactician, a pugnacious warrior, and a dashing cavalier. His daring exploits rivaled those of his mentor, Gen. James Ewell Brown "Jeb" Stuart. Under Mosby's leadership, this band of a few hundred partisan rangers instilled fear and confusion with their quick, precise raids against the supply lines of the Union army. Operating from Fauquier and Loudoun Counties in northern Virginia, they would appear from nowhere in small bands to strike against much larger opposing forces, only to seemingly vanish in the mist, leaving Federal soldiers dazed and demoralized while Mosby's Rangers exulted in yet another victory.

The rangers never fought in the grand campaigns and battles of the Army of Northern Virginia, but they accomplished the limited tactical goals of guerilla warfare. With a force of fewer than 400 men at any one time, Mosby's Rangers killed, wounded, or captured some 2,900 Federal soldiers. Their raids diverted troops from the front to guard the rear and supply lines. Their actions confounded Union generals, including Ulysses S. Grant, Philip Sheridan, and George Custer. The psychological effect of capturing soldiers, sutler wagons, and over 3,500 horses and mules lifted the spirits of a war-weary Virginia. Not surprisingly, Northern newspapers demonized the rangers and vilified their exploits while Southern papers glorified these heroes of the Confederacy.[1]

Much has been written about Mosby. Proud, confident of his abilities, and well aware of the role he played in history, Mosby left a prolific record of writings for historians. Even as the war drew to a close, he collaborated with John Scott to publish a history of the rangers. Some of the ordinary soldiers who served with Mosby, aware, too, of their place in history, also provided accounts of their exploits—men named J. Marshall Crawford, Aristides Monteiro, James Williamson, John Munson, and John Alexander. Less is known about Mosby's officers—Lt. Col. William Henry Chapman, Maj. Adolphus Richards, and company commanders James Foster, Thomas Turner, William Smith, Robert Walker, Richard Montjoy, Alfred Glascock, Samuel Chapman, Walter Frankland, and Thomas Richards. Their exploits fill the pages of the history of Mosby's Rangers, but unlike their prolific commander, they left little written legacy.[2]

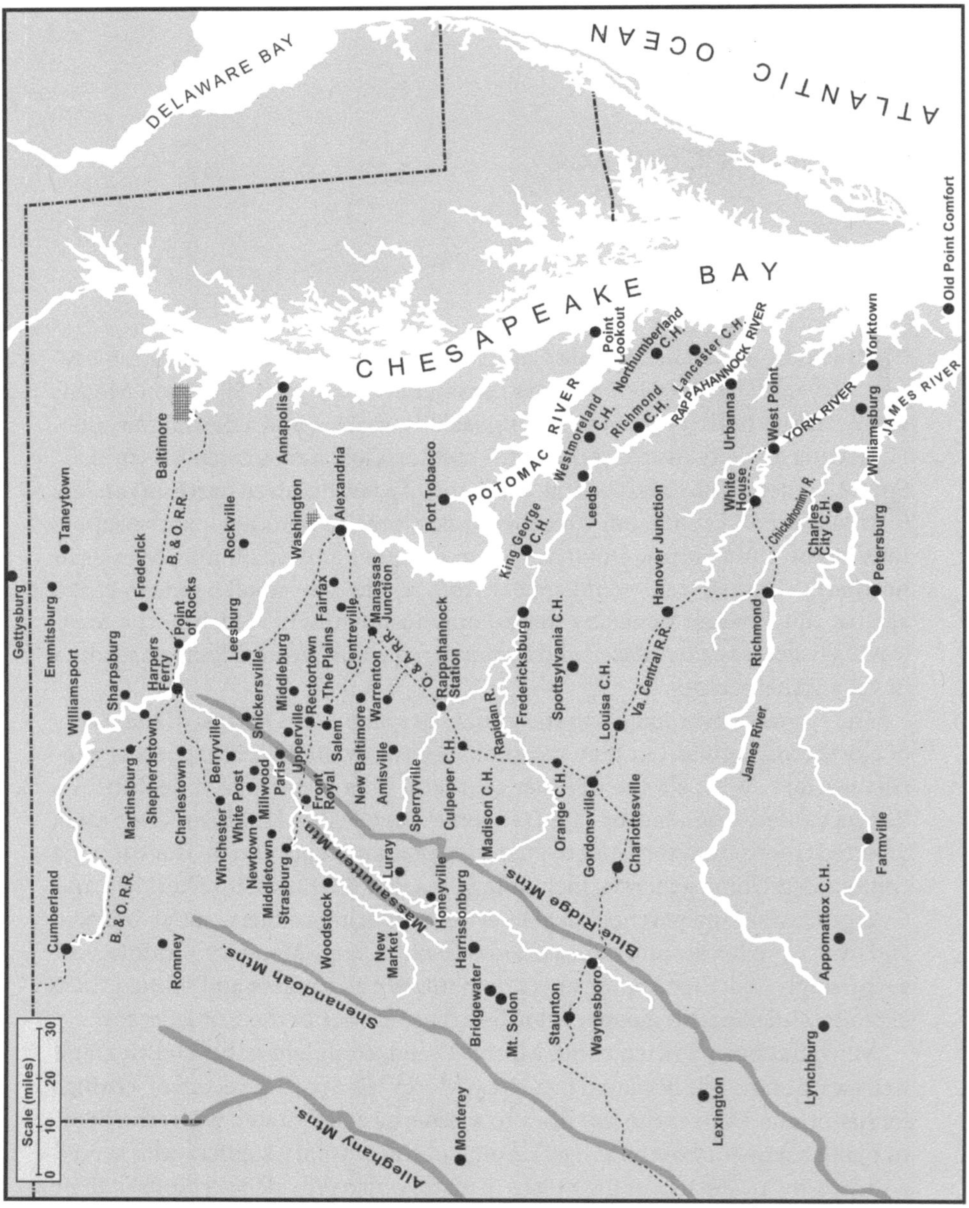

Map 1. Virginia and Maryland, 1862. From a map Chapman carried during the war (Virginia Historical Society).

One officer in particular is an enigma. Mosby's writings and all the other histories of the rangers are replete with references to William Henry Chapman, second in command. Yet the details of his life are largely unknown, limited to a few facts or brief sentences—often in error—that summarize his service record as part of larger such compilations.[3]

Chapman stood five feet ten inches tall with dark hair and dark eyes. He sported a long, dark beard as a young lieutenant in the Confederate artillery service and continued to wear a flowing beard throughout his life. Aristides Monteiro, surgeon in Mosby's command at the end of the war, described Chapman as a quiet, modest man, reserved in demeanor, reticent to boast. When called upon at the first postwar reunion of rangers to give a speech, Chapman acknowledged that "there were other tests of a man's courage than shot and shell and one of those was making a speech." Ranger John Munson once asked Chapman to tell of the fight at Miskel's farm, but Chapman's tale left Munson disappointed: "He had nothing to say about his own behavior, and I was forced to hear it from others." Chapman was not one of the dandies found among Mosby's Rangers. He did not wear a plumed hat or tall leather cavalry boots, as did many rangers. Nor did he dress in a stylish, colorful uniform with flowing cape. Rather, his leadership came from quiet confidence and conspicuous action.[4]

As a twenty-year-old student at the University of Virginia, Chapman saved the Rotunda, the university's signature building, from destruction by fire. As a twenty-two-year-old captain commanding the Dixie Artillery during the battle of Second Manassas, he laid down a devastating artillery barrage upon advancing Federal infantrymen and helped turn the tide of battle in favor of the Confederates. He spent the last two years of the war in northern Virginia as a partisan ranger with Mosby. The acclaim he earned as a cavalryman could scarcely have been predicted from the obscurity he endured as an artillerist. At the age of twenty-three, he commanded Company C of Mosby's Rangers. He soon became Mosby's trusted lieutenant, second in command, rising to the rank of lieutenant colonel when only twenty-four years old. In "Mosby's Confederacy," savage partisan warfare and its requisite counter-guerilla reprisals subsumed abstract debating points of states' rights and Southern nationalism. Yet when the war ended, when Mosby could not bring himself to surrender, Chapman accepted defeat with dignity and led the negotiations with the victorious Federal army that had so feared and yet so ruthlessly pursued the rangers. A meeting to negotiate terms of surrender left Union general Winfield Hancock favorably impressed, and he informed Secretary of War Edwin Stanton that Chapman "is as important as Mosby, and from conversation had with him I think he will be valuable to the Government hereafter."[5]

Chapman, like Mosby, spent the remaining sixty-four years of his life rebuilding the new South while preserving the memory and valor of the Confederate soldier. He embraced the Republican Party, and with Mosby's influence he befriended Presidents Ulysses S. Grant and Rutherford Hayes and found employment in the federal government. When Hayes needed a strong man that Southerners would respect to enforce the laws, he turned to Chapman, who faithfully served in that role for over thirty years as a revenue agent for the Internal Revenue Service. Housed in Atlanta during the 1880s and 1890s, the former Confederate went to work enforcing federal law for a government led by the Republican Party. There, he battled Southern corruption and the rise of the Ku Klux Klan. He was wounded, not in defense of his Southern homeland during the Civil War, but as a Republican administering federal law in the South. The tenacity with which he used his considerable energy and moral courage to fight corruption in the region ultimately hindered his career and thwarted his professional advancement.

Chapman was not typical of field officers in the Army of Northern Virginia. The median age at appointment was thirty years old; fewer than one in five was younger than twenty-four. Prewar political experience was a good path to attain an officer's commission; 40 percent practiced law or politics before the war. Chapman's education at the University of Virginia was important. Slightly more than one-third of field officers attended the Virginia Military Institute (18 percent) or the University of Virginia (17 percent) and close to one-half studied at other Virginia colleges. One fellow officer who also attended the University of Virginia was Mosby. Thirty percent of field officers attended military schools, though less than 10 percent were professional soldiers. After the war, 39 percent found careers as politicians at the state or national level; 9 percent became lawyers or judges. Fewer than 2 percent were civil servants for the United States government. About one-quarter of the men who attained the rank of field officer died during the war in battle or from accidents or disease. Chapman lived a long life, well past the year 1898, by which time one-half of his fellow field officers had passed away. When he died in 1929, only one-half of 1 percent of field officers still lived. History has not been kind to these field officers of the Confederacy, and most have long since been forgotten.[6]

It is easy to romanticize the Civil War era, especially now, several generations removed from the conflict and turmoil. Yet to those who fought its battles, the war was far from glamorous. Mosby himself believed that "war loses a great deal of its romance after a soldier has seen his first battle." "It is a classical maxim," he observed, "that it is sweet and becoming to die for one's country; but whoever has seen the horrors of a battle-field feels that it is far sweeter to live for it."[7]

Mosby and his rangers, lords of their own Confederacy, have been especially susceptible to romantic idealization as chivalrous Southern cavaliers, but the real life of a ranger and of those who protected him was unsettling, the future uncertain, death and destruction at hand with hardly a moment's notice. A sudden engagement with Federal soldiers could easily result in gruesome wounds, instant death, summary execution, or perhaps even worse—imprisonment in one of the wretched camps. Northern troopers killed, wounded, or captured some 40 percent of the men who rode with Mosby over the course of the war. Their bullets felled Mosby three times and Chapman's brother Sam, a ranger compatriot, twice. Company commanders William Smith, Richard Montjoy, and Thomas Turner died in battle. A Federal patrol captured James Foster two days after he received command of Company A, and he spent the remainder of the war rotting in prison. For civilians in "Mosby's Confederacy," a Federal scouting party might mean summary arrest, theft of valuables, destruction of property, and loss of livelihood.[8]

Chapman emerged from the war unscathed physically, but the relentless bloodletting of partisan combat and the strain of Northern reprisals drew a toll mentally. The nature of partisan warfare, existing and operating behind enemy lines and housing with civilians, promoted atrocities against combatants and civilians alike. His raids preyed upon supply wagons and soldiers in the enemy rear. He ruthlessly destroyed enemy patrols and mercilessly shot down Northern marauders. Federal troopers, unable to counter the Confederate rangers, sometimes exacted their revenge on civilians. Chapman succumbed to the inhumanity of this warfare and took up the battle cry "No quarter, no quarter today!" in a cycle of pillaging, house burning, hanging, and execution in the summer and fall of 1864.

We cannot today fully understand the motivation of these soldiers, what principles and beliefs sustained them through four years of conflict, although surely patriotism, ideology, and concepts of duty and honor contributed to their service. As someone born to wealth gained from the labor of slaves, Chapman's service to the Confederacy was likely in defense of the homeland and the mores to which he was reared; it was the burden expected of an educated young Virginian. The radical abolitionists and secessionists could argue the evils or righteousness of slavery as radicals are wont to do; and now, with a century and a half of hindsight, the institution of slavery is particularly peculiar. But in 1861 it represented the economic and social foundations of Southern society.[9]

History has not been kind to the Confederate soldier. The Confederate battle flag, with its blue St. Andrew's cross in a field of red, is today not equated with the military creed of duty, honor, and country under which so many Southerners fell. Segregationists long ago usurped the flag, and it now represents racism, hatred, and oppression. Mosby understood this battle for the legacy of the Southern soldier. "Soldiers fight for their country—right or wrong," he wrote Sam Chapman. "Let Southern soldiers get rid of the idea that their honor rests on the right of secession; or the righteousness of the pro-slavery cause. I prefer to let its ghastly memories pass away; but I know that the memory of the men who followed me will never die."[10]

In an age when defenders of the Confederacy are often zealots preserving not the memory of their ancestors but rather the divisiveness of that long-ago era, Chapman's life story provides a different legacy. He aspired to be an officer and achieved that status as an artillerist, though the fame he sought eluded him. He found that acclaim riding with Mosby, but the adventure of partisan raids on picket posts and wagon trains gave way to the horrors of man's savagery as combatants raised the "black flag" in an escalating cycle of vengeance and retaliation. Yet when the war ended and the cause was lost, Chapman, like Mosby, resumed being a citizen of the United States, unashamed of his service to the Confederacy and proud of his service to the federal government.

Chapman's life is a story of nationalism and reconciliation; liberty and slavery; chivalry and vengeance; honor and shame—contradictions found in the rise and fall of the Confederacy. His is a story of the exuberance and certainty of youth, transformed by the grimness of war, renewed in defeat, who with the maturity of age set out to rebuild that which he had sought to destroy as a young man. That we cannot now fully understand what sustained men and women through four years of civil war is a testament to the strength of our Union and the melded nation we have become; that the Confederate battle flag is a symbol of racism and hatred is a reminder that the divisiveness of one and a half centuries past has still not been overcome.

2 | Liberty and Union

William Henry Chapman was born to well-established families who had accumulated ample wealth, land, and slaves along the eastern and western flanks of the Blue Ridge Mountains of Virginia in the one hundred or so years since his forebears had settled in colonial America. His mother, Elizabeth Forrer Chapman, was two months shy of twenty-nine years old when she bore her second son. She was the granddaughter of the Swiss immigrant Christian Forrer, was raised in the town of Luray, and returned there to raise her own family after a brief foray across the Blue Ridge Mountains to Madison County. His father, William Allen Chapman, was thirty-two years old at the time of Chapman's birth, a native of Madison County, and a farmer. Chapman was brought up in a family and a community that accepted slavery as part of the norms of society. He came of age in an era when slavery, states' rights, and Southern independence dominated political discourse. Family circumstances and the events of his childhood undoubtedly conditioned him for war.

Christian Forrer had arrived in colonial America from Switzerland at the age of seventeen with his twenty-five-year-old sister, Christina, and twenty-year-old brother, Daniel. Their parents had died when Christian was a child, and the three Swiss emigrants left their homeland in 1754 for the frontiers of America. They settled in Lancaster County, Pennsylvania, where Christian successfully plied his trade as a clockmaker. He married Elizabeth Kendrick six years after settling in Pennsylvania, and they had three sons (Henry, Daniel, and Christian) born between 1761 and 1765 and later a fourth, Samuel, born in 1773. Christian died in 1783 at the age of forty-six. The family remained in Lancaster County for some years, and Elizabeth remarried, but after she being widowed a second time in 1792, she and her sons Henry, Christian, and Samuel moved to Virginia. They joined thousands of other immigrant men, women, and children on the Great Philadelphia Wagon Road, traveling by foot, horse, and wagon from Pennsylvania to the fertile farmland of the Shenandoah Valley.[1]

The Forrers settled in a region of the eastern Shenandoah Valley known as the Page, or Luray, Valley. This narrow valley is separated from the main valley by Massanutten Mountain, a wide ridge located between Front Royal and Strasburg in the north and extending some fifty miles southwest to Harrisonburg.

To the west of the mountain, the main valley extends to the Allegheny Mountains and is drained by the North Fork of the Shenandoah River. To the east, between Massanutten Mountain and the Blue Ridge Mountains, lies the Page Valley along the South Fork of the Shenandoah River. Here, the meandering Shenandoah River and Hawksbill Creek, a large branch of the Shenandoah, create a rolling topography of wide, fertile farmlands at elevations of 800–1,000 feet. From this river bottomland, the Blue Ridge Mountains rise precipitously to 4,000 feet or more. Massanutten Mountain is lower, with peaks rising to more than 2,500 feet. The early settlers from Pennsylvania, of Swiss, Scottish, Irish, and German descent, built a rich agricultural community dotted with sawmills and flourmills powered by flowing streams, as well as tanneries, forges, foundries, and furnaces.[2]

Samuel and Christian purchased a large farm just south of present-day Luray in an area known as Mundellsville. At the time, it was the largest settlement, with a few mills, a tannery, a blacksmith shop, and several houses. Their farm, acquired in 1795, consisted of 1,400 acres of land on Hawksbill Creek and Dry Run. The brothers divided up the farm in 1807 and worked the land separately. However, Christian Forrer's family did not permanently settle in Virginia. His oldest son, Samuel, moved to Ohio in 1817 and became a well-known civil engineer, instrumental in early surveys of the state and principal engineer for the Miami and Erie Canal. In 1828 the sixty-three-year-old Christian uprooted his family to join his son in Ohio.[3]

His brother Samuel married Catherine Ebersole shortly after moving to Virginia, and they had six children. They lived in a log house constructed by the original landowners and occupied by the Forrers when they purchased the farm. Samuel's family remained in Luray and became leading citizens of Page Valley. Samuel was a successful farmer and entrepreneur and grew quite wealthy. In addition to running his farm, he owned or operated a mill, tan yard, distillery, sawmill, and hotel. His youngest child, Elizabeth, born in 1811, was William Chapman's mother.[4]

The following year, 1812, the Town of Luray was established. Its early growth and settlement arose due to its location at the crossroads of major travel routes. At that time, Page Valley was part of Shenandoah County. However, to travel to the county seat at Woodstock required crossing Massanutten Mountain. The difficulty and inconvenience of this journey led to the establishment of Page County in 1831, with Luray designated the county seat. A history of Virginia published in 1845 described Luray as consisting of several mercantile stores, two or three churches, and a population of 500. Its location as a transportation hub contributed to a vibrant economy. The Luray and Front Royal turnpike ran from Front Royal southwest along the South Fork of the Shenandoah River to Luray, continuing up the Page Valley to Waynesboro. The New Market and Sperryville turnpike heading east passed through Luray, crossing Thornton's

Gap in the Blue Ridge Mountains to Sperryville. Heading west from Luray, the turnpike crossed Massanutten Mountain to New Market. The New Market and Gordonsville turnpike crossed the Blue Ridge near Stanley through Fisher's Gap, just north of Milam's Gap.[5]

As the town of Luray prospered, so, too, did the Forrer family. In 1825 Samuel built a large brick house just south of Luray along Hawksbill Creek. The two-story home contained fourteen rooms, each with a fireplace, and two large halls. One large room, forty-eight feet long, built to accommodate religious meetings, covered the entire south side of the house on the first floor. A kitchen, dining room, wine cellar, and food pantry filled a large basement.[6]

Elizabeth's older brothers Daniel and Henry Forrer became wealthy industrialists. The region supported a thriving iron industry, and the brothers acquired an iron furnace, along with over 1,000 acres of surrounding land, that became known as the Shenandoah Ironworks, located in southern Page County at the present-day town of Shenandoah. Henry and Daniel lived there for the next several years. Then, in 1843, after inheriting part of the ironworks owned by his wife's father, Daniel moved with his family and Henry up the Shenandoah Valley to the Mossy Creek Ironworks in northern Augusta County near the present-day town of Mt. Solon. By the late 1850s, Daniel and Henry also owned or operated several other furnaces. These ironworks would supply the Confederacy with materials during the war, and iron from one of their furnaces would find its way to the ironclad C.S.S. *Virginia*. With an estate valued at $127,000 in 1860, Henry was one of the wealthiest of Page County's landowners.[7]

The Chapman family also possessed considerable wealth and land, with roots extending to colonial Virginia. Chapman's great-great-grandfather John Chapman purchased 3,540 pounds of tobacco and 295 acres of land in St. George Parish, Spotsylvania County, in 1729 and acquired an additional 200 acres in 1753. He had six children by his first wife, all born between 1739 and 1754. Within the next six years, his wife died, and he married Mary Allen (born 1739), who bore him several more children. Upon his death in 1775, John Chapman's estate included 1,003 acres of land in Spotsylvania County, more than 300 acres in Orange County, and fourteen slaves.[8]

John Chapman's first son, William, was born in 1739. In 1777, William resided in Culpeper County, which at the time included present-day Madison County. His second wife, Mary Buford, gave birth to six children—Elizabeth, William Allen, Thomas, Judith, Anne, and Simeon. Their family home was located on Quaker Run, two miles west of present-day Criglersville in Madison County. The original rectangular structure consisted of six rooms each with fireplaces, two inside chimneys made from stone, and a large, English-style basement with walls of stone. A small stone springhouse provided water. William Chapman contributed to Madison County civic affairs. He was one of several justices appointed to the first county court in 1793 after Madison County was cleaved from

Culpeper County. He also served as an overseer of local roads. At the time of his death around 1802, William Chapman owned more than 1,000 acres of land.[9]

William Allen Chapman, the oldest son (born 1777) and William Henry Chapman's grandfather, married Catherine Gaines in 1799. Four children were born from this marriage; the youngest, William Allen Chapman Jr. (Chapman's father), was born in 1808. After the death of their father, the Chapman land was divided up, and William Allen Chapman Sr. and his brothers became wealthy landowners, farmers, and slaveholders in Madison County. William Allen received a tract of land containing the family home on Quaker Run. In 1810, he possessed 10 slaves and his brothers Thomas and Simeon owned 12 and 16 slaves, respectively. In 1820 William Allen, Thomas, Simeon, and their mother, Mary, were each operating farms in Madison County. At that time, William Allen owned 7 male and 5 female slaves. Thomas and Simeon had 20 and 23 slaves, respectively; and Mary, 12. Fifteen male slaves (7 under the age of ten) and 10 female slaves labored on William Allen's farm in 1830.[10]

At some point, William Allen Chapman Jr. crossed the Blue Ridge Mountains into Page County and met Elizabeth Forrer. They married on 27 November 1837. The couple initially resided in the spacious brick house built by Elizabeth's father, who had died the previous year. It was there that their first son, Samuel Forrer Chapman, was born in 1838. Later, the family moved across the Blue Ridge to Madison County for a brief period. Their second son, William Henry Chapman, was born twenty months after his older brother, on 17 April 1840, at the family home on Quaker Run. There, William Allen lived with his wife, Elizabeth, their two sons, and his sixty-three-year-old father. Madison County relied heavily on slave labor (slaves comprised more than half the county population in 1840), and Chapman's father was no exception. He farmed his land with 20 slaves—3 boys and 2 girls under the age of ten; 3 boys and 3 girls between the ages of ten and twenty-four; 3 women twenty-four to thirty-six years old; and 5 men and 1 woman thirty-six to fifty-five years old.[11]

Sometime thereafter, perhaps after the death of his father in 1841, William Allen Chapman and family yet again crossed the Blue Ridge Mountains to settle near Luray. Eight more children (five sons and three daughters) were born into the Chapman family between 1842 and 1854—Edmund Gaines, Hannah Catherine (Kate), Mary Elizabeth (Bettie), Margaret Ann (Annie), John Newton, James Harvey, George Thomas, and Andrew Jackson. All except James, who died at thirteen months, would live full, long, and prosperous lives. Many years later, their obituaries would describe the Chapmans as "illustrious for physical and moral courage," renowned in Luray for their "courage and tenacity of purpose," civic service, and dedicated contributions to the Luray Baptist community. Samuel, William, and Edmund would serve in the Confederate army. Their brother John, too young to serve in the war, would become sheriff of Page County from 1888 to 1892. George would be remembered as an honored merchant "closely identified with the business, social, and church life of Luray for a half century."[12]

William Allen Chapman was prosperous and farmed a large tract of land located north of Luray along Hawksbill Creek. His real estate was valued at $14,000 in 1850, among the wealthier landowners in Page County. The farm consisted of 280 acres of improved land and 98 acres of unimproved land. Three female slaves between the ages of eleven and forty-six and eight male slaves ranging in age from four to fifty-five labored on the farm. Livestock that year included 9 horses, 9 milk cows, 4 working oxen, 20 cattle, 30 sheep, and 62 swine. The Chapmans grew wheat, corn, oats, and hay, along with potatoes and sweet potatoes, and produced 300 pounds of butter and 100 pounds of cheese. The Chapman house was originally the home of Peter Ruffner, one of the first settlers in Luray. It was a two-story brick house, forty-two feet by forty-seven feet, with four chimneys and eight fireplaces. The walls were twelve inches thick. Its large rooms had ceilings ten feet high. A ten-foot-wide hall extended through the house. An English-style basement kitchen, dining area, and servant quarters extended under the length of the house.[13]

By 1860 William Allen Chapman's wealth had increased to $20,000 in real estate and $11,000 personal property, among the richest 1 percent of county households. The farm had grown by 82 acres, and Chapman had 7 male slaves ranging in age from four to sixty-two and 4 female slaves aged nine to thirty-four. One slave, Evelina, was baptized into the family faith, at the Luray Baptist Church, in 1858. Seven years later, several African American members of the Baptist church would be expelled for "having left their homes and gone to the Yankees and not returned." Among them was Evelina. Within two years, during the summer of 1862, Federal soldiers would enter Page County and confiscate horses, livestock, and food. A number of slaves ran away. Soldiers forcibly detained men and made them swear an oath of allegiance to secure their release. The Chapmans "suffered very much," a neighbor reported.[14]

Slaves comprised about 10 percent of the Page County population, a low percentage compared with counties east of the Blue Ridge Mountains, and slave ownership was concentrated in the hands of a few individuals. In 1840, 189 slaveholders owned 781 slaves, for an average, or mean, of 4 slaves per owner; but the median was 2, meaning roughly half of the slaveholders had more than 2 slaves and half had less. Among slaveholders, 16 of them (8 percent), each with 10 or more slaves, held 36 percent of the slave population (278 slaves). One family, the Blackfords, possessed 68 slaves who worked an iron furnace. The Forrers used 31 slaves in their ironworks. The slave population increased to 957 and slaveholders to 229 in 1850, when 24 slaveholders (10 percent) had 10 or more slaves and held 39 percent of the slave population (373 slaves). Henry Forrer was the leading slaveholder, with 77 slaves. By 1860 the slave population had dropped to 850 slaves owned by 199 slaveholders. At that time, 23 slaveholders (12 percent) had 10 or more slaves and held 36 percent of the slave population (302 slaves). William Allen Chapman was among the few people with 10 or more slaves.[15]

During the 1856–57 academic year, William Henry Chapman attended the Mossy Creek Academy in Augusta County. The academy had grown out of a school that Daniel Forrer, Chapman's uncle, had organized at his Mossy Creek home for his six children and for Henrietta and Judah Forrer, children of his brother Christian, who died in 1846. The instructor was a young Jedediah Hotchkiss, who would gain fame as topographical engineer and mapmaker for Stonewall Jackson during the Civil War. Hotchkiss began instructing the eight Forrer cousins in November 1847. In 1850 eleven-year-old Samuel Forrer Chapman arrived at the Mossy Creek home of his uncle for instruction during the five-month session from January to June.[16]

Schooling under the tutelage of Hotchkiss was so successful that the Mossy Creek community invested in building a larger school, and the Mossy Creek Academy opened in 1854. The academy featured a large (forty-three feet by sixty feet), multistory, brick building built at a cost of $4,000. The lower level held a main classroom for instruction, a library, and a laboratory for chemistry experiments. A large public hall and an additional classroom occupied the upper level. An observatory capped the roof of the building. The campus included a boardinghouse with space for fifty students located at the base of the hill below the main building, overlooking a lake formed by a mill dam. The curriculum prepared students either for a career in education or for classes at the University of Virginia and other colleges. Hotchkiss remained at the academy until the close of the 1856–57 session, when he resigned and moved up the Shenandoah Valley to organize another school.[17]

The 1856–57 term began in early September and continued through June, with a two-week break for Christmas. Hotchkiss instructed students in languages and mathematics, Sara Hotchkiss, his wife, tutored them in modern languages, and J. T. Brodt taught the natural sciences. Rules prohibited card playing, possessing tobacco, alcohol, or firearms, reading novels, and using profane language. Students attended regular religious services held every morning in the chapel as well as church on Sunday. Friday afternoon brought required exercises in composition and public speaking for all students. Friday afternoon was also the time for weekly seminars on the natural sciences by regular instructors or invited speakers. Sixty-six students (55 boys and 11 girls) enrolled in academic departments. Forty-four students (29 boys and 15 girls) enrolled in the primary department. Chapman attended the academic departments, which offered instruction in ancient languages, modern languages, mathematics, natural sciences, and common English. He took classes in all but one of these departments, ancient languages, and was one of only ten students to study in four of the academic departments.[18]

The academy held its semiannual exhibition featuring student recitations, singing, and theatrical productions on 19 December 1856 in the large public hall, which overflowed with parents, family, and friends. Chapman played the showman P. T. Barnum in an original comedy performed with several other students. He was also one of thirty-nine students engaged in public speaking. Few students addressed the issue of secession, though there was an oration entitled "Union Linked with Liberty" and two other recitations of speeches by Daniel Webster on "responsibility of the American citizen" and "peaceable secession." Chapman tackled the political and social tempest of secession directly when he recited a speech on "liberty and Union" that had been given before the U.S. Senate by Daniel Webster on 26 January 1830. The sixteen-year-old boy stood in the crowded hall and spoke these words:

> I have not allowed myself, Sir, to look beyond the Union, to see what might lie hidden in the dark recess behind. I have not coolly weighed the chances of preserving liberty when the bonds that unite us together shall be broken asunder. I have not accustomed myself to hang over the precipice of disunion, to see whether, with my short sight, I can fathom the depth of the abyss below; nor could I regard him as a safe counsellor in the affairs of this government, whose thoughts should be mainly bent on considering, not how the Union may be best preserved, but how tolerable might be the condition of the people when it should be broken up and destroyed. While the Union lasts, we have high, exciting, gratifying prospects spread out before us, for us and our children. Beyond that I seek not to penetrate the veil. God grant that, in my day, at least, that curtain may not rise! God grant that on my vision never may be opened what lies behind! When my eyes shall be turned to behold for the last time the sun in heaven, may I not see him shining on the broken and dishonored fragments of a once glorious Union; on States dissevered, discordant, belligerent; on a land rent with civil feuds, or drenched, it may be, in fraternal blood! Let their last feeble and lingering glance rather behold the gorgeous ensign of the republic, now known and honored throughout the earth, still full high advanced, its arms and trophies streaming in their original lustre, not a stripe erased or polluted, nor a single star obscured, bearing for its motto, no such miserable interrogatory as "What is all this worth?" nor those other words of delusion and folly, "Liberty first and Union afterwards"; but everywhere, spread all over in characters of living light, blazing on all its ample folds, as they float over the sea and over the land, and in every wind under the whole heavens, that other sentiment, dear to every true American heart,—Liberty *and* Union, now and for ever, one and inseparable![19]

Webster's speech was an outgrowth of sectional conflict in the late 1820s and early 1830s. A high tariff passed by Congress to help Northern manufacturers compete with foreign goods was thought to hurt the Southern economy. John Calhoun of South Carolina strongly opposed this interference by the federal government. Instead, he advanced the doctrine of *nullification* and the notion of *states' rights*, which privileged the rights of states over the power of the federal government, including the right of a state to defy an act of Congress. In 1830 Congress bitterly debated nullification, and Daniel Webster, then a senator from Massachusetts, gained oratorical fame from his debate with Senator Robert Hayne of South Carolina in which he defended a strong federal government and rejected the concept of nullification. Sectional disputes again arose in the 1840s and 1850s over the issue of slavery in the new territories.[20]

As these uncontrollable political events rushed toward a tumultuous, catastrophic culmination, Chapman embarked on a new stage of his life. Like his brother Sam, who attended Richmond College, Chapman was drawn away from Luray by higher education. In the fall of 1859, at the age of nineteen, Chapman made the journey east over the Blue Ridge Mountains to Charlottesville to begin two years of study at the University of Virginia. There, the political discourse of states' rights and secession took on new meaning.[21]

Chapman attended the thirty-sixth (1859–60) and thirty-seventh (1860–61) sessions of the University of Virginia, where he studied mathematics, moral philosophy, chemistry, physics, and modern languages. Slightly over 600 students, all white males at least sixteen years old, attended the university, more than half from Virginia and almost all from Southern states.[22]

Chapman left a notable mark at the University of Virginia one morning in March 1861. The centerpiece of Thomas Jefferson's academic village is a long, rectangular, terraced green space known as the Lawn. A row of contiguous rooms connected by inward-facing colonnaded walkways flanks each length of the Lawn, providing dormitories for students, residences for faculty, and classrooms for instruction. The domed Rotunda, modeled after the Roman Pantheon, stands at the head of the Lawn and, at that time, housed classrooms and a library. On that spring morning, Chapman was in the library when he heard someone cry, "Fire!" Plumbers working atop the building had dropped burning coal on the roof. Chapman ran to the upper gallery and tried to break open a door leading to the roof of the Rotunda. The librarian shortly arrived with the key to the door, and Chapman climbed out onto the roof.[23]

Chapman slid down the roof to its eaves, where the flames were visible. Chemistry professor Socrates Maupin and several students gathered on the roof and lowered buckets of water to Chapman. In a precarious position, braced only by using a gutter along the eaves as a foothold, Chapman extinguished the exposed flames and then cut away part of the woodwork to reach smoldering embers. Fearing Chapman's tenuous foothold, Maupin lowered a rope, which Chapman secured around himself while Maupin and students held the other end. Chapman's labors had left him exhausted, and the support of the rope provided much comfort. Soon, another student slid down and relieved the fatigued Chapman.[24]

Chapman's efforts that morning quickly extinguished the fire and saved the university's signature building from serious damage. That afternoon, Maupin, who as faculty chairman also oversaw management of the university, extended a special resolution commending Chapman for his "prompt and efficient services." The leadership qualities that would serve Chapman well in war—readiness to take quick, decisive action; ability to inspire and command men—were already present.[25]

While Chapman attended the University of Virginia, the dominant talk was likely politics and secession. John Brown's seizure of the arsenal at Harpers Ferry on 16 October 1859 inflamed Virginians. For weeks afterwards, rumors abounded of slave uprisings and armed abolitionists invading Virginia. Volunteer militia companies organized throughout the state to counter the threat. A vigilance committee formed in Page County to guard against abolitionists. On the afternoon of 21 November, university students, after several eloquent and patriotic speeches, unanimously offered the services of the entire student body to the governor. Secessionist rhetoric swelled, and students in the university's literary societies debated in January 1860 whether a state had the right to secede. The verdict, as more and more Southerners were concluding, was in the affirmative.[26]

Histories of the University of Virginia written long after the passions of the era had ebbed claimed that the faculty separated their personal views on secession from their roles as instructors. However, one Virginia newspaper, Charleston's *Kanawha Valley Star,* described the university in 1859 as a proponent of Southern nationalism, instructing students in "devotion to Southern rights, Southern institutions, Southern manners, and Southern chivalry." Two professors were particularly vocal supporters of secession.[27]

Albert Bledsoe, who taught Chapman mathematics, would later serve as assistant secretary of war in the Confederate government. Bledsoe was a strong advocate of Southern nationalism, saw secession as a constitutional right and slavery as a moral obligation, and often interrupted his lectures with discussions of states' rights. In an essay published in 1856, Bledsoe claimed that "the institution of slavery, as it exists among us at the South, is founded in political justice, is in accordance with the will of God and the designs of his providence, and is conducive to the highest, purest, best interests of mankind." Bledsoe argued that "no fact is plainer than that the blacks have been elevated and improved by their servitude in this country," and he believed that "if the abolitionists can conceive a better method for their enlightenment and religious improvement, we should rejoice to see them carry their plan into execution."[28]

Law professor James Holcombe was also a passionate defender of slavery and a proponent of states rights' and secession. Many students left their classes to hear his lectures, and very likely his views were widely known in a university with only thirteen professors. Holcombe believed slavery was the "debt of Christian humanity towards this degraded race." Slavery, he argued,

> surrounds the black man with a protection and salutary control which his own reason and energies are incapable of supplying, and by converting elements of destruction into sources of progress, promotes his physical comfort, his intellectual culture, and his moral amelioration. Emancipation . . . would either destroy the race through a wasting process of poverty, vice, and crime, or sink it into an irrecoverable deep of savage degradation. . . . [Slavery] has weaned a race of savages from superstition and idolatry, imparted to them a general knowledge of the precepts of the true religion, implanted in their bosom sentiments of humanity and principles of virtue, developed a taste for the arts and enjoyments of civilized life, [and] given an unknown dignity and elevation to their type of physical, moral and intellectual man.[29]

Holcombe counseled a local assemblage in January 1860 of the dangers of a Republican victory in the fall presidential election. "This Union cannot endure," he said, "if it is to be preserved by submission to a fixed policy of injustice, and acquiescence under an accumulating burthen of reproach." He informed the crowd that "we are willing to give much for Union" but also warned that "much as we value it, we will not purchase it at the price of liberty or character."[30]

In the fall of 1860, the upcoming presidential election undoubtedly occupied the minds of students and faculty. Three days before the election, on 3 November, students in the Washington Society debated the consequences of a Republican victory and decided by a vote of thirty-three in favor to six opposed that Southern states should secede if Lincoln was elected. Student debaters in the Jefferson Society concurred. William Pegram, then studying law, wrote to his sister four days after the election that disunion was certain, and he expected the faculty would soon suspend classes.[31]

The presidential contest was actually two elections divided by geography—between Abraham Lincoln and Stephen Douglas in the North and between John Breckinridge and John Bell in the South. Breckinridge represented Southern Democrats, who, in contrast to Douglas and his Northern Democrats, would guarantee the constitutional rights of slaveholders. Bell represented the Constitutional Union Party, which advocated compromise and preservation of the Union. Lincoln won seventeen of the eighteen free states. Breckinridge prevailed in eleven of the fifteen slave states. Bell had his greatest showing in the Upper South, winning Kentucky, Tennessee, and Virginia.[32]

The election in Virginia was between Breckinridge and Bell. Douglas polled about 10 percent of the vote; Lincoln received only 1 percent. Bell won by less than 0.1 percent of the vote. Voters in Page County overwhelmingly chose Breckinridge, with 81 percent of the vote. Albemarle County, home of the University of Virginia, narrowly divided between Breckinridge and Bell, but chose Bell.[33]

The sectional strife that had divided the nation finally reached the boiling point. Events rapidly escalated, and though Lincoln would not be inaugurated until March, the hopes of secessionists, the fears of unionists, and the growing likelihood of conflict were soon realized. Just days after the election, the South Carolina legislature called a special secession convention to consider withdrawing from the Union. That dream, long hoped for by radical secessionists, came to fruition on 20 December. Six days later, the Federal garrison at Charleston moved to the safety of Fort Sumter in the harbor. Secession fever quickly spread throughout the Lower South. Mississippi was the next to leave the Union, followed by Florida, Alabama, Georgia, Louisiana, and Texas. Delegates from these seven states met at Montgomery on 4 February to form a new nation. Over six days, they drafted a constitution, established a Congress, and elected Jefferson Davis as president of the Confederate States of America.[34]

The state of Virginia followed a more deliberate path to civil war. On 4 February, Virginians elected delegates to their own secession convention. The vote overwhelmingly favored moderation at that time. Some Virginians, however, held a different view and looked south to a new future, seeing in the fledgling Confederacy the birth of a nation rising against a coercive government, just as their forebears had done eighty-five years earlier. Among these secessionists were the people of Page County. They elected Peter Borst, a thirty-four-year-old wealthy lawyer and slaveholder, to represent them. He was an ardent secessionist, but the citizens of Page County were not entirely comfortable with entrusting in him their future. By a vote of 520 to 430, they required the actions of the convention be subject to their approval. Albemarle County sent a mixed delegation to the convention. Law professor James Holcombe brought his fervent secessionist views to Richmond, while Valentine Southall, a seventy-one-year-old lawyer and former Speaker of the House of Delegates, was a moderate. An initial vote to adopt a secession ordinance was easily defeated on 4 April with 45 delegates in favor of secession and 88 opposed. Borst voted in favor of secession, as did Holcombe.[35]

The outbreak of war eight days later, on 12 April, at Fort Sumter in Charleston harbor converted the majority of delegates to Borst and Holcombe's position. On 17 April, by a vote of 88–55, the State of Virginia joined the Confederacy. Borst again voted in favor of secession. He explained his stance by saying that war had been declared and his vote was in defense of Southern rights and liberty. The noble and patriotic people of Page County, he insisted, were "fully alive to the crisis, and prepared to meet it, come what may." The elder Southall, too, was swayed and voted for secession. News of secession reached Charlottesville that same day, and students suspended their studies.[36]

It is widely accepted that votes cast during the secession convention reflected regional differences in the prevalence of slavery. This is because most of the 88 delegates in favor of secession on 17 April hailed from counties east of the Blue Ridge Mountains, which held 87 percent of the slave population, and from southwest Virginia, where slavery was also prevalent. Delegates from the

Shenandoah Valley and northwest Virginia, where slavery was less common, cast most of the 55 votes against secession.[37]

In the sixteen-county region of the Shenandoah Valley north of the James River, there was not as clear a relationship between secession and the prevalence of slaves. In the two votes on secession during April, the 26 delegates from the northern valley decidedly opposed secession. Twenty-four delegates cast votes on 4 April; 20 opposed secession. Delegates from Shenandoah County and Page County, both with low numbers of slaveholders (about 10 percent or less of white families had slaves), and Warren County, where more than 20 percent of white families had slaves, cast the 4 votes in favor of secession. Of the 9 delegates from the six counties with the highest slave population, only the delegate from Warren County voted for disunion. Thirteen days later, the vote was 17–7 against secession. Support for secession again came from the 4 delegates from Shenandoah, Page, and Warren, now joined by 3 delegates from the counties of Rockbridge, Rockingham, and Morgan.[38]

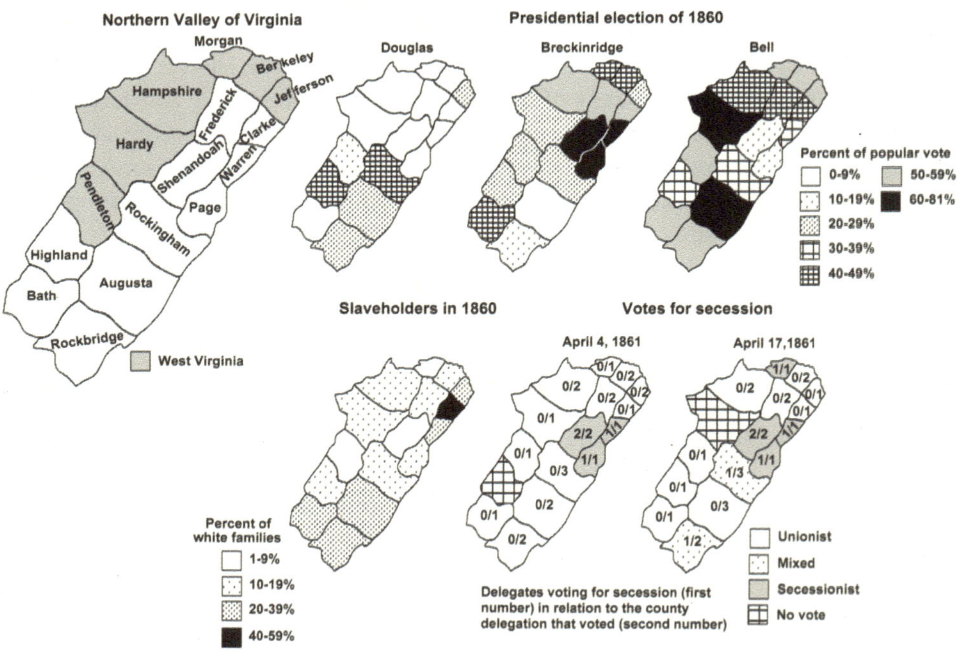

Map 2. Slaveholding, 1860 election, and secession in the Shenandoah Valley. Data are from the sixteen-county region north of the James River. From H. T. Shanks, *The Secession Movement in Virginia, 1847–1861* (Richmond: Garrett and Massie, 1934); G. H. Reese, ed., *Proceedings of the Virginia State Convention of 1861, February 13–May 1*, 4 vols. (Richmond: Virginia State Library, 1965); W. H. Gaines Jr., *Biographical Register of Members: Virginia State Convention of 1861, First Session* (Richmond: Virginia State Library, 1969); W. D. Burnham, *Presidential Ballots, 1836–1892* (Baltimore: Johns Hopkins University Press, 1955); R. A. Wooster, *The Secession Conventions of the South* (Princeton: Princeton University Press, 1962).

The staunch support in Shenandoah, Page, and Warren Counties for secession is reflected in the 1860 presidential election. The sixteen-county northern valley region favored Bell (45 percent of popular vote) over Breckinridge (37 percent) and Douglas (18 percent). Douglas fared best in southern counties, winning a plurality of votes in two counties. Bell won 8 counties. Breckinridge garnered 6 northern counties. Of the 6 counties where slavery was most prevalent, 4 favored Bell and 2 opted for Breckinridge. Breckinridge's greatest support was in Page, Shenandoah, and Warren, where he polled 81 percent, 76 percent, and 62 percent of the popular vote, respectively. A vote for Breckinridge was not necessarily a verdict for secession. However, statewide analysis of the voting record of delegates to the secession convention shows that counties that voted for Breckinridge tended to favor secession while Bell counties were overwhelmingly unionist or moderate. This is also seen in the northern Shenandoah Valley, where only 2 of 11 delegates (18 percent) from the 8 counties that favored Bell voted for secession on 17 April, while 4 of the 9 delegates (44 percent) from the 6 counties carried by Breckinridge opted for secession.[39]

The picture that emerges from this analysis is that Shenandoah, Page, and Warren were consistent as the primary supporters of Breckinridge and secession despite a generally low occurrence of slavery. Whether this represented staunch support for disunion or merely support of Southern unity is unclear. Shenandoah County's support for secession may have been an attempt to show a united front that would force the North to adopt a more favorable position toward the South. Indeed, a public meeting held on 12 November 1860, six days after the presidential election, resulted in just such a pronouncement. The citizens of Shenandoah County had advocated a similar stance ten years earlier.[40]

The low number of slaves in Page County may misrepresent the importance of slavery to the economic, social, and political structure of the county. Slaves were the primary source of labor to run the local iron industry. The Blackfords had 68 slaves who worked their iron furnace in 1840. That same year, Chapman's uncles Daniel and Henry Forrer had 31 slaves working their ironworks. In 1850 Henry Forrer was the leading slaveholder in Page County, with 77 slaves. Moreover, the slave population was concentrated in the hands of a few wealthy families. These families likely had influence and social standing in the county that far exceeded their numbers. Chapman's was one of these elite families.[41]

Yet it may be misleading to overplay the importance of family wealth and privilege. Chapman may have seen the conflict not as a means to preserve wealth and slavery per se, but rather in light of Southern nationalism. If, as many of his generation believed, the values, society, culture, and economy of the South were superior to those of the North, then the war was justified as a defense against Northern aggression and in preservation of the prevailing social, moral, and political order. Slavery was an accepted part of the social hierarchy that distinguished rich from poor, planter from laborer, white from black. Citizens in his native Page County, strident in their secessionist views, reinforced these sentiments. At the University of Virginia, Albert Bledsoe, James Holcombe, and others, too, spouted the fiery rhetoric of fervid secessionists and Southern nationalists.

In many respects, Chapman's decision to lend his service to the Confederacy was likely simple and foregone: to defend Virginia, her people, and the society and values he had known all his life. As the crisis grew and armed conflict loomed, he volunteered for military service, as did his fellow students. Of some 600 students enrolled at the University of Virginia for the 1860–61 session, more than 500 joined the Confederate army. Chapman may have been motivated to act in defense of slavery, in defense of Southern liberty, or against the unfair usurpation of states' rights, or from desire to preserve the homeland and the Southern way of life, or out of sympathy with the patriotic fervor of the day. It may have been for the same reasons that young men have always exposed themselves to the horrors of combat: youthful exuberance, adventure, devotion to comrades, the quest for honor and glory, and duty to country. Quite likely it was for all these reasons, and quite likely it was simply what was expected of an educated young man in Virginia during the spring of 1861.[42]

3 | A Much Pleasanter Service

Following the 1860 presidential election and the secession of South Carolina, students at the University of Virginia organized two military companies comprising over one-quarter of the student body. Student military companies had been part of the academic culture since the founding of the university, but the faculty had disbanded them in an era of student riots. Now, the faculty granted permission for students to again form military companies. Law student Capt. Edward Hutter commanded the Southern Guard, ninety-nine students strong. They wore black trousers, light blue shirts trimmed with brass buttons and dark blue collars and cuffs, and light blue or gray caps. The Sons of Liberty, named by law professor James Holcombe and comprising seventy-four students, wore black trousers and red shirts trimmed with black velvet. Chapman joined the Southern Guard as a private. Among his fellow students was Robert E. Lee Jr., whose father expressed displeasure over the rush of the young students to join the coming war. The students gathered every afternoon except Sunday to drill on the Lawn and Carr's Hill. There, equipped by the governor with old flintlock muskets, bayonets, and cartridge boxes, but without flints or cartridges to fire their weapons, the students were instructed by officers in infantry drill. At some point, military fever also intoxicated the faculty, who gathered to practice in their own drill.[1]

During the 1860–61 session, Chapman lived in a boardinghouse and roomed with law student Wayland Fuller Dunaway. As Dunaway later recalled, John Brown's raid on Harpers Ferry and the election of Lincoln aroused martial fervor. Speeches by James Holcombe, Albert Bledsoe, and John Buchanan Floyd, former governor of Virginia (1849–52) and secretary of war in the cabinet of James Buchanan, further inflamed passions. Several students broke into the Rotunda one night in early March to raise the first Confederate flag over the university. The next morning, as dawn broke, the sight of the Confederate flag fluttering in the breeze caused a sensation. A large crowd of students abandoned their classes and gathered at the Rotunda to hear speeches in favor of secession. Though faculty chairman Socrates Maupin ordered the flag removed, students and faculty alike, including Dunaway, could not help but be inspired by this symbol of the new nation flying defiantly in the wind.[2]

On 13 April 1861, the university held its annual Founder's Day celebration of Thomas Jefferson's birthday. The two student military companies united with two companies of local militia, the Albemarle Rifles and Monticello Guards, in a military parade. To a throng of onlookers, Chapman and some 400 other men displayed their military proficiency in an afternoon parade and drill on the Lawn. During the celebration, a telegram arrived from Richmond announcing the fall of Fort Sumter. The crowd erupted in cheers as Edward Hutter, given honorary command of the combined military companies, proclaimed, "Fort Sumter has surrendered and the Palmetto flag now floats over its walls."[3]

Four days later, on 17 April, Virginia seceded from the Union. Securing arms and munitions became an immediate concern of the state government, and the arsenal at Harpers Ferry, nestled at the fork of the Shenandoah and Potomac Rivers, presented a tempting target. On the night of the sixteenth, when it became evident that secession was likely, military authorities hatched a plan to size the arsenal. With the approval of the governor, the Staunton Artillery, led by Capt. John Imboden, and the West Augusta Guard left Staunton for Harpers Ferry late in the afternoon of the seventeenth by way of the Virginia Central Railroad. The Albemarle Rifles, Monticello Guard, and the two student companies joined the expedition when the train pulled into Charlottesville. The students so enthusiastically supported the plan that the faculty did not intervene. Maupin granted students a leave of absence of one week, but in the rush of preparations Chapman and many other students did not obtain their leave. Late that evening, with their old flintlock muskets in hand but neither flints nor ammunition, the students gathered at the railroad depot to board boxcars. Before embarking, Holcombe read the announcement of secession to the eager young warriors.[4]

Without rations, blankets, overcoats, haversacks, or canteens, the students huddled in two dark boxcars. They passed through Gordonsville and headed north on the Orange and Alexandria Railroad, picking up another infantry company in Culpeper. They reached Manassas Junction early the next morning and then boarded a westbound train for the journey to Strasburg along the Manassas Gap Railroad. Cold, tired, and hungry, the young soldiers eagerly climbed out of the cramped boxcars when the train arrived in Strasburg a few hours later. After some welcome food, the students formed ranks and began the eighteen-mile march to Winchester. They reached Winchester in the evening and boarded a train for Harpers Ferry.

The student warriors arrived at Harpers Ferry before daybreak on 19 April not knowing what to expect. They were too late to prevent the destruction of the arsenal by Federal soldiers but did help secure its firearms. Over the next few days, several false alarms roused the students from their camp to defend against expected attacks. One night they climbed the imposing Loudoun Heights, rising some 1,000 feet, south of Harpers Ferry and across the Shenandoah River, to support Imboden's battery, only to return the next morning, exhausted, but still not having fired a shot. For the most part, however, they settled down in an old depot near the end of the railroad bridge across the Potomac and, in the words of one student, "fared badly."

After a few days, Gov. John Letcher, acting on behalf of faculty chairman Maupin, ordered the student soldiers to return to Charlottesville. Upon reaching Charlottesville, members of the Southern Guard petitioned the governor to accept them into the growing Virginia army. Letcher, however, refused their services. He believed that many of the young men were capable of becoming fine officers, and their concentration in a single unit would limit their effectiveness. Instead, the governor advised them to return to their homes and aid in organizing military companies. On 8 May, without having ever fired a shot in combat, the Southern Guard and Sons of Liberty disbanded. However, their brief military service had not gone unnoticed. Chapman's excursion to Harpers Ferry inspired Wayland Fuller Dunaway, his roommate, to leave the university for military duty.[5]

After Confederate authorities issued an order for mobilization on 4 May, Page County organized several volunteer companies for the war effort. The Page Grays (Company H, 33rd Virginia) and Capt. Macon Jordan's Company (Company D, 7th Virginia Cavalry) enlisted on 1 June for one year. The Page Volunteers (Company K, 10th Virginia) enlisted the next day as the second infantry company from Page County. Among the Page Volunteers were Chapman's brother Edmund (nineteen years old) and cousin Samuel Jacob Forrer (twenty-four years old).[6]

Other cousins also enlisted for service, though not in a rush. John Forrer (thirty years old) and Samuel Forrer (twenty-three years old), sons of Daniel Forrer of Mossy Creek, enlisted as privates in the 52nd Virginia from Augusta County on 30 July. Judah Forrer (twenty-six years old), Samuel Jacob Forrer's brother who lived at Mossy Creek, joined his Chapman cousins in the artillery in August. Christian Forrer, brother of Samuel Jacob Forrer and Judah Forrer, was the last to serve, enlisting in the 33rd Virginia in March 1862 at the age of nineteen. Of the eight Chapman and Forrer cousins who served in the Confederate army, Christian was the only one to die, mortally wounded at Second Manassas.[7]

Chapman's older brother, Sam, was the most impetuous of the Chapman and Forrer boys. He abandoned his studies at Richmond College, but almost twenty-three years old and eager to join the army, Sam did not wait for companies to organize in Page County. He traveled to Front Royal to join the Warren Rifles (Company B, 17th Virginia) on 3 May as a private. The company was stationed in Alexandria at the end of May, saw the town abandoned to the Federal army, and then set up camp with the Confederate army gathering near Manassas.[8]

Unlike his older brother, Chapman followed a deliberate, rather than headstrong, path to service in the Confederate army. After returning to the University of Virginia from Harpers Ferry, Chapman left Charlottesville toward the end of May. Early June found him in Luray, where he aided in drilling the Page Grays. However, Chapman chose not to enlist in this unit. Instead, he joined John K. Booton and William Crisp in organizing an artillery company that came to be known as the Dixie Artillery. Booton had previously commanded the county's disbanded artillery company. Crisp was a Shakespearean actor from England living in Luray. A proficient swordsman, he instructed officers in the local infantry companies on the art of swordplay.[9]

The pathway to artillery service was an uncommon one. Only some 5 percent of soldiers in the Confederate army served in the artillery. Perhaps his brief experience as an infantryman in the Southern Guard did not appeal to Chapman. Indeed, Edward Porter Alexander, the famed Confederate artillerist, compared the artillery service to other branches of the military as a "much pleasanter service, free from all guard and picket duty." Chapman's commander in the Southern Guard, Edward Hutter, also transferred to the artillery with the rank of major. The artillery corps was a technical branch of the army. Later regulations for a commission as a captain of artillery for ordnance duty would require proficiency in algebra, trigonometry, mechanics, and chemistry. Chapman's coursework at the University of Virginia in mathematics and science was consistent with these future Confederate regulations. But the basic reason Chapman helped organize the Dixie Artillery was simple: with two infantry companies and one of cavalry having already been organized in Page County, forming an artillery company provided Chapman the opportunity to procure a commission as an officer. It would prove to be a wise choice.[10]

Equipping the company posed an immediate problem for the aspiring artillerists. The county possessed two old cannons, probably small 12-pounder mountain howitzers, and these formed the nucleus of the battery. Uniforms had to be made and horses, harnesses, wagons, and equipment procured to make the guns serviceable. The money county commissioners had raised could have helped, but these funds had been used to arm, equip, and uniform other companies. Instead, Booton used his own money to finance the battery, but vast supplies of equipment were still needed.[11]

Booton, Crisp, and Chapman held their first recruitment meeting for the newly formed Dixie Artillery on 21 June. Sixty-six volunteers, including the three organizers, enlisted for one year. The Cubbage family contributed four soldiers to the battery; the Cameron and Stroop families, three each. In accordance with procedures of the day, elections were held to choose officers. Booton was elected captain; Crisp, first lieutenant; Chapman, second lieutenant; and Francis Conrad, first sergeant. Monthly pay for the captain was $140; first lieutenant, $100; second lieutenant, $90; first sergeant, $20; sergeant, $17; corporal, $13; and private, $12.[12]

With little training or equipment, the men of the Dixie Artillery eagerly awaited their assignment to the growing Army of the Shenandoah at Winchester, commanded by Gen. Joseph Johnston. By the end of the month, this army consisted of 10,010 infantrymen and 334 cavalrymen. The artillery consisted of 15 officers and 263 men organized into four batteries. On Friday, 19 July, almost one month after being formed, the long-awaited orders to join Johnston at Winchester arrived. The following morning, the citizens of Page County sent their fourth company of soldiers to war. However, the march from town was more comical than martial. A childhood accident prevented Booton from riding a horse, and he led the men away not mounted on a noble steed, but rather conveyed in a one-horse sulky. The battery had neither horses nor harnesses to transport its meager equipment. Instead, a hired team hauled the two small guns, caisson, and other equipment. The men reached Winchester on Sunday. They had hoped to get authority from Johnston to purchase horses and harnesses, but their dream of finally being attached to the army and equipping the battery was dashed. Johnston had already moved out of the Shenandoah Valley to join fellow Confederate general P. G. T. Beauregard and his Army of the Potomac at Manassas.[13]

Orders to join Johnston at Manassas did not arrive for another month. In the meantime, the company settled into camp in a warehouse and continued drilling. Permission to requisition horses and harnesses did not come until later, and the would-be artillerists maneuvered their two guns by hand as best they could. Instruction in artillery drill without horses to maneuver the guns, though unbecoming, was in fact a drill in light artillery tactics. In one such exercise, a race back to camp between the crews of the two limbered guns, one commanded by Chapman and the other by Crisp, Chapman fell and was run over by a gun carriage but escaped serious injury. Thirteen recruits joined the company while stationed in Winchester. One of the new recruits was Chapman's cousin Judah Forrer. Another was Henry Brent, a student from the Virginia Military Institute who had studied artillery tactics. He became a second lieutenant and the battery's drillmaster.[14]

The battery eventually received orders to join Johnston at Manassas. On 27 August, the men harnessed horses to the guns, traveling forge, and other wagons, and the small battery marched out of Winchester to join the Confederate army. They reached Manassas three days later and took a station near Johnston's headquarters at Portici, the plantation home of Francis Lewis. Then, on 11 September, Johnston relocated the battery to a post near the railroad. The spirits of the men were high, discipline was good, and the men kept busy drilling. The Dixie Artillery had finally joined the Confederate army, though the small battery remained independent, unattached to a particular infantry brigade or the growing reserve artillery corps.[15]

The Dixie Artillery was not among the elite of the artillery corps. That honor rested with the men who had battled the enemy at Manassas. One such group of artillerists was the famed Washington Artillery from New Orleans, led by

Maj. James Walton. This battalion of four companies, replete with four color guards, two buglers, and an eleven-member band, had arrived at Richmond in June. A twenty-one-car train carried the officers and their horses, the enlisted men, six 6-pounder bronze guns, two 12-pounder howitzers, and one 8-pounder rifle. Local newspapers heralded the coming of these men from New Orleans, and they enthralled Richmond society, including Jefferson Davis. Upon completing their outfitting, they reached Manassas with some 275 men and thirteen guns, fired their first shots at the enemy on 18 July at Blackburn's Ford, and helped turn the tide in favor of the Confederates during the heated fighting on the afternoon of the twenty-first. Brig. Gen. James Longstreet, whose infantrymen the Washington Artillery supported at Blackburn's Ford, observed that "our young artillerists proved themselves equal, if not superior, to the boasted artillerists of the enemy." The Louisianans enjoyed the accolades of victory, saw minor adventures in the months following the battle, and by mid-October had settled into camp, called Camp Hollins, near Beauregard's headquarters. There, regimental bands provided merriment, and hot punch warmed the soul on cool evenings. Longstreet and fellow general "Jeb" Stuart frequented the festivities.[16]

The officers and men of the Dixie Artillery saw no such gaiety in their camp. They were a small battery, lacking many of the essential tools of their trade, unrecognized by the military command, uncertain of their prospects. But the fortunes of the aspiring artillerists from Page County would soon be linked to that of the dashing cannoneers from New Orleans.

The Dixie Artillery most likely had two small mountain howitzers, making them underarmed compared with other batteries. More common were the model 1841 6-pounder field gun and model 1841 12-pounder field howitzer. These weapons comprised 26 percent and 18 percent, respectively, of the Confederate arsenal early in the war. The 6-pounder field gun used a 66-inch bronze barrel that weighed 884 pounds and had a 3.67-inch bore. The gun fired solid spherical shot a distance of 1,523 yards with a 1.25-pound powder charge. The 12-pounder field howitzer used a 59-inch bronze barrel that weighed 788 pounds and had a 4.62-inch bore. A 1-pound powder charge fired shell 1,072 yards. In contrast, the smaller model 1835 12-pounder mountain howitzer had a 37-inch bronze barrel that weighed 220 pounds with a 4.62-inch bore. A 0.5-pound powder charge fired shell 1,005 yards.[17]

Three newer pieces were introduced at the beginning of the war and quickly gained favor in both the Northern and the Southern armies. The model 1857 12-pounder field gun, commonly called the Napoleon, was superior to the 6-pounder field gun and the 12-pounder field howitzer. Its bronze barrel had a 4.62-inch bore, was 72 inches long, and weighed 1,220 pounds. A 2.5-pound powder charge fired solid shot 1,619 yards and spherical case shot 1,135 yards. A smaller, 2-pound charge fired shell 1,300 yards. The model 1861 10-pounder

Parrott field rifle had a cast-iron barrel 78 inches long, a 2.9-inch bore, and weighed 890 pounds. It used a 1-pound powder charge to fire shell and case shot to a distance of 2,000 yards. Another weapon was the model 1861 3-inch ordnance rifle. Its 73-inch wrought iron barrel had a 3-inch bore and weighed 816 pounds. A 1-pound powder charge fired shell and case shot to a distance of 1,835 yards. By September 1862, the Napoleon, 10-pounder Parrott, and 3-inch rifle comprised 12 percent, 18 percent, and 19 percent, respectively, of the Confederate arsenal.[18]

A small number of men and horses serviced the meager armament of the Dixie Artillery. When the battery arrived at Manassas, it carried 5 sergeants, 4 corporals, and 65 privates on its muster roll under the command of Booton, with Crisp, first lieutenant, and Chapman and Brent, second lieutenants. The effective strength was less, however. Five enlisted men were absent, 1 had deserted, and 2 men were rejected as unfit for service when the battery mustered into the Confederate army in September 1861. Poor fitness led to the discharge of 3 men, and another died of illness. At least 2 men joined the battery during the fall. The Dixie Artillery, though small in numbers, was comparable to other batteries at that time. The number of horses, however, barely constituted an effective transport. The battery reached Manassas with 45 horses and within several days had obtained 8 more. A four-gun battery supported by four caissons, one forge, and one battery wagon, each pulled by 6 horses harnessed to a limber, required a minimum of 60 horses, not including reserves and horses for officers, though many batteries used only 4 horses to haul guns and caissons.[19]

Camp life during the Civil War was notoriously unsanitary. When tens of thousands of men gathered together in close quarters, filth, sewage, and lack of potable water fostered poor health. More men died of disease than in battle. The health of the men of the Dixie Artillery, as with the army in general, was poor during the fall of 1861. Three officers and seventy-six enlisted men were present in camp during November; one-quarter of these men suffered from poor health. Illnesses continued to plague the men of Page County into winter.[20]

Conditions were no better for horses. The mortality rate of horses in the artillery service was high due to inadequate shelter, meager rations, and long marches hauling heavy guns and caissons over poor roads caked with thick mud. Cold weather during the winter of 1861–62 made for especially trying circumstances. The allotted daily ration for a horse was 14 pounds of hay and 12 pounds of corn. The 66 horses in the Dixie Artillery in early January needed 924 pounds of hay and 792 pounds of corn each day. By the middle of January, the ravaged land surrounding the Confederate encampments made hay and fodder increasingly difficult to find. The Dixie Artillery's horses often had to subside on less than their allotted hay. Horse shelters consisted of wood plank roofs filled with brush along the sides, feeble protection from the cold and wind. In early February, the battery had only 57 horses. The horses of the

Washington Artillery, winter campmates of the Dixie Artillery, were also in poor condition from lack of forage, and many died. Inclement weather and lack of proper forage had been a problem for the Louisianans as early as November, when they condemned 48 of 248 horses as unfit for service.[21]

This period of quiet in the Confederate army brought notable changes to Chapman and the Dixie Artillery. Sam Chapman joined the battery in October. This was the beginning of a close association between the Chapman brothers that would last throughout the war. Cousin Judah Forrer left the battery in January to assist in his uncle's ironworks. He would later rejoin his cousins in their exploits with Mosby.[22]

The weeks before the end of the year saw command of the battery pass from Booton to Chapman. Booton had been elected to the Virginia House of Delegates the previous May and resigned his commission on 21 November to attend the 1861–62 session, which began on 2 December. An election was held, and Chapman became captain of the battery on 8 December. William Crisp retained his position as first lieutenant, and Henry Brent was second lieutenant. Francis Conrad, first sergeant, became second lieutenant to fill the vacancy created by Chapman's promotion. Crisp had assumed command in Booton's absence. He was not pleased with the elections and left the battery in early January 1862.[23]

Early in the war, light artillery companies were typically attached to infantry brigades, serving under the command of the brigadier general, or were assigned to the reserve artillery. The Dixie Artillery was unattached and independent of any infantry brigade or the reserve artillery upon reaching Manassas and remained unattached throughout the fall. The middle of October found the battery encamped at Camp Pickens, the Confederate fortification at Manassas Junction. The battery was still unattached in November, but neighbored the Washington Artillery at Camp Hollins near Beauregard's headquarters, just west and south of Centreville. And by the end of January, the men were ensconced in snug cabins in winter quarters with the Washington Artillery at Blackburn's Ford, a few miles southwest of Centreville on Bull Run.[24]

At this point in time, an artillery battery was assigned to each of fifteen infantry brigades. These fifteen batteries had four to six guns each. The reserve artillery was divided into two separate organizations. Col. William Nelson Pendleton, chief of artillery, commanded nine batteries totaling forty-four guns. James Walton led a separate reserve command of the four-company Washington Artillery. The Dixie Artillery fell into favor with Walton and joined his command. It was the beginning of a long association throughout the year with Walton and the Washington Artillery as Longstreet's reserve artillery. The fate of Chapman and his men, and their future as artillerists, was now linked to Walton.[25]

Pendleton and Walton were rival commanders in the artillery service. Pendleton, promoted from captain to colonel in July, had been chief of artillery for Johnston's Army of the Shenandoah. Walton, then a major, was chief of artillery for Beauregard's Army of the Potomac, later known as the First Corps when the two separate armies combined following Manassas. Pendleton had attended West Point with Jefferson Davis and rose quickly in the Confederate army. His promotion to colonel subsequently led to a special act of the Confederate Congress to increase the number of field officers in the artillery corps, necessitated in part to recognize the distinguished service of Walton, who had been repeatedly recommended for promotion by Beauregard and Longstreet. Walton eventually gained promotion to colonel under that act, but by then Pendleton had been given command of the reserve artillery and received the rank of brigadier general under the same act of Congress. However, history has not been kind to Pendleton, and fellow Confederate staff officers as well as historians viewed him as unequal to the task.[26]

Cold, damp weather in the fall of 1861 made for difficult camp life and exacerbated the poor health of the army. October was cold and rainy, with a hard frost at the end of the month, and the cold, rainy weather continued into early November. November and December brought more cold and snow, with roads deep in mud and nearly impassible. Cold nights spent on guard duty with no overcoats or shelter left many men in Pendleton's reserve artillery sick. Thin tent walls and a shortage of blankets offered scantly better conditions for men seeking warmth in their tents. Log cabins soon sprung up to provide winter quarters.[27]

The men of the Washington Artillery, too, began constructing winter quarters at the end of December to escape the recurring cold and snow and provide better refuge for their horses. The camp, called "Waltonville," was located at Blackburn's Ford on Bull Run. Instead of flimsy canvas tents, the men built log huts with planked roofs and floors, glass windows, and doors. Two rows of covered shelters running along the front of the camp protected the horses from wind and cold. Guns were parked to the front, under tarpaulins to shield them from the weather. Under Walton's authority, the Dixie Artillery joined in the construction, erecting cabins next to Waltonville in the early part of January. Chapman was likely in Luray during this time, but returned to camp toward the middle of the month and oversaw completion of the cabins and horse shelters. The camp was in all likelihood festive, with thoughts of war far removed as the men gathered in the warmth of their cabins. Indeed, the men of the Dixie Artillery enjoyed the merriment of the Washington Artillery during its Mardi Gras celebration. However, the grim realities of warfare intruded after just a few short weeks.[28]

4 | We Suffered Considerably

The Confederate army around Centreville began stirring from winter encampments in early March. With the coming of spring, and concerned about the expected Federal offensive on Richmond, Confederate commander Gen. Joseph Johnston evacuated the Centerville positions during the weekend of 8–9 March for better defensive lines along the Rappahannock River. Johnston had good reason to fear a Federal offensive. Maj. Gen. George McClellan, commanding the Federal army, intended to move the army by ship to Urbanna on the Rappahannock, below the Confederate army at Centreville. From there, he would be in position for an overland strike at Richmond. However, the Confederate fallback forced McClellan to change his base of operations from Urbanna to Fort Monroe, still in Federal hands at Old Point Comfort on the tip of the Virginia Peninsula formed by the York and James Rivers. The artillerists of Page County, underarmed and ill-equipped, had prepared for war as best they could. The coming weeks would test their readiness.[1]

The men of the Washington Artillery and their Dixie Artillery campmates began preparations to leave their winter quarters on 6 March. They formed the reserve artillery for Maj. Gen. James Longstreet's division while Pendleton's reserve artillery supported Maj. Gen. Gustavus Smith's division. The men filled their wagons with quartermaster stores and destroyed what could not be carried. On the eighth, they began the long march along the Warrenton turnpike to Warrenton and south to Orange Court House. The march was arduous, in cold, wet weather over muddy roads. The Dixie Artillery brought fifty-five horses and two mules, all in poor physical shape from lack of forage; all suffered through undue strain. Taking proper care of horses was difficult, if not impossible, under these miserable conditions. Both man and beast struggled to extricate heavy wagons, caissons, and gun carriages from mud that was at times axle deep. Several horses of the Dixie Artillery and Washington Artillery broke down and were condemned. Commanders reduced ammunition carried in limbers and caissons to half loads and forbade cannoneers to ride. The wretched circumstances made for a slow march. The soldiers reached Warrenton on the tenth. Three days later, they stopped at the Hazel River (a tributary of the Rappahannock between Warrenton and Culpeper) to rest for a few days.[2]

The artillerists arrived at Orange Court House by the nineteenth, and Walton's command remained there with Longstreet's division for the next few weeks. The Washington Artillery, with the Dixie Artillery nearby, pitched their tents in a grove of pine trees on a local farm. Longstreet's headquarters was nearby at the farm of Erasmus Taylor. The men trained in artillery drill daily, weather permitting. A festive attitude prevailed in camp. Men feasted on the newfound bounty of food in a land not yet ravished by the army. Fair young women appealed for the attention of decorous officers. The more mannered officers of the Washington Artillery, along with some of Longstreet's staff, organized a dance club at a local tavern, where they were entertained by the battalion band.[3]

The gaiety of camp life shortly lapsed, though, as the specter of war resurfaced. The enemy was reported in the area of Fredericksburg, and as the sun set on Sunday, 6 April, Pendleton's reserve, the Washington Artillery, and others of Longstreet's artillery fell in behind Longstreet's infantrymen and began a difficult march along the plank road to Fredericksburg. The men marched all night and into the early hours of Monday morning. The march resumed that morning after a brief rest. A winter storm blanketed the region with cold, dismal weather; snow, sleet, and rain made for poor conditions. The men bivouacked that wintry night without rations for nourishment, tents for shelter, or wood for fires. After passing an uncomfortable night, they awoke Tuesday morning to more snow, sleet, and rain. The reports of the enemy advancing on Fredericksburg proved wrong, and the men, cold, wet, tired, and hungry, retraced their steps before turning off toward Louisa Court House. They marched all day Tuesday in chilly, freezing rain. It was a hard march, along a road thick with mud and through swollen streams. Tuesday night was again spent under wretched conditions in pouring rain and without shelter. The march began anew Wednesday morning over even worse roads and in even heavier rain and sleet. Frozen, drenched, and covered with mud, the exhausted soldiers and their horses finally reached Louisa Court House the next day, 10 April. But there was little rest for the weary. The artillerymen continued on to Richmond, reaching that city by the thirteenth and setting up camp in the surrounding countryside.[4]

The cause of this discomfort was McClellan and his army gathering at Fort Monroe. From there, the Federal army began advancing up the Virginia Peninsula toward Yorktown on 4 April, but after encountering an apparently larger than expected force, which only reinforced his view that he faced a vastly superior Confederate army, McClellan opted to lay siege to Yorktown. In fact, however, only a small force stood in McClellan's way. The delay allowed portions of Johnston's army to reach Yorktown by the seventh and reinforce the beleaguered Confederates. The next weeks brought a standstill as McClellan's engineers wrestled the heavy artillery into position. All was in place, ready to open fire, on Monday, 5 May. However, the long days of digging trenches, felling trees, and building roads and earthworks were for naught; the Confederates had evacuated their positions Saturday night.[5]

Inadequate defenses on the Virginia Peninsula, between the York and James Rivers, forced a long retreat by the Confederates back to Richmond during the month of May. Federal naval supremacy posed the danger that the Confederates could be outflanked along these rivers. The Confederate army reached Williamsburg on the afternoon of Sunday, 4 May, after a hard march mired in mud and rain-soaked. In a clash the next day, Longstreet's infantrymen delayed the advancing Federals while the Confederates evacuated Williamsburg. By 9 May, Johnston's army was safe beyond the head of the York River, and by the fifteenth, Johnston had positioned the army across the rain-swollen Chickahominy River. The remainder of the month saw cautious advances toward Richmond by McClellan.[6]

The men of the Washington Artillery and their Dixie Artillery comrades saw much marching but little action during this time. They reached Richmond on 13 April, encamped four miles from the city, and boarded transports down the James River to the Peninsula on the twentieth. The soldiers disembarked the next day at King's Mill Wharf below Williamsburg and in a heavy rainstorm bivouacked near Lebanon Church, about nine miles east of Williamsburg near the right flank of the Confederate lines along the Warwick River. Pendleton's reserve artillery and Rogers's Loudoun Artillery, Stribling's Fauquier Artillery, and Dearing's Lynchburg Artillery, all batteries of Longstreet's division, were also at Lebanon Church. The Washington Artillery fell back to Williamsburg on the twenty-fifth, and by 2 May bivouacked at Burnt Ordinary, on the road to Richmond about ten miles beyond Williamsburg. On the fifth, the men marched in heavy rain with axles deep in mud. The sixth of May found the Washington Artillery near Forge Bridge (also known as Jones's Bridge) on the Chickahominy River, which the artillerists crossed the following day at Long Bridge. They marched twenty-three miles in six hours, encamping at Blakey's Millpond on the outskirts of Richmond on the eighth.[7]

Walton's command at this time included Chapman's Dixie Artillery, with four 6-pounder guns, and three companies of the Washington Artillery consisting of Charles Squires's two 3-inch rifles and two 6-pounder guns, Merritt "Buck" Miller's two 12-pounder guns and two 24-pounder howitzers, and Benjamin Eshleman's two 6-pounder guns and two 12-pounder howitzers (the battalion's other company was detached to another command). These four batteries left the artillery camp on 15 May to join the army along the Chickahominy. The artillerists awoke early, at 3:30 A.M., and advanced to Bottom's Bridge, where the Williamsburg Road crossed the Chickahominy, about twelve miles east of Richmond. From there, they fell back to Savage's Station on the Richmond and York River Railroad, camped within six miles of Richmond at

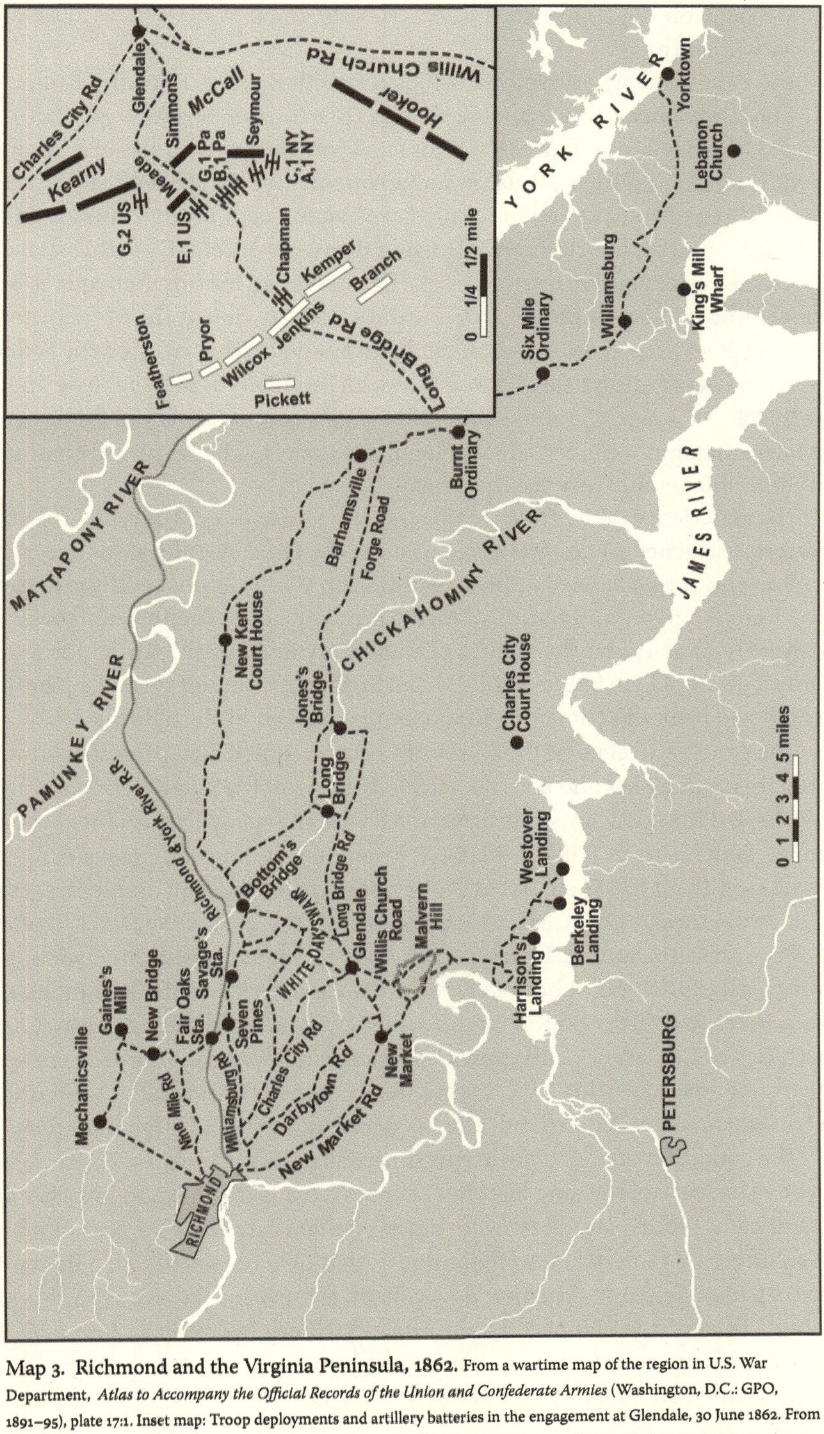

Map 3. Richmond and the Virginia Peninsula, 1862. From a wartime map of the region in U.S. War Department, *Atlas to Accompany the Official Records of the Union and Confederate Armies* (Washington, D.C.: GPO, 1891–95), plate 17:1. Inset map: Troop deployments and artillery batteries in the engagement at Glendale, 30 June 1862. From Brian K. Burton, *Extraordinary Circumstances: The Seven Days' Battles.* Bloomington: Indiana University Press, 2001), 277.

New Bridge on the sixteenth, and returned to camp at Blakey's Millpond on the seventeenth.[8]

The Federal army crossed the Chickahominy River at Bottom's Bridge on 20 May and continued advancing to the crossroads of Seven Pines, six miles distant. By the twenty-fourth, the right flank was within five miles of Richmond at Mechanicsville. Then, Johnston saw an opportunity to strike the Federal left flank. Three of the five Federal army corps were north of the Chickahominy, two were south of the river, and Johnston devised a potentially lethal strike to the two exposed southern army corps. His plan called for simultaneous attacks converging on Seven Pines from three directions. A violent thunderstorm the evening of 30 May flooded the Chickahominy and further isolated the Federal corps. However, the battle of Seven Pines, or Fair Oaks as it came to be known by the North, on 31 May and 1 June, was largely indecisive. Yet it did have one notable outcome. Johnston fell wounded, and Robert E. Lee assumed command of the Confederate army the next day.[9]

The experience of the Dixie Artillery during this period was typical of other batteries attached to Longstreet's division. The Dixie Artillery was in reserve and saw no action at Seven Pines. Nor did the Washington Artillery. Rogers's Loudoun Artillery and Smith's Third Company of the Richmond Howitzers also did not join the battle. Maurin's Donaldsonville Artillery saw minor action. Only Dearing's Lynchburg Artillery and Stribling's Fauquier Artillery, both of which had been in action at Williamsburg, engaged in the fighting.[10]

The first few weeks of June brought relative quiet. Lee used this time to prepare his defenses and plan his attack. Brig. Gen. Jeb Stuart, guided by John Mosby, led his audacious ride around McClellan's army that revealed the exposed Federal right flank. Maj. Gen. Thomas J. "Stonewall" Jackson's army came over from the Shenandoah Valley, and Lee devised an ambitious attack that would threaten McClellan's supply line. For the men of the Dixie Artillery, it was a peaceful time at Blakey's Millpond. The camp was located about two miles east of Richmond between Oakwood Cemetery and the Richmond and York River Railroad, and Richmond society was only a short ride away. Other batteries of Longstreet's division as well as Pendleton's reserve artillery were nearby. It was, according to William Miller Owen of the Washington Artillery, a "delightful camping-ground, and bordered by a grove of large fine trees."[11]

The condition of the horses at this time was pitiful. Able horses were always in need because of the long marches over poor roads in inclement weather and insufficient fodder, and there were never enough. The Dixie Artillery and the Washington Artillery had to make due with only 4 horses to pull a light gun, grossly insufficient for the muddy roads on the Peninsula and around Richmond. Toward the end of May, the Dixie Artillery had only 43 horses fit for service and needed 16 more to have 6 horses per gun. The four companies of the Washington Artillery lacked horses, too. Eshleman had only 34 fit horses and needed 28 more to have 6 horses per gun; Squires needed 10 horses; Miller needed 30.[12]

Throughout May and June, some 85 officers and enlisted men appeared on the muster rolls of the Dixie Artillery. Among them was Chapman's brother Edmund, who abandoned the life of an infantryman for artillery duty as his two older brothers had done earlier. Not all of these men were present for duty. Three enlisted men left camp without leave, and many more fell ill. The men present in camp to service the four smoothbore six-pounders increased from a low of 71 at the beginning of May to 81 by the end of June as the sick recovered and returned to camp. When the Seven Days' battles opened on 25 June, the Dixie Artillery was 81-men strong, though 8 claimed illness; 5 were absent; and 56 privates, 3 artificers, 4 corporals, and 5 sergeants were present for duty. The five officers were Chapman, captain; E. M. Crews, assistant surgeon; and Francis Conrad, Henry Brent, and Sam Chapman, lieutenants. William Crisp had earlier resigned his commission as first lieutenant, and Conrad filled the vacancy on 24 May. Sam Chapman, then a sergeant, was promoted to lieutenant five days later. Chapman's battery was comparable in manpower to those of the Washington Artillery and other batteries from Virginia. Chapman and the men of the Dixie Artillery would soon be put to test during the Seven Days' battles around Richmond.[13]

Longstreet led the right wing of the Southern army, and Walton, now a colonel, served as Longstreet's chief of artillery. This helped to distinguish Walton's reserve artillery from Pendleton's command, who as brigadier general was chief of artillery for the army. As the battle approached, Longstreet's division, now commanded by Brig. Gen. Richard Anderson, had ten batteries: Arthur Rogers's Loudoun Artillery, Edwin Anderson's Thomas Artillery, Victor Maurin's Donaldsonville Artillery, and Benjamin Smith's Third Company Richmond Howitzers, all attached to infantry brigades; in reserve under Walton's command were Chapman's Dixie Artillery, James Dearing's Lynchburg Artillery, and the four companies of the Washington Artillery.[14]

On 17 June, Longstreet steeled his men for the coming battle, many of whom would be seeing combat for the first time. He encouraged them to defend their Southern homeland against Northern conquest and to protect the good women of the South against "dishonor and violation." He reminded his soldiers that "if ever men were called upon to defend the beloved daughters of their country, that now is our duty." Of combat, he said, "Let such thoughts nerve you up to the most dreadful shock of battle; for were it certain death, death would be better than the fate that defeat would entail upon us all. But remember, though the fiery noise of battle is indeed most terrifying, and seems to threaten universal ruin, it is not so destructive as it seems, and few soldiers after all are slain." His advice was to "keep cool, obey orders, and aim low." Sacrifices would be required and men would die but, Longstreet urged his soldiers, "stand well to your duty, and when these clouds break away, as they surely will, the bright sunlight of peace falling upon our free, virtuous, and happy land will be a sufficient reward for the sacrifices which we are now called upon to make."[15]

The Seven Days' battles opened on Wednesday, 25 June, not with Lee's planned attack but under McClellan's initiative. McClellan hoped to advance his position to bring his siege guns within range of Richmond and struck Confederate lines between the Williamsburg Road and the Richmond and York River Railroad in an area known as Oak Grove. Compared with the days to come, it was a modest affair that produced some 1,000 casualties. The Confederate offensive began the next day, Thursday, 26 June. A 55,800-man force was to attack Brig. Gen. Fitz John Porter's 28,100-man Fifth Corps in the early morning hours. Porter's troops guarded the Federal right flank north of the Chickahominy River near Mechanicsville. By turning this flank, Lee would threaten McClellan's supply and communications lines along the railroad and force a retreat. But the Confederates lacked the command and control required for such a large, coordinated attack. The attack failed, but it did produce an unexpected outcome. McClellan, worried about overwhelming Confederate forces, pulled the Fifth Corps back to a more defensible position guarding the bridges across the Chickahominy.[16]

Friday brought the third day of battle, at Gaines's Mill, during the afternoon of 27 June on a scale heretofore never seen in Virginia. Porter deployed 27,160 men supported by 17 batteries of 96 guns along a broad plateau north of the Chickahominy. The swampy bottomlands of a slow-moving stream, Boatswain's Swamp, protected the approaches from the west and north. The initial Confederate assaults that afternoon were scattered, uncoordinated, and failed to breach the strong Boatswain's Swamp line. In the last hours of daylight and into dusk, Lee gathered his troops for a final assault. Wave after wave of Confederate infantrymen stubbornly advanced against the reinforced Federals. The Southerners faced murderous musket and cannon fire, but on they came, and though their Northern counterparts fought no less gallantly, their lines broke under the weight of determined Confederate assaults. As night fell, the Confederates held the battlefield and some 15,000 men, Northern and Southern, were dead, wounded, or missing.[17]

Longstreet's infantrymen received heavy fire at Gaines's Mill, but the men of the Dixie Artillery saw no combat. Close to the action and under fire, they endured shell bursting all around, but remained in reserve with other batteries. The Page County artillerists would have to wait three more days before their guns could reply.[18]

Saturday, 28 June, day four, was a day of relative calm. Lee sought information that would allow him to plan his next attack, and when that intelligence came—that McClellan was retreating to the James River—Lee sent out his army. His plan for the next day was to catch McClellan crossing White Oak Swamp. Jackson led his wing of the army south from its position north of the Chickahominy

River. Maj. Gen. John Magruder's three divisions advanced east along the Williamsburg Road and the Richmond and York River Railroad. Next in line came Maj. Gen. Benjamin Huger's division, advancing in a southeastward direction on the Charles City Road to the village of Glendale, south of White Oak Swamp. The two divisions of Longstreet and Maj. Gen. Ambrose Powell Hill advanced to the south of Huger, along the Darbytown Road to the Long Bridge Road and on to Glendale.[19]

However, Sunday brought little fighting other than an inconclusive skirmish near Savage's Station on the Richmond and York River Railroad, and as the morning of the thirtieth broke, McClellan's army was safely across White Oak Swamp. For Longstreet and A. P. Hill, it was a long march from their positions north of the Chickahominy on the Gaines's Mill battlefield to the Darbytown Road. They had to cross the river at New Bridge and march back toward Richmond along the Nine Mile Road before heading south to reach the Darbytown Road. Longstreet's men marched some ten to twelve miles that Sunday until dark and made camp at Atlee's farm on the Darbytown Road in a heavy rainstorm.[20]

Lee's plan for Monday, 30 June, the sixth day, was to hit the Federal army at Glendale. The retreat from White Oak Swamp passed through this crossroads town on the Long Bridge Road and then turned south onto the Willis Church Road toward Malvern Hill and the James River. Lee massed six divisions, 44,800 men, for the assault at Glendale. As originally planned, Huger's division of 12,000 men, still three miles from Glendale on the Charles City Road, would open the battle. The two divisions of Longstreet and A. P. Hill, 19,200 men still several miles from Glendale, would continue down the Darbytown Road and on to Glendale along the Long Bridge Road. Magruder's three divisions, 13,600 men, formed the reserve. Jackson, with 25,300 men in his four divisions, would support the attack, sweeping down from the north at White Oak Swamp and diverting Northern reinforcements from the Glendale battlefront. However, as was common during these seven days, failure to press the enemy hindered Lee's plan for a decisive victory. Huger did not bring his men up for attack. Nor did Jackson effectively engage the rear guard at White Oak Swamp. Magruder's divisions were diverted in a vain attempt to attack the head of the Federal column already at Malvern Hill. That attack never materialized. Instead, Longstreet's and A. P. Hill's divisions bore the burden for the Confederacy.[21]

The march of 29 June provided Longstreet's infantrymen a needed respite from the heavy fighting they had seen at Gaines's Mill, but as they closed in on Glendale on the afternoon of the thirtieth, the line of battle was formed. Three brigades commanded by Brig. Gen. Cadmus Wilcox, Brig. Gen. James Kemper, and Col. Micah Jenkins deployed perpendicular to the Long Bridge Road. Wilcox had the left of the line, north of the Long Bridge Road. Jenkins seized the land in the center, straddling the road. Kemper took the right flank, south of the road. Brig. Gen. Roger Pryor's brigade moved to near the front, to the left of Wilcox. The remaining two brigades, Brig. Gen. Winfield Featherston's and George Pickett's, led into battle that day by Col. Eppa Hunton, provided support—Featherston on the left, Pickett at the center. Brig. Gen. Lawrence Branch's brigade from A. P. Hill's division supported Kemper, while the rest of Hill's division formed the reserve.[22]

Defending the crossroads was a Federal force of 36,300 men and thirteen batteries deployed to the west of Glendale. Brig. Gen. Henry Slocum's Sixth Corps division had the right, on the Charles City Road. Brig. Gen. Philip Kearny's Third Corps division occupied the ground between the Charles City and Long Bridge Roads. Another Third Corps division, Brig. Gen. Joseph Hooker's, maintained the left flank, well south along the Willis Church Road. The three infantry brigades of Brig. Gen. George McCall's Fifth Corps division—the Pennsylvania Reserves—straddled the Long Bridge Road and held the center of the Federal line in an area known as Frayser's farm.[23]

The land was open ground some 800 yards wide and 1,000 yards deep. Brig. Gen. George Meade posted his brigade on the right at the Long Bridge Road; Brig. Gen. Truman Seymour's brigade took the left; and Col. Seneca Simmons held his brigade in reserve. Five batteries, a total of twenty-four guns, supported McCall's Pennsylvanians on the front line. Lt. Alanson Randol's Battery E, 1st United States Artillery, six 12-pounder Napoleons unlimbered with Meade on the right. Two batteries of the 1st Pennsylvania Light Artillery, Lt. Frank Amsden's Battery G, four guns, and Capt. James Cooper's Battery B, six 10-pounder Parrott rifles, supported the center. Two batteries of the 1st Battalion New York Light Artillery, Capt. Otto Diederichs's Battery A and Capt. John Knieriem's Battery C, eight 20-pounder Parrotts in all, held the left. A sixth battery, Capt. James Thompson's Battery G, 2nd United States Artillery, six guns, was nearby to the right of Randol supporting Kearny's division.[24]

In midafternoon, between 2:30 and 3:00 P.M., with his troops in position and hearing cannon fire that was thought to signal Huger's long-awaited opening attack, Longstreet ordered several of his batteries to commence firing. The Dixie Artillery supported Jenkins's brigade that day. Chapman's battery was one of the first to open fire, bringing a swift and heavy reply from the opposing batteries. In a clearing nearby, Lee and Jefferson Davis had joined Longstreet to witness the coming battle. Some of the shells burst among them and their staff. Cooper's battery was near the Confederate lines and particularly threatening. Longstreet ordered Jenkins, closest to the battery, to silence it.[25]

Col. Micah Jenkins was a twenty-six-year-old graduate of the Citadel in command of Richard Anderson's brigade (Anderson was leading Longstreet's division while Longstreet was in overall command of the right wing of the army). Jenkins had established his reputation for fighting at Seven Pines, where he led a ferocious push through the Federal lines. But the cost was high. The

6th South Carolina alone sustained a casualty rate of more than 50 percent. Jenkins was again in no mood to trifle that Monday. His men had already pushed back skirmishers as they moved up the Long Bridge Road. Now, he advanced his brigade into a vicious melee for Cooper's battery that brought on a general engagement.[26]

As Jenkins's men went forward and reached the edge of the woods, beyond which lay the open ground of Frayser's farm, the Dixie Artillery came up to provide support. It was their first action of the war. The aspiring artillerists had trained for one full year for this moment. They had perfected the "school of the battery" to maneuver the battery while marching and in action. The most important drill was to form "in battery," in which the cannoneers unlimbered their guns and prepared for action. This formation consisted of three parallel lines with guns spaced fourteen yards apart, limbers positioned six yards behind guns, and caissons placed eleven yards behind limbers.[27]

They had mastered the "school of the piece" and its carefully choreographed drill by which the gunner and a 7-man team designated by different numbers fired a cannon. The gunner, a corporal, shouted the type of projectile and range to target to Number 6 and Number 7, who prepared the timed fuses at the limber. The gunner gave the command to "load," and Number 1 sponged the barrel. Number 5 gave a round, fixed to a powder cartridge, to Number 2, who placed it in the barrel. Number 3 sealed the vent in the barrel with his thumb, and Number 1 rammed the round into the barrel. The gunner then aimed the cannon, assisted by Number 3 who moved the carriage to the left or right. When properly sighted, the gunner stepped aside, and with his command of "ready," Number 1 and Number 2 moved clear. Number 3 punctured the cartridge. Number 4 hooked the lanyard to a friction primer and inserted the primer into the barrel vent. Number 3 held the primer in place while Number 4 stepped back from the cannon. When the gunner issued the command to "fire," Number 3 moved away and Number 4 pulled the lanyard. During this time, Number 5 had gotten another round of ammunition from Number 6 and Number 7 at the limber. Well-drilled artillerists could deploy and open fire in less than one minute and could sustain fire from a smoothbore gun at a rate of about two rounds per minute in the heat of battle. Rifle cannons had a slower rate of fire because the powder cartridge was separate from the projectile.[28]

The novice Confederate artillerists deployed their guns "in battery," shielded among the trees facing the farm field, and quickly tasted the might of northern firepower. Chapman's 6-pounders could not match Cooper's six 10-pounder Parrotts and were driven off in a fierce thirty-minute artillery duel. Other Federal gunners joined the fray. As many as thirteen guns directed their fire toward the men from Page County. Chapman's own recollection of the action was terse, saying only that "we opened the fight . . . and suffered considerably." Others painted a more ghastly scene. Cooper said that his battery "replied with marked effect, as soon but one gun replied." An officer in Jenkins's brigade reported that Chapman's battery "had scarcely unlimbered before it was knocked to pieces." William Miller Owen of the Washington Artillery saw the Dixie Artillery the next day and described the battery as having been "crippled," a term also used by artillerist Edward Porter Alexander.[29]

Federal cannon fire wounded several of Chapman's men, and three did indeed suffer considerably. The rain of shot and shell left John Keyser mortally wounded; he died later that night. A projectile severed the left hand of Ambrose Rothgeb. Shell fragments mangled the right side of Daniel Brubaker's body from head to foot. A native of Page County, the eighteen-year-old had only enlisted with the battery three months previously. Now, he lost his right eye, and his right leg was permanently injured. Horses to the rear faired no better as shot and shell smashed into the animals.[30]

Jenkins had led his brigade into a maelstrom. As the South Carolinians emerged from the woods into the farmland, they faced murderous cannon fire from Cooper's six guns and Amsden's four guns. The 1st and 9th Pennsylvania Reserves poured musket balls into the oncoming Confederates. Randol's battery, too, bore down on the Southerners. The fighting here, as elsewhere along the battlefront that day, was vicious, hand-to-hand, and with bayonet, and when the bayonet did not suffice, heads were crushed with rifle butts. One of every two men under Jenkins's command fell that day—94 killed and 475 wounded in a brigade of 1,095 men. The Palmetto Sharpshooters sustained a casualty rate of 69 percent. One of its officers, twenty-one-year-old Lt. John Lee, lost both legs to a cannonball. Alone on the battlefield, he bandaged one leg but bled to death before he could wrap the other leg. Shell fragments struck Jenkins in the shoulder and chest; two horses fell from under him; a cannonball broke his sword; musket balls riddled his overcoat with holes and cut his bridle reins in two. Jenkins's opponents, the 1st and 9th Pennsylvania Reserves, fared better, but still sustained 39 killed, 197 wounded, and 77 missing. After the battle, Longstreet praised Jenkins for his gallantry, but many years later, in the hindsight of the defeat of the Confederacy and the lost opportunity it had had at Glendale, he claimed he had only ordered Jenkins to silence the battery with his sharpshooters, not to advance, and he rebuked Jenkins for being "too anxious for a dash at a battery."[31]

By now the battle had been joined by others. Kemper's brigade on the right easily drove back the picket lines, but as the Southerners stepped from the woods onto the open farmland, they faced Diederichs's and Knieriem's eight 20-pounder Parrotts supported by the 12th Pennsylvania Reserves. Kemper's men briefly overran them before being forced to withdraw. Branch's brigade arrived on the field and resumed the attack, as did Pickett's brigade, but the timely arrival of fresh reserves stemmed the Confederate advance. The Confederates fared no better on the left. Wilcox's Alabamians charged Cooper's and Randol's batteries. The 4th Pennsylvania Reserves, lying hidden in grass near Randol's guns, rose as one when the Southern infantrymen came within sixty feet and delivered a devastating volley. In the same vicious hand-to-hand fighting as elsewhere, the Confederates eventually overran the batteries, only to be beaten back in a determined countercharge. More than 450 Alabamians fell dead or wounded, yet still Cooper's and Randol's batteries were free of Confederate hands.[32]

The attack was not going well for Longstreet. The initial assaults had punched holes in the Federal lines in three places. McCall's division was utterly destroyed. In the fighting at Mechanicsville, Gaines's Mill, and now at Glendale, the division had taken some 3,000 casualties. The combat this afternoon left brigade commanders Seneca Simmons dead, George Meade severely wounded, and Truman Seymour missing from the battlefield. But the Federal lines, strengthened with reinforcements, held. Four of Longstreet's brigades—Jenkins's, Kemper's, Pickett's, and Wilcox's—had been forced back. Yet more carnage was still to come. Pryor brought up his brigade on the extreme left against Kearny's division. The Confederates advanced in the face of canister—double rounds fired without sponging as they got closer—and met the same fate as had others previously down the line. Featherston's brigade of Mississippians came up for support, but even at great cost they, too, could not push back the enemy.[33]

Finally, with darkness approaching, A. P. Hill's five remaining brigades went into action, advancing over the same ground strewn with the dead, dying, and wounded of Longstreet's division. The honor of capturing Cooper's and Randol's guns went to the Virginians of Brig. Gen. Charles Field's brigade. The fighting was no less intense for these Virginians than it had been for Jenkins's South Carolinians and Wilcox's Alabamians earlier. Among the participants in this last charge of the day was Wayland Fuller Dunaway, Chapman's roommate at the University of Virginia, whose 47th Virginia captured Randol's battery. Another prize was McCall, captured when he strayed into Confederate lines. Despite the beating his battery had taken earlier in the afternoon, Chapman witnessed the action and observed McCall as he was taken off the battlefield.[34]

However, the addition of A. P. Hill's troops, already weary from fighting at Mechanicsville and Gaines's Mill, was offset by Federal reinforcements. Jackson's idleness at White Oak Swamp and Huger's inactivity along the Charles City Road allowed Northern reserves to transfer to the Glendale front. Longstreet and Hill had come close to breaking the Federal lines but did not have enough fresh soldiers to meet these reinforcements. Weariness and nightfall brought an end to the hostilities. Stubborn resistance and timely reinforcements had saved the day for McClellan.[35]

As night fell, fallen bodies littered the battlefield. Longstreet and Hill lost more than 600 dead, 2,800 wounded, and 200 missing. Federal losses were almost 300 killed, 1,700 wounded, and 1,800 missing. Northern general Joseph

Hooker described the ghoulish scene that night: "From their torches we could see that the enemy was busy all night long in searching for his wounded, but up to daylight the following morning there had been no apparent diminution in the heart-rendering cries and groans of his wounded. The unbroken, mournful wail of human suffering was all that we heard from Glendale during that long, dismal night." One more day of suffering was still to come.[36]

Tuesday, 1 July, the seventh and final day of fighting, found the Federal army massed on Malvern Hill near the James River. Terrain restricted the Confederate attacks to a narrow front along the northern slope, where open ground rose gradually from the bottomland. Two divisions of 17,800 men and 37 guns lined this narrow battlefront. More men and guns guarded the western and eastern slopes. All told, 53,000 men and 171 guns crowded onto the hill. Into this cauldron of firepower, Lee sent Jackson's, Magruder's, and Huger's commands. The plan was to precede the infantry assaults with a coordinated artillery bombardment, but the necessary batteries could not be massed in strength. Instead, various batteries unlimbered individually only to be driven off with heavy losses in men, guns, and horses. Wave after wave of Confederate regiments and brigades marched in scattered, uncoordinated advances and were slaughtered in the face of overwhelming cannon fire and musketry. The assaults that day yielded another 8,650 casualties North and South but did not give the outcome Lee desired. McClellan again held the battlefield.[37]

Rain fell in torrents the next day, as many weary soldiers expected. A common belief at the time held that cannon fire induced rainfall—a notion that arose from the heavy rainstorms that often followed large battles. When the Confederate pursuit began in earnest the following day, McClellan and his army were safely under the protection of fortifications and gunboats in the area of Harrison's Landing on the James River. Lee pulled his men back toward Richmond, and both sides settled in for a necessary respite from war.[38]

Losses during the Seven Days' battles were horrendous. The Army of the Potomac lost more than 1,700 men killed, 8,000 wounded, and 6,000 missing from an effective strength of about 90,000 men. As the aggressors, Confederate casualties were higher, with about twice as many dead and wounded. Seven days of fighting left more than one in every five Southerners—some 20,000 men—dead, wounded, or captured. Longstreet's division suffered the highest casualties. In two days of fighting at Gaines's Mill and Glendale, almost one-half of the division fell dead or wounded.[39]

Chapman's experience during the Seven Days' battles, engaged only at Glendale with a loss of one man killed and two severely wounded, was not much different than that of other batteries in Longstreet's division. Smith's Third Company of the Richmond Howitzers supported Featherston's brigade at Gaines's Mill. It was in action again with Featherston at Glendale where one man was wounded. Maurin's Donaldsonville Artillery saw action at Gaines's

Mill, where it was attached to Pryor's brigade and joined with Smith's battery to support Longstreet's attacks, and it may have been in action again at Glendale. The battery lost one killed and three wounded. Anderson's Thomas Artillery lost one man killed at Gaines's Mill, where the battery supported Wilcox's division, and another man killed and two wounded at Glendale. Dearing's Lynchburg Artillery laid down heavy fire in support of Pickett's division at Glendale. Rogers's Loudoun Artillery saw no action at Gaines's Mill, though the battery was under fire, and though posted with Kemper's brigade at Glendale saw no action. Stribling's Fauquier Artillery had been detached from Longstreet's division following Seven Pines. The battery rejoined the division in time for Glendale, where it was exposed to heavy fire but did not go into action. The four companies of the Washington Artillery, sixteen guns in all, fired no shots during those seven days. For their trials, the batteries in Longstreet's division received three captured Napoleons, three 3-inch rifles, one 12-pounder howitzer, and one Parrott rifle. A 3-inch rifle, gained at Glendale, augmented the meager armament of the Dixie Artillery.[40]

In the days following the fighting, Longstreet's artillery settled into camp near Richmond. Camp life provided a needed diversion from combat, but war still intruded on several occasions. Throughout the month of July, light artillery batteries were sent on various forays to the James River to interfere with Federal shipping. Squires's company of the Washington Artillery and Rogers's Loudoun Artillery had participated in one such action near Charles City Court House earlier in the month. The Dixie Artillery participated in another such affair. Walton sent eight batteries to the vicinity of New Market to support Brig. Gen. Robert Toombs's infantry brigade at the end of July. Among the batteries detached to the outpost were the Dixie Artillery, the Loudoun Artillery, and the Fauquier Artillery. At some point, two armed side-wheel ships anchored nearby on the James River. The Dixie Artillery along with other batteries under the command of Maj. John Garnett marched to the banks of the river to drive them off, but the ships turned around without the batteries firing.[41]

The "long arm of Lee" was poorly utilized during the Seven Days' battles. Infantry commanders launched attacks without preliminary artillery bombardment and in some cases without artillery support. In part, the terrain around Richmond, with dense forest cover, did not favor artillery. However, organizational deficiencies in the artillery corps contributed to its poor showing. Confederate artillery was not organized into battalions but rather commissioned as independent batteries. Infantry brigades had an attached battery, and other batteries formed a divisional reserve. Pendleton, as chief of artillery for the army, commanded a larger general reserve. This scattering of commands made it difficult to mass artillery so as to concentrate fire as needed. Indeed, Pendleton's reserve artillery did not participate in much of the fighting. Instead, individual batteries often opened fire in a piecemeal basis and were easily knocked out by devastating counter fire. A reorganization of the artillery service in June had reduced the number of undermanned batteries and had provided a chief of artillery for each division, who led divisional reserves to support brigade batteries. However, better organization was still needed.[42]

5 | Opportunely Delivered Fire

The seeds of the Manassas campaign were sown on 26 June 1862, even before the fighting around Richmond had reached its conclusion, when Maj. Gen. John Pope gained command of the newly organized Army of Virginia. This army, 51,000 men strong, consisted of remnants of the forces Stonewall Jackson had earlier defeated in the Shenandoah Valley. Its task was to move against Gordonsville and Charlottesville to disrupt the Confederacy's link to the Shenandoah Valley along the Virginia Central Railroad. The army soon advanced to the Rappahannock and Rapidan Rivers in a line extending from Fredericksburg west to Culpeper Court House and Sperryville. So began the events that over the following weeks would elevate Chapman's Dixie Artillery to the heights of success yet in the end bring the disbanding of his battery and loss of command.[1]

The strategic situation in July did not favor the Confederate army around Richmond. McClellan's Army of the Potomac still threatened the capital from its base on the James River, and Pope readied his Army of Virginia to advance south. To counter this threat while still defending Richmond, Lee sent 14,000 men to Gordonsville under the command of Jackson. Without sufficient numbers to attack, Jackson settled into a wary watch. A. P. Hill's division later joined Jackson, but still Jackson waited for his opportunity to strike. That came on 6 August, when Pope began moving his army on Culpeper. Pope's troop movements left the army scattered, and Jackson found his opportunity at Cedar Mountain, eight miles south of Culpeper. There, on the ninth, he engaged the Federals, but though Jackson held the field, the position was not secure, and the Confederates fell back across the Rapidan River to Gordonsville two days later. By that time, Lee had discerned that McClellan no longer threatened Richmond and was in fact abandoning his position on the James River. It was John Mosby who secured evidence of this movement and brought it to Lee's attention. Lee left a minimal force around Richmond and moved the remainder of the army to Gordonsville.[2]

The end of July found the Dixie Artillery still attached to Longstreet's division. Together, the Dixie and the Washington batteries formed the artillery reserve. Yet as the men prepared for the march to Gordonsville, they suffered from losses in the ranks—a persistent trend that would ultimately lead to disbandment. Three men had been lost from service at Glendale, 1 man transferred, 4 men were medically discharged, and 1 man died of chronic diarrhea.[3]

Walton's command prepared to leave camp on Saturday, 9 August, and began the march late Sunday afternoon. Unlike their brethren in the infantry, who enjoyed a quick passage to Gordonsville by train, the artillerymen labored under a difficult march, covering some 70 miles in the oppressive heat and humidity of central Virginia in August. Temperatures in excess of 90°F restricted marching to early morning and evening. Midday relief was sought in whatever shade could be found. The artillerists reached Louisa Court House Tuesday evening and Gordonsville Wednesday morning. The next day, the fourteenth, they set up camp 3 miles from Gordonsville. There, the weary men rested, but their respite was brief.[4]

The fifteenth of August found Lee, Jackson, and Longstreet at Gordonsville planning strategy. Jackson commanded the left wing of the army, 24,000 men organized into three divisions. Longstreet commanded the right wing, 30,000 men organized into five divisions. The commanders knew that if they had any hope of victory they must quickly defeat Pope's army before McClellan's arrived. Pope's Army of Virginia was situated between the Rapidan and Rappahannock Rivers. The latter river presented a formidable barrier. The Confederates could gain a decisive victory by blocking the river crossings and pinning the Federals along the Rappahannock. Lee set the attack for three days later, 18 August.[5]

Longstreet's command had grown considerably from his old division of six brigades. In this campaign, he commanded fifteen brigades. Richard Anderson, who had led the division during the Seven Days' battles, now held the rank of major general and led a division of three brigades. Brig. Gen. John Hood led a second division of two brigades—his Texas brigade and Col. Evander Law's brigade. Four other brigades had joined the command—three organized into a division led by Brig. Gen. David Jones; the fourth, an independent brigade of Brig. Gen. Nathan Evans's South Carolinians. Longstreet split his old division into two separate divisions. Cadmus Wilcox commanded his own, Roger Pryor's, and Winfield Featherston's brigades. James Kemper commanded his own brigade, Micah Jenkins's brigade, and Pickett's brigade, still led by Eppa Hunton. Longstreet had 23 batteries. Col. Stephen D. Lee commanded a battalion of six batteries attached to Anderson's division along with two independent batteries. Walton, who was named chief of artillery for the right wing, commanded the other 15 batteries. Three of these batteries operated with Hood's division. Walton assigned the remaining 12 batteries to the ten other brigades and kept 2 batteries in reserve. He placed Chapman's Dixie Artillery with Featherston's brigade.[6]

The army began its advance to the Rapidan River on 16 August. That Saturday night found Jackson's left wing north of Orange Court House approaching

Somerville Ford. Longstreet, on the right, advanced on Raccoon Ford. Walton's artillerymen had spent Friday and Saturday morning preparing for the rigors of the march, including cooking three days' rations of bread and meat to be carried in haversacks. In a long march that began at 3:30 P.M. Saturday and continued into the night until 1:30 A.M., the artillerists approached Orange Court House. The march resumed Sunday, and following an eleven-hour march on Monday, 18 August, the command bivouacked near Raccoon Ford on the Rapidan at 11:00 P.M.[7]

However, before the Confederates could attack, Pope learned of their presence and made his escape across the Rappahannock River. Lee responded by directing his army to cross the Rapidan on the morning of the twentieth. The men again prepared to march, with the now familiar cry to cook three days' rations. The twentieth of August dawned early for the men in Walton's artillery, who marched at three o'clock in the morning. By the end of the day, Jackson's men approached Brandy Station north of Culpeper. Longstreet's men advanced on Kelly's Ford, several miles downstream of Rappahannock Station.[8]

The next days found the Federal army ensconced safely behind the Rappahannock River in a line extending from Kelly's Ford on its left flank upstream to Rappahannock Station and beyond. It was a strong position, the few fords and bridges across the river being easily guarded. The bridge at Rappahannock Station on the Orange and Alexandria Railroad was particularly well-defended. Artillery lined the banks of the river, and a small bridgehead of infantry and artillery remained across the river. Pope maintained contact with Fredericksburg, from where McClellan's first troops were to arrive, and left the crossings above Rappahannock Station—Beverly's Ford, Freeman's Ford, Fauquier White Sulphur Springs (known locally as Fauquier Springs), and Waterloo—lightly defended. Lee saw this opportunity and moved his army upriver over the next few days. Jackson's corps extended as far as Fauquier Springs; Longstreet's covered Freeman's Ford, Beverly's Ford, and Rappahannock Station.[9]

The morning of 23 August brought the first action of the campaign for the Dixie Artillery. As dawn broke, seventeen long-range guns from Walton's artillery readied to drive the Federals from the crossings at Beverly's Ford and Rappahannock Station. Walton had personally selected the positions the night before. Seven guns held the Beverly's Ford line, placed on a hill overlooking the river some 1,000 yards distant—on the left, Edwin Anderson's Thomas Artillery, one 10-pounder Parrott; in the center, Arthur Rogers's Loudoun Artillery, two 10-pounder Parrotts; and on the right, four 12-pounder Napoleons of Buck Miller's Third Company, Washington Artillery. Walton positioned a second line of ten guns nearby in front of Jones's divisional headquarters on a hill overlooking Rappahannock Station. Here, one 3-inch rifle and three Napoleons of Robert Stribling's Fauquier Artillery, a 3-inch rifle and a Napoleon of Chapman's Dixie Artillery, and four 3-inch rifles of Charles Squires's First Company, Washington

Artillery, prepared to drive the Federals away from the bridge. Two Blakely guns of Victor Maurin's Donaldsonville Artillery shortly joined the batteries at Rappahannock Station. These nineteen Confederate guns were opposed by twelve Federal guns across the river at Beverly's Ford, eighteen guns across the river at Rappahannock Station, and two guns at the bridgehead. Longstreet later called the ensuing duel "quite a spirited artillery combat."[10]

Heavy rain the previous night enshrouded the river valley in fog and mist during the early morning hours. At six o'clock, as the sun rose and the fog lifted, Miller fired the first shot. The other Confederate guns immediately opened fire and drew a quick reply. The return fire was heavy, accurate, and deadly. Smoke filled the river valley as cannons belched forth round after round in rapid succession. Shells screamed overhead and sprayed their deadly fragments. It was "a dreadfully hot reply," said Napier Bartlett of Miller's company. "Every shot they fired tore through our ranks, killing and wounding the men, and smashing the pieces." Shell fragments wounded one of Rogers's men in the lower body, chest, and arm; buckshot struck his head. The steady stream of shot and shell forced Rogers and Anderson to withdraw their guns after less than an hour. Miller's company remained in position and endured a devastating barrage as the Federal batteries concentrated their fire on his sole remaining guns. After some time, Miller, too, withdrew. The stubborn and unflinching artillerists from New Orleans had fired 356 rounds of ammunition and lost five men killed, eight wounded, and twenty-one horses killed. Among the dead was Lt. Isaac Brewer, wounded in the groin and his left arm shot off at the shoulder.[11]

The action was just as hot on the right, where the Confederate guns fired upon the bridgehead and the batteries on the opposing bank. A well-positioned Federal battery on the left enfiladed the Confederate guns. A section of the Washington Artillery changed front and engaged the battery along with Maurin's two guns. The firing was fast and furious. One of Squires's guns became so hot it exploded and killed a man. These twelve guns fired a total of 1,172 rounds of ammunition. The two guns of the Dixie Artillery fired one-quarter of the rounds—299 shots. It was just the second combat experience for the Dixie Artillery, and the men from Page County performed with "great coolness," Squires reported. Casualties were heavy. Squires's company lost four men killed and five wounded—one, shot through the heart with spherical case; another, part of his head blown away by shell. The Dixie Artillery suffered four wounded. Stribling's battery, too, took casualties and was rendered nearly immoveable from the loss of horses.[12]

After two hours of dueling, Longstreet sent two brigades of infantry to clear out the bridgehead. At the sight of these Confederates advancing, the Federals quickly abandoned their positions and crossed over the bridge. The artillery on the opposing banks that had plagued the Confederate guns turned their attention on the advancing southern infantrymen. Boyce's Macbeth Artillery came up to support the infantry. Murderous cannon fire drove the Confederate artillerists off in just two minutes with a loss of seven men wounded and seven horses killed. The Confederates had forced back the bridgehead, but the Northerners still held the bridge, which they set ablaze at noon.[13]

The twenty-third of August was also a day of action for Jackson's men upriver at Fauquier Springs. The heavy downpour the previous night swelled the river and trapped a Confederate expeditionary force across the river. Pope saw an opportunity to strike and shifted his army upriver on the morning of the twenty-third to attack. However, the Confederates hastily built a bridge across the river and crossed back to safety late that night and into the following morning. Lee was denied yet again in his attempt to cross the river, and worse, Pope was marching upriver to block future attempts. By nightfall on the twenty-fourth, Pope confronted Jackson in force at the upper crossings at Fauquier Springs and Waterloo. To match this movement, Longstreet abandoned the Rappahannock Station position and marched upriver to Jeffersonton that day. Time was not on Lee's side. Delay worked to Pope's advantage because elements of the Army of the Potomac were arriving from Fredericksburg. More came south from Alexandria by way of the railroad.[14]

Out of this strategic stalemate, Lee hatched one of his most daring maneuvers of the war. On 24 August he proposed to split his army in two. Jackson was to march north around the far right of the Federal army, turn east and pass through the Bull Run Mountains at Thoroughfare Gap, and strike the Federal rear along the Orange and Alexandria Railroad. Longstreet would defend the Rappahannock line, later linking with Jackson. Dividing the army was a dangerous gambit, and Pope could easily crush either of the two isolated army wings. But battles are not won without risk, and on that Sunday evening, Longstreet's forces quietly replaced Jackson's along the Rappahannock River. Over the next two days, Longstreet's artillery poured heavy cannon fire across the Rappahannock to deceive Pope about the Confederate strength while Jackson marched through Thoroughfare Gap.[15]

Jackson's march of 25–26 August was uneventful, and he arrived in Pope's rear unopposed with some 24,000 men. He struck the Orange and Alexandria Railroad during the evening of the twenty-sixth, first at Bristoe Station and then at Manassas Junction. Pope responded to this threat by turning his army around from its lines along the Rappahannock River and moving toward Gainesville. Jackson settled into a site a few hundred yards north of the Warrenton turnpike in the vicinity of Groveton near the old Manassas battlefield to await the arrival of Longstreet. It was a strong defensive position. Thick woods and a deep, unfinished railroad cut offered protection while allowing Jackson to watch for the expected Federal advance east along the turnpike. Moreover, the position was close to Thoroughfare Gap, from which Longstreet's force would soon emerge and link with Jackson's right flank.[16]

Longstreet's command, joined by Lee and his staff, began the march to join Jackson on the twenty-sixth. Anderson's division and Stephen D. Lee's artillery battalion remained behind to guard the river. Longstreet followed the same path as Jackson, but at a more leisurely pace. Clear skies and hot weather baked the men. They made camp at Orleans on the first night and along the Manassas Gap Railroad at The Plains (also known as White Plains) on the second night. On the twenty-eighth, the march did not resume until 11:00 A.M. Longstreet's soldiers reached Thoroughfare Gap by 3:00 P.M., at which time they secured the gap and bivouacked west of the mountain.[17]

The second battle at Manassas opened on 28 August. Brig. Gen. Rufus King's Federal division marched east on the Warrenton turnpike toward Centreville late that Thursday afternoon. Near the Brawner farm in the vicinity of Groveton, the four brigades tangled with Jackson's Confederates. It was not a particularly large affair, but the opposing lines were close, in some places separated by tens of yards, and fallen bodies littered the fields stretching from the Brawner house toward Groveton over the course of two hours. One of every three men engaged in the fighting fell, including two of Jackson's division commanders. It was by no means a victory for Jackson, but King still moved his division back toward Manassas later that night. The fighting resumed the next morning as more Northern soldiers massed on the battlefield. Federal infantrymen advanced along a two-mile-long battlefront throughout the morning, but their attacks were uncoordinated and poorly managed. They damaged the Confederates, but Jackson fended off the attacks, and the action on the morning of the twenty-ninth, though at great cost of life, was indecisive.[18]

Longstreet's command arrived on the scene around 10:00 A.M. and deployed over the next two hours. In contrast to the previous day, the march from Thoroughfare Gap to Haymarket and Gainesville and onto the Warrenton turnpike began early, at 6:00 A.M. for the lead division. The weather was hot, and the men suffered from thirst in air choked with dust kicked up by tens of thousands of troops marching on dirt roads. Before reaching Gainesville, the soldiers heard the din of combat and approached the battlefield knowing that another fight was at hand. Hood's division—his brigade and Law's—arrived first and positioned along the Warrenton turnpike, supported by Evans's brigade. Stribling's Fauquier Artillery assisted as the Confederates pushed back the forward Federal lines. Kemper's three brigades deployed to the right of Hood, extending toward the Manassas Gap Railroad. Rogers's Loudoun Artillery unlimbered on the right near the railroad, along with Bachman's German battery, which fired on Federal troops advancing along the Manassas–Gainesville road. Jones's three brigades went into line on the right flank along the railroad. Wilcox's division, at the rear of the march, formed along the Warrenton turnpike. In all, Longstreet's line stretched south one and a half miles from the right of Jackson's line near the Brawner house, perpendicular to the Warrenton turnpike.[19]

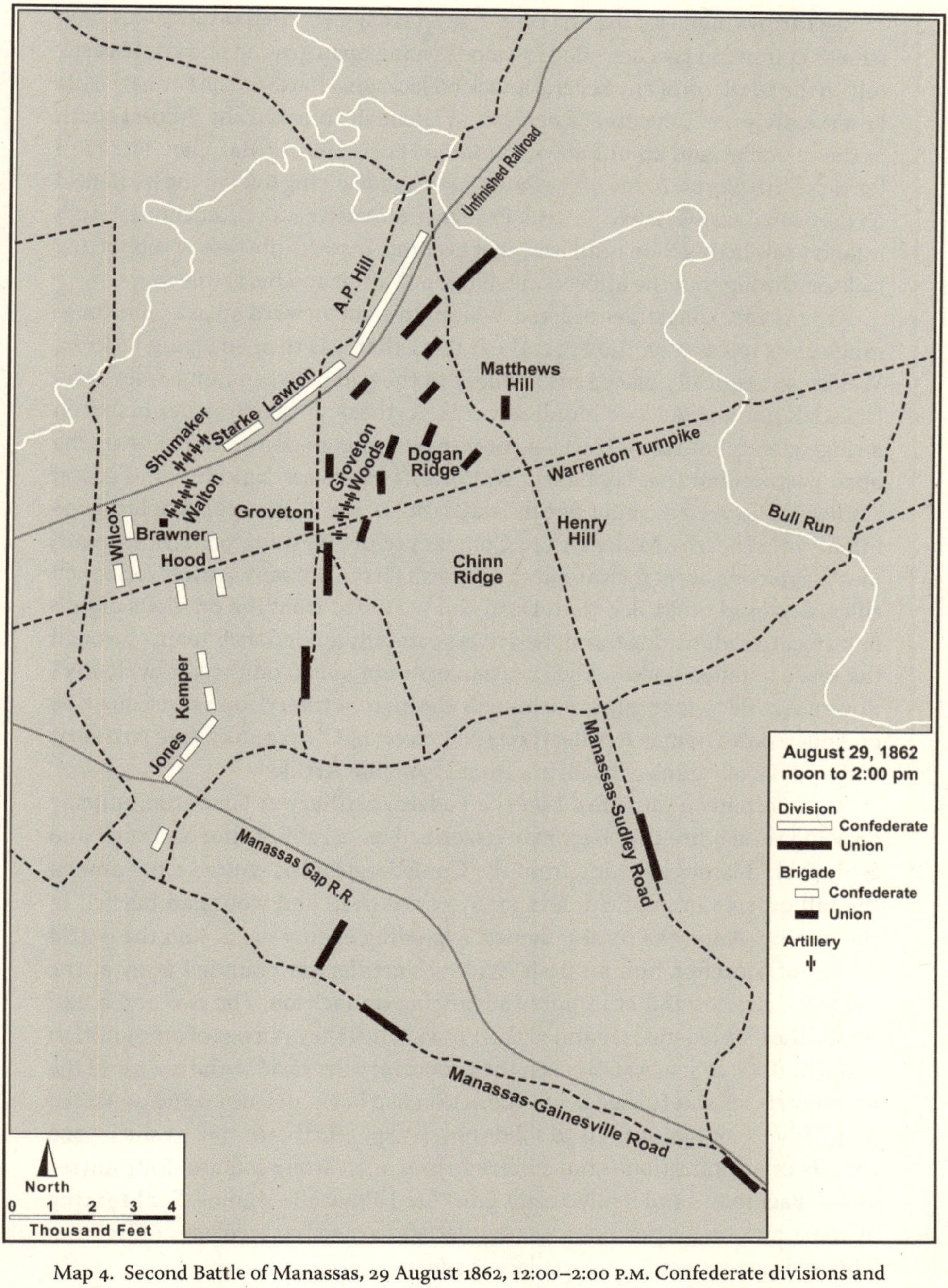

Map 4. Second Battle of Manassas, 29 August 1862, 12:00–2:00 P.M. Confederate divisions and artillery are labeled by commander. From John J. Hennessy, *Second Manassas Battlefield Map Study* (Lynchburg, Va.: H. E. Howard, 1991), map 5.

Lee's army, united for the first time in several days, was well-positioned. Longstreet's command lay concealed in woods facing open ground and could easily roll up the left flank of any Federal attack on Jackson. However, the Pennsylvania Reserve division, Longstreet's nemesis at Glendale, blocked the ground south of the turnpike, and an unknown but large Federal force (Maj. Gen. Fitz John Porter's Fifth Corps, Army of the Potomac) was advancing toward the battlefield on the Manassas–Gainesville road. Prudence dictated caution, and Longstreet's infantry saw little action until later that evening. Instead, the task of supporting Jackson throughout the afternoon fell upon Walton and his artillery.

At 1:00 P.M. Longstreet ordered Walton to send forward all available long-range guns to open on the Federal left flank that was then engaging Jackson. Walton strategically placed his artillery in the gap between Longstreet's and Jackson's lines, about two hundred yards northeast of the Brawner house on a ridge cleared of trees. It was a prominent vantage point, higher than the open pastureland that lay below. Walton's cannoneers could fire on Federal artillery at Groveton, about one mile distant, as well as in support of Jackson's infantrymen nearby. Miller's Third Company of the Washington Artillery, with four Napoleons, went forward first. Squires's First Company, with three 3-inch rifles, deployed on Miller's left. Dead and wounded from the previous night's fighting littered the ridge, and the drivers carefully guided their teams through the maze of fallen bodies. The Louisianans were joined on the left by: Reilly's Rowan Artillery, four guns; Bachman's German Artillery, four guns; one rifle of Anderson's Thomas Artillery; one Napoleon of Chapman's Dixie Artillery; and two Blakely guns of Maurin's Donaldsonville Artillery.[20]

These nineteen guns fired on the Federal artillery at Groveton, quickly drawing return fire that Bachman described as "a rain of shot and shell and schrapnel." Flames belching from the Confederate guns ignited a fire among the tall grasses in the field, and many of the dead and wounded burned in the inferno. Amid the smoke, flames, exploding enemy shells, and the putrid stench of scorched human flesh, Walton's artillerists pounded away at the Federal batteries and at infantry advancing on Jackson. For two and a half hours, the Confederates manned their guns, until they ran out of ammunition and withdrew at 3:30 P.M. By then the Federal artillery had withdrawn and the infantry attack was turned back. The action had been furious up and down the line. Miller's four guns fired 76 solid shot, 117 spherical case, and 33 shell—226 rounds of ammunition—and suffered three men wounded and four horses killed. Bachman's and Reilly's eight guns fired about 100 rounds. For breaking up the attack on his positions, the artillerists earned the accolades of Jackson, who told Longstreet, "your artillery is superior to mine."[21]

Pope ignored reports of a strong Confederate presence on his left flank—Longstreet—and instead clung to the belief that Porter, advancing on the Manassas–Gainesville road, would strike Jackson's right flank. He initiated a series of assaults designed to keep Jackson occupied, his attention away from the expected threat from Porter. Some of these attacks had initial success that if supported might have broken Jackson's lines, but all were disjointed and uncoordinated and were repulsed in savage, hand-to-hand combat with rifle butt and bayonet, at great cost to North and South. As the fighting wound down with the coming of darkness, little had been settled that afternoon. Pope's indecisive clashes with Jackson only left the battlefield littered with men dead, dying, and wounded numbering in the thousands. And still one more day of fighting, more horrific than that Friday, was yet to come. It was a day on which Chapman's guns would butcher and maim hundreds of Northern men.[22]

The morning of 30 August found both armies in essentially the same positions as the previous day. Jackson occupied the unfinished railroad cut. Longstreet's line extended perpendicular to Jackson, reaching south to the Manassas Gap Railroad. Anderson's division, along with Stephen D. Lee's artillery battalion, had arrived during the night and was in reserve. After the engagement the previous afternoon, Walton had pulled his guns back from the ridge near the Brawner house. Now, Stephen D. Lee placed eighteen guns in the same location, ready to enfilade any Federal attack on Jackson. Pope lacked a firm grasp of the strategic situation that day—he clung to a misguided belief that the Confederates were retreating from the field of battle—and the fate of the Federal army hinged upon an ill-conceived attack on Jackson's right flank.[23]

The burden of attack that Saturday afternoon fell upon Fitz John Porter. Two brigades of Brig. Gen. Daniel Butterfield's division—Col. Henry Weeks on the left and Col. Charles Roberts in the center—led the attack. King's division, now commanded by Brig. Gen. John Hatch, provided additional support. These four brigades took the right, led into battle by Col. Timothy Sullivan's brigade, followed by Brig. Gen. Marsena Patrick's brigade, with Brig. Gen. John Gibbon and Brig. Gen. Abner Doubleday in the rear. Two brigades of Brig. Gen. George Sykes's division were held in reserve, ready to exploit the successes of Butterfield and Hatch. In all, some 10,000 infantrymen maneuvered into position in and around Groveton woods.[24]

The woods offered some cover from which to launch an attack, but Stephen D. Lee's cannoneers harassed the Federals as they took their positions. Skirmishers exchanged musket fire, and all recognized the daunting task before them. Weeks's and Roberts's brigades had to cross up to 600 yards of open farmland before they hit the Confederate lines. Hatch's division on the right had to advance across 300 yards. Without any cover to conceal them, men all along the battlefront would be exposed to murderous flanking fire from Confederate artillery. The task would get no easier once the troops had crossed the field, for they were advancing directly into some of the best infantrymen in the Confederate army. Butterfield spurred his men to step out of the woods that afternoon with a rousing three cheers. Others in his command saw the

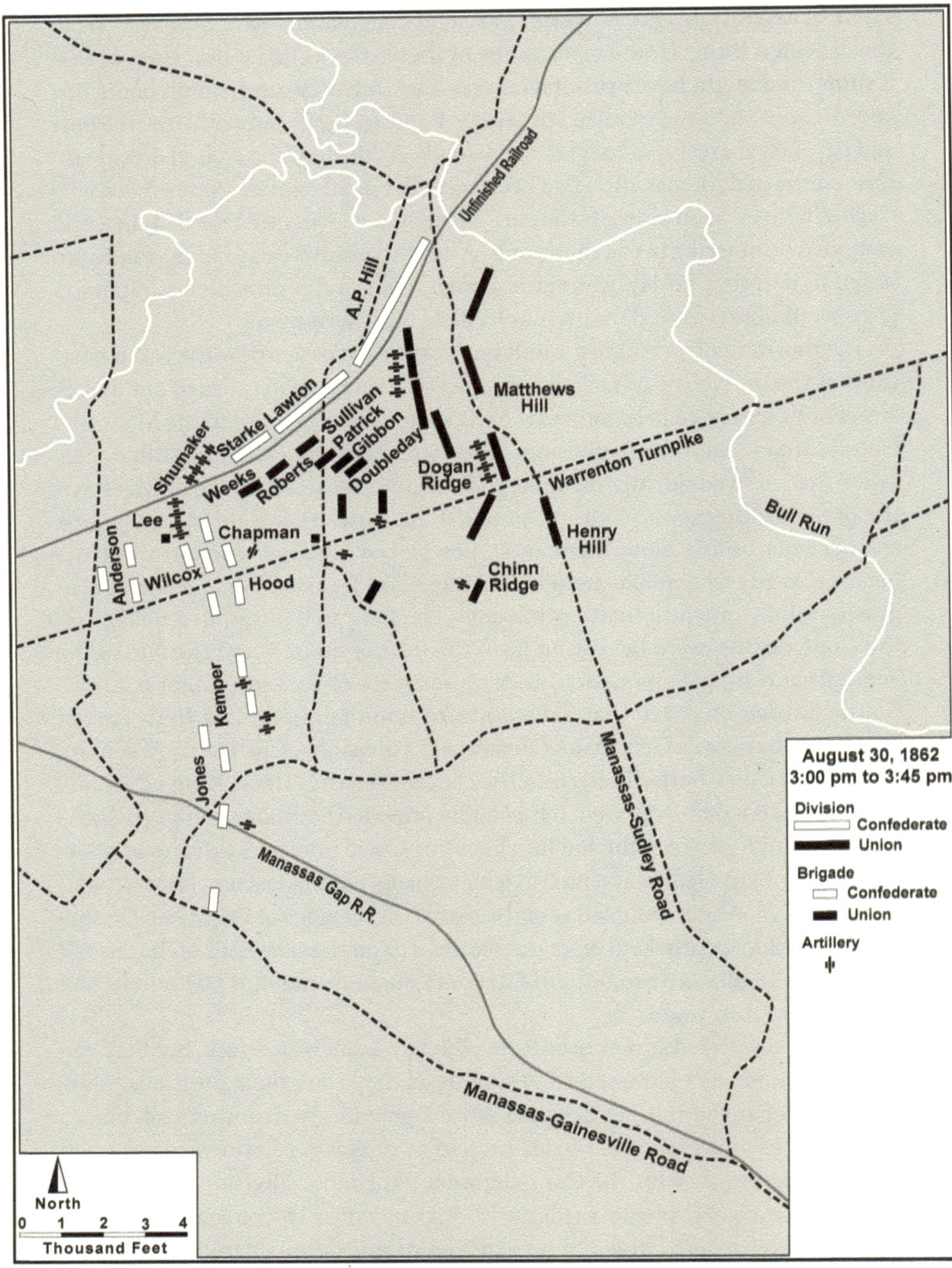

Map 5. Second Battle of Manassas, 30 August 1862, 3:00–3:45 P.M. Confederate divisions and artillery are labeled by commander, as are Federal infantry brigades that participated in the attack. From Hennessy, *Second Manassas*, map 11.

cauldron of fire that they were about to enter and were less optimistic. "Even privates realized that they were going into the jaws of death itself," reported Charles Roberts. Col. Horace Roberts of the 1st Michigan told his troops to "remember what Michigan and our friends at home expect of us." The Michiganders did do what was expected of them and paid the price. Horace Roberts himself died in the charge.[25]

At 3:00 P.M. the Federals emerged from the woods. It was a spectacular advance with men aligned shoulder to shoulder, muskets and bayonets gleaming in the sun, flags waving. Hatch's four brigades on the right were to advance in six lines, each separated by fifty yards, but only Sullivan and Patrick left the woods. Sullivan's four regiments advanced in lines of two—the 24th and 30th New York, followed by the 22nd and 84th New York. Musket fire met the lead New Yorkers, but on they advanced, transformed, recalled one man, "from a lot of good natured boys to the most bloodthirsty of demoniacs." The second line stepped from the woods only to crumble before a storm of shot and shell. Patrick's 21st and 35th New York struggled across the field in what one Confederate called a "slaughter." Only the 80th New York advanced in the next line; the 23rd New York reached the edge of the woods but did not step beyond it into the field. Roberts's brigade advanced along the center in a line of three regiments—the 18th Massachusetts, 13th New York, and 1st Michigan, trailed by the 2nd Maine. Weeks's brigade on the left struggled onto the field under heavy cannon fire. The 17th New York advanced in the first line, followed by the 44th New York, 83rd Pennsylvania, 12th New York, and 16th Michigan.[26]

The military creed of duty, honor, and country spurred the Northerners to cross the open field into murderous musket and cannon fire. Lee's cannons wreaked havoc with Weeks's and Roberts's brigades leading the left and center of the attack. Exploding shells cut down wide swaths of men, but the gaps closed, and the men pressed on across the field. Many reached the Confederate lines along the railroad cut, and a fierce firefight ensued. Porter's infantrymen pushed the Confederates back, only to lose the contested land following a determined Southern countercharge. Jackson's men were holding the line but were hard-pressed and needed help fast.[27]

That help came from the Dixie Artillery. The battery was toward the rear along the Warrenton turnpike. Earlier, Chapman had ridden forward to Featherston's brigade, to which his battery was assigned, and saw Porter's infantry advancing. When he returned to his battery, Chapman saw Longstreet and his staff riding toward the front. Anticipating Longstreet's request for artillery to move up and support Jackson, Chapman readied his men to move. Within a few minutes, a staff officer hurriedly came back with a request for batteries. Longstreet had indeed seen that Jackson needed help and had called for artillery. The Dixie Artillery responded and instantly moved to the front at a gallop. Longstreet personally directed the placement of its Napoleon, 3-inch rifle, and smoothbore 6-pounder at a prominent point on the left of the turnpike. The position offered an unobstructed view of the assault from which enfilading fire could devastate the advancing troops. As the three guns of the Dixie Artillery formed "in battery," the Federal infantrymen passed within 400 yards.[28]

The artillerists from Page County quickly found the range and poured devastating fire into the advancing Federal lines. Sam Chapman recalled that "a line of battle from the enemy was advancing in fine order for an attack" as the Dixie Artillery deployed. "The order to fire upon them was given, and as the guns were on their left flank a most destructive enfilade fire was given. Behind this line of battle came another, and still another. The first had halted under the fire that ploughed their ranks. The second and third line was soon mixed with the first and the work of destruction went on more fiercely as shot and shell tore to pieces all formation of this body of men."[29]

Wilcox described a similar scene as the second line emerged from the woods: "The fire of this battery [Chapman's] was most opportunely delivered upon this advancing line of the enemy. They were caught in the open field. The effect of every shot could be seen. A rapid fire of shot, shell, and spherical case, delivered with admirable precision, checked their advance. As the shells and spherical case would burst over in front and near them their ranks would break, hesitate, and scatter. This artillery fire alone broke regiment after regiment and drove them back into the woods." Thomas Church Haskell Smith of Pope's staff witnessed the action. He watched as "every shot went through the ranks" and later told Chapman that "it was the firing of your battery that turned the tide of the battle." Capt. William Huson, commanding the 12th New York, was exposed to the fire of the Dixie Artillery. "We marched into the open field," he reported, "where we were met by a terrible fire from a masked battery of three guns, throwing shell, grape, and canister in quick succession, woefully thinning our ranks at each discharge."[30]

There were few Federal batteries in position to return fire, and the Dixie Artillery was most likely initially mistaken for a Northern battery. Its guns were positioned to the left and rear of the advancing infantrymen, and its shots ricocheted into Jackson's lines. This may well have confused the Northerners, who did not return fire for several minutes. Indeed, Maj. Freeman Conner, commanding the 44th New York, afterwards complained of friendly artillery fire from the rear.[31]

With ineffective return fire from opposing Federal batteries, the Confederate artillerists—Stephen D. Lee's eighteen guns and Chapman's three guns—quickly decimated the Federal ranks moving across the field. And when those in the first line that had reached the railroad cut began to retreat back across the field, they were trapped among the shot and shell with their oncoming comrades. A witness to the artillery barrage described the carnage: "As shell after shell burst in the wavering ranks, and round-shot plowed broad gaps among them, you could distinctly see through the rifts of smoke the Federal soldiers flying and falling on every side. With the explosion of every bomb, it seemed as if scores dropped dead or writhed in agony upon the field. Some were crawling upon their hands and knees; some were piled up together, and some were scattered around in every attitude that imagination could conceive." In a short time, perhaps thirty to forty-five minutes since the first battle line had advanced from the woods, the assault was broken.[32]

Longstreet romanticized the battle scene in his remembrances: "The heavy fumes of gunpowder hanging about our ranks, as stimulating as sparkling wine, charged the atmosphere with the light and splendor of battle." For the Northerners who made the assault, it was anything but romantic. Roberts lost 103 men killed, 374 wounded, and 99 captured from his brigade. Weeks's brigade lost 70 killed, 357 wounded, and 163 missing. Confederates killed, wounded, or captured one of every three men in the 290-man 16th Michigan. About one-half of the 17th New York, including 5 company captains, fell that afternoon. The 44th New York brought 160 men onto the field; 71 were killed, wounded, or captured. The 83rd Pennsylvania—224 men strong—suffered 97 casualties.[33]

The collapse of Porter's attack provided the opportunity to crush the Northern army. In the few hours of daylight remaining, Longstreet unleashed his brigades on the weakly defended Federal left flank. The Confederate advance rolled onto Chinn Ridge and then on toward Henry Hill, which dominated the Warrenton turnpike and the Federal retreat across Bull Run. Though Longstreet's infantrymen pressed the Northerners hard, indeed wreaked many casualties, the Southerners could not gain control of the all-important Henry Hill. As darkness fell, the fighting abated. The turnpike still lay in Northern hands, and the Federal army trudged off the battlefield across Bull Run to fight another day.[34]

Longstreet's batteries advanced to support the infantry during these attacks. Stribling's Fauquier Artillery assisted the assault on Chinn Ridge and then joined Rogers's Loudoun Artillery and Eshleman's Fourth Company, Washington Artillery during the attack on Henry Hill. Richardson's Second Company, Washington Artillery also operated on the right flank. Bachman's German, Garden's Palmetto, and Reilly's Rowan batteries advanced along the Warrenton turnpike to the area around Groveton. Boyce's Macbeth battery, too, moved forward. All fired on the Federal batteries at Dogan Ridge, which threatened the left flank of Longstreet's advance. The Dixie Artillery joined in the advance up the turnpike. The battery took position in an orchard near Groveton, where it fired at the retreating infantry for about thirty minutes, and then advanced beyond Groveton. In both positions, the battery came under heavy fire from Federal artillery massed on Dogan Ridge, and Chapman had two horses shot from under him. At the orchard position, a cannonball crushed both hind legs of Chapman's horse. At the next position, Chapman escaped injury when a shell exploded in front of him, but fragments from the shell killed his horse.[35]

Longstreet's men spent the night encamped among the dead and wounded. Weapons, equipment, and bodies—men and horses—lay scattered across the fields. The fighting yielded more than 3,000 dead and 15,000 wounded. One of the Confederate casualties was Chapman's cousin Christian Forrer, a private in the Stonewall Brigade, shot in the lungs along the railroad cut. He never recovered from this wound and died within a few months. Longstreet's command sustained more than 650 dead and 4,000 wounded, most in the frantic few hours late in the afternoon of the thirtieth. During the night and into the next day, as the army went about the tasks of caring for the wounded, burying the dead, and sorting through the spoils of victory, the skies opened with a steady downpour of rain. But this misery was to be expected after a major battle.[36]

The second battle at Manassas was a great victory for the South. History has lauded the role Stephen D. Lee's eighteen guns played in repulsing Porter's attack but has largely forgotten the effort of the Dixie Artillery and its three guns. Poor records hurt Chapman's claim to history. Longstreet and Wilcox mentioned that an unknown battery participated in the attack but did not identify it in their reports, and Featherston said of the Dixie Artillery only that "it performed good service during the day." Longstreet's writings on the battle also confused the affair. He wrote in his official report that he called up two unnamed batteries and that the attack had been broken before the second arrived. His later recollections changed to mention Reilly's and Boyce's batteries in addition to Chapman's. Chapman's place in history was probably greatly hurt by an 1878 article in the *Southern Historical Society Papers* in which Longstreet claimed that Reilly's six-gun battery unlimbered first, later joined by several other batteries, and that these batteries single-handedly threw back Porter's assault. This drew the wrath of Stephen D. Lee, and a bitter series of letters resulted. It was not until 1887 that Chapman finally contacted Longstreet and clarified the events of that long ago day. Chapman spent the rest of his life defending the glory his battery earned that afternoon of 30 August.[37]

The respite from war was brief, and within a few days the Confederate army was on the move into Maryland. The Manassas campaign had greatly strained the artillery corps. Pendleton's reserve artillery was absent from the campaign, but the hard marching and heavy fighting left brigade and divisional batteries depleted in men, horses, and supplies. Many batteries were too weak to cross into Maryland. Among these were Stribling's Fauquier, Rogers's Loudoun, Anderson's Thomas, and Leake's Goochland batteries, all of Longstreet's right wing, which were sent along with other batteries to Winchester to refit. Rogers had only 48 healthy men in his battery; Stribling, less than 40 men; Anderson, 29. All lacked sufficient horses to haul guns, caissons, and wagons.[38]

Longstreet's command was significantly reorganized following Manassas. Richard Anderson now commanded his three brigades, those of Wilcox, Pryor, and Featherston, and four artillery batteries. David Jones commanded his three brigades and Pickett's, Jenkins's, and Kemper's brigades. Depletions in Stribling's, Rogers's, and Leake's batteries meant that only one battery, Brown's Wise, traveled with the division into Maryland. Nathan Evans and John Hood retained their commands of one and two brigades, respectively, with Boyce's Macbeth battery assigned to Evans, and Bachman's German, Garden's Palmetto, and Reilly's Rowan batteries assigned to Hood. The four-company Washington Artillery formed one divisional reserve under the command of Walton. Stephen D. Lee led the other six-battery reserve. Two brigades led by Brig. Gen. John Walker joined Longstreet's right wing of the army with two new batteries. Maj. Gen. Lafayette McLaws also brought his four brigades to the command along with five batteries. During the Maryland campaign, the Dixie Artillery joined one of those brigades, that of Brig. Gen. Joseph Kershaw. It crossed into Maryland with a Napoleon and a 3-inch rifle, both in short supply in the Confederate arsenal, but saw little or no action until the Confederates retreated across the Potomac River.[39]

The ensuing battle on 17 September at the town of Sharpsburg was the single bloodiest day of the war. The fighting began early in the morning and continued throughout the day. The two armies together sustained some 23,000 casualties in the day's combat. The Dixie Artillery traveled with McLaws's troops to Sharpsburg, but saw no action. Other batteries were, however, heavily engaged in the fighting and suffered significant losses. Stephen D. Lee's artillery battalion lost 10 men killed and 75 wounded. The Washington Artillery took 34 casualties. After resting the next day, the Confederates withdrew across the Potomac River on the evening of the eighteenth and into the morning of the nineteenth.[40]

The Dixie Artillery received fire, but saw no action at Sharpsburg. The battery did, however, participate in the defense of Boteler's Ford as the army retreated across the Potomac River. Located about a mile downstream of Shepherdstown, the shallow crossing provided an important route from Maryland back into Virginia. Pendleton had previously lined the heights on the Virginia side with batteries from his reserve. As other batteries forded the river during the retreat, he gathered them into his defenses and soon had forty-four guns in place. The Dixie Artillery, with its Napoleon and 3-inch rifle, was one of the last to cross the Potomac early in the morning of the nineteenth and joined Pendleton in the defense of the crossing.[41]

The previous day, Chapman had moved the battery back from the Confederate lines at Sharpsburg to obtain forage. That night, he did not sleep well, awoken by the rumbling of wagons and gun carriages passing by. Chapman assumed it was another of Jackson's flanking maneuvers when in fact it was the Confederate army retreating from Sharpsburg. He arose the morning of the nineteenth to find two cavalrymen riding across the field with the warning that there were no troops between them and advancing Federals. The artillerists hastily harnessed their horses, hitched them to the guns, and stole through the woods to the ford. There, with the ominous report of approaching Federals—indeed under fire from skirmishers—they crossed the river with transportation wagons under the watchful eyes of Stonewall Jackson.[42]

Pendleton placed the Dixie Artillery's two guns in line on the bluffs with nine other guns about 200 to 300 yards from the river. The haste was well founded because Federals came up to the river by eight o'clock and positioned artillery and sharpshooters to fire on the Confederates. Pendleton's artillerists remained in position throughout the day in the face of ever-increasing cannon and musket fire that left 3 men dead, 4 wounded, and 26 horses dead or disabled. The batteries kept up their counterfire, and by dusk had run low of ammunition. Pendleton ordered the batteries to retire, just as Federal infantrymen pushed across the river. The Confederates lost four pieces of artillery in the confusion. The Dixie Artillery escaped unscathed, without casualties.[43]

After crossing the Potomac, the Dixie Artillery and the Confederate army retreated up the Shenandoah Valley to Winchester. There, the army encamped to rest and replenish. Straggling plagued the army throughout the Sharpsburg campaign, and the force that assembled around Winchester was greatly reduced in strength. The Dixie Artillery had only 32 men present for duty. Chapman, under orders from Longstreet, returned to Page County to recruit men and purchase horses for the battery.[44]

The artillery was in an especially poor state after weeks of campaigning. The long march from Richmond to the Rappahannock, thence to Manassas, across the Potomac into Maryland, and back across the river to Winchester had exacted a toll. Underfed and overworked hauling guns, caissons, and supplies over long distances on poor roads, the horses many batteries had were no longer sufficient. Men, too, suffered from the incessant marching and fighting. Most batteries were significantly undermanned. Confederate regulations soon to be established called for a light artillery battery of four guns to be manned by 1 captain, 1 first lieutenant, 2 second lieutenants, 1 first sergeant, 1 quartermaster sergeant, 4 sergeants, 8 corporals, 2 buglers, 1 guidon, 2 artificers, and 64–125 privates. Few batteries met these requirements in late September.[45]

Lee recognized the inefficiency of having many small batteries and initiated a reorganization to consolidate the artillery into fewer but larger batteries. At this time, each infantry brigade had an attached artillery battery under the command of the brigadier general. Other batteries formed a reserve for the division under the command of the chief of artillery for the division. Still more batteries, led by the chief of artillery for the army, formed a larger reserve for the entire army. This organization was inefficient because the numerous separate commands hindered concentration of artillery fire. Lee's reorganization was part of an ongoing effort that had begun before the Seven Days' battles and continued into the following year. The new army organization placed the brigade artillery into battalions of several batteries each. Every infantry corps had several artillery battalions that served under the overall command of the chief of artillery for the corps.[46]

Acting on recommendations from Pendleton, Lee, on 4 October, disbanded nineteen light artillery batteries, one-quarter of the army's artillery. The officers were relieved of command, and the men, guns, and horses were redistributed among the remaining batteries. Some were disbanded because of incompetent officers, some because they were too small, and some because despite laudable service they were reduced in strength and unlikely to come up to service standards. Lee ordered the Dixie Artillery, with only thirty-two men present for duty, disbanded for being "greatly below the service standard," and its men were assigned to William Pegram's Purcell Artillery. Other disbanded batteries in Longstreet's corps, all under Walton's command as chief of artillery, included Rogers's Loudoun Artillery, Anderson's Thomas Artillery, Leake's Goochland Artillery, and Brown's Wise Artillery. Pendleton proposed to reduce the four-battery Washington Artillery to two six-gun batteries, but this was not enacted.[47]

Chapman was in Luray when the Dixie Artillery was disbanded. Upon returning to Winchester, he personally appealed to Lee to revoke the order, but to no avail. Robert Stribling, whose Fauquier Artillery survived the reorganization intact, noted the injustice to the brigade batteries, which had seen much action over the past two months and endured many forced marches with irregular issues of rations and forage. The reserve batteries, he bitterly complained, "had seen but little service, had made regular marches and had issued to them rations and forage with comparative regularity."[48]

William Pegram, to whose battery the men of the Dixie Artillery were transferred, looked upon the disbanded units unkindly and believed that "General Lee is getting rid of all incompetent officers and cowards." The result was that "the whole army is in a much better state of discipline than heretofore, and . . . there will not be the same amount of straggling and cowardice." Pegram was quite pleased with the outcome. "My battery is in as good, if not better order, than ever," he informed his sister. "I have two Parrotts and two Napoleons, with plenty of men, and the probability of getting out all six pieces. If you know anything about guns, you will pronounce this a pretty battery."[49]

Chapman and Walton believed that Pendleton purposely disbanded the Dixie Artillery because it was under Walton's command. There is some merit to this reasoning. Walton had feuded with Pendleton over command of Walton's reserve artillery while on the Virginia Peninsula and around Richmond. Walton, himself, later suffered a similar ignominious fate. Though chief of artillery in Longstreet's corps, Walton's command was tenuous. In a February 1863 letter to Lee, Pendleton effusively praised many commanders of Longstreet's artillery. Of Edward Porter Alexander, who led one of Longstreet's artillery battalions, he gushed that "we have no more accomplished officer." Yet of Walton,

Pendleton said simply that "Colonel Walton, of course, remains as long as he wishes in command of this [the Washington Artillery]. He is known to be from Louisiana." Relations were also tense with Alexander. Alexander, not Walton, directed the tactical deployment of Longstreet's artillery at Fredericksburg in December 1862 and at Gettysburg in July 1863. Pendleton again rebuked Walton in a reorganization of the artillery proposed in November 1863. Although Pendleton called Walton a "meritorious officer," he advised Lee that "some other sphere of duty seems required." Alexander was promoted to brigadier general, a rank long coveted by Walton, and made chief of artillery in Longstreet's corps. Walton was eventually placed on other duty as inspector general of artillery and resigned his commission in July 1864.[50]

The year 1862 witnessed the rise of epic clashes between the Army of Northern Virginia and the Army of the Potomac. The Confederates thoroughly defeated the Federals in their attempt to capture Richmond in the spring of 1862, outwitted them along the Rappahannock River in August, and defeated them again on the plains of Manassas during the last days of August. Only at Sharpsburg did the Federals finally turn back the Confederate tide. Some 51,000 Confederates fell dead or wounded in the Peninsula, Manassas, and Maryland campaigns. Federal commanders lost 41,000 killed or wounded and 14,000 captured during this period. But for Chapman, campaigning on this grand scale was over. The impersonality of cannon fire was foregone. He would spend the remaining two years fighting the more intimate close-quarter combat of cavalry raids on horseback, where the weapon of choice, the six-shot .44 caliber Colt army revolver, required personal contact with the enemy.[51]

Chapman was not a professional soldier. His Dixie Artillery is barely mentioned in histories of "the long arm of Lee," but it served the Confederacy well on 30 June at Glendale, 23 August at Rappahannock Station, 29–30 August at Manassas, and 19 September at Boteler's Ford. For this devoted service, Chapman lost his command. His career as an artillerist was over. His career as a cavalier was about to begin. His exploits with John Singleton Mosby would be remembered and saluted by his fellow Rangers, by historians, and in newspapers and would give Chapman the recognition that had alluded him as an artillerist.

6 | A Thrilling Sensation

After disbanding the Dixie Artillery in October 1862, the Chapman brothers became enrolling officers for conscripts in Fauquier County. Their job entailed enrolling all men required by law to serve in the army, arresting deserters and stragglers, and paroling Federal prisoners. It was not an assignment that men of action—men who had endured withering fire at Glendale and Rappahannock Station and who had helped turn the tide of battle at Manassas—accepted lightly. Sam Chapman said the work was "not at all to my taste" and derisively described it as "gathering men who were very unwilling to leave their homes to become soldiers." Following a visit to Luray for Christmas, William Chapman was in Warrenton during January and February. As fate would have it, Warrenton was exactly the right place for independent-minded men looking for adventure in the spring of 1863.[1]

The path to conscript duty had begun many months earlier. The Confederate Congress passed the first conscription act in the spring of 1862. The law required all white males between the ages of eighteen and thirty-five to serve in the army for three years. A revised law, passed five months later, increased the age limit to forty-five. In practice, however, many men obtained occupational, family, medical, and religious exemptions; others hired substitutes. Conscription was not popular—many people saw the draft as an infringement upon personal liberty—but it was necessary to sustain the war. The Army of Northern Virginia had suffered tremendous losses in 1862 and needed replacements to fill the depleted ranks. Enrolling officers were central to that task. "If you are zealous and active we shall make our enemy taste the bitterness of war; if you are negligent we shall continue to witness its ravages on our own soil," they were informed. Col. John Shields, formerly of the Richmond Howitzers, was appointed commander of Camp Lee, the camp of instruction for recruits at Richmond, and later commandant of conscripts for the State of Virginia.[2]

In general, disabled officers no longer fit for active military service performed conscript duties, but many of these officers were incompetent, and in early November Shields requested that he "be permitted to select from the regular service such officers as I know will render efficient service in enrolling and reporting the conscripts promptly into camp." Two of these officers, former artillerymen as was Shields, where William and Sam Chapman. The Chapman brothers were assigned to Fauquier County, operating out of Warrenton. Robert E. Lee had personally singled out Fauquier County earlier in September as having a high number of available conscripts. As winter set in, the army, reduced in strength by desertion and straggling, needed more recruits to fill the ranks, and the Chapman brothers began their new duties. However, enemy raids often interrupted their work. And there was a new breed of Confederate soldier in Warrenton—John Singleton Mosby, whose bold attacks on enemy camps attracted their attention.[3]

Mosby was a scout on Jeb Stuart's staff. It was he who led Stuart's ride around McClellan's army before the Seven Days' battles. That raid taught Mosby the value of preying on the enemy's rear. The Confederate Congress saw similar merit and authorized formation of partisan rangers to operate behind enemy lines. Mosby got his chance to conduct this style of warfare following a cavalry raid at the end of December 1862 that passed through Middleburg. Stuart allowed Mosby to remain behind in Loudoun County with 9 men. From Middleburg, Mosby conducted three raids over two days on outposts of the 5th New York Cavalry and the 1st Vermont Cavalry in western Fairfax County, capturing 20 cavalrymen and their horses, arms, and equipment before returning to Stuart's camp.[4]

Mosby returned to the Middleburg area toward the end of January 1863 with 15 men. Posted across western Fairfax County along the outermost picket lines of the Washington, D.C., defenses were 3,300 Federal cavalrymen and 5,200 infantrymen. Mosby's plan was to prey upon the loosely protected rear; attack isolated outposts and wagon trains; create fear and anxiety among the enemy; and divert more soldiers to protect the lines around Washington. This he did. In his report to Stuart dated 4 February, Mosby described his capture to date of 28 cavalrymen, their horses, and arms. Stuart forwarded the report to Lee as "additional proof of the prowess, daring, and efficiency of Mosby."[5]

Mosby's reputation was growing, and 27 men gathered at Rector's Cross Roads, four miles west of Middleburg, on 25 February for a raid on the 18th Pennsylvania Cavalry. Some 40–50 troopers occupied a schoolhouse on Ox Road at Thompson's Corner, three miles from Chantilly. In cold, freezing rain—miserable weather that he knew would lessen the likelihood of detection—Mosby struck at four o'clock on the morning of the twenty-sixth. His report claimed the Confederates killed 4 men, captured 5 others, and brought out 39 horses. Two days later, Lee heralded Mosby's successes to all in the Army of Northern Virginia.[6]

The Federals followed with a raid on Middleburg. Late in the afternoon of 1 March, Maj. Joseph Gilmer of the 18th Pennsylvania Cavalry led 200 men along the Little River turnpike to Middleburg. Early the next morning, the troopers surrounded the town, searched the houses, and detained a group of

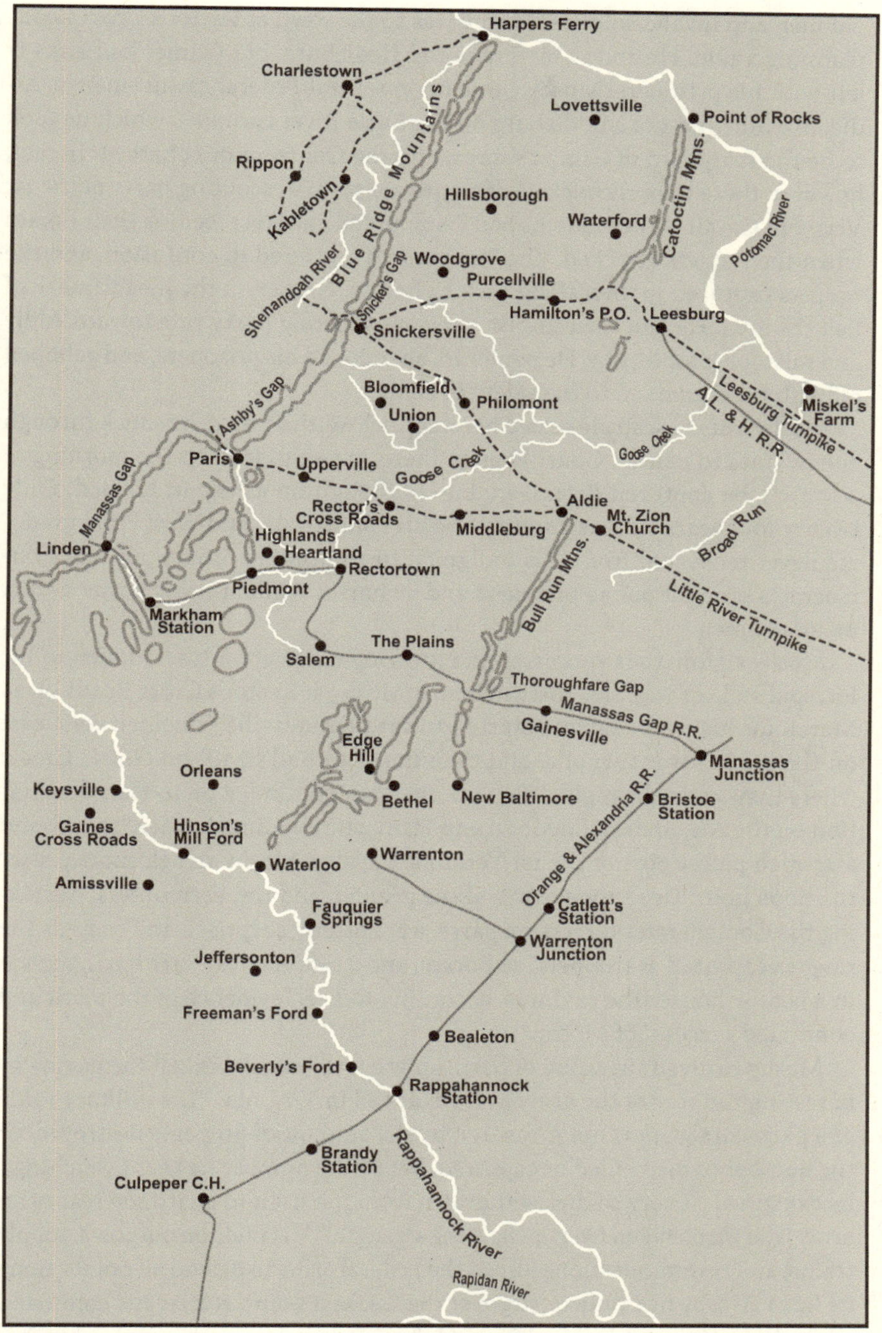

Map 6. Mosby's Confederacy in Loudoun and Fauquier Counties. From a wartime map of the region in Richard W. Stephenson, *Civil War Maps*, 2d ed. (Washington, D.C.: Library of Congress, 1989), 306 (map H11); and the Eugene M. Scheel map, John Singleton Mosby Heritage Area, Inc., Middleburg, Va.

old men and invalid soldiers. Mosby was to the west, at Rector's Cross Roads planning a raid. He and 17 men rode to Middleburg, but Gilmer had already left with his prisoners. Mosby came upon several Federal cavalrymen at Aldie, five miles east of Middleburg on the Little River turnpike, which he took to be the rearguard of Gilmer's force, and the Confederates charged. In fact, however, these were the pickets of a separate 50-man scouting party of the 1st Vermont Cavalry. The troopers had dismounted and were feeding their horses when the rangers attacked. The Vermonters scattered in confusion, and the rangers captured 19 men along with 23 horses. Gilmer, in the meantime, had fled the area. He had seen the 1st Vermont scouting party ride toward Aldie and mistook it for Mosby. He panicked, abandoned his prisoners, and galloped off with his command to the safety of camp.[7]

Mosby's next escapade sealed his standing. With 29 men, he snuck through enemy lines to Fairfax Court House. There, at two o'clock on the morning of 9 March, he captured Brig. Gen. Edwin Stoughton asleep in his bed. Only twenty-four years old, the infantry brigade commander and West Point graduate never recovered from this indignity. In addition to Stoughton, the Confederates brought out 32 prisoners and 58 horses without firing a shot and at no loss of men.[8]

Mosby's numerous successes and growing notoriety attracted men to his intrepid style of warfare. Forty men met Mosby at Rector's Cross Roads on 16 March for his next raid and started toward Dranesville. The men rode east on the Little River turnpike and then north to Ball's Mill on Goose Creek, where they spent the night. The next day, they continued on to Herndon Station on the Alexandria, Loudoun and Hampshire Railroad, where they found a 25-man picket post of the 1st Vermont Cavalry. Mosby struck shortly after the noon hour. Deep snow covered the ground, and the Vermonters, mistaking the Confederates for a relief party, were utterly surprised and routed. The rangers captured 21 troopers, 26 horses, and 4 officers who were having lunch in a nearby house. The raid was, according to Lee, "evidence of the merit and continued success" of Mosby.[9]

Mosby realized the value of partisan warfare was to weaken the enemy by harassing the rear of the army as it advanced in Virginia. "The military value of a partisan's work is not measured by the amount of property destroyed, or the number of men killed or captured, but by the number he keeps watching," he explained. "Every soldier withdrawn from the front to guard the rear of an army is so much taken from its fighting strength." His raids on outposts, supply trains, and communications forced the Federal army to defend all points along its lines. Mosby had only to strike at the weakest point, scatter his command while the enemy searched for him, and then regroup for another raid in another location. The area of Fauquier and Loudoun Counties had good farmland to feed his men and their horses. He had the broad support of the people to house his men and to warn of approaching Federal cavalry. And the nearby Blue Ridge Mountains provided sanctuary, if needed.[10]

Mosby's operations in Fairfax County during January–March 1863 accomplished much of his goals. Washington newspapers reported alarming tales of pickets "gobbled up" in the darkness of night. Federal authorities relieved Col. Percy Wyndham, commander of the cavalry brigade, of duty and increased the cavalry screen at Fairfax Court House from one brigade to two and later to a division of three brigades. The men of the 18th Pennsylvania Cavalry, frequent victims of Mosby, were demoralized and frustrated with ineffective weapons; one company mutinied rather than go out on picket duty.[11]

The Confederate command praised Mosby and promoted him for his triumphs. Lee informed Stuart on 12 March that "Mosby has covered himself with honors." That same day, Stuart commended Mosby for his "boldness, skill, and success." Southern newspapers lauded Mosby, and he noticed a different attitude toward him from the citizens of Middleburg. Whereas previously they had asked him to stop his raids, the sentiment changed with his successes, and the people now wanted him to remain. Mosby was promoted to captain on 19 March and was authorized to organize a cavalry company. Shortly thereafter, he received appointment to major, effective 26 March 1863.[12]

Sam Chapman first saw Mosby in January, following his initial raids, when Mosby spent the night in Warrenton before rejoining Stuart's cavalry. Mosby was twenty-nine years old, clean-shaven, almost boyish in his looks. Small and thin, he stood 5 feet 8 inches tall and weighed 128 pounds. Later, Sam recalled "how youthful he looked and how thin he was." It was a deceptive appearance that startled many, friend and foe alike. Yet there was something in Mosby's attitude that attracted Chapman—certainly raiding Federal outposts was more exciting than enrolling conscripts—and he rode with Mosby on 2 March during the skirmish with the 1st Vermont Cavalry at Aldie. Sam evidently liked what he found, and so, too, did William Chapman upon hearing his brother's tale. In their duties as enrolling officers, they faced the indignity of fleeing from recurring enemy raids on Warrenton. Mosby was just the man to provide needed action, and the Chapman brothers joined the growing band of rangers for his next venture.[13]

Fifty-five men met at Rector's Cross Roads on 23 March. It was, as Sam Chapman described, a "raw, chilly day." They rode east along the Little River turnpike toward Chantilly. A few miles distant, the band of rangers turned off the turnpike and rode across muddy fields and woods, parallel to the road. The Confederates approached Chantilly at around five o'clock in the afternoon, hoping to surprise a large picket post of the 5th New York Cavalry. However, vedettes spotted the rangers as they approached the camp. The alarm raised, 70 New Yorkers mounted their horses and rode out after the Confederates. The rangers had ridden 23 miles along poor roads and over mud-soaked fields, and their horses were in no condition for a sharp fight. Mosby turned the command around and withdrew along the turnpike, but not before his men killed 1 of the pickets and captured 6.[14]

A few miles back, the turnpike passed through a large body of woods. There, Federal soldiers had felled trees across the road at two locations one-quarter mile apart as part of their defenses to prevent Confederate raids. Mosby saw an opportunity to turn on the approaching cavalrymen. Between the barricades, Mosby wheeled the command around and ordered the charge when the New Yorkers closed within 100 yards. Sam Chapman was apprehensive about this, his first cavalry charge. He asked a compatriot what to expect. The reply startled him: "Oh, beside the possibility of a sabre stroke or a pistol shot, you have a good chance of being knocked from side to side by friend or foe, or knocked down, horse and rider, and being run over." But the fighting that day was one-sided.[15]

The Confederates surged forth with sabers drawn, not, according to Mosby, because of their effectiveness as weapons, but rather simply to keep the men from firing their revolvers too early. The startled New Yorkers broke in fear; the gleeful hunters had become the scared fox. The rangers were amid them in an instant, now with sabers sheathed and revolvers blazing. The Confederates followed in pursuit over a few miles before a larger body of cavalry rode up and the rangers hastily withdrew. Mosby claimed 5 Northerners killed, many wounded, and 36 prisoners, along with numerous horses captured. The New Yorkers admitted to 3 dead, 1 man mortally wounded, and 1 captured. Sam Chapman's remembrance of the action likely summed up the experience for both brothers. It was, he recalled, a "thrilling sensation I had in this first cavalry charge," more satisfying even than the artillery barrage laid upon Fitz John Porter's infantrymen at Manassas some months earlier.[16]

The next raid began on 31 March. Sixty-nine men, the largest force to date, met Mosby at Rector's Cross Roads. Most of these men were new to the command. Mosby had no formal lieutenants around to organize them. Instead, he relied on a few trusted aides: John Underwood, his scout who knew the woods and roads of Fairfax County like no other man; Richard "Dick" Moran, a forty-nine-year-old father of ten and one of the oldest rangers; and William Hibbs, affectionately called "major," forty-six years old, father of eight children. James "Big Yankee" Ames deserted from the 5th New York Cavalry and proved his mettle in many a fight. Men flocked around these strong figures, men like Sam and William Chapman, veteran soldiers searching for adventure. So, too, did Capt. Bradford Smith Hoskins, a British officer who served in the Crimean War and fought as a soldier of fortune with Giuseppe Garibaldi in Sicily in 1860; and Capt. William Kennon, who served in Wheat's Louisiana Tigers infantry (1st Louisiana Special Battalion) until it disbanded. Both men had joined Mosby for the Chantilly raid and now looked for more adventures. Wounded soldiers and deserters from the regular army also filled the ranks. Others were in search of horses, only to disappear after the raid.[17]

The last day of March was cold—snow fell steadily for most of the day—and the men plodded along on roads and fields muddy and laden with snow. The objective was a cavalry camp at Dranesville, nearly thirty miles distant. They reached Herndon Station around sunset and learned that the encampment had withdrawn closer in toward the Federal lines. The rangers continued on to Dranesville and turned west on the Leesburg turnpike, looking for a place to camp for the night. They rode for several miles until, around midnight, they came upon Miskel's farm, situated far back from the turnpike along the Potomac River. The men were cold and tired from the long march. They wearily dismounted their horses in the dark, corralled them in the stable and barnyard with food, and stumbled into bed in the barn and farmhouse. Those in the house, Mosby among them, were fortunate and nestled before a warm fire for the night. Those in the barn, including the Chapman brothers, burrowed into the hay, yet found scant protection from the cold and passed an unpleasant night. Mosby was unsure of his authority over the men and did not set out pickets to warn of danger. Besides, the nearest enemy camp was miles away.[18]

Around sunrise Dick Moran raced across the fields waving his hat and shouting, "The Yankees are coming!" A Union sympathizer had seen Mosby pass through Herndon Station and alerted the Federal cavalry to his presence. Capt. Henry Flint and 150 troopers of the 1st Vermont Cavalry picked up the chase, searching for the raiders in Dranesville and continuing along the turnpike through the night. Moran had spent the night away from the command and had seen the cavalrymen ride by as he arose. He stole through the fields on his horse and shouted the warning that alerted the Confederates to the coming danger.[19]

From the woods along the turnpike, a farm lane led through a narrow gate off the road to the Miskel farmhouse a few hundred yards distant. Flint led his Vermonters through the gate. Anticipating an easy rout, the cavalrymen closed the gate to prevent any rebels from escaping. It was a mistake that proved costly to the Green Mountain men. Flint continued down the lane with 100 men directly toward the farm buildings while a squadron of 50 men circled through the fields to the rear. There were few options for escape. The farmyard was in full pandemonium as Confederates rushed about to saddle and mount their horses. Those in the farmhouse raced to the barnyard about 100 yards distant. Around the barnyard was a tall plank fence that offered some protection, but nestled as they were in the fork of the Broad Run and the Potomac River, the only way for the Confederates to escape was to move forward, headlong into the mass of cavalrymen pouring through the gate. Across the Potomac, soldiers in a Federal encampment heard the early morning sounds of shouting men, galloping hooves, and gunfire and lined the embankments of the river to watch the anticipated slaughter with glee.[20]

Both Chapmans arose at daylight. They had spent the night in the barn, and the cold night air—below freezing at Washington, D.C.—had made sleeping difficult. Chapman fed his horse and then put on its saddle and bridle, leaving the bit hanging so that the horse could continue feeding. He and Sam went into the farmhouse for warmth. Some men had found hard apple cider, which lessened the bite of the cold morning air. Chapman was cooking corncakes and bacon over the fire in the farmhouse with Sam and other men when he heard Moran's cry. At first he thought it was a joke, but as he watched from the doorway, he saw the approaching Federals. Chapman rushed to the stable and mounted his horse. Others joined in a mad scramble to saddle and mount the many horses in the barnyard. With the Federal cavalrymen now within 50 yards of the barnyard, Mosby swung the gate open and ordered the charge.[21]

Men rushed from the walled enclosure with what Mosby described as "one of those demoniac yells which those who once heard never forgot." Mosby, on foot until one ranger dismounted and gave him his horse, led about 20 mounted Southerners out of the barnyard with revolvers blazing. Among them were the Chapman brothers. Six bullets struck Flint early in the action, and he fell dead. Chapman described the commotion as the Confederates charged forth: "I was on the extreme right of this party of men, and the first cavalryman I came in contact with was near the fence, and we were not more than a yard apart. This cavalryman turned immediately towards me from the line and our pistols almost touched. A fierce wind was blowing from the west, and the brim of my Confederate cloth hat flapped down over my eyes. I knocked my hat from my head with my left hand still holding my pistol in my right and aiming at my antagonist, whose pistol snapped and mine went off. He fell at that point." Four more cavalrymen fell to Chapman's pistol that day.[22]

The Northerners that survived this onslaught panicked and fled back up the lane toward the turnpike. The Confederates followed on their heels, pistol shots remorselessly felling bluecoats from their horses, sabers swinging wildly when pistols were emptied. The closed farm gate blocked the exit onto the turnpike, and the Vermonters piled up into a mass of hysteric men. Sam Chapman, who Mosby described as "a sort of military Calvin, singing the psalms of David as he marched into battle," emptied both his pistols, and then drew his saber, standing up in his stirrups to get better leverage as he slashed left and right at the fleeing enemy. "I doubt whether he prayed that day for the souls of those he sent over the Stygian river," Mosby said. Eventually, the gate swung open, and the Green Mountain men spilled onto the turnpike.[23]

Dead and wounded troopers fell strewn along the turnpike beyond Dranesville as the rangers hunted down their quarry. In the melee, Sam Chapman came upon two cavalrymen. They turned on him with their sabers, and one struck Sam on the head before another ranger came to his rescue. His brother fared only slightly better. After keeping up the pursuit for about a mile, William

Chapman's horse broke down. He transferred his saddle to a captured horse, but by then the main body of Confederates had sped down the turnpike. Chapman spotted a small squad of enemy cavalrymen in a field to the left of the turnpike. He set off in pursuit with another ranger, but was instead himself captured. "My pistol, which was a captured one, missed fire [*sic*]," Chapman explained, "and my antagonist, seeing this, closed in upon me. But one barrel of six went off. I was taken back to the woods about 400 yards from the pike, where there was another group of cavalrymen. After being held there a few minutes, I was rescued by a party of my friends who had heard of my misfortune, and, with a number of prisoners captured there, we proceeded to join our comrades."[24]

Mosby reported his men killed 9 Federals, severely wounded 15, and captured 82 men and close to 100 horses. One of the wounded was Lt. Josiah Grout, severely wounded by bullets in the hip and abdomen. Grout later became governor of Vermont and reunited with Mosby and Sam Chapman at the inauguration of William McKinley in 1897. But there were few thoughts of happy reunions on that April Fool's Day. More than two of every three Vermont cavalrymen were killed, wounded, or captured by a force less than half its size. Mosby's own losses were a comparatively scant 1 dead and 3 wounded.[25]

The army needed a scapegoat for the missed opportunity to capture Mosby, and Maj. Gen. Julius Stahel, commanding the Federal cavalry division, squarely placed the blame on Captain Flint in his report the next day. "Had a proper disposition been made of our troops," he wrote, "Mosby could not by any possible means have escaped." He claimed that Flint ordered his men to fire at some distance from the house and that the volley was ineffective; that Flint then ordered a charge with sabers drawn, which was itself ineffective because of the high fence around the barnyard. The failure to capture Mosby, Stahel concluded, "is only to be ascribed to the bad management on the part of the officers and the cowardice of the men." The dead Flint could not defend his actions. Mosby himself painted an image of Federal cavalrymen armed with useless sabers cut down by Confederates charging with revolvers in both hands. "The remorseless revolver was doing its work of death in their ranks, while their swords were as harmless as the wooden sword of harlequin," he wrote in his reminiscences.[26]

Forty-seven years after the battle, an unlikely voice rose to the defense of Flint. Flint's sister wrote to Chapman asking him for information about the fight at Miskel's farm. With respect to the claim that Flint had ordered an ineffective volley from too great a distance, Chapman informed her that "this is an error. I had heard no shots fired when I came out of the house, and the Federal cavalry was then nearing the house." Nor did he recall a saber charge, "because the first men we met after we had passed through the gate had their pistols drawn and were still making the movement to encircle us and not making a charge directly on us." Chapman should know. He had met the enemy face-to-face, revolvers aimed, ready to fire, and survived only because of a misfire.[27]

Chapman told Flint's sister that he "never heard any of our officers or men attribute the failure of the Federal cavalry to lack of courage upon the part of Capt. Flint, or even of his men." Chapman attributed the Confederates success that morning to their desperation—they had been cornered and could either surrender or fight—and to the fact that they had rested during the night while the Vermont cavalrymen were cold and tired from being in the saddle all night. The Confederates also had better weapons. They were armed with Colt army revolvers; the Federals had Remingtons. According to Chapman, many of the Remingtons failed to fire because, claimed some of the captured Vermonters, the pistols had gotten wet during the night. "The importance of our advantage and their disadvantage in this respect is shown by my own experience," Chapman wrote. "In the first encounter the failure of the Remington pistol to fire saved my life, while later, the failure of the Remington pistol that I had captured resulted in my being made a prisoner."[28]

The astounding failure at Miskel's farm prompted Federal authorities to step up their efforts to capture Mosby and his rangers. The Federal cavalry in the vicinity of Fairfax County had grown to ten regiments and an artillery battery, organized into three brigades under the overall command of Stahel. Brig. Gen. Joseph Copeland, who commanded a brigade of three Michigan regiments, led a retaliatory raid to Middleburg on 3–6 April. He failed to make contact with the rangers but netted 61 civilian and military prisoners and 53 horses.[29]

Throughout the month of April, the Army of the Potomac, led now by Maj. Gen. Joseph Hooker, prepared for its anticipated spring offensive. Hooker's plan was to send the cavalry, some 10,000 men, on a raid around the Confederate army toward Richmond. The bulk of the infantry would march up the Rappahannock River and turn the Confederate left flank while the remaining infantry crossed the river at Fredericksburg and hit the Confederate lines there. By the twenty-seventh, all was ready, and the Federals left their encampments around Fredericksburg, marching west, upriver. The two armies met at Chancellorsville on 1–3 May.[30]

During the prelude to Chancellorsville, the Confederates needed information on Hooker's intentions. Lee turned to Mosby for that intelligence. Then, on 26 April, Stuart suggested that Mosby strike the enemy rear at Warrenton Junction. Mosby was to disrupt operations along the Orange and Alexandria Railroad and gather information on troop movements. About 80 men met Mosby at Upperville on the twenty-ninth for the raid. However, an ill-organized expedition of some 2,000 troopers and an artillery battery that Stahel had mounted two days earlier disrupted the plan. Stahel's cavalrymen pressed past Aldie and Middleburg toward Upperville before turning south to Rectortown and Salem. Mosby knew of the raid but planned to elude Stahel by passing through Salem and crossing the Bull Run Mountains at Thoroughfare Gap. Purely by coincidence, the two commands met near The Plains on the afternoon of the twenty-ninth and warily watched each other until nightfall.[31]

Mosby's next opportunity to support the Chancellorsville campaign was on 2 May. Ninety-eight men met Mosby and rode on to Warrenton. They reached the town around dusk and received a warm reception—dinner for the men, forage for horses—before encamping nearby for the night. The rangers continued on toward Fredericksburg the next morning. Mosby's plan was to strike Hooker's supply wagons near the fords across the Rappahannock River. The gunfire at Chancellorsville could be heard as the men rode east. With martial ardor raised, action, not marching, was the call of the day, and as the rangers approached the railroad, they came across a Federal cavalry camp at Warrenton Junction. The temptation to fight was too great that morning, and Mosby ordered the charge. Yet, while the Confederates carried the day at Chancellorsville in one of Lee's greatest displays of military strategy, the rangers were for the first time soundly defeated and suffered an inglorious day. "I committed a great error in allowing myself to be diverted by their presence from the purpose of my expedition," Mosby later admitted. "They were perfectly harmless where they were, and could not help Hooker in the great battle then raging." He had not scouted the cavalry camp and knew nothing of the whereabouts of surrounding troops. "I learned wisdom from experience," Mosby said, "and after that always looked before I took a leap."[32]

The morning of 3 May was warm and sunny. The Federal troopers, 100 men of the 1st West Virginia Cavalry of Stahel's division, had just returned from a scout. Their horses were unsaddled, being groomed and fed, and weary men lounged in the warm sun. As the Confederates rode across an open field toward the camp, the troopers at first mistook them for a returning scouting detachment, but wild battle cries and the thundering of 400 hooves across the field alerted the West Virginians to the approaching danger. The rangers rode into camp with pistols firing and quickly captured some of the enemy, but a large body of men took refuge in the two-story station depot. Some crouched for safety; others lined the windows and doors, carbines and pistols poking ominously outward; all hoped to hold out until reinforcements arrived.[33]

Mosby ordered the charge, and heavy gunfire erupted from within the building. Several rangers immediately fell in a hail of bullets. Chapman was there that day with his brother and narrowly escaped the rain of lead balls, but his horse died in the charge. Mosby reached the depot and poured shots from his two Colt revolvers through a window. Sam Chapman, too, safely reached the building. He crept to a window and, protected under the windowsill, struck with his sword at those who were brave enough to lean out to fire. Then, he burst through the door with Richard Montjoy and two others, and it was all over. Those on the first level surrendered. The West Virginians on the second story dared the Confederates to come up to capture them, but hastily surrendered when Mosby ordered the building set on fire.[34]

Rangers scattered across the fields, rounding up horses and sorting through prisoners and weapons. Suddenly, seventy Federal cavalrymen appeared 200 to 300 yards distant. It was men of the 5th New York Cavalry under the command of Maj. John Hammond. They were camped nearby and had heard the gunshots. Now, they swiftly swept onto the battlefield. With no time to organize resistance, the rangers scattered and fled in every direction. All was abandoned in haste. Sam Chapman had just come out of the depot with an armful of pistols, so many that he could barely walk. A Federal captain fell upon him, and the two combatants exchanged saber blows until Richard Montjoy shot the challenger. Hammond's troopers pursued the rangers to Warrenton, joined by the 1st Vermont Cavalry. "The pursuit was so hot," Sam Chapman described, "that I left the road and broke through the pines, getting my face dreadfully scratched. That was better than getting killed, however. My pursuers passed me, as the pines screened me from their view. I caught up two captured horses that our men had let go, and by a roundabout way got back to Salem, twenty miles distant." His brother, too, escaped to safety.[35]

Federal losses were 2 dead and 15 wounded, including Maj. Josiah Steele, who had rallied the West Virginians and fell mortally wounded. Stahel crowed in his report that his troopers captured over 30 of Mosby's men, 16 of whom were badly wounded, and 40 horses. Among the captured was Dick Moran. Mosby confirmed heavy losses in his report but still claimed to have taken back 8 prisoners and some 25 to 30 horses.[36]

Mosby's presence in northern Virginia had caused Federal authorities to station infantry guards along the railroads. His rangers, lightly armed with pistols and lacking ammunition for their carbines, were not sufficiently strong to attack these heavily guarded routes. Instead, Mosby requested a mountain howitzer from Stuart on 19 May. "I think I could use it with great effect, especially on the railroad trains," he informed Stuart. "I have several experienced artillerists with me." Ten days later, with gun in hand, about forty men heeded Mosby's call for action and met near Middleburg. Sam Chapman took command of the gun and duly drilled some men in its operation. There was no caisson and only fifteen rounds of ammunition in the limber, but Mosby determined to put it to use against the railroad. The rangers stopped for dinner at Greenwich and continued east a few more miles toward the railroad before making camp for the night. Rest did not come easy. All around were Federal camps, and the men awoke on the thirtieth to the sound of reveille from a nearby encampment. That morning, Mosby selected a point north of Catlett's Station to make the attack. The rangers cut the telegraph line, loosened a rail, and attached the telegraph wire so that they could pull the rail away as a train approached. Then, they hid in the woods and waited.[37]

In due time, a ten-car train carrying forage and sutler's stores came barreling down the track. A squad of twenty-five to thirty infantrymen rode as guards. As the train approached, some rangers pulled on the wire and the track came apart. Before the engineer could halt the train, the engine slid into the gap in the track and derailed. The stunned infantry guards fired a ragged volley that did no harm. Chapman and Montjoy worked the cannon and fired a round into a car; the guards fled in panic. A second shell tore through the boiler of the engine, exploding the cab. The rangers quickly appropriated what stores they could find. Among the bounty were fresh shad, oranges, candy, leather, and mailbags. They set the train ablaze, and the Confederates, loaded with their rewards, mounted and started back to safety.[38]

Col. William Mann of the 7th Michigan Cavalry commanded a cavalry post at Bristoe Station. He heard the firing of the cannon at about nine o'clock and suspected an attack upon the railroad—indeed, he had learned a few days earlier that Mosby was in possession of an artillery piece. He hastily organized a 170-man detachment of the 5th New York Cavalry, 1st Vermont Cavalry, and 7th Michigan Cavalry to join the pursuit. Troopers from the 5th New York Cavalry raced across the fields to intercept the rangers. Mann took the remainder to investigate the wreck site. Lt. Elmer Barker and about 25 New Yorkers found the fleeing Confederates and blocked their advance along a road. Sam Chapman unlimbered the howitzer and fired a shell. Barker's New Yorkers scattered, and the rangers rode on, but Barker rallied his men and followed in pursuit. Again, the Confederates stopped, unlimbered the howitzer, and Chapman fired another shell. The New Yorkers again fell back. This time, Mosby remained behind with several rangers to cover the retreat. Barker rallied his men and charged. The ensuing combat left several men dead and wounded, among them Hoskins, the British veteran of Crimea and Sicily, mortally wounded by a gunshot.[39]

More cavalrymen arrived on the scene, and Mosby realized that he faced a ruthless pursuer that day. The howitzer limited his ability to scatter his command and flee across fields. He opted instead to make a final stand. If the Federals wanted his howitzer, it would come at a price. "If I had to lose it, I was determined to exact all that it was worth in blood," Mosby explained. As the rangers approached the Grapewood farm in the vicinity of Greenwich, Mosby ordered Sam Chapman to place the howitzer in a narrow lane on a nearby hill. The Federals would have to advance along the lane, which was lined by fences on both sides, to capture the howitzer. By now, many of his men, unwilling to face the enemy, had fled. "Some of the men who had joined me, thinking that they were going on a picnic, had already left to fry their shad and eat the confectionaries they had got on the train," Mosby derisively wrote in his reminiscences. But some stayed to defend the howitzer with Mosby; among them were Sam Chapman, Richard Montjoy, and Fount Beattie.[40]

Sam Chapman fired a shell at about 200 yards, but Barker was relentless and rallied his men. "We can get that gun before they can fire again," he shouted, and led his New Yorkers up the lane. As the bluecoats approached, Chapman fired canister at close range. The hail of lead balls killed three men and wounded seven, including Barker, struck by two balls in the thigh. Mosby ordered the charge, and the New Yorkers fell back. But by then Mann had arrived on the scene with his detachment. Chapman worked the cannon as fast as he could, but the Federals would not be denied. As the howitzer spurted out its last round, Mann's cavalrymen pressed in, firing revolvers at close range and then swinging their sabers. Mosby and Beattie were lucky to escape, but the Northerners captured Montjoy. A bullet struck Sam Chapman, and he fell to the ground wounded, still swinging with the rammer to the gun before being captured. His wound was serious, thought to be mortal, and he was paroled on the field. Federal losses were 4 killed, 15 wounded, and 11 horses killed, but Stahel had another victory to crow about. "We whipped him like the devil, and took his artillery," Stahel announced.[41]

The close of May ended the initial adventures of the Chapman brothers with Mosby. Sam Chapman remained on the field of battle after being wounded and recovered at a nearby home for ten days until well enough to move. Then, when he had improved, he returned to duty in the artillery service. It was a period of inactivity, and he spent much of the time serving on courts-martial in Petersburg before rejoining Mosby in February 1864. His younger brother, too, left the pages of ranger histories, but resurfaced in the fall of 1863 and began his rise to become Mosby's lieutenant and lifelong confidant.[42]

William H. Chapman, c. 1861–62, when he served with the Dixie Artillery (Archer Ellis Hansen).

Col. James B. Walton, commander of Battalion Washington Artillery, chief of artillery in Longstreet's corps and Chapman's mentor. Undated photo from Jennings Cropper Wise, *The Long Arm of Lee* (Lynchburg, Va.: J. P. Bell, 1915), 1:192.

William H. Chapman, 1863. From James J. Williamson, *Mosby's Rangers* (New York: Ralph B. Kenyon, 1896), 327, and John Singleton Mosby, *The Memoirs of Colonel John S. Mosby* (Boston: Little, Brown, and Co., 1917), 270. The frock coat is at the Greensboro Historical Museum, Greensboro, N.C.

John S. Mosby in the uniform of a major, c. March 1863–January 1864 (Library of Congress).

Mossy Creek Academy, Augusta County, Va., which Chapman attended in 1856–57
(Special Collections, University of Virginia Library).

The Lawn of the University of Virginia, looking towards the Rotunda, c. 1868
(Special Collections, University of Virginia Library).

Fight at Miskel's farm, 1 April 1863. From Williamson, *Mosby's Rangers*, 53.

Rangers attack Federal soldiers burning the residence of Colonel Morgan, 20 August 1864. From Williamson, *Mosby's Rangers*, 214.

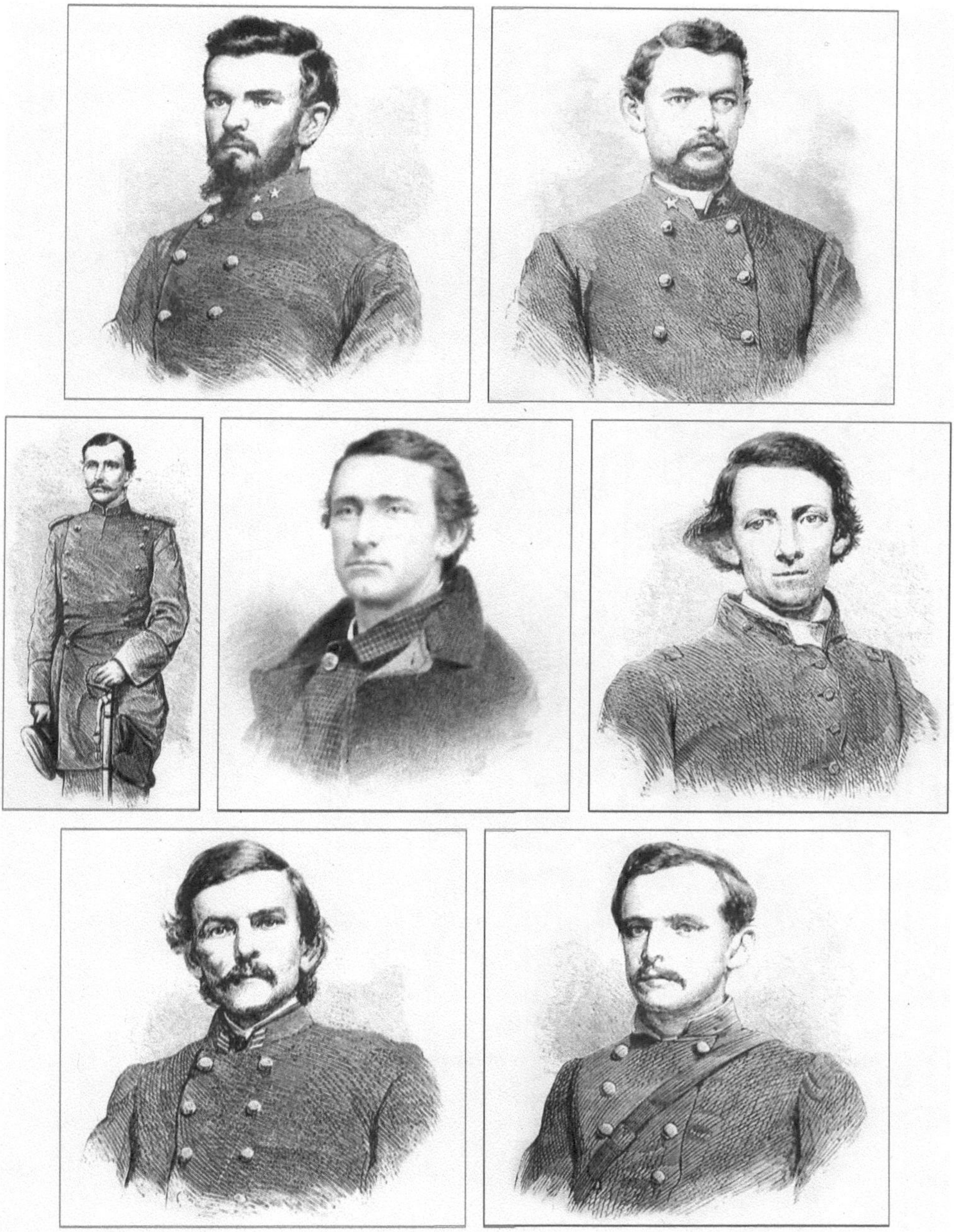

Col. John S. Mosby (*center*) and (*clockwise, from top left*) Lt. Col. William Chapman, Maj. Dolly Richards, Capt. William Smith, Capt. Richard Montjoy, Capt. Sam Chapman, and Baron Robert von Massow. From John Scott, *Partisan Life with Col. John S. Mosby* (New York: Harper, 1867).

Mosby's Rangers as depicted on the cover of *Harper's Weekly,* 5 September 1863.

Josephine Jeffries (Chapman) in her early teens, c. 1860 (Archer Ellis Hansen).

Josephine at age 46, c. 1892 (T. Ritchie Sampson).

Josephine in her later years, undated photograph (Alice Sampson Bonan).

Mosby Returning from a Raid (Berryville), oil painting by Armand-Dumaresq depicting the aftermath of the Berryville wagon train raid, 13 August 1864. (The Museum of the Confederacy, Richmond, Va. Photograph by Katherine Wetzel).

The three oldest Chapman children, c. 1875: Esther, Elizabeth, and William (T. Ritchie Sampson).

The two youngest Chapman children, c. 1886: Samuel and Mary (Archer Ellis Hansen).

Esther at sixteen years of age, photograph labeled "to my dear Father, from his eldest daughter," 25 December 1883 (Archer Ellis Hansen).

Chapman in San Francisco after the war, undated photograph (Peter Brown).

Chapman in Atlanta, 3 September 1890 (Carolyn and Chris Russell).

Chapman in his later years, undated photograph (Carolyn and Chris Russell).

The Chapman family at Clifton, 24 June 1899. (*From left to right, standing*): Samuel, John, Katherine, William H. Chapman, Mary, and James. (*Seated, second row*): Esther Jeffries, Elizabeth Chapman Pendleton, holding daughter Elizabeth, and Josephine Jeffries Chapman. (*Sitting on the grass*): Esther Brooking, William H. K. Pendleton (*blurred*), Josephine Brooking, William Brooking, and Esther Chapman Brooking. The Chapman's oldest son, William, was not present. (Archer Ellis Hansen).

Four generations of Jeffries and Chapman women, c. 1899. (*Left to right*): Esther Jeffries, Esther Chapman Brooking, Josephine Brooking, and Josephine Jeffries Chapman. (T. Ritchie Sampson).

Matching studio photographs of William H. Chapman and Josephine Jeffries Chapman, undated. The photograph of Chapman appeared in his obituary. (*Left*, Carolyn and Chris Russell. *Right*, T. Ritchie Sampson).

7 | A Fascinating Life

Nearly fifty years removed from the events of the spring of 1863, Chapman stood before a crowd of men and recalled those days. The legend of Mosby's Rangers had long been secured, and Chapman was asked to recite some of those tales. "I appreciate the compliment you have paid me in expressing the thought that I could relate anything that might interest or entertain," he began, but he chose not to tell of his personal adventures. Instead, he believed the audience would be "interested in knowing how this unique band of soldiers was organized, how it existed, and how it subsisted in a territory that for most of the time was in the rear of the Federal army."[1]

Mosby's base of operations was upper Fauquier County and lower Loudoun County from the Bull Run Mountains west to the Blue Ridge Mountains, in a region that became known as "Mosby's Confederacy." Rich farmland protected from Federal raids was abundant to sustain the rangers. The Manassas Gap Railroad ran along the southern stretch of this land, through the Bull Run Mountains at Thoroughfare Gap west past the towns of The Plains, Salem, Rectortown, and Piedmont before dropping into the Shenandoah Valley at Manassas Gap and continuing on to Front Royal. North of Thoroughfare Gap was the town of Aldie, a key point of access between the Bull Run Mountains to the south and the Catoctin Mountains to the north. East along the Little River turnpike lay the Federal lines in Fairfax County; west lay the heart of Mosby's Confederacy and the towns of Middleburg, Rector's Cross Roads, Upperville, and Paris. From Paris, the turnpike passed through the Blue Ridge at Ashby's Gap, across the Shenandoah River at Berry's Ferry, and on to Winchester. Access to the riches of the Shenandoah Valley was also gained by the next gap to the north—Snicker's Gap, adjacent to the town of Snickersville.[2]

Mosby's strategy was to harass Federal communications and supply lines, forcing troops to be diverted from the front lines. He could strike anywhere with a small body of cavalry, any point where he found a weakness, while Federal commanders had to guard against attack at all locations along their lines. His men scattered throughout the countryside after a raid, living in the homes of sympathizers. Herein was a key element of Mosby's success. "Having no fixed lines to guard or defined territory to hold," he explained, "it was always my policy to elude the enemy when they came in search of me, and carry the war into their own camps." Mosby understood that "to have fought my own command daily, on equal terms and in open combats against the thousands that could have been brought against it by the North, would soon have resulted in its entire annihilation." Yet this style of warfare was unconventional, and Northern commanders and newspapermen derisively called Mosby a guerilla, a thief, and a bushwhacker. He defended his actions, saying that "to destroy supply trains, to break up the means of conveying intelligence, and thus isolating an army from its base, as well as its different corps from each other, to confuse their plans by capturing despatches, are the objects of partisan war. It is just as legitimate to fight an enemy in the rear as in front."[3]

The rangers lived and operated mostly north of the Confederate army, in the rear of the Army of the Potomac, and at all times in close proximity to Washington, D.C. By the summer of 1864, the Army of Northern Virginia was entrenched around Petersburg. Mosby's band of rangers was the only Confederate force in northern Virginia, situated between the Army of the Shenandoah, led by Philip Sheridan, and the Army of the Potomac, led by Ulysses S. Grant. The typical ranger at that time was about twenty-three years of age; Chapman was twenty-four. Some were only teenagers, several less than sixteen years old. Mosby favored youths because of their adventurous spirit and fearlessness. Yet it took special men, men of steely courage, alert to lurking danger, independent and self-reliant, to survive in this contested land.[4]

The Confederate Congress passed the partisan ranger act on 21 April 1862. This legislation authorized the organization of bands of rangers to conduct guerilla warfare. Rangers received the same pay and followed the same regulations as the regular army, but were also paid for arms, munitions, and horses captured from the enemy. Partisan rangers were not, however, highly regarded in the Confederate political or military establishments. Many authorities believed that such commands consisted of little more than hoodlums and thieves who plundered the homes of Southerners more often than their enemies and that their ranks were filled by deserters from the regular army. Brig. Gen. Thomas Rosser, who commanded a brigade of cavalry in the Shenandoah Valley, wrote to Lee in early 1864 that partisans in the valley lacked discipline and did not fight. He described them as a "band of thieves, stealing, pillaging, plundering, and doing every manner of mischief and crime. They are a terror to the citizens and an injury to the cause." He mocked their efforts and informed Lee that "they sleep in houses and turn out in the cold only when . . . they are to go upon a plundering expedition."[5]

The partisan act was eventually repealed, though an exception was made for Mosby, who retained Lee's confidence. Yet Lee and Stuart held out hope that Mosby would eventually join the regular army. Indeed, in authorizing Mosby to organize a permanent command in the spring of 1863, Stuart warned him that the term *partisan ranger* was "in bad repute." Instead, he advised Mosby to "call your command 'Mosby's Regulars,' and it will give it a tone of meaning and solid worth which all the world will soon recognize, and you will inscribe that name of a fear-less band of heroes on the pages of our country's history, and enshrine it in the hearts of a grateful people. Let 'Mosby's Regulars' be a name of pride with friends and respectful trepidation with enemies."[6]

Men joined Mosby for a variety of reasons. One was for adventure. High-spirited men seeking excitement could find no better release than to ride with Mosby. Epic battles ensued when the Army of Northern Virginia and the Army of the Potomac clashed, but these were infrequent contests that punctuated longer periods of inactivity in camp, marked by the monotony of drill and guard duty. When the rangers struck, the action transpired on a much smaller and more intimate scale, but the raids were incessant, with often just a scant few days rest between encounters. Mosby understood this and knew that the life of a partisan ranger appealed to men of action. "The true secret was that it was a fascinating life, and its attractions far more than counterbalanced its hardships and dangers," he admitted. "They had no camp duty to do, which, however necessary, is disgusting to soldiers of high spirit. To put them to such routine work is pretty much like hitching a race-horse to a plow." Nor were Mosby's men satisfied with simply scouting and reconnaissance, the traditional roles of cavalry. "In order to retain them," Mosby acknowledged, "it was necessary for me to stimulate their enthusiasm with something more tangible. War to them was not an abstraction; it meant prisoners, arms, horses and sutler's stores."[7]

Others sought more noble aspirations. Mosby's Rangers were the gallant cavaliers protecting defenseless women and the elderly from marauding Northerners. This was certainly true late in the war, when Federal raids exacted an increasingly harsh toll on civilians. In describing one raid on Middleburg, Mosby said, "To avenge the wrongs of distressed damsels is one of the vows of knighthood; so we spurred on to overtake the Federal cavalry." In another tale, Mosby told of a band of enemy marauders who stole the horse and medicines of an elderly doctor who was making his rounds to the sick. The marauders then plundered families of their valuables. Mosby and his rangers swooped down to avenge these depredations and returned the medicines and valuables to their rightful owners.[8]

Many rangers expressed similar sentiments in their memoirs. James Williamson said that although dangerous "there was a fascination in the life of a Ranger; the changing scenes, the wild adventure, and even the dangers themselves exerted a seductive influence which attracted many." John Munson wrote that joining Mosby was "an irrevocable good-bye to regular army life and to camps, bugle calls, drills and picket duty. It meant the abolition of winter-quarters and the end of idleness." Nor, Munson boasted, did the rangers suffer camp food. "The idea of making coffee, frying bacon, or soaking hard-tack was never entertained. When we wanted to eat we stopped at a friendly farm house, or went into some little town and bought what we wanted." About the action, Munson said, "Every affair in which Mosby and his men figured had in it something novel, something romantic, something which is worth the telling." J. Marshall Crawford described the ranger lifestyle as "far preferable to a position in the regular army, where men stand up like posts to be shot at, and where there is little or no opportunity for the display of personal courage." When he left the regular army to join Mosby as surgeon late in 1864, Aristides Monteiro encountered many officers and soldiers hoping to join him. One such soldier was willing to leave the safety of conscript duty in Richmond. The allure of partisan life was tempting, and the man was "easily seduced from duty by its charm of novelty and romance, with the spice of avarice attached." Adolphus "Dolly" Richards, captain of Company B and later promoted to major, said simply, "No conscripting was necessary."[9]

To be sure, part of the allure was that their captures enriched the rangers. Raids upon enemy camps and supply trains brought fast horses and weapons to sustain the war effort, and the rangers largely armed, equipped, and supported themselves, with little aid from the Confederate government. Captured sutler stores provided food, clothing, and money, which rangers shared with civilians as payment for housing and to foster loyalty in a countryside ravaged by war. Mosby recognized the importance of plunder and its cohesive bond. He used it to reward individual merit and to encourage competition. He awarded those who participated in a raid a share of the spoils, the most fearless ranger of the day receiving first share. Indeed, the ability to keep or sell captured armaments, horses, and supplies has been widely credited with enabling Mosby's successes.[10]

Supply wagons were a favorite target, and John Munson acknowledged that his fellow rangers "had a decided weakness for Yankee sutlers." A popular ranger song expressed their attitude:

> When I can shoot my rifle clear,
> At Yankees on the roads,
> I'll bid farewell to rags and tags
> And live on Sutlers' loads.

One raid netted a large supply of boots; a bounty of clothing, coffee, tea, sugar, and cheese; cans of meat, oysters, sardines, and fruits; and boxes of cakes, crackers, and tobacco. The excesses befuddled the rangers, James Williamson confessed. "Each man helped himself to what pleased him best, and it was amusing to see the men pick up one thing and then throw it away to take something else which took their fancy. We could not take all, and it was hard to decide what was most necessary or profitable."[11]

Many rangers sported gold braid on their uniforms and ostrich plumes in their hats—a lifestyle supported by riches gained from raids. Dolly Richards was considered the most stylish in the command. He invested greatly in his look, and when Federal raiders surprised him at his home and stole his uniform, he hunted them down. John Munson visited Lee's headquarters near Petersburg late in the war. Amid the mud and filth of the trenches, Munson was bedecked in a splendid uniform that contrasted starkly with the rags of the Confederate army. "My boots came half way up my thighs, and my spurs were hand-made with silver rowels. My entire suit was gray corduroy trimmed with buff and gold lace, my hat had a double gold cord and an ostrich plume on it, and I carried a pair of high gauntlets carelessly in one hand, while with the other I toyed with a handsome enamelled belt and a pair of Colt's revolvers."[12]

A theatrical production in Alexandria known as "The Guerrilla; or, Mosby in Five Hundred Sutler-Wagons" celebrated these raids. Northern opinion was less flattering. The 5 September 1863 cover of *Harper's Weekly* featured a derisive sketch of rangers destroying a sutler train. It depicted a drunken mob of hoodlums looting a wagon train as merchants fled for their lives. The accompanying article reported that "instead of 'Stonewall Jackson' with his dashing achievements, the rebel cavalry in Virginia have now nothing better to show than the performances of Moseby [*sic*] and his guerrillas, 'citizens by day and soldiers by night.'" Lee, too, tired of these raids in August 1863. Though he continued to support Mosby, Lee criticized him for being too interested in the capture of sutler wagons and the rumored sale of plunder in Charlottesville, which later turned out to be false. Lee wanted Mosby to stick to attacking outposts and communications and to raiding railroads.[13]

Mosby espoused a philosophy of individuality among his men that, at the same time, promoted camaraderie and cohesiveness. He did not drill his rangers relentlessly as a unit that would break down without its commanders. Partisan warfare required freethinking men who could survive by wit and quick action. There were no official formalities—no saluting or addressing officers by their rank; no inspections, guard duty, or drills—as in the regular army. Marches were carefree. Pranks, jokes, songs, and tales relieved the tedium of a long march and the stress of looming conflict. Yet the command was not without discipline. For a ranger to be on Mosby's wrong side meant banishment to the regular army, a fate that many saw as worse than death.[14]

Men quickly learned that Mosby's physical stature was deceiving and that they must perform to high expectations. When John Munson first saw Mosby, his reaction was one of disappointment. He looked over a crowd of soldiers seeking "a big man with a showy uniform, a flowing plume and a flashing saber." Instead, Munson found "a small, plainly attired man, fair of complexion, slight but wiry, standing with his arms behind his back, talking quietly to one of his men." Munson confessed that "the total absence of visible might, the lack of swagger, the quiet demeanor of the man, all contributed to my astonishment and chagrin. He did not even strut." But that disappointment changed when later Munson approached Mosby. "He turned upon me suddenly, meeting my full glance. At that instant the secret of his power over his men was disclosed. It was in his eyes, which were deep blue, luminous, clear, piercing." James Williamson related a similar encounter with Mosby. "I could scarcely believe that the slight frame before me could be that of the man who had won such military fame by his daring." Yet he, too, observed Mosby's "keen, restless eyes" that cut though a man and quickly assessed his character. Grant, as well, upon meeting Mosby for the first time after the war beheld "a different man entirely from what I had supposed," but he also instinctively realized that few men could have conducted partisan warfare as effectively.[15]

The rangers rarely united into a single command. More commonly, Mosby sent out companies individually. At war's end there were eight such companies. This required strong captains who possessed good military acumen and who commanded the respect of their men. Only a select few rose to the inner circles of Mosby's command. The privilege of leading a company came solely on merit, and the best way for advancement was to show courage in battle. Law required that the enlisted men vote for officers, but Mosby acknowledged, "I really appointed the officers, and told the men to vote for them." The Chapman brothers were among the chosen few. Both served as company commanders. William Chapman gained Mosby's highest respect and became part of his innermost staff. By the latter part of 1864, the rangers operated in two squadrons commanded by Chapman and Richards.[16]

Raids required the rangers to stealthily wind their way through enemy lines, surrounded by pickets and encampments. The slightest noise would warn their opponents of the lurking danger. As the men approached their target, silence fell among the ranks. Not a noise was to be heard—no clanking of canteens, sabers, or carbines; only the hushed whispers of commands. Dolly Richards recounted that during these tense moments, "it would be surprising to see with what noiseless secrecy these manoeuvers [*sic*] could be accomplished. Only whispered commands were necessary from the officers, and the presence of danger insured silence in the ranks." Many of these raids occurred at night to aid in stealth, to catch the enemy unprepared, and to instill fear. Mosby playfully acknowledged that the depth to which his foes despised him "was more on account of the sleep I made them lose than the number we killed and captured."[17]

Mosby favored pistols over sabers. The standard tactic was to gallop on horseback into close quarters and fire at close range. Indeed, Mosby admonished his men not to fire until closely engaged, when pistol shot was sure to find its mark. Each ranger carried at least two revolvers, most commonly the six-shot Colt .44 caliber army revolver, and each was an expert shot when riding at a gallop. Use of the saber by Federal cavalrymen bemused Mosby, for he considered it an antiquated weapon. Mosby described how at Miskel's farm Confederate revolvers did the remorseless "work of death" against Federal troopers charging with "harmless" swords. In another encounter, Mosby related how charging troopers fell to Confederate bullets: "They had drawn sabres, that hurt nobody, and we used pistols." And of the British captain, Hoskins, who was mortally wounded at Grapewood farm, Mosby said that "it was a point of honor or of military etiquette with him to use his sword and not his pistol. In this way he lost his life."[18]

Friend and foe alike envied rangers for their fast horses. Indeed, Mosby once presented Stuart with a fine sorrel to replace his worn-out horse. Each ranger had two horses, and many kept more, to allow a continual supply of fresh mounts. Upon joining the rangers, surgeon Aristides Monteiro was advised by Mosby that "it was neither proper nor safe to engage in his peculiar methods of warfare with an indifferent steed." Dolly Richards expressed a similar sentiment and attributed the adeptness of the rangers to "knowledge of the country and the swiftness of their steeds."[19]

Once in battle, the rangers charged headlong into the fray. Mosby's theory of warfare was "not to stand still and receive a charge, but always to act on the offensive." This tactic served the rangers well at Chantilly, Miskel's farm, and in other affairs. The clashes were short and rapid, violent encounters at close quarters, where opponents looked each other in the eyes, men thrashed wildly through a haze of smoke, and the din of battle deafened the ears. John Munson described these contests as "fast and furious and quickly over, one or the other side withdrawing at a dead run when the pistols were empty." Monteiro said that one clash "lasted only a few minutes, and the road, for nearly one mile, was literally covered with dead and wounded men and horses."[20]

Every day brought the chance of violent death, and those men who emerged unscathed from two years of partisan life did so by taking quick and decisive actions. Munson related that "very few of the fights of Mosby's men were pitched battles. Most of them were little affairs hardly worth writing about. Yet they were part of the almost daily experience of some of the men." Munson described one such encounter by Charles Hall and John Puryear, typical of countless such affairs during the war. Riding one night deep in Mosby's Confederacy along the Snickersville turnpike, the two rangers stopped to water their horses at a stream. The sky was dark, and soon two other men came up and did the same. There was a moment of panic when Puryear realized they were Federals, but then instinct overcame fear. The rangers "quietly drew their pistols and, each selecting the nearest man, fired. There were cries of pain; a splash in the little stream; two riderless horses dashing by them down the pike; and the clatter of hoofs back of them. That was all. War is not play."[21]

Support of civilians was vital to the success of the rangers. A regular, fixed encampment so close to enemy lines would have only led to the rangers' capture. Instead, they lived among the local citizens in their homes, gathered for raids at a known rendezvous on a prearranged date or when summoned by courier, and then dispersed upon return. Mosby described his operations as similar to "the Children of the Mist." His rangers would appear from nowhere to strike a weakly guarded point and then hastily retreat with their captures. When the enemy mounted a chase, it was generally to no avail; the pursuers "were striking at an invisible foe." When enemy patrols approached, rangers fled to safety in the woods or mountains, or, in the face of imminent capture, scurried into secret closets or trapdoors common to most safe houses. Women actively protected their houseguests and concocted clever ruses. One coolly hid a ranger under her hoop skirt as Federals searched her home. Another ranger posed as a sick girl, clothed in a nightgown and nightcap under covers in bed.[22]

The civilians in Mosby's Confederacy who supported the rangers were repeatedly subjected to arrest, their homes ransacked, and their horses and livestock confiscated. The spring of 1863, as the populace adjusted to Mosby's presence, was particularly unsettling for some residents. Catherine Cochran of Middleburg recorded in her journal that "silver was put out of sight and money buckled on like armor" when bluecoats were seen approaching. Ida Dulany, who lived at "Oakley" in Upperville, observed that the presence of Mosby's Rangers brought undue hardship. "The impression in the army seems to be that we are protected from Yankees by them," she wrote in her journal, "but I fear it is just the reverse, as every raid Mosby has made had produced a retaliatory raid from the Yankees in which the citizens suffer severely." Upon hearing of an approaching patrol, "instantly everything was confusion, horses had to be hurried off, meat concealed, silver, jewelry, etc. secreted . . . and every preparation made to escape the rapacity of the enemy." The Dulany family had so few supplies and valuables left that any rumor was taken seriously to avoid losing more. A state of weariness set in that spring, patience worn thin by raids real or rumored. "We have all the meat taken from the meat house and concealed, the stock all run off to a safe place, the silver, money, arms, etc. concealed, and generally it amounts to nothing," Ida Dulany grumbled.[23]

The town of Warrenton, too, was not without hardship. Federal troops occupied Warrenton during the winter of 1863–64. To thwart incursions by rangers, the troopers ringed the town with picket posts. Outsiders could not enter; residents could not leave; no one was permitted to cross picket lines. All trade with outside markets ceased. Food was in short supply and could not be obtained from the military. The Federal occupation left the once-vibrant Southern town impoverished and desolate, its young men long gone, replaced by a large population of suffering women, children, and old men.[24]

Not all families supported Mosby. The northwest section of Loudoun County was home to many Quakers and German Americans who remained loyal to the Union. Yet those who did aid Mosby retained their faith even in the face of hardship as raiding Federal troopers exacted revenge. Mosby claimed "the stubborn faith of the people never wavered. Amid fire and sword they remained true to the last, and supported me through all the trials of the war." Indeed, late in the war, Catherine Cochran still believed that "every man, woman, and child black and white was true to the South and would die rather than see the Union restored."[25]

Mosby was the uncontested leader who ruled all aspects—military and civilian—of his Confederacy. He provided the law and order that was lacking, settled legal disputes, and protected his supporters from pillaging by stragglers and deserters, as well as by Federal soldiers. Many families welcomed rangers into their homes for just such protection and for the bounty of livestock and supplies they brought. The importance of this support for a beleaguered population was not lost on Stuart and Lee.[26]

The rangers bred fear among Northern cavalrymen. Their lurking presence caused a lingering wariness for soldiers on picket duty, on patrol through Mosby's Confederacy, or guarding supply trains as they wound their way over country roads. Mosby's specter was everywhere and in everyone's mind. Lt. Rawle Brooke of the 3rd Pennsylvania Cavalry, on picket duty one night in August 1863, confessed that he "never passed a more anxious night, expecting to be 'gobbled.'" Capt. Walter Newhall, also with the 3rd, said that "nobody ever saw one [of the rangers]; they leave no tracks, and they come down upon you when you least expect them." Col. Henry Gansevoort, 13th New York Cavalry, was stationed in Fairfax County in the fall of 1863. Picket duty and its many encounters with Mosby left Gansevoort rattled. "The whole country, in our rear, front, and flanks, is full of guerrillas," he wrote his father. "These chaps murder, steal, and disperse." One week later, he was even more uneasy. "We are surrounded by the enemy. He makes frequent dashes here and there, surprising, capturing, and destroying." Darkness after the sun set was most unsettling. "The night does not know what the morning may disclose," Gansevoort admitted.[27]

Rangers trailed patrols or wagon trains like hunters stalking their prey. Newhall, safely ensconced in Warrenton during December 1863, said that "even now, from the tops of the neighboring mountains, his hungry followers are looking down upon our weak points." James Taylor was an artist with *Frank Leslie's Illustrated Newspaper* traveling up the Shenandoah Valley in the summer of 1864 with the Federal army. Unaccustomed to their methods, he spotted a group of seven rangers along a distant stream tracking his movements. Their vigilant surveillance unnerved Taylor. "One of the rangers, on a powerful black in the run, standing out in relief against the bank, especially attracted," Taylor described in his diary. "His was the face of a Devil may care, not yet out of his teens who with eyes strained eagerly scanned us while fingering his Colt as if tempted despite the distance, to salute us with a leaden compliment."[28]

Herman Melville accompanied the 2nd Massachusetts Cavalry on a patrol from Vienna to Aldie, 18–20 April 1864. He later wrote a poem about his experience entitled "The Scout toward Aldie." In it he captured the depth to which Mosby had penetrated the psyche of Northern soldiers posted throughout Fairfax County. Their camp was within sight of the Capitol dome, yet was a monument to fear, and there the soldiers were imprisoned:

> The cavalry-camp lies on the slope
> Of what was late a vernal hill,
> But now like a pavement bare–
> An outpost in the perilous wilds
> Which ever are lone and still;
> But Mosby's men are there–
> Of Mosby best beware.
> Great trees the troopers felled, and leaned
> In antlered walls about their tents;
> Strict watch they kept; 'twas *Hark!* and *Mark!*
> Unarmed none cared to stir abroad
> For berries beyond their forest-fence:
> As glides in seas the shark,
> Rides Mosby through green dark.[29]

Mosby was a furtive ghost, romanticized yet dreaded:

> All spake of him, but few had seen
> Except the maimed ones or the low;
> Yet rumor made him every thing–
> A farmer–woodman–refugee–
> The man who crossed the field but now;
> A spell about his life did cling–
> Who to the ground shall Mosby bring?[30]

Mosby's lurking presence was sensed by all—beyond the next hill, around the next bend in the road, behind the next tree. The rustling of leaves, the snap of a twig, a bird flurrying into the sky—any noise spooked the troopers as they rode through the woods on patrol. A night spent in Mosby's Confederacy was a night without sleep. Charles Humphreys, regimental chaplain, wrote that men slept next to their horses, reins in hand, ready to mount in an instant should the rangers spring an attack. Melville painted a similar image of men worn from a day's ride yet fretful still in their sleep:

And so till night, when down they lie,
Their steeds still saddled, in wooded ground:
Rein in hand they slumber then,
Dreaming of Mosby's cedarn den.[31]

And as have others who traversed this contested land, Melville captured the doubt and unease that swelled through each man upon sighting rangers in the distance, watching the column, searching for the right moment to pounce:

By peep of light they feed and ride,
Gaining a grove's green edge at morn,
And mark the Aldie hills uprear
And five gigantic horsemen carved
Clear-cut against the sky withdrawn;
Are more behind? an open snare?
Or Mosby's men but watchmen there?[32]

In Melville's poem, rangers ambush the patrol, kill its young colonel, and leave his new bride at camp widowed. Returning from one of these patrols brought welcome relief. Chaplain Humphreys recounted that "we had been out three days and two nights, and I had slept only two hours, and was so stiff from a cold caught the first night that it seemed as if I could count by its special ache each muscle in my body." Melville captured a similar sense of dejection:

The weary troop that wended now–
Hardly it seemed the same that pricked
Forth to the forest from the camp:
Foot-sore horses, jaded men;
Every backbone felt as nicked,
Each eye dim as a sick-room lamp,
All faces stamped with Mosby's stamp.[33]

The highest levels in the Federal army, too, felt frustration in dealing with irregular combatants. Ten months of operations against the rangers left Henry Halleck, general in chief of the army, bedeviled. "If these men carried on a legitimate warfare no complaint would be made. On the contrary, they fight in citizens' dress and are aided in all their rascalities by the people of the country. As soon as they are likely to be caught, they go home, put out their horses, hide their arms, and pretend to be quiet and non-combatant farmers." This style of warfare fomented bitterness, and "it is not surprising that our people get exasperated at such men and shoot them down when they can," he acknowledged.[34]

Conventional tactics were not useful to counter the rangers. Capt. Newhall returned from a patrol empty-handed and concluded that "hunting guerrillas with four regiments of cavalry and four pieces of artillery was very much like shooting mosquitoes with a rifle." Maj. Gen. Wesley Merritt commanded a large expedition into Mosby's Confederacy late in the war and echoed similar sentiments. He reported that "the guerillas, being few in numbers, mounted on fleet horses and thoroughly conversant with the country, had every advantage of my men."[35]

Col. Henry Lazelle, 16th New York Cavalry, was stationed in Fairfax County. He faced the rangers on numerous scouting expeditions and knew well the damage they inflicted. By July 1864, he realized that the traditional methods of the regular cavalry were unsuccessful against the rangers. He proposed a new method of operations based on "plain common sense." Small patrols of 50, 100, or 150 men were too vulnerable to ambush, he argued. He knew from personal experience the fate of such patrols. "Their steps are dogged, their approach heralded, the warning given, the assembly sounded by the enemy, and ten to one the party is followed and overwhelmed, or ambuscaded." Only large forces of several hundred men could safely scour the countryside for rangers, and even then "the few captures made and extent of damage inflicted on the enemy in nowise compensate for the destruction of horse-flesh and loss of men which ever attends such visits." Lazelle recognized that Mosby's success stemmed from knowledge of the countryside, which rangers used to their advantage to move at night, trail patrols, find concealment in forests, flee when necessary, and set ambushes when advantageous. Lazelle proposed to operate in a similar manner, led by scouts knowledgeable of the country and abetted by families that provided reliable information. The only way to successfully counter the rangers was to act like the rangers.[36]

Countering the threat posed by Mosby's Rangers was hard work that brought little glory. It was irregular warfare rather than epic clashes of tens of thousands of men formed in line of battle with flags crisply fluttering. It was anxious scouts and searches of homes and destruction of property. Col. Charles Lowell commanded a cavalry brigade of the 2nd Massachusetts, 13th New York, and 16th New York regiments stationed in Fairfax in the summer and autumn of 1863. Twenty-eight years old, from a prominent Boston family, educated at Harvard, and an abolitionist, Lowell did not relish chasing partisans. "It brings me in contact with too many citizens, and sometimes with mothers and children," he confessed. Yet he considered Mosby "an honorable foe" who should be treated as such. His dislike of serving against "bushwhackers" only increased over the next year as both sides locked into a cycle of increasing atrocities and retaliation. After several of Mosby's men were hung at the end of September 1864, Lowell divulged to his wife that "the war in this part of the country is becoming very unpleasant to an officer's feelings." Ironically, Lowell was mortally wounded just a few weeks later not by a partisan's bullet but in a grand battle of 53,000 soldiers at Cedar Creek in the Shenandoah Valley.[37]

8 | Efficient Services

Mosby organized his first company of rangers, Company A, on 10 June 1863. Enough men had joined these rangers by the fall to form a second company. The command gathered at Scuffleburg, in the Blue Ridge Mountains between Paris and Markham, on 1 October. There, sixty men enrolled in Company B. As he had done four months previously, Mosby gave command of the company to someone who had conspicuously distinguished himself on the battlefield. For captain, he selected William Smith, twenty-seven years old, the father of four children, and a lieutenant in the famed Black Horse troop of the 4th Virginia Cavalry. The new command went into action the following day.[1]

Forty rangers set off from Salem toward Warrenton on 2 October. Chapman was among the rangers that day. He had on two previous occasions safely approached Warrenton and captured pickets within a few hundred yards of the garrison quarters. Now, Chapman planned to enter the town unnoticed at night and hide in a safe house during the next day while scouting enemy strength and positions. He would relay this information to Smith, who would lead a nighttime attack. The rangers passed the night near Smith's home, some four to five miles north of Warrenton, while Chapman rode on, skirting Federal pickets posted on the roads leading into town. The plan went awry when an alert sentinel spotted Chapman sneaking into town. The two men exchanged gunfire. Chapman's pistol shot found its mark, and the sentinel fell wounded, but Chapman abandoned the raid.[2]

The following day, 3 October, the rangers regrouped, and forty-five men set off for another raid to Warrenton. At dusk, Smith stopped the men a few miles from town and then after dark proceeded around the town to a point about a mile south of Warrenton. There, the rangers rested while Smith, Chapman, and Richard Montjoy scouted an encampment of four cavalry companies nearby on Lee's Ridge. Though vastly outnumbered, the rangers used the element of surprise to their advantage and attacked at four o'clock on the morning of 4 October. They quickly routed the groggy bluecoats, but the Northerners were well disciplined and rallied to drive off the Confederates. The rangers did not leave empty-handed; 6 prisoners and 27 horses accompanied them back to Salem.[3]

Following its retreat from Gettysburg, the Army of Northern Virginia resumed the offensive in October. Lee launched the Bristoe campaign on 9 October, when his troops crossed the Rapidan River in an attempt to turn the right flank of the Army of the Potomac, but its commander, Maj. Gen. George Meade, foiled the plan in a well-executed retreat. By the thirteenth, the Confederates had entered Warrenton, but then lost a poorly planned battle at Bristoe Station the next day. Lee concluded that his army was overextended and started back to the Rappahannock River on the eighteenth. The Confederates safely crossed the river that day and the next. Meade reoccupied Warrenton and then cautiously moved southward. On 7 November he forced a sharp clash at Rappahannock Station, in response to which Lee retreated further south across the Rapidan. By 10 November both armies occupied essentially the same positions they had several weeks earlier, with Meade in Culpeper County north of the Rapidan and Lee in Orange County to the south. Mosby conducted operations in Fairfax County throughout this time. During the period 15–19 October, the rangers captured over 100 horses and mules, between 75 and 100 prisoners, and several wagons.[4]

As the Army of the Potomac followed Lee southward back to the Rappahannock River, the rangers harassed its supply trains and communication lines. One such raid occurred on 26 October. Mosby left Salem that evening at six o'clock with about fifty men. Near New Baltimore, the rangers found a large train of supply wagons on the turnpike from Gainesville to Warrenton. A strong guard of cavalry, infantry, and artillery escorted the column at the head and rear, but the center of the train was unprotected. Chapman led a group of ten rangers and, while the remaining rangers waited concealed in woods along the road, struck the unguarded center. Chapman stopped the wagons by pretending to be a provost marshal. He approached one wagon and asked the driver for the officer in charge. Upon finding the lieutenant, Chapman promptly arrested him. He then ordered the wagons to the side of the road and the drivers to unhitch their teams. Chapman stopped some forty to fifty wagons in this manner, and the rest of the raiders poured out of the woods along the turnpike to gather the bounty. However, before they could set fire to the wagons, the cavalry escort came upon the scene. The Confederates carried off 145 horses and mules and 30 prisoners without firing a shot. Stuart described this as "but another instance of Major Mosby's skill and daring." The Confederate secretary of war, James Seddon, received the report with "admiration at the fearlessness and skill of this gallant partisan."[5]

Chapman's growing stature within the rangers was evident one week later. Mosby had the men meet at Rectortown on 2 November. An increasing number of deserters and stragglers had arrived in Mosby's Confederacy, pretending to be part of his command. Mosby issued signed certificates of membership to the legitimate members. Then, as the rangers formed in line, Chapman read letters from Lee and Stuart that complimented them on their actions. In the spring months, Sam Chapman had garnered Mosby's unflinching respect. Now, William Chapman, too, had earned Mosby's trust. "By his intelligence and courage he has so won our leader's confidence as to be frequently sent by him in command of expeditions," ranger historian John Scott explained.[6]

In November, Meade moved his army southward across the Rappahannock River toward the Rapidan in preparation for an offensive before the onset of winter. Then, for seven days, from 26 November until 2 December, Meade launched an offensive against the Army of Northern Virginia. His Mine Run campaign was an attempt to strike the right flank of the Confederate army south of the Rapidan River, but Meade found the Confederate lines too strong and withdrew his army. Thereafter, both armies settled into winter encampments.[7]

The rangers harassed the Federal rear during this time. Operations in the first three weeks of November netted about 75 prisoners, over 100 horses and mules, 6 wagons, and considerable arms and equipment. During this period, Chapman commanded a company of men and further garnered Mosby's respect. In a report to Stuart, Mosby commended Chapman for his "efficient services."[8]

One raid occurred on 20 November. Seventy-five rangers left The Plains that evening. They spent the night between New Baltimore and Warrenton and headed for Bealeton Station on the Orange and Alexandria Railroad between Warrenton Junction and Rappahannock Station the next day. The air was cold, and rain poured from the skies. Cold and wet, the rangers lay in the woods waiting for a wagon train. Shortly after noon, five wagons guarded by about 30 cavalrymen came down the road. The cavalry escort quickly scattered, and the Confederates found a rich trove of medical supplies in two ambulances among the wagons. The rangers gathered what they could before leaving the scene. The raid yielded 12 prisoners and 27 horses and mules, but much of the supplies were left behind because the wagons had to be abandoned. A 250-man cavalry patrol of the 2nd Massachusetts Cavalry and 16th New York Cavalry under the command of Col. Charles Lowell subsequently descended upon Mosby's Confederacy, led by ex-ranger Charles Binns. Binns had been arrested for drunkenness and deserted to escape punishment. They captured some 18 rangers, mostly in their homes.[9]

The rangers struck the Orange and Alexandria Railroad again on 26 November. The air was frosty with the temperature below freezing as 125 men plodded on horseback from Rectortown south across the Rappahannock River. At Brandy Station they found a large wagon train guarded by infantry. After personally scouting the camp, Mosby planned an attack in the growing darkness of night. He divided the command into four squads. Montjoy led one group to burn the wagons; Smith and Chapman each led detachments to drive off the mules; Lt. Thomas Turner, commanding Company A, held the remainder of the rangers in reserve. The teamsters, many of them African American, ran in panic as the Confederates stole into camp. Chapman drew his revolver and exclaimed he would shoot the first one who made a noise. The infantry guard proved ineffective, and flames from scores of burning wagons soon lit the cold night sky. The rangers left with over 100 mules and horses and a number of prisoners.[10]

Mosby officially recognized Chapman's leadership on 7 December. On that day at Rectortown, the command grew to three companies. Mosby appointed the twenty-three-year-old artillerist-turned-cavalryman the captain of Company C. Subsequently, Chapman, who was still a commissioned officer in the artillery, formally obtained a transfer to Mosby's command. Dolly Richards, nineteen years old, was named first lieutenant. Richards was a native of Upperville and an experienced cavalryman. He had been a lieutenant with Turner Ashby's 7th Virginia Cavalry and a staff officer with Mosby's former cavalry commander, William "Grumble" Jones, before joining the rangers. Richards was of like build to Chapman—both stood five feet ten inches tall—but there the similarities ended. Chapman was stern and serious. Richards was a fearless combatant, but he was also a dandy who wore a stylish uniform with a feather in his hat. The two men became rivals for leadership in the rangers, and their mutual ill-will continued well beyond the end of the war.[11]

Chapman resided at the "Highlands" home of John Blackwell Jeffries near Piedmont during this time. With Chapman were fellow rangers cousin Judah Forrer, Richard Montjoy, and Robert von Massow. Upon his return to the rangers in February 1864, Sam Chapman joined them. In the household, too, were Jeffries's seventeen-year-old niece Josephine Jeffries, her widowed mother, and her grandmother. As in other homes throughout Mosby's Confederacy that boarded rangers, romance blossomed when young men and young women met among the trials of war.[12]

Josephine Macrae Jeffries was born on 28 October 1846. The family home was "Edge Hill," five and one-half miles northwest of Warrenton on the western slope of the low-rising Pignut Mountain, along the road from Warrenton to Salem in the vicinity of Bethel. It was a large, two-story stone house with a wide center hall and stairway to the second floor, large rooms with high ceilings, and deep windowsills. She was the only child of James Eustace Jeffries and Esther Helm Foote. They had married that same year, but the family was not to be blessed for long. James Jeffries died three years later, in 1849, at the age of thirty from typhoid. Twenty-eight years old, Esther Jeffries found herself a widow with a large estate to manage and a young daughter to raise.[13]

James Jeffries was the eldest of five sons and one daughter born to Enoch Jeffries and Agatha Conway Blackwell. The Blackwell family was wealthy and owned considerable land in the Bethel community. In 1850 Agatha Jeffries was widowed and living at "The Meadows," near Bethel to the east of Pignut Mountain, with her sons Joseph and Eustace Jeffries, daughter Lucy Jeffries, and fifteen slaves. The original frame house had four rooms, and later the family added a stone structure with two large rooms, a bedroom, and two large halls. Agatha Jeffries's brother James Blackwell also lived with his family at The Meadows, which was valued at more than $32,000 in 1850. He farmed the land with thirty-six slaves. His eighteen-year-old son Joseph Hancock Blackwell had an additional sixteen slaves. James Blackwell gave part of the estate as land for the Bethel Methodist Church. A small school for the Blackwell children, which later grew into the Bethel Academy, was nearby.[14]

Joseph Hancock Blackwell, Josie's first cousin once removed, later endeared himself to the rangers during the war. At that time he had moved to an estate known as "Heartland," located about one mile east of Piedmont. The farm was home to his wife, their two young children, and four slaves, and it was valued at almost $41,000 in 1860. Heartland was frequently visited by Mosby and served as an unofficial headquarters for the rangers. For this, Joseph Blackwell was designated Mosby's unofficial chief of staff and was affectionately known as "The Chief."[15]

The brothers of James Jeffries were also entitled land owners. Josie's uncles Joseph and Eustace Jeffries farmed 2,000 acres of land valued at close to $60,000 in 1860. They had 30 horses, 16 milk cows, 12 working oxen, 180 cattle, 580 sheep, and 190 swine. The farm produced 1,200 bushels of wheat, 1,400 bushels of corn, 2,200 bushels of oats, 2,000 pounds of wool, 100 tons of hay, 500 pounds of butter, and 100 pounds of honey that year. Later, the bachelor uncles occupied "Road Island," located in the community of Bethel south of The Meadows. The sixteen-acre estate with large, two-story frame house, built around 1800, had been owned by their father. Mosby lived in this house after the war from 1865 to 1867 while practicing law in Warrenton. Enoch Jeffries, another uncle, was a farmer and slaveholder who lived near Warrenton with his family and had an estate valued at almost $67,000 in 1860.[16]

In 1850 the newly widowed Esther Jeffries lived with her four-year-old daughter, Josie, and her widowed mother, Esther Foote, at Edge Hill. The estate, managed by John "McCrae" (as his name appears in the records) of the neighboring Macrae family, was not nearly as prosperous as those of her brothers-in-law, valued at only $6,000. She had 5 male slaves, six to twenty-eight years old, and 6 female slaves, 3 under the age of four years. The farm consisted of 345 acres of improved land and 290 acres of unimproved land. The land supported 4 horses, 4 milk cows, 2 working oxen, 11 cattle, 150 sheep, and 27 swine. Crop production that year was a paltry 300 bushels of wheat, 750 bushels of corn, 480 pounds of wool, 400 pounds of butter, and 78 pounds of honey.[17]

Farming was perhaps too much for the small family of three women to successfully manage, and Esther Jeffries turned to her late husband's brother John Blackwell Jeffries for assistance. In 1860 the three women were living with him at Highlands, about one mile northeast of Piedmont and one mile northwest of Heartland. John Jeffries was a bachelor. Missing one arm, he ran a thriving farm with 22 slaves, 18 of whom were fourteen years old or younger, and his combined real and personal estate were worth close to $62,000. He farmed 800 acres of land. Livestock included 16 horses, 5 milk cows, 2 working oxen, 70 cattle, 52 sheep, and 56 swine. The farm produced 1,000 bushels of wheat, 2,500 bushels of corn, 300 pounds of wool, 33 tons of hay, and 350 pounds of butter that year.[18]

At that time, Esther Jeffries owned $11,000 worth of real estate and personal property. Josie, thirteen years old, possessed more than $15,000 worth of real estate and personal property. The Jeffries women owned 15 slaves, though 4 were fugitives from the state. Esther Jeffries had a twenty-two-year-old male, two boys (eight and three years old), an eleven-year-old girl, and a newborn girl. Josie had three boys aged one, three, and seventeen years and three girls aged seven, eleven, and thirteen years.[19]

Chapman met Josie one day, most likely in the fall of 1863, while he was riding with three other rangers to Highlands. They splashed across Goose Creek and came upon Josie at a nearby walnut tree, supervising the gathering of nuts. The seventeen-year-old woman made a striking impression on the battle-hardened Chapman. The following weeks were filled with walks together through fields. A large rock outcrop provided sanctuary from the war. There, Chapman and Josie would meet and "feel all the bliss that lovers are wont to feel."[20]

Life in Mosby's Confederacy was filled with romantic adventure for young lovers. One day in the fall of 1863, Chapman and Josie were riding near "Oak Hill," the family home of John Marshall between Piedmont and Salem. There, a lone horseman dressed in the uniform of a Prussian cavalry officer interrupted the courtship. He was Robert von Massow, a baron, and he carried a letter of introduction to Mosby from Stuart. About twenty-five years old, he had come to the Confederacy looking for adventure. Stuart suggested he seek out Mosby. With piercing black eyes, a heavy moustache, and outfitted with a large plumed hat and red-lined cape draped over a sparkling uniform, his persona and actions befitted an aristocratic Prussian cavalry officer. He was an accomplished swordsman and carried a large German saber into battle. On one occasion, as Massow joined the front of the line in anticipation of a charge, ranger Ben Palmer advised him, "Baron, unless you are ready to die this morning, use your pistols and put back that sabre." Massow wryly replied, "Palmer, a soldier should always be ready to die." In partisan warfare, he found the adventure he was seeking and told Chapman that "this beats the fox-hunt."[21]

Other young women in Mosby's Confederacy, too, found the presence of the rangers enthralling. The "Belle Grove" home of Amanda "Tee" Edmonds, near Paris, was frequented by rangers. Twenty-four years old and single, she confided in her diary to "have become perfectly devoted to the society of the Rebels, too much so for my own happiness." The soldiers brought "many happy days full of change, variety and romance," and she admitted that she loved them "for their heroic valor and fortitude and some very pleasant, agreeable and fine company." These would surely be "some of the happiest moments of my life," she confessed, "even amid the terrible war with all its sorrow and grief."[22]

Chapman must have presented a striking figure to a young woman of seventeen years like Josie Jeffries. Her family heritage included the well-known Blackwell and Edmonds families of Fauquier County and other notable Virginian families, including Ball, Conway, and Lee that made her distantly related to George Washington and James Madison and directly descended from Mayflower passengers Isaac Allerton and Fear Brewster. Her forefathers were prominent in county and colonial government and several served in the Revolutionary War. To Josie, whose father died while she was young, the twenty-three-year-old Chapman would have been a romantic hero, a gallant knight from the pages of literature, a defender of liberty and founder of a new nation, as in the pages of her own illustrious family history.[23]

To Chapman, Josie would have been a vision of splendor among the deprivations of war. Her affections must have eased the pain of long hours in the saddle on cold, dark nights; the terror from flashes of gunpowder, the explosive reports of discharging revolvers, bullets whizzing in all directions, and the haze hanging over the field in the chaos of close-quarter battle. She and her family added a new dimension to the war—an innocent family to protect from marauding Yankees. Concern for Josie's safety and well-being certainly personalized a conflict that Chapman had previously seen through the eyes of a carefree young man with obligations only to his fellow rangers. The romance between Chapman and Josie blossomed, and both found comfort in each other. It did not take Chapman long to realize that Josie was the partner he needed in his life.

9 | Much Obliged to You

The year 1863 ended with a warm spell. Morning temperatures at the Naval Observatory in Washington, D.C., during the last five days of the year were above freezing, and afternoon temperatures were mild, though it did rain heavily on three of those days. The populace awoke to a balmy New Year with morning temperatures in the upper 40s. Then, that afternoon, a cold front passed into the region, and by midafternoon temperatures fell below freezing. On 2 January 1864, the morning low temperature was in the single digits, and mornings dawned with temperatures below freezing for the next several days. During the eleven-day period 2–12 January, the sun rose with temperatures hovering near 10 degrees or colder on five days. Afternoon temperatures just barely broke the freezing point on only four days. Several inches of snow blanketed the region on the afternoon of the fourth and again on the evening of the seventh and continuing the following morning.[1]

The cold weather did not deter the rangers from conducting operations. William Smith led 32 rangers in a New Year's Day attack on 80 cavalrymen near Rectortown, killing, wounding, or capturing 57. These were the men of Maj. Henry Cole's battalion of Maryland cavalry stationed at Harpers Ferry. They had entered Loudoun County on a scout, stopping first at Upperville and continuing on to Rectortown. Mosby had called an assembly there that same day, and the gathering Confederates warily watched the Federals at a distance. When the Marylanders left, Smith followed them through the countryside. He eventually gained a favorable position and launched the attack. Thomas Turner led another attack early in the morning of 7 January west of Warrenton. Troopers of the 3rd Pennsylvania Cavalry manning an outpost at Lee's Ridge on the road to Fauquier Springs were huddled around their campfires in a vain attempt to find warmth in the harshest night of the cold snap when Turner and 32 rangers slipped through the picket line and attacked from the rear at half past four in the morning. The rangers utterly routed the surprised Pennsylvanians, wounding 8, capturing 18 prisoners, and securing 43 horses.[2]

The largest and most costly engagement of the period occurred early in the morning of 10 January. Frank Stringfellow, who had served as a scout for Jeb Stuart and had previously accompanied Mosby on a raid, proposed an attack on

Cole's cavalry camp near Harpers Ferry. Cole's battalion was encamped on the eastern slope of Loudoun Heights, guarding the road between Harpers Ferry and Hillsborough, in Loudoun County, against Confederate excursions from Loudoun County. It was a strong location. The only way to attack was from the south, along the Hillsborough road. Cole placed his pickets there while he headquartered in a house and his men camped nearby in tents.[3]

About 100 men met Mosby at Upperville on the afternoon of the ninth and began the 22-mile trek to Harpers Ferry. The night air was bitterly cold. Temperature dropped to near single digits in Washington, D.C., and was considerably colder in the heights around Harpers Ferry. Snow covered the trees, fields, and pathways, and the crunch of feet and hooves as men and horses tramped through the wintry landscape ringed through the night air. Many men cut holes in blankets and draped the cloth over their heads and shoulders to stay warm. Others, their limbs numb from hours in the saddle, dismounted and walked to keep from freezing. Chapman recalled that "the snow was quite deep and as the weather was intensely cold the sufferings of the men were very great, many of the men having their hands and feet frostbitten during the night." As night fell, warm fires and a meal of hot coffee, bread, butter, and meat at the home of a fellow ranger helped to stave off the cold, but the march resumed at ten o'clock and continued through the bitter night. Chapman rode part of the night with William Smith. The two most senior company commanders talked not of the upcoming fight but of family, and Smith showed Chapman a gold watch his wife gave him as a birthday present.[4]

As the rangers approached the camp, Stringfellow and a squad of 10 men joined them. About 110 Confederates were set to face 175–200 Northerners, but Mosby had the element of surprise and the darkness of night on his side to even the odds. After scouting the camp, Mosby and Stringfellow led the rangers north to the Potomac, then westward along the riverbank to a path that rose steeply onto a plateau and the Hillsborough road. It was a difficult trek, on a narrow path deep with snow and up a steep slope. The men dismounted and led their horses single file. Instead of attacking along the road from the south as Cole expected, Mosby had his rangers poised to sweep in from the north. Mosby sent Richard Montjoy with a group of men south to capture the pickets posted along the road. Stringfellow and his 10 men approached the headquarters house to capture Cole and his staff. Smith was to lead a detachment of men to capture horses. Mosby would take the bulk of the rangers into the camp to capture the soldiers while they slept in their tents. In the wee hours of the night, between three and four o'clock, the rangers crept into position.[5]

The plan went disastrously awry from the start. The retort of a Federal carbine, perhaps fired by an alert sentinel, awoke the camp to the danger. Then, Stringfellow's squad charged through the camp on horseback. Believing them to be Federals, Smith's rangers charged into the camp from the opposite side as

Stringfellow. The two groups mistook each other for the enemy and exchanged gunfire. The remaining rangers rushed into the encampment. The commotion roused more of Cole's men from their slumber. They hurriedly found their carbines in the cold darkness and fired a volley from their tents.[6]

Soon there was a large melee of Confederates on horseback and Federals on foot. Barehanded men, gloves removed to better grasp their weapons, shortly found hands and fingers numb from the bitter cold. Yet their aim was sharp, and the night sky was ablaze with the flash of carbines and pistols. Bodies fell to the snow, and men called to comrades to be carried from the field. A bullet to the abdomen mortally wounded Thomas Turner, and he fell with the cry, "I am shot." Charles Paxson, shot off his horse with a mortal wound, pleaded, "You are not going to leave me here on the field?" Cole's men were driven back but still poured withering fire into the rangers. After about fifteen minutes, Mosby realized the attack was not in his favor. He heard a signal gun fired at Harpers Ferry and knew reinforcements would shortly arrive. He ordered a retreat.[7]

Several Confederates lay dead, dying, or injured on the ground in snow soaked with blood. The shrieks and moans of the wounded filled the night air and echoed off the mountain. Men raced about to gather their comrades before leaving camp. Among them was the Prussian officer Robert von Massow. He had joined Mosby looking for adventure and now, in the midst of a fight for his life, gallantly gave his horse to a wounded ranger. In the confusion, Chapman thought that Mosby was wounded and left behind. He found Smith, who was helping a wounded ranger to safety, and the two officers rode back among the tents searching for Mosby. A third ranger joined them, and the three Confederates rode deeper into the camp. They came across Paxson, lying on his back, incapable of moving. He cried out to be removed to safety. Chapman sent the third ranger back for a horse, but before help could arrive someone in a group of Cole's men some twenty steps distant spotted the two officers and fired a shot. Chapman and Smith returned the fire, and the Federals responded with a large volley.[8]

The flash from the weapons momentarily blinded Chapman, but then "a feeling of thankfulness" overcame him upon finding he was unharmed, Chapman later admitted. Not so, Smith. Chapman looked to see if his comrade was safe and saw him leap into the air and fall off his horse, dangling with his head in the snow and his feet caught in the stirrups. Chapman leapt from his horse to assist Smith, but could not lift him back into the saddle. Realizing Smith was dead, Chapman pulled him out of the stirrups and placed his body on the ground. He attempted to recover Smith's watch as a remembrance for his wife and four children, but he had removed his gloves before going into the fight and his hands were so numb from the cold that he could not unbutton Smith's overcoat. All he could do was mount his own horse, gather Smith's horse, and ride away. The memory haunted Chapman, and he found little comfort in his own deliverance: "While this was going on the group of men who had fired the volley, whom I could distinctly see in the same position as when they fired, made no further demonstration towards me, neither by firing at me nor by trying to capture me. I never could understand why they did not close in upon me."[9]

Mosby claimed to have brought out 6 prisoners and 50 to 60 horses, but the price was high. The rangers lost 4 men killed, 4 more mortally wounded, 3 others wounded, and 1 captured. Blood soaked the snow to mark the path of their retreat. Among the casualties were senior leaders including Turner, who died the next day, and Smith, killed two days short of his twenty-eighth birthday. Cole lost four enlisted men killed and sixteen wounded. Also wounded was Capt. George Vernon, who was stuck by a bullet in the head that destroyed his left eye, but still rallied his men as he fell. Despite the defeat, Stuart and Lee praised Mosby and recommended his promotion to lieutenant colonel.[10]

The loss of Turner and Smith cost the rangers dearly. Mosby eulogized the commanders of Companies A and B in his report, saying they were "two of the noblest and bravest officers of this army, who thus sealed a life of devotion and of sacrifice to the cause that they loved." They were "the first to go into a fight" and "the last to leave," James Williamson wrote. "Both men were universal favorites . . . and their loss was regretted by all."[11]

Chapman and Montjoy later returned to the battleground under a flag of truce to gather the dead and wounded Confederates in exchange for Federal prisoners, but Cole denied the request. Smith's body was not recovered until some days later when his wife, father, and mother ventured to the Federal camp; they found the corpse stripped of clothes and his watch stolen. Yet the day was not without some mercy. Paxson's family lived nearby in Loudoun County, and his father had assisted some of Cole's cavalry who had been wounded in an earlier fight. He requested no payment for his aid, only that they return the favor if his own son in the Confederate army was wounded. Now, that obligation was fulfilled as Cole's troopers tended to the twenty-two-year-old Paxson until he died.[12]

Despite the loss, the rangers remained active during the month of January, raiding enemy camps and patrols and capturing men and horses. One such affair occurred toward the end of the month, when a deserter arrived in Mosby's Confederacy. He had a plan to attack a Federal camp at Vienna and offered to show Mosby the route. But the rangers treated strangers suspiciously; the life of a ranger could end abruptly or wither away in a Federal prison at a moment's notice. Chapman was wary and thought the deserter would lead Mosby into a trap. Instead, Chapman proposed to go forth with the guide and scout the camp himself. Another ranger accompanied them with orders to shoot the deserter guide if he was not reliable. Mosby remained behind with twelve men in some woods about 400 yards distant.[13]

The night air was cold and snow on the ground crunched under foot as the three men crept into the camp at about one o'clock in the morning. Chapman could see soldiers huddled around campfires and heard them talking and laughing. Barricades surrounded the camp, which proved too strong to attack, but Chapman found a large unguarded stable of horses. Each man quickly gathered a horse and rode out of camp without raising the alarm. Chapman returned to the camp with a second and third detail to claim more horses. Massow accompanied Chapman in the second detail. The aristocratic Prussian proclaimed, "This is not fighting; this is stealing."[14]

Mosby left the rangers in early February to visit his wife in Charlottesville and attend to administrative duties in Richmond. Chapman, the most senior officer, commanded the rangers in his absence. On 5 February he crossed the Shenandoah River with 14 men and proceeded to Berryville. There, he learned that an equal number of enemy had just left town heading toward Charlestown. The rangers caught up to the patrol and killed, wounded, or captured several men during the pursuit. From the prisoners, Chapman learned that the garrison at Charlestown had left for a raid on Winchester. Anticipating the easy capture of a large supply of military stores, Chapman hastily returned across the Blue Ridge Mountains to gather more rangers to attack the lightly guarded camp. However, Chapman abandoned the attack when the rangers, approaching Charlestown, came across the garrison returning to camp. Yet the expedition was not without some gains. Federal soldiers straggling on the march heard voices calling them into the woods along the route back to Charlestown. The men, thinking that they were to share the spoils of their comrades taken during the Winchester raid, hastened off the road and found themselves instead surrounded by rangers.[15]

Despite his military successes that day, a more pressing matter was at hand. Chapman needed a ring to propose marriage to Josie. Later that day he wrote to Sam, then in the Richmond area. "I just returned from a scout near Charlestown," he informed his brother. "Met with a party of Yankees and attacked them, killing three, wounding several and capturing three Yankees and four horses. Do not get the ring I wrote to you about a day or two ago as I am going to send to Richmond today."[16]

The dawn of 18 February revealed yet again just how perilous was the well-being of a ranger. The previous night, 350 Federal cavalrymen had left the confines of Warrenton for a raid into Mosby's Confederacy. A deserter, John Cornwell, claimed Mosby was at Markham Station on the Manassas Gap Railroad and offered to guide the Northerners to Mosby's hideaway. Cornwell had had a dispute with Mosby and quartermaster Walter Frankland over payment for expenses. Frankland had earlier sent Cornwell to Charlottesville to obtain ammunition for the command. Cornwell presented a list of expenses upon his return, but Mosby thought that the amount was excessive and refused payment. Outraged, Cornwell slipped into Warrenton to seek his revenge. Maj. Gen. Alfred Pleasonton, commanding the Army of the Potomac cavalry corps, eagerly believed Cornwell, but warned that Cornwell should be shot if he led them into a trap.[17]

As cavalrymen of the 1st New Jersey, 1st and 3rd Pennsylvania, and 1st Massachusetts under the command of Lt. Col. John Kester, 1st New Jersey, rode deep into the countryside, they launched a three-pronged assault on the ranger homeland. At Salem 50 men turned north to Upperville and thence on to Paris. Another 150 men broke off at Piedmont to scour the countryside north to Paris. The remaining 150 men marched on to Markham. The night air was bitterly cold. Temperatures dipped to the single digits and remained below freezing throughout the day. By noon the three squadrons reunited at Paris with 28 prisoners.[18]

Many rangers narrowly escaped capture that day. Chapman awoke that cold winter morning at the Highlands home of John Jeffries. With him were fellow rangers Montjoy, Massow, and cousin Judah Forrer, new to the command. Sam Chapman was there, too. Mosby had secured his transfer from the artillery, and he had just returned to serve as Mosby's adjutant with the rank of lieutenant. The Chapmans were lucky that day; the Northern cavalrymen did not stop at their residence. James Williamson, who also eluded capture that morning, thought that the troopers were burdened by the intense cold and not anxious to loiter.[19]

Chapman and Montjoy collected about 25 men and pursued the raiders to Paris. There, two of the cavalry squadrons reunited. Chapman and Montjoy edged toward town to reconnoiter, but sharp firing from Federal marksmen forced them back. More sharpshooters armed with carbines hid behind stone fences and fired into the rangers. A third squadron soon came up from Markham to Paris. Chapman and his rangers charged their rear, but to little avail. With the raiding party united and too strong to attack, Chapman dismissed the men with orders to gather more rangers and meet again at Piedmont in the afternoon. The Northerners shortly left Paris, followed by about 30 rangers who harassed their rear. Mosby rejoined the command that afternoon at Piedmont and with about 60 men followed the raiders back to Warrenton.[20]

Just two days later, on the twentieth, the alarm was again raised. This time the raiders came from the west, about 250 men of Cole's Maryland battalion along with men of the 1st New York Veteran Cavalry riding from Harpers Ferry. They captured several rangers during the expedition, which penetrated as far as Piedmont. Mosby was eating breakfast that morning at the Heartland home of Joseph Blackwell. With him were rangers John Munson, Jake Lavinder, and John Edmonds. The four Confederates mounted their horses and followed the raiders. From a distance, they harassed the expedition with carbines until more rangers joined them.[21]

Near Upperville, Cole halted to rest and feed his horses. By then about 50 or 60 rangers had joined Mosby. The Confederates charged the rear of the column and pressed Cole's men up the road. A running fight ensued over several miles. Combat was fierce. The rangers would charge the rear guard; Cole's men would countercharge. With the threat driven away, the march resumed. Shortly, the rangers would regroup and dash off on another charge into the rear guard. And so it went, charge and countercharge. In one such clash, Montjoy killed Capt. William Morgan, 1st New York Veteran Cavalry, in a hand-to-hand duel. Mosby witnessed the combat, and when Montjoy emerged victorious, rushed over to congratulate him and proclaim that he had just won his commission.[22]

At Blakeley's Grove School, north of Upperville on the road to Bloomfield, Cole made his stand. Stone fences lined the crossroads, and behind these Cole positioned his troopers armed with carbines. The rangers charged the defenses, but Colt revolvers were no match against carbineers. Mosby gallantly led his men, a conspicuous target for sharpshooters, mounted on a gray horse, wearing a plumed hat and dark overcoat with a cape lined in red cloth thrown over his shoulder. Tactics, not firepower, won the battle that day, when a flanking maneuver by the rangers eventually forced Cole's men to abandon their positions and flee up the road for safety. The rangers chased the panicked cavalrymen as far as Bloomfield along a road littered with strewn clothing and equipment.[23]

In his report, Mosby claimed Cole lost 6 men dead and 7 captured. The rangers lost 2 men wounded. After the stinging defeat at Loudoun Heights six weeks earlier, the repulse of Cole's raid into their homeland was especially gratifying. Many rangers shared in the glory of the day. Among those singled out for exceptional gallantry were the Chapman brothers—Sam in his first action since rejoining the command—and their housemate Montjoy. The rangers gained another recruit that day. Henry Cabell "Cab" Maddux was in class when the fighting spilled past the Blakeley's Grove schoolhouse. Not yet sixteen and standing only five feet five inches tall, the boy threw away his schoolbooks for the adventures of partisan warfare.[24]

The rangers gathered at Piedmont the next morning for the funeral of Joseph McCobb, killed the previous day when thrown from his horse while fleeing before Cole's advance. Mosby was at the Jeffries's farmhouse writing a report to Stuart when a scout rushed in with urgent news. A 150-man patrol, mostly Californians of the 2nd Massachusetts Cavalry under the command of Capt. James Reed, commonly referred to as the California Battalion, was at Rector's Cross Roads. The notorious deserter Charles Binns guided the patrol. The rangers, some 160 men strong, promptly abandoned the funeral and proceeded in search of the scouting party. Chapman brought up the command, while Mosby went ahead to reconnoiter.[25]

Mosby soon learned that the Californians had already vacated Rector's Cross Roads and were headed to Mountville, on the Snickersville turnpike between

Philomont and Aldie. From there Reed proceeded on toward Leesburg. Mosby's plan was to intercept the Federals on their way back to their camp at Vienna, and he ordered Chapman to march the command toward the turnpike between Leesburg and Dranesville, while he continued to follow the patrol. Mosby's reconnaissance confirmed that it was Reed's intention to march from Leesburg to Dranesville, and he sent a message by courier for Chapman to close up on the turnpike. There, the rangers camped for the night. Campfires blazed to provide warmth in the late winter cold. Sleep was hard to find. Reed was encamped up the turnpike and sure to resume his march in the morning. Moreover, another body of some 150 men of the 16th New York Cavalry had joined Reed's camp during the night. The ranger camp bustled with excitement in expectation of a clash in the morning.[26]

The rangers awoke early the next morning, 22 February, and moved further to a spot near Anker's blacksmith shop about two miles from Dranesville. There, Mosby awaited word that Reed had resumed his march. The road forked further back, and Mosby was uncertain which path the cavalrymen would take. He and the rangers waited anxiously for the approaching enemy. Toward the middle of the morning, ranger Walter Whaley rode up with the all-important news. The California Battalion was indeed proceeding along the turnpike, and the New York troopers had split off at the fork.[27]

Now, Mosby plotted his attack. Pine woods that lined the turnpike provided concealment for the rangers, and a slight hill rose up in the distance. His scouting had revealed that 3 men led the front of Reed's column, followed by some 25 men about 200 yards further back, and the bulk of the column another 200 yards back. Mosby divided the rangers into three groups positioned along the south side of the road concealed in the woods. Montjoy led 20 dismounted carbineers in the center. On the right, over the small hill, Mosby placed about 70 men under the command of Lt. Frank Williams, Company B, to charge the front. Chapman took the remaining 70 men to the left, about 80 yards up the turnpike from Williams, to charge the enemy rear. A loud whistle from Mosby was to signal the charge. To Frank Rahm and 2 other men, Mosby assigned an important task. They were to stall the advance scouts in conversation while the bulk of the column approached into the ambush. Mosby was confident of success. In the moments before battle, Mosby gave his final orders: "Men, the Yankees are coming and it is very likely we will have a hard fight. When you are ordered to charge, I want you to go right through them. Reserve your fire until you get close enough to see clearly what you are shooting at, and then let every shot tell."[28]

Tension mounted as the Californians approached. "We sat motionless on our horses, holding our breaths, with heads thrown forward and ears strained, watching and waiting in anxious expectation for the approach of the enemy and the signal for the attack," James Williamson remembered. "There was an unnatural, an unearthly stillness around us at that moment—a stillness which seemed to creep over our flesh like a chill, and to be seen and felt." In the distance, siege guns around the capital echoed in salute to the birthday of George Washington. The 3 lead men passed by Chapman's rangers without noticing them. Rahm performed his task well. Sitting on his horse astride the turnpike on the rise of the hill, he stalled the scouts until one became suspicious and raised his carbine to fire. At that moment, Mosby blew his whistle and signaled the charge.[29]

The ranger carbineers instantly opened fire on the 25 men at the front of the column. The withering hail of bullets devastated these lead scouts. John Munson put down his carbine just long enough to watch as the men "halted and wavered, some of them throwing up their hands as if to ward off a sudden slap in the face." To their left and right, 140 rangers erupted into a wild yell and charged the startled Federals. Mosby, along with Sam Chapman, led the charge of Williams's detachment down the hill to the head of the column. Chapman's men also spilled out onto the turnpike, hitting the main body, which had not yet caught up to the advance guard. The Californians were some of the best fighters the rangers faced, and they made a valiant stand, but the weight of the ranger onslaught crushed them. Men broke and fled in all directions. Many were driven into the Potomac River in panic, and bodies were still being found in the river for days after the battle. Munson observed that "the road was rapidly filled up with dead and wounded men and horses, and riderless horses were galloping in terror everywhere."[30]

Typical of such affairs, the fighting was close-quarter, individual contests amid a field of many such encounters, where a man could look his opponent in the face and feel his breath. It was vicious, hand-to-hand combat. James Chappalear was riding in his first raid. While awaiting the signal to attack, he told a friend that he had hidden a large sum of money in his boots. That money should be taken to his father if he died. He did indeed fall to Federal bullets. His cousin, Monroe Robinson, rode up to the man who had killed him and dispatched him with a point blank pistol shot. John Munson forced a Californian to surrender, but did not stop to disarm him. As Munson rode past the trooper in search of more quarry, he shot Munson in the back, the bullet missing his spine by only half an inch. Ludwell Lake witnessed the shooting and promptly killed the man. A fellow ranger reached out to hold Munson on his horse as he toppled over, but then Harry Sweeting, at Munson's side, was also shot. The same ranger reached over to hold him, too. A .44 caliber bullet struck John Edmonds in the thigh. A Bible that he carried at the insistence of his mother likely saved his leg from amputation. He carried the Bible in his pants pocket that day. The bullet passed through the Bible and lodged in his leg without shattering the bone.[31]

Chapman's friend and housemate Robert von Massow also suffered a career-ending wound. He rode with Chapman's group into the battle and presented a striking figure in his Prussian uniform, with long, redlined cape, an ostrich feather in his hat, and carrying his trusty German saber. He soon discharged his pistol and then used his sword as his weapon. Massow spotted Reed among the masses of bluecoats and charged at him with his sword raised. Reed was armed with a pistol, and as he saw Massow lumbering toward him, sword outstretched, Reed raised his hand to surrender. Massow was in too much of a hurry to stop and disarm Reed. Federals were fleeing in all directions, and there was more prey to hunt down. It proved to be a costly mistake. As Massow charged past Reed, Reed turned and shot him. Chapman watched as his friend fell to the ground, severely wounded in the lung. He spurred his horse toward Reed, who tried to get away, but Chapman overtook him. Chapman closed within three feet of Reed, deliberately aimed his pistol, and shot down the Federal commander. Reed fell next to Massow. He tried to raise his pistol to shoot Chapman, but life ebbed away and he fell forward on his face, dead. Upon hearing of his assailant's death, Massow replied, "I am much obliged to you."[32]

The fight at Anker's shop was another brilliant victory for Mosby. He reported that his rangers killed 15 Federals, wounded a considerable number, and captured 70 prisoners. Mosby lost 1 man killed—Chappalear—and 4 wounded. Mosby commended the Chapman brothers, along with Lt. Frank Williams and Lt. William Hunter, Company A, for their actions that day. Federal commanders sent out a cavalry patrol when word of the ambush reached camp, but to no avail. Mosby and his rangers had already retreated to the safety of their Confederacy.[33]

With the fight over, Chapman's thoughts turned from the heat of battle to more humane concerns. He had fought three hard battles in a period of five days. The long rides, fierce combat, and scores of dead and wounded soldiers likely left him physically and emotionally exhausted. Now, his good friend Massow was severely wounded and needed urgent care, and he still had one more important detail to which to attend. He was to marry Josephine Jeffries in three days.

The twenty-fifth of February dawned unlike other days in Mosby's Confederacy. It was the day Chapman and Josie would be wed in a military ceremony at Highlands. The day began early because the ceremony was held at sunrise to prevent a surprise attack. For Chapman, there were logistics and planning. The war could not wait for the fortunes of two young lovers, and a wedding attended by Mosby and his officers would provide a prime opportunity to capture the elusive rangers. Outside, in a large cordon surrounding the house, vedettes watched for approaching danger. For Josie, it was a day of romance. Amid the devastation and deprivation brought by three years of war, she gathered with her family. Women in their finest silk dresses and soldiers outfitted in their best uniforms filled the house. As they awaited the beginning of their new life together, the realities of war intruded. The minister who was to perform the ceremony was captured on his way to the wedding. Another minister was soon found, and the ceremony proceeded. Dick Buckner and his ranger band likely entertained family and guests with music and dancing. Later that day, Federal troopers arrived at the house, but the wedding party had already dispersed—the Chapmans, to enjoy a brief honeymoon; Mosby and his rangers, to fight again.[34]

As night fell, Chapman had new obligations, to his bride, her mother, Esther Jeffries, and grandmother, Esther Foote. The exhilaration of exploits with Mosby and attacks on Federal troops would be tempered by concern for Josie's safety. As the wife of Mosby's most trusted officer, second in command, Josie would become a much-sought-after prize, but she evaded capture through the loyalty of friends and faithful servants. In one such case, family history maintains, Josie fled to the mountains to escape approaching Federals—a hurried, anxious escape that caused her to lose an unborn child. Northern soldiers, hoping to capture her and force her to ride a supply train to protect against raids by Mosby, had chased Josie into the mountains, where a local mountain man befriended her. Pregnant, flushed, and feverish, and with the house surrounded by enemy soldiers, she evaded capture when the man put her to bed and claimed she was his sick daughter.[35]

The newlyweds maintained their home at Highlands along with John Jeffries, Josie's mother, and her grandmother and remained there for the duration of the war. Only after the war did the family return to the Edge Hill estate. It was at Highlands that Massow, after first being ministered to by daughters of a local farmer, recovered under Josie's attentive care. In the summer of 1864, he left Mosby's Confederacy and returned to Europe, where he served a distinguished career as a general in the German army.[36]

The rangers fought a different war than those in the regular army. They did not establish encampments, but rather lived in their homes or with sympathetic supporters. For this they were derisively called "featherbed soldiers," but it meant that Chapman and Josie were never separated for more than a week at a time until January 1865, when Chapman took his squadron to the Northern Neck for three months.[37]

When Chapman did go to the Northern Neck, Josie suffered the pain and heartache of parting. "It is a week today darling since you left me," she wrote him, "and oh you don't know how I miss you, and how very hard I struggle not to feel desolate and heartsick, lonely I must feel, and always am when you are away." Yet Josie's faith steered her through the lonesome weeks. "We both know we love each other, and must not think so much about our separation, but of the time when we may meet again. I think of that so often, and almost begin to look for you already." She saw brighter days beyond the despair of war, as young lovers can, in a future sustained by love and companionship. "I think if the war was only over and you and I might be together for the rest of our lives I would be perfectly happy no matter how humble might be our lot." The separation tore at Chapman, too. He confessed to Josie: "It seems that every thing around me at all times reminds me of my loved one at home, oh how I feel as if I would like to pour out my whole soul to you and wish that I had the language, this it seems would bring us nearer together and then I feel so much happier."[38]

Chapman received a thirty-day furlough following his wedding. Dolly Richards commanded the company in Chapman's absence. Weather and poor roads in March and April limited operations mainly to small bands of men, but the rangers still succeeded in capturing prisoners and horses. Collecting forage and horses in Loudoun County occupied much of the time. Mosby himself scouted for Lee, providing needed intelligence on troop movements. Ulysses S. Grant was the new commander of the Federal army, and Lee was anxious to know his intentions for the coming spring campaign. One of Mosby's successes was anticipating the Federal advance up the Shenandoah Valley.[39]

Cavalry raids from Warrenton kept pressure on the rangers. One such large raid was expected on the night of 19 April. Some 180 men, each armed with every conceivable weapon that could be found, gathered after dark to protect their homeland, concealed in the woods near Piedmont. Pickets were posted to warn of the approach, wire was strung across the road to dismount riders, and all waited anxiously for the raiders. The Federals did not come that night, nor the next night, nor again the following night. Three sleepless nights of vigilant watch left the rangers weary and edgy, but that was a better fate than being sent to Old Capitol Prison in Washington, Point Lookout in Maryland, or other prisoner of war camps. However, raids by Col. Charles Lowell and his 2nd Massachusetts Cavalry during the month of April rounded up some 50 rangers and 30 to 40 horses.[40]

This period also saw notable changes in the organization of the rangers. Mosby formed Company D at Paris on 28 March. He appointed Montjoy captain, his long-awaited officer commission having been earned at Blakeley's Grove School. One month later, Mosby promoted Richards to captain of Company B to fill the vacancy created by Smith's death at Loudoun Heights.[41]

10 | Catch Those Fellows

With the weather improving and roads again passable, Grant launched his expected spring offensive. The main advance in Virginia was by the Army of the Potomac. In a series of battles at the Wilderness, Spotsylvania, and Cold Harbor, Grant drove the Confederates back to Richmond, and the middle of June found both armies entrenched around Petersburg. In the Shenandoah Valley, Maj. Gen. Franz Sigel advanced with 6,500 men. The intent was to capture the town of Staunton, but Sigel never made it that far. A 5,000-man Confederate army turned Sigel back at New Market on 15 May 1864 in a battle that immortalized the young cadets of the Virginia Military Institute.[1]

The rangers harried Sigel as he advanced up the Shenandoah Valley. Mosby took 10 men across the Blue Ridge Mountains, struck a supply train near Bunker Hill on 1 May, and then proceeded on with 20 men to Martinsburg for another raid. While Mosby next turned his attention toward the Rappahannock River to raid wagon trains in the wake of Grant's advance, Dolly Richards and Chapman took 15–20 men each into the Shenandoah Valley to operate in the rear of Sigel's army. Richards crossed the Shenandoah River and killed or wounded several Federals in a skirmish near Winchester on the ninth.[2]

Chapman, too, found successes in the Shenandoah Valley. Accompanied by his brother, he crossed the Shenandoah River with Richards's men. The two groups parted, and Chapman attacked a detachment of the 1st New York Cavalry near Berryville. His rangers killed 2 men and captured several others in a brisk skirmish. The approach of the full regiment forced the rangers to retire from the field, but not before Sam Chapman inflicted 3 more casualties in an impetuous charge on the advance guard. He came away from this encounter unscathed, though his horse was shot.[3]

Chapman returned to the Shenandoah Valley on 11 May and scouted along the Valley turnpike north of Strasburg with 20 men. Late in the day, the rangers captured a 5-man cavalry patrol coming from Strasburg. Early the next morning, the rangers moved off toward the town. Soon, they came across a large supply train guarded by 300 infantry and 80 cavalry traveling along the turnpike from Winchester. It was raining that morning, and the Confederates wore dark overcoats to stay dry. None of the guards were concerned as Chapman and his men fell in and followed the rear of the train.[4]

A few miles south of Strasburg, along the banks of the Shenandoah River, the road climbed sharply up a steep hill before crossing a bridge over the river. There, as the wagons ascended Fisher's Hill and the accompanying guard was strewn out along the narrow road, Chapman attacked the rear. Details of the clash are vague. Mosby reported that Chapman captured about 30 prisoners and a like number of horses. John Scott, in his history of Mosby's command, wrote that the rangers killed or wounded 12 men, captured 19, and escaped with 23 horses. Another history put the Federal losses at but 2 killed, 4 prisoners, and a number of horses captured. The rangers escaped unscathed to Luray, abetted by a local woman who convinced the pursuing cavalrymen that they had little chance of overtaking the fleet partisans. Chapman turned his prisoners over to the provost marshal at Luray and dismissed the command.[5]

After the defeat at New Market, Maj. Gen. David Hunter replaced Sigel as leader of the Federal army in the Shenandoah Valley. He assumed command on the evening of Saturday, 21 May, and Mosby quickly initiated him to the nature of partisan warfare. The day before, Mosby and 103 rangers had assembled at Paris and dropped into the Shenandoah Valley through Ashby's Gap. They reached the Shenandoah River at nightfall but found the river swollen with floodwaters and too dangerous to cross in the dark, so the rangers made camp for the night. They crossed the river Saturday morning in boats, driving their reluctant horses across or tying them to the crafts and towing them. The rangers continued on toward Front Royal, where at a point on the turnpike from Front Royal to Winchester, along a prominent ridge known as Guard Hill on the north bank of the Shenandoah River, 150 troopers of the 15th New York Cavalry garrisoned an outpost. Thirty men led by Capt. Michael Auer manned a forward picket post. The remainder of the squadron was one-half mile to the rear.[6]

The rangers reached Guard Hill after dark. When informed of the strength of the outpost, which was more than he had expected, Mosby replied that it meant only a larger capture of horses. In the early morning hours of Sunday, Sam Chapman led a detachment of 15 rangers on foot to the rear of the forward camp, armed with carbines. Their volley signaled the attack, and the other rangers rushed into camp on horseback. The rangers caught the New Yorkers completely by surprise and unprepared for the attack and routed them before the groggy Northerners could return fire. The Confederates captured 11 men and 45 horses. Among them was Auer, who had spent the night away from his picket post. Upon arriving at the scene, Auer enquired of the nearest man he could find what was happening. That man happened to be Sam Chapman, who replied, "It means that Mosby has got you." The stunned Auer could only respond, "Well, this beats hell, don't it." Hunter promptly discharged Auer for incompetence, as well as Maj. Henry Roessle.[7]

The next raid began six days later, on 28 May. That Saturday, 144 rangers heeded Mosby's call to assemble at Rectortown. They passed through Manassas Gap into the Shenandoah Valley and camped near Front Royal for the night. The Confederates forded the Shenandoah River the next morning and proceeded on toward Strasburg. There, they spent that Sunday watching the Valley turnpike. A large wagon train passed by, but it was too heavily guarded to attack. Later, a troop of 100 cavalrymen was seen, which Mosby let pass by without attacking. With little results to show for the day, the command marched north to Middletown in the evening. The rangers entered the town Monday morning to a warm reception and continued on to Newtown. Other Southern partisans, notably Harry Gilmor, also operated in the area, and the rangers came across the burning remnants of a supply train captured by Gilmor during the night.[8]

Eventually, the rangers spotted wagons moving along the turnpike from Winchester, and the command formed for the attack in woods along the road. A large cavalry force of 600 troopers escorted the wagons. Mosby remained on the road with a few men to draw off the escorts. Company A was to charge the front while Companies B and C cut off any escape from the rear. With the troopers separated from the wagons, Chapman was to take 40 men and attack the wagons. However, the plan went awry from the start. The Northern troopers did not fall for Mosby's feint. They fell back toward the wagons before Company A charged. Richards charged with Companies B and C as directed, but instead of striking the rear of the cavalry, his rangers encountered a second escort of 100 infantrymen deployed behind a stone wall along the roadside. The Northern muskets roared in unison, and the volley drove off the rangers at a loss of 1 man killed, 1 wounded, and 2 horses killed. With their cavalry escorts retreating upon them and infantrymen fending off an attack, the wagoneers wasted little time in turning around and scurrying back to Winchester. Chapman and his 40 men charged out of the woods. A brisk skirmish netted 5 prisoners taken and 2 Northerners killed, but the wagons escaped unharmed.[9]

Hunter understood only too well the threat partisans posed to his supply lines and dealt harshly with guerilla activities. On 24 May, after someone in the town of Newtown on the Valley turnpike shot at a passing wagon train the previous night, Hunter ordered the house from which the shot came and surrounding buildings torched. He then informed the inhabitants of the town that all homes within five miles would be burned if the offense occurred again. Hunter attempted to enforce this threat on the thirtieth. He ordered the burning of the town and all buildings between Newtown and Middletown, sparing only churches and the property of those loyal to the Union, but his men were more sympathetic and absolved the townfolk. At some point, though, Chapman captured a house-burner. Amid the ruins of the scorched estate, the rangers executed the soldier. Attached to his back was a placard announcing "shot for house-burning."[10]

Hunter was decidedly more forceful than Sigel and shortly resumed the offensive. He brushed aside an undermanned Confederate army at Piedmont on 5 June. Hunter occupied Staunton the next day and tore up the railroad and destroyed bridges, depots, and factories. The army of 15,000 men proceeded on to Lexington, where Hunter torched the buildings of the Virginia Military Institute and the home of former Virginia governor John Letcher on the twelfth. Hunter then crossed out of the Shenandoah Valley to march upon Lynchburg. He arrived on the seventeenth, just as Lt. Gen. Jubal Early appeared with an army of 10,000 Confederates, pulled from the front lines of Grant's advance and rushed by train to defend Lynchburg. Short of ammunition, Hunter abandoned his campaign and retreated to West Virginia.[11]

The next large operation began on Wednesday, 22 June. About 200 rangers left Rectortown to strike east, riding to The Plains and through the Bull Run Mountains at Thoroughfare Gap. The rangers arose early the next morning and resumed their march toward Fairfax at sunrise. Grim reminders of the cost of war sprang before the men as they crossed the battlefields at Manassas. Skeletons lay exposed in shallow graves, clad in decaying uniforms, white fleshless bones of arms and legs protruding outward from the ground. Rusted guns and bayonets and rotting cartridge boxes littered the field. Surely the memory of the mayhem inflicted by the Dixie Artillery on Fitz John Porter's infantrymen must have crossed the Chapman brothers' minds as they passed over the battlefield. Yet the ghoulish sights did not deter the rangers from their mission. Their weary horses needed a respite, and there, on the battlefield, amid the graves, the rangers stopped to rest. They rode on until midnight, when they bivouacked at Union Mill. Friday morning, the march resumed toward Centreville, where Mosby learned that 40 troopers of the 16th New York Cavalry had been seen. The troopers, Lt. Matthew Tuck commanding, were searching for 10 men who had attacked a 4-man patrol the previous night. The New Yorkers had vacated the town before the rangers arrived, however, and Mosby sent Company A on to Chantilly to intercept them. In fact, Tuck's detachment was close by.[12]

At eleven o'clock, Tuck's New Yorkers were resting at a farm about one and one-half miles from Centreville, weary from their early morning ride. They had failed to find the 10 men they were seeking and knew nothing of Mosby and 200 rangers lurking nearby. Their horses were unbitted, eating fresh hay. Troopers lounged and slept, some lying in the fields, some loitering in the farmhouse and barn, many climbing cherry trees that lined the lane to the house. There was an air of indifference and only one picket, poorly placed, guarded the entrance to the farm. The scene was far less calm at the headquarters of the 16th New

York Cavalry. There, Col. Henry Lazelle knew of Mosby's presence and knew Tuck was in danger. Three hours earlier, he had sent out a 150-man patrol to reinforce Tuck, but it was too late.[13]

As the rangers came upon the scene, Mosby turned to Chapman and told him to "take the men with you and catch those fellows." The rangers gathered in formation, and Chapman led the men through the gate and up the farm lane at a gallop. Revolvers were drawn as the Confederates crashed into the farm. Surprised New Yorkers, reveling in the bounty of cherries, dropped out of the trees in astonishment and were quickly corralled. Men fled the house and barn. Those in the hayfield ran for safety. Everywhere, panic-stricken men ran off in all directions. Little defense was offered. Chapman organized squads of rangers to hunt down the fleeing troopers. Soon, prisoners came back in droves. Chapman's rangers decimated Tuck's 40-man detachment. The rangers killed or wounded 6 men, captured 31, and secured 38 horses. Tuck was one of the fortunate ones and fled to safety.[14]

One game Northern trooper, Thomas "Boston" Corbett, gathered his Spencer repeating carbine and hid protected by a ditch behind a tree. Twice, ranger Bush Underwood tried to capture him; twice, Corbett valiantly fended him off. For the third attempt, Chapman led 20 rangers galloping on horseback in a sweep to the ditch. Underwood, determined to capture his adversary, was the first to reach Corbett. He dismounted by abruptly reigning in his mount and springing head first out of the saddle over his horse's head. Landing at Corbett's feet, Underwood knocked the carbine away and pointed his cocked revolver at Corbett's head, ready to shoot his foe. Chapman hastily intervened. "Don't shoot that man," Chapman shouted. "He has a right to defend himself to the last!" Later released from a Confederate prison, Corbett returned to the 16th New York Cavalry and gained immortal notoriety ten months after his capture as the man who killed John Wilkes Booth on 26 April 1865.[15]

The battalion was in the saddle again four days later for a raid on the Baltimore and Ohio Railroad near Harpers Ferry. Mosby left Upperville with Company A on the evening of 28 June and marched to near Charlestown. Chapman followed with the rest of the command and crossed into the Shenandoah Valley that same night. With them was a recently acquired 12-pounder Napoleon howitzer. When Chapman brought the rangers up on the morning of the twenty-ninth, Mosby deployed for the attack. His objective was Duffield Station between Harpers Ferry and Martinsburg. Mosby positioned Company A along the road from Charlestown to Harpers Ferry to guard the rear. He then took the rest of the command and the howitzer west to Duffield Station. Upon arriving at the station, the rangers captured 4 men and learned that a small garrison of 45–65 soldiers guarded the depot.[16]

Mosby hoped to attack a train coming from Martinsburg, but the train was delayed, and he instead opted to attack the station that afternoon. After cutting the telegraph lines, Mosby prominently posted the rangers in line of battle with the howitzer trained on the station. Deep in enemy territory, with a garrison at Harpers Ferry nearby, Mosby preferred to capture the depot without firing a shot. He hoped his line of battle and the sight of the howitzer would instill fear, and Mosby sent Richards into the camp with a flag of truce to demand surrender. This, the commanding officer readily agreed to do. The rangers reaped a bounty of dry goods, coffee, calico, and other cloths and then burned the buildings.[17]

For the return march, Richard Montjoy proceeded ahead with Company D to Charlestown, escorting the howitzer and the prisoners. Richards and Chapman followed with their companies, spaced apart at one-quarter mile intervals to kick up as much dust as possible to create an illusion of a greater force. The deception succeeded because panicked Federal reports told of 400–500 cavalrymen with two guns; some reports claimed 500–800 raiders with a battery of four guns. A Federal detachment from Harpers Ferry timidly followed the rangers. However, the rangers were eager for a fight, and Mosby turned and formed line of battle. Companies A and D were positioned in front with the howitzer. Richards and Chapman were stationed about one-half mile back to sweep in on the flanks, but the enemy did not engage, and the march resumed. Again the Federals followed, and again Mosby formed line of battle with the same result. By nightfall the command was safely across the Shenandoah River with 74 prisoners and 34 horses, and the rangers shared their bounty of captured stores with war-weary Southerners when they returned through Paris on the morning of the thirtieth.[18]

When Hunter crossed out of the Shenandoah Valley into West Virginia, the path to Washington, D.C., lay open before Early. His 15,000-man army crossed the Potomac River on 6 July and pushed aside a makeshift Federal force at the Monocacy River east of Frederick three days later. The Confederates approached the outskirts of the capital on the eleventh, but veterans from Grant's army rushed to reinforce the garrison, and Early called off the attack. He recrossed the Potomac into Loudoun County and dropped back into the Shenandoah Valley through Snicker's Gap.[19]

To support Early during his advance, Mosby opted to cut communications between Harpers Ferry and Washington. Two hundred and fifty rangers heeded the call to assemble at Upperville on 3 July and marched north to the Potomac River. The target was Point of Rocks, a prominent rock outcrop on the northern riverbank about twelve miles downriver from Harpers Ferry, where the Catoctin Mountains drop steeply to the river. There, the Baltimore and Ohio Railroad from Harpers Ferry met the Chesapeake and Ohio Canal in a narrow gap along the riverfront, from which the railroad turned north to Baltimore. Two companies of Loudoun Rangers and two companies of infantrymen guarded the small town and depot.[20]

The rangers reached the Potomac on the morning of Monday, 4 July, and crossed at a shallow ford about a mile from Point of Rocks. Richards and Chapman had by now emerged as Mosby's two most able commanders. Mosby increasingly utilized his command in a First Squadron led by Richards and a Second Squadron led by Chapman. This was Richards's day to shine. The river was about a quarter-mile wide at this point, separated by a long, narrow island. Sam Chapman, supported by Company C, placed the Napoleon on a high embankment and shelled the opposing riverbank. Dismounted rangers armed with carbines led the advance into the river, followed by Richards in command of the bulk of the rangers. The pickets guarding the ford melted before the onrushing Confederates. Once across the river, the rangers followed the towpath along the canal to Point of Rocks. There, the attack momentarily stalled. Planking on the bridge across the canal had been torn up, and an earthen fortification, brimming with armed soldiers, lay beyond the bridge. But the defenses were ineffective, and the Federals offered little resistance. Richards gamely led the charge across the bridge, and the soldiers fled the entrenchments.[21]

Few prisoners were captured that day—most deftly escaped the onslaught—but the rangers still celebrated the eighty-eighth anniversary of the signing of the Declaration of Independence in good accord. Seventeen clerks from the Treasury Department had chartered a boat for a holiday excursion. They passed through the canal just as the rangers attacked and received three shells from Sam Chapman's Napoleon. The shells fell harmlessly, but the boat became caught in a closed lock, and the clerks hastily fled for safety. Still later, a train approached from Harpers Ferry and was turned back by well-placed cannon shots. And the rangers found a bounty of treasures in the camp and stores. Men crossed back to Virginia on horses laden with calico, bolts of cloth, boots, shoes, hoops, skirts, and bonnets. Red and white bunting flew in the breeze to honor Independence Day. And the day was not without strategic success. The attack at Point of Rocks disrupted communications between Washington and Harpers Ferry, heightened the fear created by Early's advance to Maryland, and diverted troops from defense of the capital.[22]

A squadron of 230 troopers of the 8th Illinois Cavalry arrived at the scene on Tuesday and traded gunfire with rangers from the opposing riverbank. However, a bigger threat to the rangers loomed in their rear. Col. Charles Lowell had sent out a large force of cavalry on Monday. From their base at Falls Church, 100 troopers of the 2nd Massachusetts Cavalry and 50 troopers of the 13th New York Cavalry led by Maj. William Forbes scouted the countryside between Aldie and Leesburg on Tuesday and Wednesday. Mosby learned of their presence at Leesburg Tuesday evening, but when he reached the town the following morning, Forbes had already marched south toward Aldie. Mosby and several others gave chase while Chapman brought up the rest of the command, some 175 men and the howitzer. The rangers caught up with Forbes at Mount Zion

Church, east of Aldie on the Little River Turnpike. There, late in the afternoon of Wednesday, 6 July, Forbes allowed his men to rest for a few hours during their march back to Falls Church. It proved to be a deadly delay.[23]

At half past six, the northern cavalrymen heard firing on their picket lines. It was Mosby's carbineers, driving back Forbes's advance guard. Forbes formed two lines of battle, one behind the other, in an open field south of the turnpike. "Their alignment was as perfect as if on dress parade," ranger John Alexander described. "Their officers were in position with their sabers drawn and the men sat on their horses with carbines ready." A rail fence lined the field along the roadway. Sam Chapman deployed the Napoleon on the turnpike, supported by Company D, and fired a shell. It burst harmlessly behind the lines, but added to the edginess of Forbes's men and horses, unaccustomed to receiving artillery fire. As the rangers closed within 225 yards, they stopped to tear down the fence, and then Confederates on horseback poured across the field. The first line of Northern troopers opened fire with carbines, followed by some in the second line with pistols. Their horses, already jittery from the artillery shot, panicked from the noise. Forbes repositioned his men to restore order.[24]

As he did so, the rangers struck the front and flank of Forbes's cavalrymen, shouting wildly and firing their revolvers. "Mosby and his rangers were upon us, swooping down like Indians, yelling like fiends, discharging their pistols with fearful rapidity, and threatening to completely envelop our little band," recounted Charles Humphreys, chaplain with the 2nd Massachusetts Cavalry. Stunned troopers saw comrades drop to the ground, killed or wounded. The onslaught was too much. The lines broke, and Northern cavalrymen fled for safety. Forbes rallied his men several hundred yards back along a fence, but the Confederates pressed on and again broke the Federal lines. Other such rallies were also in vain. The hunt was on, and rangers pursued panicked Federals for several miles.[25]

In his account of the affair, Lowell wrote that he had "only to report a perfect rout." A rout it was. Forbes lost 14 men killed and 37 wounded, 10 too badly hurt to move from the field. The rangers captured 55 men, including most of the officers, along with about 100 horses. Forbes was among those captured. He gamely attempted to strike a blow at Mosby with his saber but was captured when a pistol shot felled his horse and he was pinned underneath. Mosby's losses—1 killed and 6 wounded—were comparatively light.[26]

As darkness enveloped the battleground, bodies of men and horses littered the field. James Williamson wrote that "horses, wounded and maddened with pain and fright, dashed wildly over the battleground, while others lay trembling, or rearing and falling, unable to stand." Equipment and weapons lay strewn across the field. A nearby farmhouse served as a hospital. There, ranger surgeon William Dunn and his assistants toiled for hours to save the wounded enemy, but many were beyond repair. John Munson told how he "found a man kneeling near the fence by the roadside, with his head bent forward touching the ground in front of him and his left hand clutching a gaping wound in his side." Munson rushed to his assistance, but the man toppled over dead. John Alexander served on picket duty at the edge of the field. "I never had as bad two hours as I had that night. The groans of the wounded men and horses, the pitiful calls for relief, the prayers, the heart-rending laments for loved ones were borne to me on the quiet summer night," he remembered.[27]

Early's retreat from the outskirts of Washington brought him into Loudoun County to Leesburg on 14 July. On the sixteenth he passed through Snicker's Gap into the Shenandoah Valley. The Federal army—6th Corps, 19th Corps, and two additional divisions—followed in pursuit. Mosby divided the rangers into detachments led by Chapman, Richards, and other officers that operated independently and harassed the Federals as they traversed the countyside.[28]

One such clash occurred on 19 July. Brig. Gen. Alfred Duffié marched from Snickersville to Upperville with his cavalry division, artillery, and an ambulance train on the eighteenth. He continued on to Paris the next day and into the Shenandoah Valley through Ashby's Gap. He pushed on to cross the Shenandoah River but met determined Confederate resistance and fell back to Ashby's Gap for the night. Duffié posted a squadron from the 20th Pennsylvania Cavalry, Capt. Samuel Montgomery commanding, to watch the rear of the gap. The outpost was less than one mile from the main body, surely safe from attack.[29]

Chapman found the lone outpost and routed its defenders. He divided his men into two groups led by himself and Frank Fox, his lieutenant in Company C, so as to attack the camp from opposite sides. Fox's men, however, were diverted by marauders plundering a house, and Chapman's group charged alone on horseback. His rangers captured the entire squadron of 2 officers and 50 enlisted men, along with 55 horses. Only 1 ranger died, thrown from his horse during the charge. Upon hearing the gunfire, a patrol from the main cavalry body pursued the rangers, but Chapman and a few others acted as decoys and diverted the pursuers while the rest of the rangers escaped with the prisoners.[30]

With Early pushed back up the Shenandoah Valley to Fisher's Hill south of Strasburg, Federal commanders left a small force at Winchester and returned the 6th and 19th Corps to Washington. The rangers harassed their march through Loudoun County and also the weak Northern supply lines in the Shenandoah Valley. Early, too, pressed his advantage and pounced on the garrison at Winchester. He routed the small Federal army in a battle at Kernstown outside of Winchester on 24 July and hurried on to Harpers Ferry.[31]

The month of July ended with another accomplishment for the Chapman brothers. On 28 July, Mosby organized a fifth company, Company E, at Upperville. He appointed Sam Chapman, married just that morning, captain. The rangers, 200 men and three cannons strong, then raided across the Potomac River to support Early. The operation accomplished little materially, but it confused and concerned the Federal command. Sam Chapman, in his first operation as company commander, crossed the Potomac and was nearly cut off by a large enemy presence.[32]

One significant consequence of Early's second advance to Harpers Ferry was the formation of the new Army of the Shenandoah, led by Maj. Gen. Philip Sheridan. Sheridan's instructions from Grant regarding Early were to "follow him to the death." Sheridan did, with tragic consequences for the populace of the Shenandoah Valley. The rangers, too, played a role in this final act of the Valley campaign of 1864, also at the expense of citizens of their Confederacy.[33]

11 | No Quarter

Sheridan arrived at Harpers Ferry on 6 August 1864 and took command of the Army of the Shenandoah the next day. He had nearly 35,000 infantry and 8,000 cavalry awaiting his orders, including the 6th and 19th Corps, which Grant returned to the Shenandoah Valley along with two battle-hardened cavalry divisions. It was a sizeable army that the Confederates were hard-pressed to match.[1]

Sheridan began his advance from Harpers Ferry on Wednesday, 10 August, and within three days he learned the perils of partisan warfare in the Shenandoah Valley. Early's army was at Bunker Hill, and Sheridan planned a flanking maneuver that would defeat the Confederates. He expected a short campaign and did not bring his supply wagons south. Sheridan's advance was rapid. By the next day, his army was eight miles south of Winchester, but Early's retreat up the valley prevented a decisive battle. The campaign began taking longer than he had expected. Now, Sheridan needed those wagons from Harpers Ferry, and he ordered Brig. Gen. John Kenly to escort a supply train to Winchester by Friday evening.[2]

The wagon train consisted of 525 supply and headquarters wagons. Wagons of the cavalry formed the rear of the train, with those of the Cavalry Reserve Brigade rearmost. Kenly's infantry brigade and a battery of artillery were detailed to escort the wagons, but Kenly's brigade was insufficient for such a large supply train. He positioned two companies of his 3rd Maryland Potomac Home Brigade at the head of the train and dispersed the remaining companies, one every 20 wagons. Kenly also had two regiments of Ohio National Guard to escort the train. The 149th Ohio guarded the center of the train, one company stationed every 30 wagons. The 144th Ohio watched the rear section, one company every 20 wagons and two companies posted behind the rearmost wagon. Kenly assigned one section of artillery to the head of the train, another in the center, and the third section at the rear. It was not a particularly strong guard. The Ohioans had enlisted for only 100 days, and their term of service was set to expire in just a few days; and the battery never joined the train.[3]

It took most of Friday, 12 August, to organize and outfit the supply train. Not until 4:15 P.M. were the last of the wagons ready to move. The route to Winchester followed the Valley turnpike from Harpers Ferry south through Berryville before turning west to Winchester. The head of the train reached Buck Marsh Creek, one mile north of Berryville, at ten o'clock that night. There, the wagons parked while the teamsters fed and watered their mules and the guards rested. Kenly ordered the march resumed after ninety minutes. However, the wagons were strung out and the train was so long that the cavalry wagons did not reach the creekside stop until after those of the infantry corps had left. Kenly expected these rear wagons to shortly resume the march. Instead, the drivers parked their wagons, unhitched their teams, fed and watered their mules, and slept. Confusion abounded. No one could find the officer in charge of this section of the train. The Ohioans in the rear guard lay on the ground asleep. No pickets watched for raiders. Finally, at six o'clock on the morning of Saturday, 13 August, as the head of the train approached Winchester, the rear cavalry wagons broke camp and began moving. The wagons of the Cavalry Reserve Brigade at the rear of the train were the last to move out.[4]

On the evening of the twelfth, as the train headed toward Berryville, Sheridan's army was at Cedar Creek, and Sheridan fretted about the supplies. He knew Kenly's brigade was small for the escort, but still he expected the wagons to arrive the following day. The specter of Mosby haunted Sheridan, though, and that evening he directed the 8th Illinois Cavalry to cross the Potomac River into Loudoun County "to exterminate as many of Mosby's gang as they can." Kenly, too, was anxious that night. As the lead wagons pulled out of Buck Marsh Creek and started for Berryville, he disclosed to his officers that he considered this to be "the most dangerous point in the route" and expressed concern to make sure every wagon passed through safely. Sheridan and Kenly had good reason to worry.[5]

On Friday, as the wagons slowly lumbered up the Shenandoah Valley, some 250 or more rangers with two mountain howitzers assembled at Rectortown, passed through Snicker's Gap, and crossed the Shenandoah River. Excited scouts rushed into camp that night with news of a large wagon train. Mosby, John Munson, and others rode to the scene to assess the situation and found a long line of hundreds of wagons moving along the turnpike. The rangers were seasoned veterans at gaining information from unwitting conspirators. They coolly rode among the drivers and escorts, talking to the men and obtaining information about the number of wagons and guards. Munson, brash with confidence, casually asked one guard for a match with which to light his pipe. Then, with information in hand, the rangers quietly slipped away unnoticed.[6]

Chapman brought the command up to the site before daybreak, and the rangers disposed for the attack. The artillerists among them unlimbered the howitzers on a knoll overlooking the road, but only one was operational; the other was disabled with a broken wheel. The First Squadron, led by Dolly Richards, was to attack the front of the train approaching Berryville. Chapman led the Second Squadron to strike the train further back. Sam Chapman and Company E remained in reserve with the artillery. Tension was high as the moment of attack neared. After the war, Mosby admitted to doubts about attacking such a heavily guarded train. Then, chance nearly spoiled the attack. The rangers had unlimbered the howitzer over a nest of yellow jackets, and a swarming horde of insects drove the gunners, drivers, and horses away. The attack was delayed until the rangers moved the howitzer to a new position. His men, Mosby related, "could stand bullets, but the stings of insects were too much."[7]

As dawn broke and the mist covering the countryside lifted, three well-placed shots from the howitzer fell among the wagons. This was the signal for Richards and Chapman to lead their squadrons in a charge upon the train. With cannon fire falling among them and Confederates on horseback dashing in, pistols blazing, the wagon drivers fled for their lives. The infantry escort also panicked. Some at the head of the train re-formed behind a stone fence. Others sought shelter among buildings near the town. Richards's squadron rode into heavy musket fire and drove out the defenders. Another body of infantrymen made a stand behind a stone wall. Chapman led his squadron in a charge and forced out the soldiers. One ranger fell dead; another was severely wounded. George Perkins of the 149th Ohio recounted the desperation: "We grasped our guns, leveled them over the stone wall, gave them one volley, when the captain in command gave the order to scatter and save ourselves. Well, we ran." Perkins survived only by hiding under hay in a barn.[8]

Smoke, noise, and pandemonium prevailed up and down the turnpike. Musket fire, pistol shots, and the report of the howitzer created a din of confusion. Cattle lowed in despair. The braying of mules added to the clamor. Captured wagons were set afire. Other mule teams dashed about wildly, still harnessed to their wagons. Rangers rode alongside the careening wagons and set them ablaze. Shortly, the fighting ended. Reinforcements from the 1st Rhode Island Cavalry reached the scene by 6:45 A.M., but by then the rangers had absconded with their captures.[9]

The captures that morning were astonishing. The rangers secured more than 200 prisoners, over 500 mules and horses, 200 cattle, and destroyed 75 wagons. They captured and destroyed all the wagons of the Cavalry Reserve Brigade but one. The cost was 2 rangers killed and 3 wounded. A long line of prisoners, horses, mules, and cattle stretched along the road as the rangers marched home. Flush with success, the rangers were wildly excited. Many wore newly captured uniforms. Fiddles found in one wagon filled the air with melodies and the festive strains of "Dixie." Armand-Dumaresq aptly captured the joy of victory and the despair of defeat in his oil painting *Mosby Returning from a Raid (Berryville).* In it, forlorn prisoners pass in review before Mosby, Chapman, Richards, and others while joyous rangers wave their hats and fiddlers merrily lead the procession. Chapman approved of the painting. "The portraits are good—most of them very striking—while the appearance of the prisoners is true to nature," he commented upon viewing the artist's rendering. By late afternoon, all were safely across the Blue Ridge Mountains. To the chagrin of many, however, a paymaster carrying $112,000 escaped unnoticed.[10]

Sheridan's first foray up the Shenandoah Valley had not gone well. The attack on the supply train was an embarrassment. Sheridan's initial report acknowledged only 6 wagons burned, which was later increased to 40 wagons and 200 mules captured. Exaggerated accounts in Northern newspapers only fueled Sheridan's fury. A board of inquiry later convened to investigate the disaster. And Sheridan fell back toward Harpers Ferry after timely Confederate reinforcements joined Early.[11]

Grant, too, was increasingly frustrated with the rangers. He informed Sheridan on the afternoon of 16 August that "the families of most of Mosby's men are known, and can be collected. I think they should be taken and kept at Fort McHenry, or some secure place, as hostages for the good conduct of Mosby and his men." The rangers, themselves, would be shown no mercy. "Where any of Mosby's men are caught hang them without trial." Two hours later, Grant again wrote to Sheridan, this time requesting he send a division of cavalry through Loudoun County "to destroy and carry off the crops, animals, negroes, and all men under fifty years of age capable of bearing arms. In this way you will get many of Mosby's men." Sheridan replied the following day. "Mosby has annoyed me and captured a few wagons," he reported. "We hung one and shot six of his men yesterday." If, indeed, the executions occurred, the doomed men were not rangers, but the war had nonetheless taken an ominous turn. Two days later, on the nineteenth, Sheridan boasted to Grant that "guerillas give me great annoyance, but I am quietly disposing of numbers of them." Sheridan sent the 8th Illinois Cavalry into Loudoun County to "break up and exterminate" the rangers. When the regiment returned on the twenty-second, Sheridan again bragged about having "disposed of quite a number of Mosby's men."[12]

At the start of Sheridan's Valley campaign, Grant had said that "it is desirable that nothing should be left to invite the enemy to return. Take all provisions, forage, and stock wanted for the use of your command; such as cannot be consumed, destroy." This, Sheridan did. In his letter to Grant on the seventeenth that announced the execution of seven rangers, Sheridan reported that he "burned all wheat and hay, and brought off all stock, sheep, cattle, horses, etc., south of Winchester." Two days later, he reported having "destroyed everything that was eatable south of Winchester." News of the destruction enraged the rangers. One ranger came across a soldier slaying a sheep and promptly killed the man. The ranger then cut off a foot from the dead sheep and stuck it in the soldier's mouth with a note for his comrades. "I reckon you got enough sheep now," the note read. Still more cruelty and retribution were to come.[13]

Brig. Gen. George Custer's Michigan cavalry brigade was encamped around Berryville on 18 August and had established picket posts to the east. Chapman was in the vicinity with Companies C, D, and E. He scouted the Federal lines himself that Thursday night and came across an outpost on the road to Berryville from Castleman's Ferry. Spying a lone picket—Cpl. Alpheus Day, 5th Michigan Cavalry—Chapman and a compatriot set out to capture the soldier. Chapman was to approach from the front and engage Day in conversation while the second ranger came up from behind. However, Day discovered Chapman's presence before the trap was sprung. Chapman demanded that he surrender, but the plucky Day, alone and wary of a stranger approaching on a dark night, reached for his weapon. In a brief exchange of gunfire, Day fell to the ground dead. "It was my purpose to capture, not to kill, the picket," Chapman later said of his actions, but when Day declined to surrender "the question then was which of us should be killed. We both fired and the result was the death of the picket."[14]

When his comrades came upon the body, the Michiganders assumed that Day had been bushwhacked. Two other men of the 5th Michigan were captured that same night and another wounded in the hand. Tales of these happenings spread through the cavalry camp and grew in imagination. When the incident was reported in the *New York Times* several days later, Corporal Day was said to have been killed by men dressed in civilian clothing who had calmly conversed with the pickets before treacherously pulling their weapons. It was men dressed in blue uniforms who had wounded the other picket. "Citizens everywhere about the camp were to be seen with arms in their hands," wrote the war correspondent, "and reports were constantly being made of outrages perpetrated by the bushwhackers under Mosby." Another newspaper account reported that "the enemy hovering about us are taking no prisoners, but are hanging and shooting all who fall into their hands." Custer reacted swiftly when news of the killing reached him that Friday. He ordered Col. Russell Alger, commanding the 5th Michigan, to destroy the homes of several citizens in retaliation. A detachment of 50 men led by Capt. George Drake set off on the mission.[15]

As dawn broke on Friday morning, Chapman again scouted enemy positions. Leaving his squadron concealed in some woods near Castleman's Ferry, Chapman rode toward Berryville with rangers John Hefflebower and George Lofland. The morning sky was overcast and rainy, and Chapman wore an old oilcloth over his uniform for protection. The three Confederates proceeded to the home of Hefflebower's family, in view of Custer's camp. There, Chapman captured three cavalrymen. Chapman's presence confused two of the troopers, and they rode directly up to him while he talked with Hefflebower's father. The third man, on leave from camp, mistook Chapman for a provost guard gathering stragglers. Chapman's calm demeanor so beguiled the unwitting trooper that he approached Chapman and offered a plug of tobacco without realizing who Chapman was. With prisoners in tow, the three rangers headed back to camp.[16]

Drake's Michiganders, too, were busy that morning. They had surrounded the home of Josiah Ware when Chapman passed by. Only their pursuit of Chapman spared the mansion from complete destruction. Other families were not as lucky. When Chapman rejoined his men near Castleman's Ferry, he saw smoke and flames arising from the direction of Berryville. It was the home of Province McCormick. Chapman and a few other rangers rushed to the house and learned that it had been set ablaze in retaliation for the killing of the picket during the night. Chapman rode on to another home, where the rest of the squadron joined him. There, in muted silence, the rangers saw the house and outbuildings engulfed in flames. The women and children cowered in the yard under the falling rain, crying and wailing in despair.[17]

The sights witnessed by the Southerners that rainy morning drove them to seek vengeance. John Munson wrote that the picture of "those helpless noncombatants crouching in the rain, weeping over their burning homes, wrought up the resentment of the men and we started out to even things up in real guerrilla fashion." James Williamson, too, recalled seeing "pale, upturned, pleading faces." Action, not words of sympathy or regret, was needed, he said. The victims, too, were defiant. "We are rebels still if we are burned out of house and home," cried one woman. Pointing in the direction of the next victim, Benjamin Morgan, the women urged the rangers to "smite and spare not." Spurring their horses madly, the rangers rode after their quarry "like bloodhounds on the trail," as Williamson described.[18]

Gone now were abstract debating points about states' rights, slavery, Southern independence, and the moral and social superiority of the Southern way of life. The boy who had recited Daniel Webster's essay on liberty and union was now a hardened war veteran. As Chapman saw yet another house in flames, yet another family dispossessed, and yet another mother and her children in despair, anger mounted. At two o'clock Chapman and his men caught up with the house-burners at the home of Benjamin Morgan. As the rangers approached Morgan's farm, Chapman cried, "Wipe them from the face of the earth! No quarter! No quarter! Take no prisoners!" Others, too, picked up the cry, and the afternoon air was broken by the harsh howl, "No quarter, no quarter today!"[19]

Ranger William Patteson called the ensuing action a "sharp, quick, and clean little fight; no prisoners." The rangers at first rode up slowly so as not to alarm the enemy. Chapman gave the order to charge when they closed to within 100 yards. By then the Michiganders had spotted the oncoming assault and had formed in line of battle. They waited until the rangers were within 40 yards and then fired an ineffective volley. Not a single Southerner was hit. In a moment, the rangers were upon them. "We struck their column about the center and threw them into confusion," Chapman said, "and they fled in the direction of their camp."[20]

An account of the fight that appeared in the *New York Times* told a more desperate tale. "More about the Massacre by Mosby—Rebel Treachery—Cowardly Cruelty," the headline blared. The newspaper reported a grisly story of captured and wounded soldiers executed in cold-blooded murder. The main part of the Michigan detachment remained at the ruins of Morgan's home, the war corresponded recounted, while Drake took a few men to torch another nearby house. The troopers at Morgan's farm noticed two hundred men approaching the estate, but they rode slowly and some at the head of the column wore blue uniforms. The Northerners mistook the rangers for their own men. By the time they realized their mistake, the rangers were in full charge. The men of the 5th Michigan formed in line of battle to receive the charge, but it was too late to offer effective resistance. The line broke, and men fled in panic.[21]

Stone fences lined both sides of the country lane. Many more stone fences situated perpendicular to the road hemmed the Michiganders in the farm field and blocked their escape. The only path to safety was along the lane, but the cavalrymen had earlier barricaded the route. Men thronged a narrow passageway through a fence along the road and around the barricade, but only one man could pass through at a time, and the rangers quickly descended upon the fleeing soldiers. In this maze of fences, Chapman's rangers hunted down and shot their quarry. "The enemy were upon them," the war correspondent reported, "and no mercy being shown, a majority of the men ran along a fence running at right angles with the road hoping to find another passage, but finding none and reaching a corner surrendered as a last resort. Several squads were cornered in this way, and in every instance the men who surrendered were killed after they had surrendered or were left for dead."[22]

The newspaper recounted grisly tales of execution. One victim was Samuel Davis. His captor reportedly shouted, "I will pay you for this now," and shot Davis in the face at close range. The bullet entered his right nostril and lodged under his right eye. Davis fell to the ground and feigned death while his would-be executioner rode off. Another group came along, "murdering those who might be still alive," but the Confederates thought Davis was mortally wounded and rode on, leaving Davis to survive to tell his tale. His companion was not so lucky. Rangers killed the man with four bullets to his body. Ten men were reported to have been put to death after surrendering, "nearly all of whom were shot through the head." The prisoners were executed under the exhortations of officers to "shoot the damn Yankee son of a bitch." Two bodies were found with throats slit.[23]

Even Southern accounts told a tale in which blood flowed freely. Mosby's report hinted of a dark affair. He informed Lee that "such was the indignation of our men at witnessing some of the finest residences in that portion of the State enveloped in flames that no quarter was shown, and about twenty-five of them were shot to death for their villainy. About thirty horses were brought off, but no prisoners." One woman who witnessed the fight said that the Northerners "hid behind the burning ruins, they crouched in the corners of fences, they begged for life, but their day of grace was past." John Scott reported that the rangers killed all prisoners and all the wounded men. "Twenty-nine Federal soldiers thus perished," he wrote, "victims of the bloody code of retaliation." He told the solemn tale of a prisoner executed on the return march across the Blue Ridge Mountains. The young soldier knelt in prayer to ask forgiveness for his sins and "then rose slowly to his feet, and, tearing open his shirt, with unquailing eye received the fatal shot." John Munson acknowledged that "our men were demons that day."[24]

Mosby's report described the killings as a justifiable response to the looting of private property and the burning of homes. Subsequent histories by John Scott, James Williamson, and John Munson repeated this assertion. More than thirty years removed from the events of that day, James Williamson's rage was still evident. He wrote in his history of the battalion: "The man who could stand within the glare of burning dwellings, and witness unmoved the pitiful spectacle of pleading mothers with their frightened little ones clinging around them, and see the merciless savages who wrought this ruin gloating over the wreck they had made, and proceeding to a repetition of their cruel deeds of incendiarism, and not feel an impulse which would drive him to avenge such savagery, would not deserve the name of man." William Patteson described how he killed one soldier loaded with plunder with a shot through the head. Among the items in the man's possession were jewelry, cloth, lace curtains, women's clothing, blankets, sheets, and two bottles of wine. In his papers was a letter from a girl asking him to send home looted goods. The men Patteson encountered that afternoon were not soldiers, but were thieves.[25]

In writing of why men fought in the war, historian James McPherson observed that soldiers became embittered by the loss of comrades, destruction of property, and the toll total warfare exacted on the civilian population as the war progressed. This was especially common among Southerners in whose states most of the fighting occurred. A vicious cycle of vengeance and retaliation fueled the escalating brutality of the war. Such was the case in the Shenandoah Valley that afternoon of 19 August. "Mosby," the *New York Times* war correspondent solemnly wrote, "has practically raised the black flag." Custer ordered many more houses set ablaze in retaliation, and the correspondent warned of yet more reprisals to come.[26]

Chapman returned to the Shenandoah Valley on 3 September, when he led Companies C and E through Ashby's Gap to Berryville. There, Chapman learned that a large force of cavalry had passed through town on the way to

Front Royal. Chapman followed their trail, and the next day, south of town near Gold's farm, the rangers saw a line of cavalry skirmishers formed in the distance on a hill. Chapman and his brother took Company C to reconnoiter behind the hill. Lt. Ben Palmer, with Company E, watched the skirmishers. Chapman found an entire regiment—the 6th New York Cavalry—behind the hill marching in columns of four along the roadway. He ordered Palmer to charge the skirmish line while he struck the regimental body.[27]

Palmer advanced his men up a narrow farm lane until a gate blocked the path. Under fire from the skirmishers, ranger Robert Jarman edged forward to open the gate. A Northern bullet found its mark, and he fell dead. Ben Iden then advanced, but he, too, fell in a lifeless heap. A third ranger balked at Palmer's order to swing the gate open, and Palmer, himself, dismounted to open the gate. With the passage cleared, Company E charged up the hill. At the same time, Company C hit the main body of the regiment. The New Yorkers fell back and attempted to rally in some nearby woods, but the rangers pressed on. The regiment broke and fled in disorder. The rangers killed and wounded some 15–20 Federals, captured 30 men, and secured 38 horses. The cost was several rangers slightly wounded and 2 dead. Frank Fox, Chapman's lieutenant in Company C, fell mortally wounded.[28]

Brutal, vicious individual contests marked the fighting that day. New Yorker Thomas Kiernan blocked a saber thrust with his revolver but was badly cut on the arm and head. Another ranger charged and emptied his revolver upon Kiernan. None of the bullets found their mark until the last shot, fired so close that the gunpowder burned his shirt, struck his side and exited out his back. Later, Kiernan witnessed another New Yorker, Peter Dewar, murdered. Dewar's horse had been shot and had fallen on him; he lay pinned under the horse with his leg broken. A ranger rode up and ordered Dewar to the rear. Dewar explained that he was unable to move. The ranger, indifferent to his plight, drew his revolver and shot Dewar dead. Chapman's rangers, recalled trooper Isaac Collier, "were having a great harvest in killing, wounding and taking prisoners."[29]

By 13 September the battalion was large enough to require a sixth company, Company F. Mosby then divided the command with orders to operate independently. Mosby himself took a few men to Fairfax County. A chance encounter with a 5-man patrol of the 13th New York Cavalry left him wounded in the groin. Mosby was safely escorted to The Plains, but the bullet was too close to an artery to be removed. Instead, Mosby traveled south to convalesce at his family home near Lynchburg.[30]

Chapman stayed to the west and had considerably better luck. At ten o'clock on the night of 15 September, 400 troopers of the 3rd Indiana Cavalry and 8th New York Cavalry under the command of Brig. Gen. George Chapman crossed the Shenandoah River at Castleman's Ferry on a scout. The Federal commander sent Capt. Hartwell Compson with 55 New Yorkers south to cross the Blue

Ridge Mountains through Ashby's Gap and then proceed north to Snicker's Gap along the mountain ridge. The main body, he led through Snicker's Gap to Snickersville and then south to Paris. Two local residents abetted the Northerners in their search for rangers. By sunrise on the sixteenth, the Federals arrived at Paris, and as dawn broke the weary horse soldiers saw rangers appear on distant heights. The troopers returned to Snickersville via Upperville, trailed throughout the day by rangers. They reached Snickersville at two o'clock and halted to rest. General Chapman sent a squadron of the 8th New York under Capt. James Bliss into Snicker's Gap, where they joined Compson's New Yorkers. The day was exceedingly hot, and the sixteen-hour march left the men fatigued. The two squads of New York troopers at Snicker's Gap, surely safe in their united strength, promptly fell asleep for an hour.[31]

The rangers trailing the expedition were William Chapman's men. Hearing of the raid, Chapman gathered about 40–60 rangers and reached Upperville after the Federals had left. The rangers cut across to the mountains and rode along a ridgetop trail to Snicker's Gap, where they spotted the isolated and poorly guarded patrol. Chapman's rangers swooped down from the mountains with a wild yell and routed the sleeping New Yorkers. The troopers fled in a stampede, some through Snicker's Gap toward the Shenandoah River; others scurried eastward to the safety of the main body at Snickersville. Chapman's rangers killed and wounded a number of Northerners and captured 18 men and 40 horses. They set free 12 Southerners rounded up during the expedition. Chapman lost 1 man killed, 3 wounded, and several captured.[32]

After disposing of the Federal raiders at Snicker's Gap, Chapman rushed to the side of his fallen commander. Mosby needed a strong leader to retain control of the loosely organized ranger battalion. The captaincy of Company A had never been refilled after the capture of James Foster. His other company commanders—Dolly Richards, Company B; William Chapman, Company C; Richard Montjoy, Company D; Sam Chapman, Company E; and Walter Frankland, Company F—had proved their worth in battle, but who could replace Mosby's strategic vision? Who had the necessary force of personality, the magnetism young men would unhesitatingly follow into battle? Mosby chose Chapman to command in his absence.[33]

The next few days proved to be a turning point in the conflict in the Shenandoah Valley. In the battle of Opequon, Sheridan pounced on Early's undermanned army at Winchester on 19 September. The Confederates broke late in the afternoon and fled south to Fisher's Hill. There, Sheridan pressed the attack three days later and routed Early. As part of this attack, cavalry chief Maj. Gen. Alfred Torbert led two divisions of Federal cavalry up the Page Valley. The cavalrymen were supposed to cross the Massanutten Mountain at New Market Gap to block the Confederate withdrawal from Fisher's Hill, but were turned back at Milford before reaching Luray.[34]

During this time, Chapman raided the enemy rear. He led eight rangers on a scout into the Shenandoah Valley on 21 September and returned with more than twice that number in prisoners. They first found a large supply train traveling between Harpers Ferry and Winchester and snatched three men from the heavy guard. That night, the rangers came across a house about five miles from Winchester with a number of horses tied outside. Suspecting more captures could be had, Chapman approached the house to gain information. He asked the owner if he could get accommodation for the night, but was informed the house was full. He could, however, sleep in the stable yard, where there was an army wagon. Chapman sent three rangers to the house and took the others to secure the sergeant and driver camped with the wagon.[35]

Chapman approached the wagon on horseback and leaning down to the sergeant whispered, "You have heard of Mosby's men, haven't you?" "Oh yes; I have heard of Mosby," replied the sergeant. Drawing his revolver from under his leg, Chapman said, "Well, we belong to his command." Chapman then directed the sergeant to wake the driver, who was asleep under the wagon, and unhitch the six mules. The other rangers had less luck and returned from the house empty-handed. The house was deserted; its vigilant guests, suspecting Confederates were about, had fled.[36]

As the rangers gathered the mules and secured the prisoners, they heard the clatter of horses approaching along the road. Chapman instantly determined it must be a scouting party; there had not been enough time to mount a squad of cavalry to rescue the wagon. He held his men back while one of the strangers approached from the road. "Who is that?" the man inquired. Chapman replied that an army wagon was broken. "But why are you making such a devil of a noise?" the man demanded. While Chapman continued to converse, his fellow rangers gathered at his side. At the sight of this, several other men on horseback emerged from the darkness of the night. Chapman continued to engage the man in casual conversation. "What command might you belong to?" Chapman asked. "It's a lot of us officers," came the haughty reply. Indeed, a group of five officers was traveling unescorted at night. The rangers swiftly drew their revolvers and swarmed among their prey. Maj. William Fry, 16th Pennsylvania Cavalry, was the senior officer captured. From the 1st New Hampshire Cavalry, Chapman captured Capt. Nathaniel Brown, Lt. Frederick Stone, and Lt. George Pressey. Only Lt. George Gilman, 1st New Hampshire Cavalry, escaped to report the fate of his comrades.[37]

Chapman hastened to safely return with his prisoners, their horses, and the wagon mules, but a sentinel stopped the rangers only a mile or so farther down the road. There, a detachment of soldiers and a sutler's wagon had camped for the night. Chapman drew the picket toward him in a conversation about troop movements that day. Then, Chapman called for the man to come closer. The soldier approached. He suspected nothing of this stranger on horseback at night, and feeling at ease, he placed his hand on the mane of Chapman's horse. As he had done before, Chapman leaned down close to the unknowing man's face and asked, "Have you ever heard of Mosby's command?" "Yes, I have heard of Mosby," the soldier replied. "Well, we belong to that command," exclaimed Chapman as he thrust his pistol into the man's chest. "Now," said Chapman, "I don't suppose you want your friends here to suffer, and if you will call them down here one at a time you will probably avoid the shedding of their blood."[38]

In the darkness of the night sky, the sentinel mistook Chapman's band, outnumbered by prisoners, for a large group of Confederates and readily agreed to Chapman's plan. One by one, Chapman lured each soldier from the camp fires into his snare. The prisoners accepted their fate with bemusement and actively abetted the charade. They called their next comrade from the encampment and eagerly watched the dumbfounded look on his face as Chapman informed the man he was a prisoner. Chapman captured 13 men in this way. The last man then approached Chapman. His 13 comrades crowded around Chapman and burst out laughing as the unsuspecting soldier heard his fate. The captives laughed so loud that Chapman ordered them to stop for fear that it might raise an alarm. Chapman's scout that night netted 23 prisoners. Bluecoats were so prevalent among the riders that Chapman's party was nearly mistaken for Federals as he returned to Piedmont the next day.[39]

Upon his return, Chapman immediately sent out his brother with 120 men on a raid into the Shenandoah Valley. The intent was to capture a picket post of the 6th New York Cavalry at Chester Gap in the Blue Ridge Mountains, not far from Front Royal. However, the report of the picket post was erroneous. Instead, the next morning, 23 September, Sam Chapman learned of Torbert's defeat at Milford and scouted in that direction for information. Chapman spotted an ambulance train moving toward Front Royal. One hundred and seventy-five troopers led by Lt. Charles McMaster, 2nd United States Cavalry, guarded the train. It presented a tempting target, and as the ambulances approached Front Royal, Chapman planned his attack. He divided his command and sent Walter Frankland with 45 men to hit the front of the train while he struck the rearguard with the bulk of the rangers. In fact, the ambulances were part of the withdrawal of Federal cavalry down the Page Valley to Front Royal. Unseen by Chapman, Custer's brigade followed the rear of the train. The Cavalry Reserve Brigade, commanded now by Charles Lowell, the rangers' old nemesis from Fairfax, also trailed in the rear.[40]

As the moment of attack neared, Sam Chapman observed Lowell's brigade following the ambulances and halted the assault, but Frankland struck before word could be gotten to him. Chapman's own men, seeing the battle joined, rushed into the fray. Lowell's cavalrymen swarmed upon and enveloped the rangers. The rangers charged the front, beat off attacks from the flanks and rear, and fell back toward Chester Gap. Blocking their way directly on the road to Chester Gap was McMaster and a small squad of men. What followed next was disputed for years. Ranger accounts claimed that McMaster died in action, "riddled with bullets." His body lay in the road, and the rangers rode over it in hasty flight. Federals reported that rangers shot McMaster after he was captured and robbed. The version given by ranger confidant Tee Edmonds in her diary tells a similar tale. McMaster, she wrote, was captured and killed, the rangers "giving him several shots after his begging and pleading with them not to kill him." Sam Chapman, too, recalled years later that McMaster seemed to be surrendering.[41]

What happened next, however, is not disputed. No rangers died during the fighting, but six were captured and brought to Front Royal. There, Federal soldiers executed them. A squad of soldiers marched Lucian Love and David Jones to a graveyard at the Methodist Church and summarily shot them. Others shot Thomas Anderson under a tree south of town. Soldiers marched William Overby and another ranger about one mile north of town. Before a large crowd of taunting soldiers, they hung the two rangers side by side from a large tree. A placard pinned to one of the corpses declared "such is the fate of all of Mosby's men." Two soldiers tied Henry Rhodes's arms to their saddles and dragged him through town. Rhodes was only seventeen years old, a Front Royal resident, and this was his first ride with Mosby. As the soldiers dragged Rhodes past his home, his mother ran out onto the street and grasped her nearly unconscious son in her arms. She pleaded with his tormentors to show mercy, but to no avail. They dragged Rhodes to a field north of town. Surrounded by a large crowd of soldiers, and while Custer's brigade band play the melody "Love Not, the One You Love May Die," one soldier stepped forward and emptied his pistol into Rhodes. Many of Custer's men were present, and the rangers long afterward attributed the killings directly to Custer.[42]

The following day, 24 September, William Chapman returned to the Shenandoah Valley with a small group of rangers. He encountered a detachment of 50 men from the 17th Pennsylvania Cavalry about ten miles from Winchester. They were searching for men wounded in a skirmish the day before and had stopped in an open field near a farm house. Lt. Uriah Reinhold and 4 men rode on to the house, joined shortly by Capt. James Ham and an orderly. Fate looked kindly upon those men that day. Chapman swooped down upon the remaining men deployed in the field. In short time, Chapman's rangers killed 4 Pennsylvanians, wounded 7 (one mortally), and collected 23 prisoners and 27 horses. One prisoner, John Zinn, observed that the rangers were extremely agitated over the murders at Front Royal. Some proposed to retaliate on the captives, but did not only because they were not Custer's men.[43]

The disastrous loss of the wagon train at Berryville, the killing of Alpheus Day, the tale of Samuel Davis and his fellow Michiganders at Morgan's farm, and the fate of McMaster fueled the embers of vengeance. What many rangers called the "black flag" had been raised in the Shenandoah Valley as summer ended. Now, Northern and Southern combatants alike knew that their foes would offer no mercy. "The war in this section is assuming a very savage aspect," Catherine Cochran wrote in her journal. "Where it will end," she wondered, "God only knows." Yet humanity was not entirely absent from the battlefield, and charity could still be found. Rangers killed John Walker, 1st United States Cavalry, in a clash near Charlestown. In his pocket he carried a small picture of his wife inscribed with her name and the date of their marriage. The memento so moved ranger John Watkins with sympathy that he returned the photograph to the widow. In November, after the violence had reached worse levels, Chapman still managed to return two rings taken from the captured Maj. William Fry. The Northern officer had asked Chapman to send them to Sheridan's headquarters. For two months, Chapman kept those rings until an opportunity arose to honor Fry's request.[44]

12 | Nothing but Yankees

While Chapman successfully organized and led raids in Mosby's absence, rivalry and jealousy arose among company commanders. Rather than submit to Chapman's leadership, Dolly Richards and Lt. Alfred Glascock, Company D, left their units and went on furlough to Richmond. Some of their men followed. Richard Montjoy, too, took leave from his command of Company D. A chance encounter with them at Gordonsville left Mosby thunderstruck. Sheridan's advance up the Shenandoah Valley had strained his supply and communication lines. Mosby expected his commanders to forcefully and aggressively raid these lines. He scolded his officers for abandoning their duties. "It is more disgraceful for a soldier to go home at this time than to go to the penitentiary," he informed the wayward soldiers.[1]

Mosby saw that his absence hindered the battalion, which he recognized "was going to pieces from the jealousy of the officers." He resumed command on 29 September, still hobbling on crutches. He found his headquarters at Joseph Blackwell's Heartland farm destroyed. Ranger confidant Tee Edmonds observed Mosby's black mood upon his return. He was enraged, she wrote in her diary, and "calls for every man to meet, as though he were going to do something rash." Mosby's wrath was still evident thirty-five years later. "That was a chance for Dolly to win his spurs," Mosby derisively said, "but he thought Chapman would get the credit." Instead of fighting the enemy, Richards "was enjoying a picnic in Richmond."[2]

The destruction of Heartland was at the hands of Col. Henry Gansevoort, 13th New York Cavalry. He led a force of 500 troopers from Fairfax County through Thoroughfare Gap and along the Manassas Gap Railroad toward Piedmont on 24 September 1864. The cavalrymen knew Blackwell's farm was Mosby's headquarters and burned the home, barns, and outbuildings. However, their primary objective was to assess the condition of the railroad. They found it to be in good condition to Piedmont, beyond which the tracks were torn up.[3]

The Manassas Gap Railroad ran from Manassas Junction on the Orange and Alexandria Railroad west through the heart of Mosby's Confederacy to Strasburg in the Shenandoah Valley. It had been used to transfer Confederate troops from the valley to Manassas in July 1861 and thereafter lay largely in disrepair. Following his victory over Early at Fisher's Hill on 22 September, Sheridan withdrew down the valley. Sheridan's base was now in the lower valley, and Grant issued orders on 2 October to reopen the Manassas Gap Railroad. The trains would supply Sheridan's army and also carry troops east to support Grant's Petersburg campaign. Within three days, the construction crew and its guard of some 2,000 infantrymen and heavy artillery had established camps at Thoroughfare Gap, The Plains, Salem, and Rectortown.[4]

On Tuesday, 4 October, as the Federal advance along the railroad progressed, army chief of staff Henry Halleck warned Grant of the need to "completely clean out Mosby's gang of robbers who have so long infested that district." Sheridan's cavalry should be assigned this task because the 13th and 16th New York Cavalry regiments along the Fairfax cavalry screen "have been so often cut up by Mosby's band that they are cowed and useless for that purpose." Mosby fulfilled Halleck's grim expectations the following day.[5]

Mosby gathered a force of 200 men on Wednesday and struck the construction camp near Salem. The rangers placed two cannons on a hill overlooking the camp, and the guns opened fire as sharpshooters inched forward. The railroad workers and guards fled in panic to Rectortown, leaving behind clothing, arms, ammunition, stores, and camp equipment. Chapman remained at Salem with his Second Squadron to secure the camp while Mosby took 80 men of the First Squadron to trail the retreat. Mosby's rangers captured about 50 prisoners and killed or wounded a considerable number of Northerners. Chapman's rangers looted the supplies, burned the camp, and destroyed the railroad. Federal forces entrenched at Rectortown and The Plains, and the trains withdrew to safety through Thoroughfare Gap.[6]

Chapman's men destroyed more track at Salem on Thursday. A train came up from The Plains, but a well-placed cannon shot forced it back. Shortly, the train returned and halted. Two hundred infantrymen disembarked and formed in line of battle, but cannon fire forced the soldiers back onto the train and back again to The Plains. That same day, rangers advanced upon Rectortown and shelled the camp with two cannons until evening. On Friday, 7 October, the rangers returned to Rectortown with four cannons and continued to shell the Federal camp, forcing a retreat by the main body of infantry to Salem.[7]

Reinforcements rushed to protect the railroad and construction workers. The 8th Illinois Cavalry ventured south from its post along the Potomac River, and troopers of the 13th and 16th New York Cavalry hurried west from the Fairfax cavalry screen. By Saturday, 8 October, the rangers could not operate unencumbered by Federal patrols. Mosby hid the artillery at a mountain safe site and divided the command into smaller groups. Chapman took three companies to operate south of the railroad. Mosby rode with Montjoy's company north of the track, while Richards led his rangers into the Shenandoah Valley. The railroad line reopened to Rectortown by the eighth, and trains ran to

Piedmont by the tenth. Tee Edmonds observed that "the old whistle and snort of the iron horse seems as natural as in days past." The trains ran slowly for fear of derailment, and infantry guards patrolled on foot alongside the cars. On the fourteenth and fifteenth, Maj. Gen. Christopher Augur, commanding the forces at Rectortown, informed Halleck that the trains arrived and departed on time without interference.[8]

Yet infantry escorts were not enough to ensure the safety of railroad operations. One plan that emerged at this time was to place civilians and captured rangers on the trains. Halleck himself attended to the details and ordered that the hostages "should be so confined as to render escape impossible, and yet be exposed to the fire of the enemy." Another plan was to lay waste to the land within five miles of either side of the railroad. All houses in this restricted area were to be destroyed, the women and children sent away, and livestock and crops confiscated. Any man found within five miles of the railroad was to be treated as a guerilla. All timber and brush along the railroad was to be cleared to prevent concealment. Further hostile acts would result in an additional ten miles of devastation on either side. While the use of hostages on trains was enacted, the latter measures were not.[9]

Mosby maintained that he would have still attacked trains even if he knew his own family was on board. Threats to his family did not deter Chapman either. Writing of the events that occurred in the latter days of the war, Mosby said of Chapman: "I think that if Sheridan had captured his wife and mother-in-law and sent them to prison, instead of going into mourning, he would have felt all the wrath and imitated the example of the fierce Achilles when he heard that Patroclus, his friend, had been killed and his armor had been captured. 'Now perish Troy,' he said, and rushed to fight."[10]

The violence that had begun earlier that summer in the Shenandoah Valley spread with the incessant sparring along the Manassas Gap Railroad in October. One such event occurred on 9 October, when the Chapman brothers, in Piedmont along with rangers "Big Yankee" Ames and Ludwell Lake, received word of an approaching cavalry patrol. Ames rode off to gather support, but a lone enemy scout attacked him. The Chapmans, Lake, and Lemuel Corbin came across the Northern trooper plundering Ames's body. Lake and Corbin fired at the fleeing man, but missed their mark. The Chapmans gave chase and secured the scout, and when the rangers discovered that the body was that of Ames, mortally wounded but still alive, Lake rushed at the prisoner and killed him with a pistol shot.[11]

On 11 October, Richards and 32 rangers spied an ambulance on the Valley turnpike between Newtown and Middletown, escorted by a 25-man detachment of the 17th Pennsylvania Cavalry. Riding in the ambulance that day were Lt. Col. Cornelius Tolles, Sheridan's chief quartermaster, and Dr. Emil Ohlenschlager, also on Sheridan's staff. The encounter left both officers mortally wounded.

Ranger bullets struck Tolles in the back of the head. Part of his brain was destroyed and tissue protruded from the gaping wound. Still, he clung to life for almost a month, tended to by his wife. Ohlenschlager was hit in the bowels and suffered for three days before dying. Rumors surfaced that the officers were killed after surrendering, though the rangers claimed the officers were shot while attempting to flee.[12]

Federal Brig. Gen. William Powell adopted the same approach used earlier at Front Royal to discourage ranger activity. Powell commanded a cavalry division in the Shenandoah Valley and considered Mosby and his rangers to be no more than a band of thieves and bushwhackers. He brought his cavalry across the Blue Ridge Mountains into Rappahannock County and on 13 October received reports that two rangers had killed a soldier. The southerners were in fact not rangers and had been escorting a suspected spy to the provost marshal at Gordonsville. They killed their prisoner when he attempted to escape. Powell did not know these details, and they were likely irrelevant even if he had known them. Nine days earlier, a soldier in his command had been found with his throat slit. Powell ordered two rebel prisoners shot to death in retaliation. Now, Powell again ordered the execution of a prisoner.[13]

At the cavalry camp near Flint Hill, Powell's troopers hung ranger Albert Willis in a grisly death sentence. Several men climbed to the top of a tall tree and bent it over by their weight. The executioners tied a leather strap to the top of the tree and secured the other end around Willis's neck. They released the tree, and Willis flew up into the sky. His body swung wildly back and forth until the tree stopped swaying. The troopers fastened a placard to the lifeless body: "A. C. Willis, member of Company C, Mosby's command, hanged by the neck in retaliation for the murder of a U.S. soldier."[14]

The escalating violence did not discourage the rangers from their mission. What did deter them was the presence of strong guards that prevented attacks on the railroad. Instead, Mosby turned his attention to the Baltimore and Ohio Railroad west of Harper's Ferry while Chapman struck into Maryland. Both raids embarrassed Sheridan, and Northern newspaper headlines blared of the failure to protect these important routes. Mosby's was the more profitable expedition. Between two and three o'clock on the morning of Friday, 14 October, his rangers derailed a passenger train near Duffield's Station. Among the plunder was $173,000 confiscated from two paymasters of Sheridan's army.[15]

On that same Friday, Chapman crossed the Potomac River with 80 men to raid the Baltimore and Ohio Railroad at Adamstown. The rangers crossed at White's Ford, about five miles below the mouth of the Monocacy River, and burned several canal boats loaded with freight. They continued on to Adamstown, but Mosby's raid at Duffield's had halted railroad traffic. After cutting the telegraph line and plundering two stores, Chapman led the rangers south toward the Potomac. A company of Loudoun Rangers led by Capt. James Grubb trailed the raiders on their return. Chapman decided to entrap them. He ordered his men to ride at a brisk pace as if fearfully retreating. Grubb's rangers took the bait and hurried after the Confederates.[16]

Chapman's men entered a lane through some woods, and the Loudoun Rangers followed. Chapman swiftly wheeled his rangers around and charged, killing or wounding 4 or 5 men and capturing several. Chapman, his brother Sam, Lemuel Corbin, and another ranger pursued four of the fleeing men into a wheat field. The Northerners scurried through a gate at the far side of the field. One soldier paused to close the gate. Chapman, undeterred, attempted to jump the barrier. His horse fell, and Chapman hurtled off his mount, yet he still managed to shoot the soldier while tumbling in mid-air. Chapman collected his men and hurried them along, fearful that Federal patrols were alerted to the raid and would entrap the rangers on the north bank of the Potomac. His fears were astute because as the rangers approached the Chesapeake and Ohio Canal they saw a squad of infantrymen destroying the only bridge across the waterway. The rangers dispersed the infantry, rebuilt the bridge, and crossed safely back to Virginia.[17]

The Federals did achieve one notable success that Friday. An eighteen-year-old ranger arrived in Gansevoort's cavalry camp at Piedmont. He revealed the location of the ranger artillery camp situated just one mile south on Little Cobbler Mountain. Gansevoort mounted a large expedition consisting of his 13th New York Cavalry, two squadrons 16th New York Cavalry, and two companies 5th Pennsylvania Artillery. They surprised the artillery camp on the night of the fourteenth and captured the 9-man guard and 4 artillery pieces—a 3-inch ordnance gun, a 12-pounder howitzer, and 2 mountain howitzers.[18]

Two days later, the rangers met at Bloomfield. Companies C, E, and F operated around Piedmont, watching the Federal encampment there, while Mosby took the rest of the command into Fairfax County. Mosby had little to show for the raid, but Montjoy raided the village of Falls Church with his company on the night of Monday, 17 October. Accounts by rangers of that affair claim that a citizen named Reed warned the Northern camp of the attack by blowing a horn; rangers shot him dead. Federal reports paint a grimmer tale. Reed was a member of the civilian home guard and was captured along with an African American guard. Rangers killed Reed with a close pistol shot to the back of his head. A surgeon examining the body found that "the skull at the base of the brain is blown to atoms." They shot the other man, too, in the head. He lost an ear blown off by the pistol shot, but survived and escaped to tell the tale.[19]

Chapman's Second Squadron operating along the Manassas Gap Railroad had considerably greater success. On that same Monday, a detachment of Federal cavalry left camp near Piedmont on a foraging expedition. The troopers visited the surrounding farms and helped themselves to the bounty of the land. At the Fletcher farm on the road from Piedmont to Paris, the raiders absconded with hay, calves, pigs, sheep, chickens, turkeys, geese, and apples. "One had the carcass of a calf on his saddle; another a live lamb; chickens and other poultry were plentifully distributed throughout their ranks," James Williamson related. Each trooper carried a bundle of hay on his horse.[20]

Chapman trailed the troopers and in the twilight of the coming evening stationed his men on the road leading back to Piedmont. He divided his squadron and led the charge into the front of the returning foragers. It was nearly dark as the Southerners swooped upon the unsuspecting cavalrymen with a wild yell. The foragers, laden with plunder, huddled together for safety and offered weak resistance to the rapid pistol fire of the onrushing rangers. Sam Chapman led the second detachment along the flanks and poured unopposed fire into the mass of thrashing Northerners. Chapman's rangers killed or wounded possibly 40 men in the bedlam. They captured 20 prisoners and 30 horses and rounded up another 15–20 horses the next day. Afterwards, surviving Federals spread rumors that the rangers had shot the troopers after they surrendered.[21]

Eight days later, on 25 October, nearly 400 rangers awoke at dawn at their camp west of the Shenandoah River. They had rendezvoused at Bloomfield the previous day, forded the river at Castleman's Ferry as the sun set, and continued on toward Winchester. Now, as the sun rose, the rangers resumed their march. That same morning, a detachment of 50 Northern cavalrymen rode out of Winchester returning to their base at Martinsburg. Accompanying them was a small, two-horse carriage carrying Brig. Gen. Alfred Duffié and another officer. About five miles from Winchester, Duffié became impatient with the slow pace of the cautious troopers. He detailed 10 men as his guard and spurred his carriage forward. Shortly, Duffié was one and one-half miles beyond the main escort.[22]

At about the same time, the 400 rangers halted near the turnpike and lay concealed. Mosby, Chapman, and a group of rangers moved forward to scout and spied the oncoming carriage. The chase was on. A large wagon train in the distance moved up the Shenandoah Valley from Martinsburg to Winchester, and Duffié's carriage fled down the road seeking its safety. However, Duffié was no match for the horsemanship and marksmanship of the rangers. Ranger Boyd Smith galloped along even with the carriage in an adjacent field. With a well-placed pistol shot, he struck one of the horses and then jumped his charger over the stone fence into the road and brought the carriage to a halt. Duffié, Sheridan reported, should be dismissed; the general was "a trifling man and a poor soldier. He was captured by his own stupidity."[23]

Attention turned to the oncoming wagon train, and Mosby dispatched Chapman and Montjoy to charge the front with one squadron while he and Richards struck the rear with the other squadron. The rangers easily drove in the cavalry escort, but the infantry guard and its accompanying artillery were well disciplined and repulsed the rangers with cannon fire. A subsequent attack near Winchester was more successful. Mosby sent Richards back across the Blue Ridge Mountains with a squadron to watch for raiding parties. He and Chapman remained in the Shenandoah Valley and came upon a small wagon train. Chapman scouted and determined the wagons could be captured. Mosby agreed, and Chapman deployed the men. The rangers secured the entire 7-wagon train and its 54-man infantry guard without firing a shot. Mosby and Chapman returned with 60 prisoners, including Duffié, and 45 horses and mules.[24]

Mosby maintained after the war that his operations on the railroad that autumn prolonged the war by preventing Sheridan from moving east to support Grant in the Petersburg-Richmond theatre. A wartime report to Lee claimed his rangers inflicted 300 casualties during the Federal advance up the railroad. In fact, however, reopening the railroad was never a priority for Sheridan. Indeed, he decided to send troops east through Ashby's Gap, not on the railroad, and advised that construction be halted on 11 October. Then, when Early's army reappeared and again threatened Sheridan, construction continued with renewed pace. Early's defeat at Cedar Creek on 19 October effectively eliminated Confederate threats in the Shenandoah Valley. Construction on the railroad halted by the end of month, and the tracks were torn up.[25]

The month of November began with an ominous entry in Catherine Cochran's journal. "Yankees—Yankees, nothing but Yankees—day and night they are prowling round—pillaging—burning—carrying distress and desolation thru the country," she wrote on the first of the month. By the end of the month, Sheridan's cavalry did indeed bring devastation, destruction, and ruin to Cochran's Middleburg countryside and much of Loudoun County for its support of Mosby's operations. And the cycle of violence and retaliation continued. This time it was Mosby's turn to avenge earlier executions of his rangers.[26]

From a haven in Middleburg at the end of October, Mosby informed Lee of the increasingly brutal nature of partisan warfare in northern Virginia. He described the use of hostages to safeguard the trains, the executions of the 6 rangers at Front Royal, and, lately, the hanging of Willis. Believing Custer to be the culprit behind the executions, Mosby proposed to hang a similar number of Custer's men in retaliation and as a measure to prevent further such executions. "It would be well," he said, "to come to some understanding with the enemy." Lee endorsed Mosby's plan and told him to proceed with the hangings.[27]

The executions occurred early on the morning of 7 November. The day before, the rangers gathered at Rectortown to select the 7 condemned men. Twenty-seven prisoners, all thought to be from Custer's brigade, formed in a single line. Each prisoner drew a piece of paper from a hat. Seven pieces were numbered; these were the condemned men. It was a forlorn scene that shook even battle-hardened rangers. James Williamson wrote that one prisoner "laid his head on the shoulder of a comrade and wept like a child." Another prayed for salvation until with trembling hands he drew his lot and then joyously beheld a blank slip of paper. A less-fortunate captive exclaimed, "Tell my mother I died like a man." Some rangers openly wept.[28]

A squad of 8 rangers marched the 7 prisoners into the Shenandoah Valley through Ashby's Gap. Montjoy, returning from a raid with his own prisoners, met the detail. For one of the condemned, it was a prophetic meeting. He was a Mason and, recognizing Montjoy as a fellow Mason, managed to be exchanged for one of his prisoners. The 8 rangers and 7 prisoners continued on toward Berryville. George Sowle, 5th Michigan Cavalry, and Cpl. Charles Marvin, 2nd New York Cavalry, escaped into the rainy night. Two more prisoners—Melchior Hoffnagle, 153rd New York Infantry, and Cpl. James Bennett, 2nd New York Cavalry—were shot but survived their wounds. Fate was less kind to the other 3 captives. Their bodies dangled lifeless from a tree and left the message Mosby desired. Pinned to one corpse was a note: "These men have been hung in retaliation for an equal number of Colonel Mosby's men hung by order of General Custer, at Front Royal. Measure for measure."[29]

The execution of the prisoners may well have halted the escalating cycle of revenge and retaliation, but it did not hinder Sheridan's pursuit of Mosby. One such counterguerrilla operation was a command of independent cavalry scouts, 100 men armed with the seven-shot Spencer rifle led by Capt. Richard Blazer. Sheridan had organized the scouts in August to "clean out Mosby's gang," and Blazer had successfully clashed with the rangers previously. On 16 November, as Montjoy and 30 rangers returned from a raid in the Shenandoah Valley, Blazer's scouts ambushed them. The next day, Mosby let loose his rangers in two squadrons to hunt down Blazer. Chapman led 100 men into the valley through Ashby's Gap. Operating further north, Richards took 110 men through Snicker's Gap. Richards's First Squadron had the better luck tracking and finding their quarry. Outside of Myerstown, south of Kabletown across the Shenandoah River, Richards's well-executed ambush captured Blazer and annihilated his command.[30]

Subsequently, the rangers returned to the almost daily task of raiding into the Shenandoah Valley. One such mission began on Wednesday, 23 November. John Russell led 65 men of Companies C and E from Paris, through Ashby's Gap, and across the Shenandoah River at Berry's Ferry. They continued on toward White Post, where Mosby and Chapman joined the raiding party at midnight. Chapman arose early the next morning, Thanksgiving Day, and scouted the countryside. He captured 5 prisoners and came upon 50 men and 10 wagons on a foraging expedition from a nearby brigade camp that was located about three miles south of Winchester on the road to Front Royal. Mosby brought up the remainder of the command and the chase was on. The foragers beat a hasty retreat from the onrushing Confederates, but the rangers overtook the wagons. A second wagon train approached from the nearby camp. This, too, turned back, and the rangers, in the heat of battle, carried their charge into the camp.[31]

It was about four o'clock in the afternoon and the soldiers were enjoying a Thanksgiving meal, when the Confederates rode in among them. The soldiers' initial confusion likely saved the rangers, but soon the Federals rallied and the camp turned out in pursuit. During this affair, Mosby's horse became unmanageable and frantic. With the enemy closing in, capture was almost certain until Chapman's steady leadership saved the day. Seeing Mosby in danger, Chapman rallied some men and charged headlong into Mosby's pursuers. This gave two rangers time to ride up and lead Mosby's horse away. Bullets felled Chapman's horse in the charge, but one of his men jumped from his own mount and offered it to Chapman. "Take him, captain; you are of more service to the cause than I," the ranger exclaimed. Scores of troopers, perhaps 100 cavalrymen, chased the fleeing rangers back to the Shenandoah River. In their hasty flight, the rangers lost all their prisoners and captures.[32]

Capt. Daniel Keyes's Loudoun Rangers also operated against Mosby. Montjoy, with Company D, came across one such 35-man patrol north of Leesburg on 28 November and cut them to pieces. The only Confederate loss was Montjoy, killed by a bullet to the head while pursuing the fleeing enemy. The loss of Montjoy was a tragic reminder of the grim fate faced by the rangers every day. Mosby immortalized the fallen Montjoy: "He died too early for liberty and his country's cause, but not too early for his own fame." Chapman could not help but wonder about his own fate, and that of Josie and her extended family, in that grim autumn of 1864.[33]

In addition to patrols into Mosby's Confederacy, Grant and Sheridan had a second strategy to counter guerilla warfare. They knew that the rangers had the support of many of the inhabitants of Loudoun County and relied on those people for subsistence and protection. Grant had earlier reminded Sheridan that "there is no doubt about the necessity of clearing out that country so that it will not support Mosby's gang." Sheridan concurred. He announced on 26 November that he would "soon commence on Loudoun County, and let them know there is a God in Israel." Should the citizens complain, "tell them that they have furnished too many meals to guerillas to expect much sympathy." He unleashed three brigades of cavalry led by Maj. Gen. Wesley Merritt upon the unsuspecting populace. The First Brigade and Second Brigade poured through Ashby's Gap on 28 November. The next day, the Cavalry Reserve Brigade marched east through Snicker's Gap.[34]

Tee Edmonds wrote only a single entry in her diary on the twenty-eighth: "The Yankees burned our barn!" The next day, the raiders approached Catherine Broun's farm near Middleburg. "We have had a terrible day today expecting every moment to be burned up," she related. "The farms all around us are on fire burning all the hay, corn, and wheat, driving off all the cattle, sheep, hogs, etc." Later that evening, she observed that "the whole heavens are illuminated by the fires." Broun, however, was lucky; her farm was spared. Fires still burned two days later. "Barns and mills are burning in every direction," Broun wrote. "All in fearful anxiety expecting them with their firebrand every moment." The destruction was so widespread that smoke was evident at Point of Rocks on the Potomac River. James Williamson observed that so much land was ablaze that a thick heavy blanket of smoke fell over the countryside and obscured the view.[35]

From the afternoon of Monday, 28 November, through the morning of Friday, 2 December, Merritt's troopers laid waste to farmlands and exacted their revenge upon Mosby's supporters. "We burned out the hornets," said one trooper of the 1st Rhode Island Cavalry. Mosby's rangers could offer no organized resistance. Merritt estimated that his soldiers confiscated or destroyed 5,000–6,000 cattle, 3,000–4,000 sheep, and 1,000 hogs and carried off 500–700 horses. He estimated the value of property confiscated and destroyed to be in the millions of dollars. The Cavalry Reserve Brigade alone captured 87 horses, 474 cattle, and 100 sheep and destroyed 230 barns, 8 mills, 10,000 tons of hay, and 25,000 bushels of grain valued at over $400,000.[36]

Charles Humphreys was a chaplain in the 2nd Massachusetts Cavalry. That regiment had long suffered at the hands of Mosby, including the stinging defeat at Mount Zion Church the previous July. Now, the men from Massachusetts were part of the reserve cavalry exacting vengeance on the populace of Loudoun County. Yet Humphreys believed "this was the most unpleasant task we were ever compelled to undertake." As the troopers rode up to a farmhouse, women and children shrieked and howled in fear, men cried and fell to their knees begging for mercy, but the pleading was for naught. "It was a terrible retribution on the county," Humphreys confessed. The destruction of Loudoun Valley between the Blue Ridge and Bull Run Mountains was, Merritt crowed, "most complete." By the end of the year, the people of Middleburg were reduced to "a pitiable condition," Catherine Broun recorded. "Our children, indeed all of us, nearly live on milk and butter." Catherine Cochran began the new year with a note of despair: "We thought we had fathomed the depths of Yankee malice and rapacity but we had only skimmed the surface. From every quarter came tales of brutal insolence."[37]

In early December Mosby traveled to Richmond to discuss the organization of his command with Confederate authorities. The rangers were seven companies strong, and Mosby hoped to reorganize into two battalions, each led by a field officer with the rank of major. Mosby would retain overall command, and Chapman and Richards would be battalion commanders. Instead, however, the single existing battalion was reconstituted into a regiment with Mosby attaining the rank of colonel. Chapman was promoted to lieutenant colonel to act as second in command, and Richards was promoted to major. Due to lost paperwork, Chapman's and Richards's commissions were not formally enacted until 13 March, effective to 7 December.[38]

Chapman commanded the battalion in Mosby's absence, though he and Richards largely operated as separate squadrons. Federal cavalry patrols of about 100 men journeyed daily from Winchester to Berry's Ferry on the Shenandoah River. Chapman resolved to attack these patrols. Late in the day of 16 December, Chapman led 130 rangers into the Shenandoah Valley through Ashby's Gap. They camped for the night on ground covered by snow and crossed the Shenandoah River the next morning. The exact route of the patrol varied. Some days the troopers came through Millwood and returned via White Post. Other days, they took the opposite route. Chapman split his force and deployed John Russell with half the rangers to watch the Millwood road while he took the other half to watch the White Post road. With both approaches covered, Chapman's plan was to let the scouting party pass by and then charge the front and rear simultaneously.[39]

Russell had the better luck that December morning. Capt. William Miles led 100 men of the 14th Pennsylvania Cavalry through Millwood toward the ferry crossing. His flankers in advance of the main body were wary of possible ambushes and spotted the rangers. The rangers immediately charged and drove back the advance guard. Miles, riding with the lead party, tried to rally his men but fell mortally wounded. The main body, too, fell back to Millwood, chased by the rangers. The rangers completely routed the patrol. They killed or wounded some 30 Pennsylvanians, captured the bulk of the rest, and secured scores of horses, without a single Confederate casualty.[40]

Three days later, on 20 December, 1,000 troopers of the 8th Illinois Cavalry, 16th New York Cavalry, and 13th New York Cavalry outfitted at Fairfax Court House for an expedition to Loudoun County. Lt. Col. David Clendenin, 8th Illinois, led the scout. The troopers marched through Thoroughfare Gap and reached The Plains the next day. From there, Clendenin took 400 men north to Middleburg. Maj. Douglas Frazar, 13th New York Cavalry, continued west to Rectortown with 600 men and then marched north to Rector's Cross Roads before reuniting with Clendenin at Middleburg. The troopers returned to Fairfax on the twenty-second. The patrol was uneventful—the command returned without a loss—but did round up 15 suspected guerillas, and Clendenin reported that his men mortally wounded "one rebel major." The rebel officer was Mosby.[41]

Mosby and ranger Thomas Love were eating supper at the home of Ludwell Lake, on the road from Rectortown to Rector's Cross Roads on the night of the twenty-first. Earlier that evening, while attending the wedding of a ranger, Mosby had received word of Frazar's approach and had scouted their advance. The weather was cold with rain and sleet. Mosby thought that the troopers had camped for the night, and he planned to attack the next morning. Instead,

Frazar followed his orders and pushed on to Rector's Cross Roads. At nine o'clock, his men saw horses tied outside Lake's house and stopped to investigate. They surrounded the house, and a trooper felled Mosby with a shot through a window. The bullet lodged in his abdomen, and Frazar pronounced the wound mortal. Not recognizing the fallen officer, who claimed to be a lieutenant, Frazar continued on to Middleburg and left the wounded man to die. Someone took his hat, though, and Frazar later recognized the captured hat to be that of a field officer. The identity of the fallen officer remained unknown over the next several days. Then, someone determined he was Mosby, and Federal officers clung to the belief that the wound was mortal. Patrols scoured the countryside in search of Mosby, but to no avail. When he had recovered sufficiently to travel, Mosby journeyed to his family's home near Lynchburg.[42]

13 | All Will Be Right

With Mosby absent, recovering from his latest wound, leadership of the rangers passed to Richards and Chapman, and the battalion split into two independent commands. Richards led Companies A, B, and D in operations throughout northern Virginia during the winter. Chapman commanded the rest of the battalion—Companies C, E, F, and G—which left from Salem for the Northern Neck on 3 January 1865.[1]

The Northern Neck is the land east of Fredericksburg bounded by the Rappahannock River on the south and the Potomac River on the north. It encompasses the counties of King George, Westmoreland, Richmond, Northumberland, and Lancaster. Mosby had earlier decided to send a portion of the battalion to that region for the winter. Ostensibly, the reason was lack of forage in Fauquier and Loudoun Counties to sustain the command. However, the security of the Northern Neck worried Confederate authorities. Some months earlier, Secretary of War James Seddon had asked Lee to send some of Mosby's men there to guard against marauding enemy soldiers. Lee declined, noting that any escape route on the narrow strip of land could easily be blocked. Instead, Lee believed there were sufficient men to provide for their own defense and solicited advice from Mosby on how to organize them. In August Mosby sent Thomas Richards, Dolly Richards's brother, to the Northern Neck to organize a local resistance. Richards raised a cavalry company and remained there until the end of November, when he returned to Mosby's Confederacy with the men. That company later became known as Company G.[2]

Prior to reaching the Northern Neck, Chapman traveled to Lee's headquarters at Petersburg to receive further instructions. The weather was cold and dreary; rain and sleet poured from the winter sky. Lee was in good humor and seemed "like a good old father," Chapman shared with his mother. Lee told Chapman that "he has but one want in this world and that is to whip the Yankees." The meeting moved Chapman. "No man can listen to him without feeling a kind of awe and wonder at being in the presence of such a great and good man," Chapman related. "Anyone who feels subdued, if he will listen to General Lee for five minutes he will feel satisfied that all will be right. Not that he would have you believe the power layed [*sic*] in himself and the army alone but in God and the justice of the cause. Who would not fight for such a cause when they have such a leader."[3]

But in recalling those events more than forty years later, Chapman confessed to have had reservations. He witnessed for the first time the wretched conditions in the trenches of Petersburg. "On that day I experienced my first depression and doubt of the success of our cause." The tale he recounted of that day was not one of inspiration. Lee's headquarters was barren but for some chairs and a table. A small fire barely filled the fireplace. A courier came into the room coatless and drenched by the freezing rain. Lee handed the soldier his own overcoat, and Chapman left for Westmoreland County with a "despondent feeling."[4]

The weather was cold that winter on the Northern Neck, and the Potomac River nearly froze across. However, it was to some extent a bucolic existence away from the depredations of war. As had been the practice in Mosby's Confederacy, the rangers dispersed throughout the countryside and quartered with families. Chapman's own Company C occupied Westmoreland County; Company E resided in Richmond County; and Companies F and G located in Northumberland and Lancaster.[5]

For the children of Bladensfield Plantation in Richmond County, it was a thrilling time. The family adopted several rangers who regaled the children with their tales of daring deeds, their dashing escapades on horseback, and their lively songs. The soldiers enthralled the young girls, and the rangers, hardened by battle but still youths, returned the affections. As they had in Mosby's Confederacy, youthful crushes and romances blossomed in Chapman's Confederacy. The presence of so many soldiers was an unaccustomed sight in a land with but few young men and provided a welcome sense of safety. "Everybody's corn stayed in the corn house and the wheat in the granary," a daughter of the plantation related. "The Yankees never came once that winter." The family had earlier hidden its silver in the garden for security. Now, they recovered it for dinner parties with the rangers.[6]

For Josie, though, it was a time of concern. Few rangers remained around Highlands, and she was lonely and starved for news. Rumors abounded that two companies had been captured on the march. Chapman reassured her as best he could. "I think this country is perfectly healthy and safe from the Yankees," he wrote to her shortly after arriving. But he feared for her safety. Chapman first arranged for Josie to visit his parents in Luray, and then, after settling into his command, he arranged for her to come to the Northern Neck with her mother and grandmother. Neither plan ever materialized.[7]

Yet the Northern Neck was not immune to the perils of war. Point Lookout was a desolate Federal prison camp on barren sand across the Potomac River in Maryland. Disease, starvation, and exposure to summer heat and winter cold took their toll on its unlucky Southern denizens. Chapman met some naval officers and proposed to attack the camp, but the available boats were too small and the water too rough to cross the river. The naval officers were, in fact, on the Northern Neck to assist illicit trade across the Potomac. Smuggling across the river was prevalent. With the approval of Confederate authorities, smugglers exchanged tobacco for provisions to sustain the Southern army. Sheridan and Grant were well aware of this and of the rich supply of provisions that supported the Confederate army besieged at Petersburg. Toward the end of February, they proposed to send an expedition to the area.[8]

Three Federal warships and several transport steamers carrying 1,800 infantrymen and 300 cavalrymen left Fort Monroe on the Virginia Peninsula bound for Fredericksburg on 5 March. Col. Samuel Roberts, 139th New York Infantry, commanded. The ships sailed north in the Chesapeake Bay, past the York River and Mobjack Bay, around Stingray Point, and up the Rappahannock River, joined by two more gunboats. A transport ship grounded at the village of Tappahannock, but several hours of hard labor freed the vessel, and the ships continued upriver until obstructions about six miles below Fredericksburg blocked their progress. Chapman was at Fredericksburg at the time and discovered the expeditionary force downriver. He approached the ships at dark with three men intending to learn their mission, but an alert picket wounded one ranger and drove them away. Roberts's Federals entered the city, destroyed the railroad, and seized some 45,000 pounds of tobacco. The tobacco was part of a smuggling operation, to be traded across the lines for meat, bacon, and other provisions.[9]

When Roberts returned to Fort Monroe, he informed Grant of his success and proposed to immediately set out for the lower counties of the Northern Neck. Grant gave his endorsement and personally attended to the details of the mission. At eight o'clock on the morning of 11 March, the force of infantry and cavalry left Fort Monroe on transports accompanied by warships. The expedition followed the previous passage up the Chesapeake Bay, but continued past the mouth of the Rappahannock to the Potomac River. The ships rounded Smith's Point on the Northern Neck and anchored at Piney Point, just above the Saint Mary's River on the Maryland side, at dusk. Roberts's intent was to land in a bay where the Lower Machodoc Creek empties into the Potomac and march on the village of Montross in Westmoreland County. However, a suitable landing could not be found, and instead, the warships retraced their route downriver. The ships rounded Sandy Point and proceeded up the Yeocomico River to the town of Kinsale. There, at five o'clock the next morning, the soldiers landed. One boat of cavalry disembarked first and met some rangers about a mile from town. More horses and troopers hurried out of a second boat and set off, followed by infantrymen and ambulances at ten o'clock.[10]

It was Sunday, and Chapman was some five miles to the west at a home near The Hague. He received news of the landing at eight o'clock and hurriedly sent couriers across the countryside to gather the rangers. Then, with about fifteen men at hand, he proceeded to Kinsale to investigate. At The Hague, Chapman learned that soldiers had on several occasions landed on the Northern Neck, marched up the Rappahannock side to Fredericksburg, and back down the Potomac side. That, indeed, may have been Roberts's intention, for the initial march was to The Hague and then across to Warsaw. The Federals never advanced much beyond The Hague.[11]

Chapman employed classic ranger tactics to turn back Roberts's expedition. A short way past The Hague, Chapman came across Wat Bowie with two or three other rangers escorting two prisoners. A regiment of cavalry trailed them just down the road. Chapman instructed Bowie to continue on to draw out the advance guard while Chapman concealed his rangers in some nearby woods. When the advance guard pursued Bowie, Chapman would swoop down upon them from the rear. However, Roberts's scouts spotted the tracks leading to the woods and halted directly in front of Chapman.[12]

Mosby had taught battle tactics well, and Chapman knew the element of surprise could accomplish much. "There was nothing for us to do but to charge them," he explained, "which we did with such a yell that they must have imagined we had a whole regiment." The detail of 30 Northern scouts immediately turned about and raced to the safety of the main column. Chapman and his rangers pursued at a gallop, capturing some of the men and passing others in an attempt to cut off their quarry. In their haste, the Confederates were quickly upon the main column. Chapman's horse was very fast and hard to handle in the excitement. He rode directly in among the head of the column. The flight of the advance guard had thrown the Northern cavalrymen into confusion. Many were turning to flee, and Chapman overheard a Federal officer, new to the methods of ranger warfare, "scolding his men and asking them if they were 'going to let a dozen men whip a regiment.'" Wat Bowie and another ranger followed on Chapman's heels, and as the Federals rallied, the three Confederates wheeled about to go back down the road. Lead bullets poured in their direction, showering the air with splinters from a rail fence. The three rangers passed through the remnants of the advance guard still streaming in and escaped along a side road.[13]

Roberts and his horse soldiers experienced that 12 March the same fear, apprehension, and frustration known to Federals throughout northern Virginia and the lower Shenandoah Valley. The enemy was, Roberts reported, "constantly hovering about our column, and being splendidly mounted and familiar with the roads, were able to avoid collision with anything more than our advance and rear guard." After turning back Chapman's charge outside of The Hague, the Northern cavalrymen chased the fleeing rangers into the village but rounded up few Confederates. "At every crossroad the enemy would separate," Roberts explained, "each squad taking a different path, until our cavalry found themselves pursuing only three men. These were captured and sent back toward the main column, but were retaken, together with a portion of their guard." Chapman, himself, was one of those who vexed Roberts. He, Bowie, and the third ranger came across guards escorting three captured rangers to the rear. They captured the guards, freed the prisoners, and also captured two cavalrymen escorting two slaves to the rear.[14]

Frustration mounted as the day grew longer. Roberts's raiders torched a blacksmith shop, a wheelwright shop, and a granary holding 500 bushels of wheat, but Roberts had had enough. There was little of value to be found in The Hague, few rangers had been captured, and his men were exposed to ranger ambushes. The cavalry column fell back to the infantry, and the soldiers returned to Kinsale, destroying four small storehouses filled with grain, tobacco, and bacon on the return march and gathering 26 cattle and 50 sheep. The soldiers began reembarking at 11:00 P.M., and the ships were under way four hours later. Chapman concealed his rangers in some woods and watched the village, but he lacked sufficient force to attack the beachhead. The warships lobed a few shells ineffectively at the rangers in a parting shot as they steamed away.[15]

Federal losses for the day amounted to 6 men wounded and 5 captured. They destroyed few provisions and returned with only 2 rangers and 4 citizens detained. Less than five days earlier, Roberts had brimmed with optimism, jubilant with success from his raid on Fredericksburg. "I think the greater part of the soldiers can be captured and a great many horses and cattle collected," he informed Grant. He expected the operation to last about five days. Now, from the safety of Saint Inigoes on the Maryland shore, Roberts telegraphed a different tale to Grant: "I regret to report that my expedition to the Northern Neck has not been very successful so far. I find the enemy in stronger force than I expected and superior in cavalry and a perfect knowledge of the country. I can march through the country with my present force, but I should probably lose a good many men." A return expedition would require much more cavalry and light artillery and take considerably longer, Roberts concluded. Chapman had just schooled Roberts and Grant in warfare, ranger-style.[16]

Federal bullets did, however, inflict a toll that Sunday. After the full complement of rangers had assembled, the Confederates harassed the march back to Kinsale. Sam Chapman was severely wounded in the thigh while attacking the rear of the column. Chapman, too, flirted with danger but came away luckier than his brother. At one point, Chapman and another ranger rode into an open field to draw out the cavalry from the infantry. Their presence failed to interest the cavalry escort but did draw the attention of sharpshooters. Chapman spotted the riflemen scurrying into position in some woods, but before he could get out of range, they found their mark. A bullet tore into the hind leg of his mare. The sharpshooters fired more shots, and the report of the guns spooked the horse. Chapman's horse galloped uncontrollably on three legs for over 100 yards and carried him to safety. The mare was Chapman's most valuable horse of the war, purchased from Robert von Massow after he had been wounded, and was one of the best mounts in the command. The wounded animal was taken to Bladensfield Plantation. There, the children of the plantation observed that "the poor wounded horse groaned now and then as we stood by watching it" until plantation workers led the mare away to its death.[17]

Federals never did return to the Northern Neck, but Chapman's presence continued to draw attention. A plan was put forth on 16 March to ring the area with warships along the Potomac and Rappahannock and drive the rangers out with a large cavalry force moving over land. Josie worried about just such a plan to capture her husband, but Chapman assured her that "the rumors which you have heard are more than half false. The Yankees cannot make a line across the neck. It would be ridiculous to attempt it." Yet even into early April, Federal commanders crafted plans to drive out Chapman's rangers.[18]

Toward the end of March, Mosby received orders from Lee to gather his scattered command. Lee was withdrawing his cavalry for the defense of Petersburg and Richmond. The rangers were the only remaining Confederate force operating north of Gordonsville, and Lee needed Mosby to watch and protect that region. Mosby recalled Chapman's squadron, but the rangers remained on the Northern Neck for almost two more weeks, until 9 April. Federal soldiers tracked their evacuation through enemy lines, and it took three more days of furtive marching to reach Warrenton.[19]

The state of affairs that Chapman found upon his return was chaotic. Mosby had long since sufficiently recovered from his injury to resume command and had inflicted his own wounds on Federal soldiers. He had even organized an eighth company, Company H. But Lee had evacuated Petersburg on the night of Sunday, 2 April. Federal soldiers occupied Richmond on Monday, and Lincoln himself toured the captured Confederate capital on Tuesday. Then, Lee surrendered at Appomattox on the ninth. Conflicting rumors swirled from house to house throughout Mosby's Confederacy. Any report that offered the slimmest possibility of hope was accepted as truthful. Even the Federals were confused. One report stated that Mosby was on his way to North Carolina to unite with Gen. Joseph Johnston's Confederate army. Alone, cut off from Confederate authorities, the rangers pondered their fate and searched for news.[20]

Mosby and his rangers had good reason to worry. The terms of surrender to be offered them were not clear. Southerners in Richmond thought that Mosby should be offered the same terms as Lee. Lincoln's secretary of war, Edwin Stanton, and Henry Halleck, army chief of staff, held a different opinion. A wire sent from Washington on 10 April to Maj. Gen. Winfield Hancock at his Winchester headquarters bore instructions from them. Hancock had replaced Sheridan and now commanded the Middle Military Division responsible for operations in the Shenandoah Valley—and operations against Mosby. The 3:00

P.M. telegraph directed that all detachments and stragglers of the Army of Northern Virginia could indeed surrender under Grant's terms and be paroled and allowed to return to their homes—all except Mosby. Grant, however, suggested a more magnanimous approach toward his adversary. In a telegraph to Stanton later that evening, he said that offering the same terms to Mosby would be an inducement to surrender and hoped that Hancock would do so.[21]

Hancock followed Stanton and Halleck's instructions and sent a letter by courier to Mosby dated Tuesday, 11 April. He told of Lee's surrender and stated that he was authorized to receive the surrender of Mosby's command on the same conditions. He would send an officer of equal rank as Mosby to arrange details, should Mosby so desire. The correspondence Mosby received also contained another important detail. Hancock had printed and distributed an announcement to the public. Mosby was not included in the parole, the notice proclaimed. Nor were people to continue sheltering and abetting the rangers. Further aggression by Mosby would bring utter devastation to the countryside. Hancock then anxiously awaited Mosby's reply.[22]

Hancock was not optimistic. He reported to Halleck Wednesday morning that he had offered to receive Mosby's surrender but had not yet received a reply. "It is quite as likely that Mosby will disband as that he will formally surrender," he informed Halleck, "as all his men have fine animals, and are generally armed with two pistols only. They will not give up these things, I presume, as long as they can escape. I will employ the cavalry force here in hunting them down." Thursday passed and still no word from Mosby. Hancock's patience had worn thin by Friday. He prepared a force of 8,000 infantry and cavalry to sweep into Loudoun and Fauquier Counties from the west across the Blue Ridge Mountains and simultaneously from the Fairfax perimeter in the east. Hancock was set to unleash his force the next day, but Lincoln was assassinated that same night, and Hancock postponed the operation.[23]

Mosby finally replied on Saturday, 15 April, the same day Lincoln died. He was well aware of Lee's surrender. Indeed, the rangers had heard the deafening cannonades of the victors. Mosby had sent men to Richmond to ask for Lee's advice but wanted to continue so long as Johnston had not surrendered. In his response to Hancock, Mosby noted that he had had no official communications from Confederate authorities nor "has the emergency yet arisen which would justify the surrender of my command." Instead, he asked for a suspension of hostilities during which time he could decide a course of action.[24]

Mosby delegated Chapman, surgeon Aristides Monteiro, Adjt. William Mosby, and Capt. Walter Frankland to deliver the reply. The latter three officers stopped at Highlands later that evening to summon Chapman. They found Chapman and Josie in the parlor room. Josie reacted hysterically upon hearing of the mission to Winchester. A trek to the enemy camp would only lead to the imprisonment or murder of her husband, she protested. There was no danger now that the war was over, Chapman assured her. Josie only became more agitated and more inconsolable, fearing her husband's imminent death. The strain in the parlor room was unbearable. The four officers were somber in their duty; they were soldiers and answered to a higher obedience than a wife's nervous pleading. Josie sensed the futility of her appeals. Chapman had emerged unscathed from the harsh combat of ranger warfare that had killed or wounded so many comrades. He had survived the incessant raids that had swept up scores of rangers, some never to return from Northern prisons. The months of separation on the Northern Neck had left her nerves severely frayed. Now, at war's end, she was powerless to save her husband from certain death. She fainted from despair. Chapman gathered his wife's limp body and carried her to the bedroom. Food was then prepared, and the four officers quietly stepped from the warm house into the darkness of a cold, rainy spring night.[25]

The reception Chapman received was not at all what Josie feared. The officers spent the night at a farmhouse four miles from Winchester. There, they learned of Lincoln's assassination and that Mosby was suspected of involvement. Uncertain of the greeting that awaited them, the four men continued on the following morning. Soon, they came across a picket post of the 12th Pennsylvania Cavalry. They attached a white handkerchief to a stick as a flag of truce, but still regal in military bearing and not willing to succumb to defeat, Chapman, Mosby, and Frankland were unwilling to carry the token of submission. The humiliating task fell upon Monteiro. He approached the picket post and to the query "What command, Major?" replied "Mosby's." The response was unexpected. There was not the humiliation and taunts of victors. There was simply the joy of war-worn soldiers, exposed on the picket lines, fearful of death. "Thank God!," one man exclaimed. "The war is over. I know the end has come when Mosby's men surrender."[26]

An officer escorted the four rangers to the quarters of regimental commander Col. Marcus Reno. It was a comfortable tent stocked with fine liquors and Havana cigars. These Reno proffered to the Confederates, and as they sipped several glasses of strong whiskey, Reno engaged his former enemies in conversation. Reno knew well of the rangers, having battled them just a few weeks earlier. He first engaged Chapman in polite conversation about the number of rangers and their condition. It was an awkward conversation. Chapman was, according to Monteiro, "a much better fighting man than conversationalist."[27]

Shortly, two colonels arrived to escort Chapman and Monteiro, the ranking officers, to Hancock's headquarters. News of Mosby's imminent surrender had spread like wildfire through the encampment, and masses of soldiers eager to catch a glimpse of the elusive gray ghost thronged the road to Winchester. The two Confederates had some difficulty guiding their horses through the dense sea of bluecoats. Headquarters was a large brick house on Main Street. Their escorts stopped in front and directed Chapman and Monteiro through an iron gateway over which hung a large United States flag. Pride still burned in their rebellious souls, however, and both rangers instead entered through a small gate to the side rather than yet submit to the Federal government. A small flag attached to a staff draped this gate, too. Monteiro removed the flag, wrapped it around its staff, and placed the flag down on the iron fence. The two escorting officers looked on in bemusement and remarked that "the rebellion was dying hard" as Chapman and Monteiro strode into the entrance hall.[28]

The two Confederates had no idea what to expect of Hancock. He might refuse to meet them. Or worse, they might not be permitted to return home. They were entirely at the mercy of their conqueror, but the man who stepped into the hallway was not harsh or haughty or belittling. The conqueror that shook the hands of the two rebel officers was benevolent and cordial, kind, considerate, and gentle in demeanor. He began the solemn meeting with dignity and courtesy. "You have fought bravely," Hancock said, "and have nothing to be ashamed of. You have, like gallant soldiers, left your cause to the God of battles, and the arbitrament of the sword has decided against you. Let us once more kneel down at the same altar and be like brothers of the same household." Choice wines and cigars came forth, as well as several glasses of strong whiskey, and the soldiers sat down to business.[29]

Hancock was magnanimous, but he was also the victor and reminded Chapman and Monteiro of that fact. He received Mosby's letter and in a steely tone informed them that he had been waiting for the reply for some days. It was better to receive it late than not at all, he said. He then told of his planned excursion into Loudoun and Fauquier, a terrible last resort necessitated by Mosby's delay but now averted by their visit. And he penned his response to Mosby. He agreed to allow Mosby time to gather more information, though he cautioned that Lee was no longer in authority. The day was Sunday, 16 April, and Hancock gave Mosby forty-eight hours, until Tuesday at noon. Both sides would refrain from hostilities until that time, when Mosby was to meet an officer of equal rank at Millwood to arrange the details of surrender. He also warned Mosby that Chapman "has been furnished with such evidence as will undoubtedly satisfy you that further resistance on the part of your command can result in no good to the cause in which you have been engaged."[30]

The pleasantries concluded with a dinner hosted by cavalry chief Maj. Gen. Alfred Torbert. By now the street in front of Hancock's quarters was packed with soldiers seeking a glimpse of Mosby. Chapman and Monteiro exited through a back alley, but throngs of soldiers still crowded their way to Torbert's residence. The two gray-clad soldiers passed through a mob of bluecoats during which they were harassed with the catcalls, razzing, and taunts of the common soldier. These, the rangers endured with stoic humor. To the repeated query of which was Mosby, Monteiro bemusedly pointed to Chapman; Chapman returned the compliment and pointed to Monteiro. The dinner was a feast of turkey, chicken salad, lamb, veal, fish, fowl, tropical fruits, and vegetables all washed down with costly wines—food that had not been seen in Mosby's Confederacy for ages. But the setting was awkward and the conversation forced. Chapman remained quiet during much of the meal. In his stead, Monteiro fawned and made polite conversation.[31]

The excursion to Winchester was not at all what had been expected. Chapman and Monteiro were treated as officers and as gentlemen, not as vanquished foes. The generosity overwhelmed Monteiro. He tried to be thankful and polite with Hancock and Torbert. In contrast, Monteiro's portrayal of Chapman during the visit told of impassive indifference. He variously described Chapman as "my laconic friend," "my silent companion," "not a talking man," employing "his usual marked economy of language," maintaining "his usual quiet way." Monteiro explained how during the return home Chapman informed him that the surgeon had "talked too much." Chapman considered Monteiro's conduct, conversation, and behavior to be "a most sublime exhibition of human impudence," Monteiro confessed.[32]

The meeting convinced Hancock that Mosby would indeed surrender. He wired the news to Halleck in Washington. Halleck replied that Grant now authorized that favorable terms of surrender similar to that which he had agreed upon with Lee should be extended to Mosby and all his men. Stanton, too, wired Hancock on the same day. He had read too many reports about Mosby over the past two years and had formed a harsh opinion of him as a cutthroat, marauder, and bushwhacker. He cautioned Hancock to watch for treachery. Hancock responded that he had no intention of meeting Mosby himself, but he would send a high-ranking officer as a compliment to Mosby. Brig. Gen. George Chapman, second in command of Hancock's cavalry, was to meet Mosby at Millwood. Hancock was so certain of the outcome that he had blank parole forms prepared for all to sign and attended to details of the surrender.[33]

The 18 April meeting at Millwood was cordial, though it did not have the outcome Hancock expected. Mosby and 15–20 officers attended. Mosby made clear that he had no intention of surrendering. There was no immediate danger to his men, and he still had no information that the Confederacy was lost. Should he hear that Johnston had surrendered, Mosby would end the conflict. However, he had no desire to formally surrender his battalion. Rather, he would simply disband, advising each man to give his parole if he so desired. Mosby, himself, expected to leave the country. The meeting did result in an extension of the truce for another forty-eight hours, until noon on the twentieth, and conditionally for ten days thereafter, subject to approval. Hancock now understood that Mosby would not surrender until he learned the fate of Johnston in North Carolina. Indeed, he likely would not formally surrender at all.[34]

Mosby was earnest during the meeting. He remarked that he was anxious to avoid further bloodshed and destruction of property. He had already informed his men that they could come in individually to receive their parole if they so desired. He and his fellow officers uniformly offered their condolences over Lincoln's death. The meeting, according to General Chapman, was "characterized by good feeling." Yet Mosby misjudged the graveness of the situation. Stanton implicated Mosby in the plot to assassinate Lincoln. Grant, too, had had enough of Mosby's antics. He notified Hancock that "if Mosby does not avail himself of the present truce end it and hunt him and his men down. Guerillas, after beating the armies of the enemy, will not be entitled to quarter." Hancock denied Mosby's request to extend the truce an additional ten days. The truce would end at noon on the twentieth. An officer bearing a flag of truce would wait at Millwood until the noon hour to accept Mosby's surrender. If that hour passed, Hancock would not offer terms of surrender again.[35]

The meeting two days later was not as cordial as the first. Mosby again rode into Millwood shortly before the truce was to expire accompanied by a cadre of some twenty officers. A like number of Federal officers awaited them. This time Hancock sent not a general but simply a staff officer. That officer told Mosby that Loudoun and Fauquier Counties would be destroyed if Mosby did not surrender. And when the sun reached its noon zenith, he informed the Confederates that the truce had expired; they were no longer under its protection. The summit of the eighteenth had been conducted with an air of respect. Now, the Confederates were deliberately taunted. Mosby rose from his chair and replied that "if we are no longer under the protection of our truce we are of course at the mercy of your men. We shall protect ourselves." He gave a hand sign that his commanders instantly recognized as the silent battle signal to attack. All rose and followed Mosby out of the room. "Mount and follow me" were the only words he spoke, and the rangers rode away, trailed one last time by Federal cavalry. Later that evening, Hancock concluded that the command was disbanded, but for Mosby he was less certain: "If Mosby is in Loudoun Valley I will hunt him out."[36]

Mosby called one last meeting of the rangers at Salem for noon the next day. The weather on that 21 April was cold and misty from an earlier rain, and a thick fog rolled over the land as the soldiers gathered in an open field. All knew what was to come, and the dismal weather matched the downtrodden look of despair worn by each man. At the appointed hour, all mounted, and the companies formed in line. Mosby rode up and down in review but could not bear to read the words he had penned earlier that morning. Instead, Chapman and Dolly Richards read his farewell address to their respective squadrons:

> Soldiers—I have summoned you together for the last time. The vision we cherished of a free and independent country has vanished, and that country is now the spoil of a conqueror. I disband your organization in preference to surrendering to our enemies. I am no longer your commander. After an association of more than two eventful years, I part from you with a just pride in the fame of your

achievements and grateful recollections of your generous kindness to myself. And now, at this moment of bidding you a final adieu, accept the assurance of my unchanging confidence and regard. Farewell!

Three cheers echoed across the countryside, and then the soldiers surrounded their leader. Tears streamed down their faces as the former warriors bid goodbye. "Men would silently grasp each other's hands and then turn their heads aside to hide their tears; but at last it became so general that no pains were taken to conceal them," ranger James Williamson related.[37]

The task fell upon Chapman to lead the rangers to Winchester to receive their paroles. It was his duty as a soldier; his honor was at stake. Chapman announced that he would go there the next day. He had personally met Hancock, had heard him be generous in his terms, and advised that it was better to surrender according to form, as expected by the rules of war, than disband. Any man who wished to accompany Chapman could meet at Paris. Yet all did not go willingly. Catherine Broun of Middleburg recorded the sentiments of the rangers regarding paroles. "It was really heartbreaking almost to see the young men," she confessed in her diary. "I saw them in tears and heard some said they would rather be shot than take it but they are compelled for every one would be taken as a prisoner of war and the houses burned."[38]

Some 200 rangers including company captains Walter Frankland, Alfred Glascock, and Sam Chapman marched with Chapman across the Shenandoah River one last time. They knew not what to expect. The truce had expired, and Hancock had vowed to offer no terms of surrender. Pickets stopped the rangers at Millwood, but then allowed them to proceed. Two miles from Winchester, pickets again stopped the rangers, this time for twenty minutes before proceeding on. Within a mile of Winchester, Chapman halted and rode into town with 15–20 men to arrange terms. He returned with a provost marshal carrying prepared paroles. On 22 April, five days past his twenty-fifth birthday, Chapman signed a slip of paper pledging to not take up arms against the United States until regularly exchanged. He was permitted to return home after swearing: "I will conduct myself as a good and peaceable citizen, and will respect the laws in force where I reside, and will do nothing to the detriment of, or in opposition to, the United States Government." Hancock telegraphed the good news to Stanton. And he informed Stanton that Chapman "is as important as Mosby, and from conversation had with him I think he will be valuable to the Government hereafter."[39]

14 | A Sense of Duty

With the war over, Chapman, twenty-five years old, and Josie, not yet nineteen, faced the difficult task of rebuilding their lives. The country they had fought for no longer existed. The South was impoverished; its economic system in shambles; its social and political order destroyed. Virginia was under military occupation, its citizens subject to harassment and arrest. Indeed, authorities arrested Sam Chapman in the summer of 1865 for journeying to Washington, D.C., without a signed parole. In these uncertain times, Chapman and Josie, along with her mother Esther Jeffries and grandmother Esther Foote, reclaimed the Edge Hill estate.[1]

A letter from Josie to Chapman's sister Kate in Luray provides a glimpse into the Edge Hill household in the spring of 1867. Son William Allen "Willie" (born 1865) was a mischievous little boy, enjoying candy from his father and pleased when his uncle John Jeffries brought apples. Josie was caring for daughter Esther Foote "Hettie," one month old and sick. Esther Jeffries and Chapman worked in the fields sowing seed, worried about the late spring. Chapman was "looking very well, fatter than I ever saw him," Josie proudly proclaimed. Yet it was also a frightful time of poverty, privation, and turmoil during Reconstruction. Josie's faith helped steer her through the troubled times. "How well it is that God mercifully conceals from us the future, nor gives us to taste in anticipation the bitterness of death," she wrote her sister-in-law. "Did we know that dark storms would overtake us on the sea of life, might we not shrink back from the path we must necessarily pursue?"[2]

Two more Chapman children were born at Edge Hill—Elizabeth Forrer "Libbie" (1869) and James Jeffries (1873). Sam Chapman lived nearby in Rectortown and taught in the school system. Chapman farmed the land. In 1870 the farm comprised 534 acres, of which 234 acres were forest, and was worth almost $11,000. Chapman's personal estate was valued at slightly over $2,000. Chapman raised 107 sheep that produced 370 pounds of wool that year. Other livestock included 8 horses, 5 milk cows, 2 working oxen, 6 cattle, and 6 swine. That year, the farm produced 800 bushels of corn, 300 bushels of oats, 250 bushels of wheat, 75 bushels of potatoes, 3 tons of hay, 200 pounds of butter, and some fruit. Three farm laborers assisted Chapman in the fields, and a servant helped Josie run the household. However, after eight years of togetherness, the year 1873 brought events that forever changed the Chapman family. Chapman sought an alternative to farming and turned to Mosby for help.[3]

Following the war, Mosby practiced law at Warrenton. He initially resided at Road Island, the Jeffries's estate down the road from Edge Hill near Bethel. However, military authorities harassed and even arrested Mosby, and it was not until Grant, at the behest of Mosby's wife, wrote his own personal order exempting Mosby from military arrest and allowing him to travel unhindered that Mosby was made a free man. Mosby eventually befriended Grant and supported his reelection in 1872. For Rutherford Hayes's election in 1876, Mosby openly declared that he was a Republican. His support of the Republican Party was pragmatic, to help gain favorable influence for Virginia in the government, but it was an act of defiance that dismayed Virginians. He was shunned, his law practice failed, and Mosby moved to Washington, D.C., in 1876. Two years later, Hayes appointed him consul at Hong Kong, a position he retained until 1885.[4]

In June 1873, with Mosby's influence in the Grant administration, Chapman and his brother Sam received appointments as railway post office clerks at an annual salary of $1,200. They served on the Washington, D.C.–Lynchburg, Virginia, route. One year later, Chapman and Josie exchanged the 534-acre Edge Hill farm, valued at $8,000, for property in Alexandria bounded on the east by Patrick Street and extending west to Henry Street and between King and Prince Streets. The Chapman family maintained residence in Alexandria for the next seventeen years. Four more children were born—John Henry (1875), Katharine Neal "Katie" (1877), Samuel Forrer (1879), and Mary Eustace (1881). Esther Jeffries, her mother Esther Foote, and a servant completed the Chapman household. Sam Chapman, too, sold his property near Rectortown and moved to Alexandria, where he also served as a minister at a local Baptist church.[5]

Shortly after moving to Alexandria, Chapman began a short-lived venture in the tavern and hotel business with his brother Edmund. They briefly operated the City Hotel, today known as Gadsby's Tavern, located on North Royal Street between King and Cameron Streets. The establishment dated to colonial America and was known for the presidents, foreign dignitaries, and prominent citizens who had sought food, lodging, and entertainment in the confines of the tavern and hotel. In March 1875 Chapman used the Patrick Street property to borrow $3,000 to purchase the lease and furnishings, and he ran the enterprise with his brother for the next year and a half. However, the tavern and hotel business was not successful. Chapman relinquished his interest in August 1876, when Edmund partnered with another investor and continued his proprietorship for the next several months.[6]

Employment as a railway postal clerk provided stable income but required Chapman to be away from his family. It was a separation that he found difficult, and he longed for the warmth of home. "You can't imagine how lonely I feel,"

Chapman confessed to Josie from Petersburg. "I find my thoughts constantly turning to you and our little ones. I would undoubtedly be a miserable creature without the enjoyment of my family. If deprived of them, this life would be a blank to me." The election of Hayes as president in 1876, and Mosby's growing influence in the Republican Party, first with Grant and then with Hayes, provided hope for a better future for the Chapmans. Like Mosby, Chapman aligned with the Republican Party, and as the new administration took office in March 1877, Chapman sought appointment as consul at Bradford, England. That position never materialized, but another appointment in Hayes's administration, as a revenue agent for the Internal Revenue Service, did.[7]

In the years following the war, enforcement of law in the former Confederacy was oftentimes difficult. Many Southerners despised the federal government and the influx of carpetbaggers that it brought. Taxes on alcohol and tobacco were an important source of revenue for the government during this time (accounting for nearly 90 percent of internal revenue from 1868 to 1913), yet the collection of taxes on alcohol was particularly difficult and dangerous in the rural postwar South. Illicit distilleries proliferated throughout the region, and Internal Revenue officers, guides, and witnesses often met armed resistance while attempting to collect taxes. From July 1876 to the end of August 1879, authorities seized 2,831 stills and arrested 5,462 persons in twelve Southern states. Twenty-two officers and employees died in these raids and 37 were wounded.[8]

Hayes needed a strong ex-Confederate that Southerners would respect to enforce internal revenue laws in the South. He turned to Mosby as that man. Mosby declined but suggested Chapman in his stead. Chapman became a revenue agent on 13 July 1878 at a pay of $7.00 a day plus expenses. At that time, 35 Internal Revenue agents were employed "subject to orders." Their job was to aid in the prevention, prosecution, and punishment of fraud, and oftentimes this involved raiding and seizing unlawful distilleries where taxes were unpaid.[9]

Chapman was initially stationed in Statesville, North Carolina (1878–79), and later Atlanta (1880) and New York City (1881). While in North Carolina, Chapman's work took him to South Carolina. His efforts there gained the attention of Hayes, who informed Mosby that Chapman "is the very man for the place and has done more than anyone else for the government in South Carolina." In the spring of 1880, Chapman assisted the Internal Revenue collector in Rabun County, in the mountains of Georgia along the North Carolina border. His actions invoked fierce resistance but gave hope to law-abiding people who had previously cowered under fright, and Chapman was optimistic of success. "I went into and all through the county enforcing the laws in a quiet way where circumstances would admit of it, and wherever resisted, in such a fierce way as to quickly overcome all resistance," he described to Josie. "The result has been very encouraging and if my recommendations are carried out, which I have no doubt they will, the country will not hear much more of resistance to officers and burning of property by lawless moonshiners in northeast Georgia." Chapman's efforts drew the praise of a federal court officer in North Carolina who remarked, "who would have thought that a rebel guerilla would have come down here and done so much for the poor mountain people." The work was satisfying, and Chapman was pleased that "our efforts to do right are appreciated by our friends and by those with whom we come in contact and by those whom we look up to."[10]

Though Chapman found satisfaction in his duties, the family struggled under the strain of distance. Visits were rare, and Chapman, Josie, and the children could not unite to celebrate birthdays and holidays or enjoy the warmth of companionship. Nor could a father's love and pride in his children be expressed except through letters. The hardship of separation was evident early. "All the wealth of India would not compensate me, if it were given on condition that we be separated from each other, and I pray that this may always be my feeling," Chapman confessed to Josie just a few months into his duties. "Any place becomes attractive to me when you are with me, but without you, I fail to see the attractions which others see. During the week, when in pursuit of my duties, I get along without heartache but when Sunday comes, that blessed day of rest and thought, and all alone in my room, my thoughts constantly turn toward my wife and children and other friends at home. They turn to my wife whom God gave me the heart to love and to wed, more than fourteen years ago, and to the dear children who have blessed our wedlock. Don't think it womanly even if I should drop a tear on these occasions."[11]

Chapman's embrace of the Republican Party was not a popular position in the postwar South. During Reconstruction and the years that followed, many Southerners abhorred the Republican Party and its policies. A few notable ex-Confederates, however, adopted a more pragmatic approach toward rebuilding the South and aligned with the Republicans. One was Mosby, who was vilified for his close relationships with Grant and Hayes. Another was James Longstreet, for whom Chapman had served while in the artillery. Like Mosby, Longstreet received appointments from Grant, Hayes, and James Garfield, including appointment as United States marshal in Georgia, and was similarly reviled for his postwar embrace of the Republican Party and maligned in the mystique of the "Lost Cause."[12]

Chapman's support of the Republican Party was likely pragmatic, to build a better future for his family. He owed his appointment as postal clerk to Grant's patronage and Mosby's friendship with Grant. (Chapman himself befriended the former president and in 1881, while working in New York City, visited Grant and reminisced about family and Mosby.) Now, Chapman's appointment as revenue agent was due to Hayes's patronage and Mosby's influence with Hayes. With Hayes not running for a second term, Josie, in 1878, professed hope that Grant would reenter politics to seek a third term in the presidential election of 1880. Grant's election, she believed, would allow Chapman to obtain a better position in the government and one close to home. Grant did not run for office that year. Instead, James Garfield was elected the twentieth president of the United States, but it was likely that hope that inspired Hettie and Libbie Chapman to send a congratulatory card to Garfield upon his election. And it was that hope that on the eve of Garfield's inauguration in March 1881 led Josie to believe that "our influential friends" will find Chapman a better position.[13]

Chapman never did gain a better position in the government. He remained a revenue agent, active until at least the age of seventy-eight. He was stationed mostly in Atlanta from 1882 to 1895, except for duty in San Francisco for parts of 1883, 1884, and 1885 and in Baltimore in 1883. Other locations included: St. Louis (1895–96), Greensboro, North Carolina (1896–98), Atlanta (1899), Lynchburg, Virginia (1899–1901), Nashville (1901–4), Greensboro (1904–5), and Richmond (1906–15). He continued serving as a revenue agent for several more years, with assignments in Greensboro (1915), San Francisco (1916–17), Salt Lake City (1917), Philadelphia (1918), and Richmond (1919).[14]

A sixteen-month assignment to San Francisco in 1884–85 was particularly trying for the family, and though Josie paid an extended visit with Mary, both husband and wife yearned for an appointment closer to home. By May 1885, Chapman was transferred to North Carolina and then back to Atlanta in the fall, where he remained employed until 1895. In 1889, with the upcoming inauguration of Benjamin Harrison as president, Josie and Chapman speculated that with Mosby's assistance Chapman could be appointed to a coveted position as Internal Revenue collector in Virginia. However, that position was given to another agent. Chapman and Josie always expressed hope that they would eventually be together, but the burden of separation was borne for thirty-some years. Only late in life did Chapman and Josie have the pleasure of companionship.[15]

Chapman's longest posting was in Atlanta, where he worked continuously from 1885 to 1895. His duties included raids on illegal distilleries in Georgia, Alabama, and Florida. When moonshiners and law enforcement officers clashed in rural backwoods locations, violence flared. On 8 April 1888, Josie received the news she had long feared. She had endured countless anxious days and nights when Chapman was on patrol as a ranger, all the time fearing for his safety. She had suffered the pain and loneliness of separation during his excursion to the Northern Neck toward the end of the war. She had fainted upon hearing that he would travel to Winchester to negotiate surrender terms, anticipating his certain capture or execution. Yet Chapman had emerged from the war unscathed. Now, he was a former Confederate turned Republican, enforcing federal law near Florence, Alabama, when a bullet finally left its mark.[16]

Chapman had entered what he called a "bad neighborhood" and, as in his days as a ranger, he split his team of 8 men into two groups to flush out his quarry. Chapman's group soon confronted 5 men and captured 3, but the encounter spooked his guides, and they deserted him. Unable to watch over his prisoners, Chapman reluctantly set them free and continued searching for the distillery with his 2 remaining aides. That he found, but the moonshiners had been forewarned by their accomplices. Chapman walked toward a suspect, calmly talking to him as he had so often done during the war to put his enemy at ease. A second man lurked behind a tree about 35 yards distant and fired his weapon as Chapman approached. The bullet found his left wrist, nearly severing his artery and tendons, but Chapman had the presence to fire back at the assailant as both suspects fled. The wound proved to be more painful than serious, but still Chapman now felt the distress that his brother, Mosby, and so many other wounded rangers had undergone before. "I long to be with those I love most dearly," he wrote Josie, "whose ministering hands would soften every pain and whose presence would so gladden my heart."[17]

Chapman investigated a particularly horrific affair in Choctaw County, Alabama, in 1891. In August of that year, marshals arrested a man, Bob Sims, for operating an illicit distillery. Sims was the leader of a local religious sect that county residents greatly disliked and harassed, and subsequent actions escalated into violence that further alienated the citizenry. Sims's brother and son rode into the town where he was being held and came to his aid, wounding a guard and killing a bystander in an escape attempt. A mob of local citizens, enraged by the killing, themselves killed the son and shot and then lynched the brother. The search for Sims, who had nonetheless escaped, was unsuccessful, and the vengeful mob instead plundered the homes of his immediate family and relatives and forcibly evicted them. The harsh treatment of his family left Sims embittered, and some months later he viciously slaughtered a neighboring family. Eventually surrounded and caught by a mob on Christmas day, Sims was lynched along with three of his followers. Later, a brother and a nephew were also caught and hung.[18]

Chapman's sense of duty to investigate fraud did not always endear him to fellow revenue officers. While in Atlanta, Chapman determined that the Internal Revenue collector there was using the position to favor his own political advancement and to aid his friends, to whom the collector oftentimes gave appointments as deputy collectors. Chapman believed that many of these appointees were incompetent and neglected their duties; one trafficked in untaxed whiskey. A physical altercation, duly noted in the local newspapers, erupted when Chapman confronted the collector. However, Chapman's most significant challenge, one in which his zeal to enforce the law to the fairness and equity of all clashed with local corruption, occurred in 1894–95.[19]

Moonshiners proliferated in Georgia. In the six-month period from November 1892 through April 1893, Internal Revenue officers raided more than 140 illicit distilleries in the state. More than 248 seizures took place in Georgia during a three-month period in 1895. These raids were at times violent, and the guides and witnesses that led agents to the stills could meet a harsh fate.[20] Some of the worst violence occurred in Gilmer and Murray Counties in the mountains of northwestern Georgia, where the Ku Klux Klan, or "whitecaps," were active and protected moonshiners, aided and abetted by local and state officials. Mobs murdered, whipped, or beat those who took a stance against these activities. They raped women, destroyed property, and forcibly evicted families. One man was saved from lynching only to be shot in broad daylight several days later by a gang of men. A few weeks later, a mob shot another man six times and threw him into a pit nearly sixty feet deep, but he miraculously survived to tell the tale.[21]

James Hetherington, who assisted Chapman in the investigation, described the nightmarish scenes:

> Usually a crowd of from twenty to fifty and often double that number of men would meet near the proposed victim's house. They would prepare balls of cotton saturated with oil, battering rams, etc. Arriving at the house of the victim, usually a small cabin, every door would be simultaneously battered down; then the fire-balls would be lighted and thrown into the house so that every move of the doomed wretch would be overlooked. If he offered resistance he would be shot down in the midst of his shrieking family. In most cases the persons attacked would surrender themselves to their persecutors without attempting resistance. After securing their victim he would be taken some distance from his house, stripped to the skin and then held with his face to the ground while two or more of his tormentors lashed his bare back with hickory writhes. Scores of men have been treated in this manner, and confined to their beds for weeks by the punishment; the scars they will carry to their graves.[22]

Chapman's investigation revealed that, in addition to numerous local officials, the Internal Revenue collector participated in these outrages—indeed was a member of the Ku Klux Klan along with another revenue officer—and that he hindered the prosecution of these cases. This time, however, the forces of local politics and corruption were too strong for Chapman to beat back. The collector and his cronies emerged from the affair unscathed, protected by Secretary of the Interior Michael Hoke Smith, from Georgia, who waged a public war against Chapman in the local newspapers. Instead, Internal Revenue authorities forced Hetherington and Chapman's clerk to resign and revoked the appointment of Andrew Chapman, Chapman's youngest brother who had found employment with the Internal Revenue Service in Georgia. For his role, Chapman was transferred to St. Louis in June 1895. It was a bitter defeat for a man who prided himself in enforcement of the law and fair treatment and who had so faithfully served as a revenue agent for seventeen years. Yet Chapman was not discouraged and continued to fight against corruption during the latter days of his career.[23]

Chapman returned briefly to Atlanta in the winter of 1898–99, only to meet further professional disappointment. Revenue agents employed guides, posses, and informers on raids. Funds to pay these employees came from the office of the commissioner of Internal Revenue. This system of reimbursement could lead to misappropriation of funds or outright fraud. Chapman returned to Georgia in November 1898 to investigate just such a case concerning problems with compensation of employees in the Atlanta office. He determined that the current revenue agent misappropriated money for his own use that should have been paid to employees. For this, the agent was dismissed.[24]

While in Atlanta, Chapman sought appointment as deputy commissioner of Internal Revenue. The promotion of the current deputy had vacated the position, and many of Chapman's political and professional acquaintances urged him to apply. Chapman obtained the support of numerous prominent Republicans throughout the South, including the states of Virginia, North Carolina, Georgia, Alabama, and Florida, where he had served, as well as influential Republican senators from North Carolina, West Virginia, and Iowa. One official described Chapman as "one of the purest and best men that I ever knew." Another said Chapman's government service "has been a bright official career of probity, usefulness and devotion to duty." Yet a third government officer described him as "a man of perfect integrity, the highest courage, and of absolute attention to duty."[25]

Chapman's own letter to the secretary of the Treasury noted that in his nearly twenty-one years of service as a revenue agent he had "suffered the privation of being separated from my family, endured many hardships, and exposed to danger of bullets (having been severely wounded while in the discharge of duty)." But his many years of government service and his longtime support of the Republican Party were not enough to secure the appointment. Perhaps grudges from the Ku Klux Klan controversy four years earlier still lingered, and Chapman's participation in the killing of Northern soldiers at Morgan's farm was not forgotten; another revenue agent received the position.[26]

Though Chapman may have met disappointment in his professional life, his family was a source of joy and satisfaction. He endured the shortcomings of a career as a revenue agent for them. "When I get to thinking about home something seems to be tugging at and wringing my heart," Chapman confided to Josie after five years of separation. "You perhaps will never know what a struggle I have between a sense of duty to my family and a desire to give up my position and live with my family the rest of my life. But I must tug on for a year or two yet until some of them are educated and we can see our way to educate the others. God bless them they are all dear to us and may He give us the will and the power to raise them as they should be raised."[27]

In his letters home over these years, Chapman never failed to express his love for Josie and the children, his pride in their accomplishments, and his admiration of Josie for raising the children into responsible citizens. Willie became a doctor and medical officer in the army. He served in Cuba during the Spanish-American War and in France during World War I. James and John were ministers in the Episcopal Church. James was a longtime missionary in Japan; John was a chaplain with the army in France during the war. Hettie and Libbie married ministers in the Episcopal Church. Sam followed his father's footsteps as a civil servant in the Internal Revenue Service at Philadelphia and later Pittsburgh. Mary married and raised a family. Katie never married and lived with her parents until their death.[28]

Though Chapman abandoned the Edge Hill farm after only a few years, farming remained a lifelong enterprise. He and Josie purchased a 551½-acre farm in Orange County for $4,500 in 1880. The farm, called "Clifton," was located along the railroad tracks about two and a half miles from Gordonsville toward the town of Orange. The house stood on high ground overlooking the farmland. It was a two-and-a-half-story frame structure, about 45 feet by 20 feet, that with additions had seven rooms, hall, attic, and pantry. The farm had several outbuildings including barns, stables, carriage house, smokehouse, chicken coop, kitchen, and dairy. Later, Chapman expanded the stables to hold 20 horses. About 300 acres of land were cleared, with the rest forested in oak and chestnut trees. Chapman grew wheat, corn, rye, oats, tobacco, timothy, and clover on 60 acres; another 60 acres were suitable for meadow. Springs and running streams watered the fields. Peaches, apples, cherries, pears, and grapes grew in an orchard. The Chapman family eventually moved to Clifton from Alexandria, but initially Chapman found it difficult to maintain and hoped to sell the farm in 1886. Chapman later sold the 551½-acre Clifton farm and an adjoining 609 acres of land for $15,500 in 1911. Still later, while residing in Greensboro, he owned a farm at Milton, North Carolina, near Danville along the Dan River.[29]

One of Chapman's less successful ventures at Clifton involved a colt named "Wealth." Wealth was foaled in 1897, and Chapman believed that the colt could be a successful trotter. He trained Wealth in Kentucky and entered him in races in Kentucky, Michigan, Indiana, Illinois, Ohio, Tennessee, Connecticut, and Rhode Island. However, Wealth never met his expectations, and by 1901 Chapman had accumulated several thousand dollars in debt. His attempts to sell Wealth for $5,000 failed, and Chapman put Wealth to stud at Clifton, where he sired several horses for Chapman's stock farm.[30]

A wave of nostalgia swept through the country in the years following the war. Many notable leaders penned their memoirs and filled the pages of monthly magazines and the *Southern Historical Society Papers* with accounts of the war. In the South, the myth of the "Lost Cause" arose, and former Confederate generals debated who was to blame for their defeat. Mosby became a lightning rod for some of this debate. Blame for the Gettysburg defeat had been placed upon Jeb Stuart, and Mosby rose to the defense of his commander. His implicit criticism of Robert E. Lee ensured that ex-Confederates would yet again disparage Mosby for turning his back on the South.[31]

Chapman, too, contributed to this nostalgia. Until his death, and even in his death, he defended the history of his small Dixie Artillery, a largely forgotten battery in the "long arm of Lee." While in Atlanta in the 1880s, Chapman befriended James Longstreet, who served as United States marshal and had an office adjacent to Chapman's. The two men frequently met and talked of the war; at some point the conversation turned to the fighting at Second Manassas on 30 August 1862. Though Confederate reports credited Stephen D. Lee's artillery with turning the tide of battle, Longstreet's and Cadmus Wilcox's reports of the action that day mentioned that an unknown battery had broken up the Federal advance. Chapman explained that his was the unknown battery that had so devastatingly enfiladed Fitz John Porter's troops that afternoon. With the 1886 opening in Washington, D.C., of Theophile Poilpot's cyclorama depicting the battle, Chapman sought to correct the official history. The massive painting was housed in a large circular building and received critical acclaim from the press and veterans for its authenticity and detail. True to wartime accounts, Porter's troops valiantly advanced into the Confederate lines, pounded by Stephen D. Lee's artillerists, but the panorama did not depict Chapman's Dixie Artillery in its critical position along the Warrenton turnpike.[32]

Chapman penned a letter to Longstreet on 27 August 1887 in which he recounted the events of that day twenty-five years earlier. He received Longstreet's endorsement the next day and had the letter published in the *Atlanta Constitution* two weeks later. The story resurfaced in 1904 in the *Richmond Times-Dispatch,* owned by Chapman's former ranger comrade Joseph Bryan. The latter retelling of the tale was at the request of Chapman and in response to an earlier feature in the newspaper on Manassas that yet again mentioned the prominent role of an unknown battery. That same year, Chapman sought to have the story of his battery included in a history of the artillery of the Army of Northern Virginia being gathered by John Daniel, a Confederate veteran and United States senator from Virginia.[33]

However, Chapman's search for a place in history was largely unfulfilled. The poor standing in the annals of Confederate history of Longstreet, who had publicly feuded with Stephen D. Lee in the pages of the *Southern Historical Society Papers* and had dismissed the prominent role of Lee's artillerists, undoubtedly hurt Chapman. The *Southern Historical Society Papers* eventually published Chapman's version of the events in 1914. He undertook another effort in 1922 to officially mark the position of his battery at the battlefield. In his latter years at Greensboro, he retold the story of the Dixie Artillery at Manassas yet again to a local newspaper, and it featured prominently in his obituary, but not until 1985 did the Dixie Artillery receive its due recognition, when the National Park Service published a detailed account of troop movements during the battle.[34]

Chapman found considerably more success in the glory of Mosby's Rangers. Mosby maintained a lifelong close bond with both Chapman brothers. The depth of respect is seen in a letter to Chapman shortly after Mosby published his war reminiscences in 1887. The daring exploits of Sam Chapman at Miskel's farm, Warrenton Junction, and Grapewood farm filled the pages of Mosby's book, but Mosby mentioned Chapman only once. This omission offended Chapman. Mosby responded to Chapman's criticism with an apology. He explained that he had hastily written the manuscript and described it as merely a series of newspaper accounts assembled into book form. As for calling the roll of all those who had participated in the events therein, Mosby said that "it was as unnecessary to say that about you as to call Hercules a strong man." He went on to tell Chapman that "although you are only mentioned once, I really say more in your favor in that single sentence than I do about all the others I mention." The particular sentence acknowledged the role of the Dixie Artillery at Second Manassas.[35]

In the early 1890s, while in Atlanta, Chapman wrote his recollection of wartime events at the request of Mosby. It was during this period that Mosby mounted his spirited defense of Stuart. Longstreet, who had placed the blame for the Gettysburg defeat squarely upon Stuart, fell prey to Mosby's venom. Clearly relishing the fight, Mosby told Chapman that he would "make Longstreet ashamed that he ever attacked Stuart," and a few months later spouted that "he will be sorry he ever wrote a word against Stuart," but later relented and claimed to have only faulted Longstreet as a historian, and not as a soldier. Chapman, ever the faithful soldier, served as Mosby's intermediary in his oftentimes virulent attacks on Longstreet.[36]

On 16 January 1895, the first reunion of Mosby's command took place at Alexandria. Mosby attended along with notable officers, including William Mosby, Dolly Richards, surgeon William Dunn, and the Chapman brothers. Mosby, Chapman, and Richards strode into the hall together. A deafening rebel yell and thundering ovation from about 150 former rangers greeted the three leaders. The reunion epitomized the contradictions inherent in the memories of the Old South and the actuality of the emerging New South, and Mosby's address that night touched upon both sentiments. He acknowledged the irony of meeting along the shores of the Potomac River, in sight of the Capitol. Where before pickets and gunboats had challenged them, now the rangers gathered in peace as citizens of a united country. He paid bittersweet tribute to the dead, remembered their valiant deeds, and spoke of his love for Virginia.[37]

Other reunions followed, but Mosby never again partook in the gatherings. He was unapologetic for his conduct during the war and told Sam Chapman that "I mourn over every Southern defeat; I exult over every Southern victory";

but the spirit of the reunions troubled him. "Nobody enjoys a talk over the old days more than I do," he explained to a former ranger, "but I can't stand the speeches and the prayers that are made at these conventions. I prefer healing the wounds of the war; I do not enjoy making them bleed afresh. Let those who take pleasure in such things listen to them; but excuse me."[38]

Chapman, however, basked in the glory of the rangers. Eighteen months after the first ranger gathering, in July 1896, a three-day grand reunion of Confederate veterans filled the streets of Richmond. Chapman, then in Greensboro, attended the event with Josie. Sam Chapman, too, was present. Crowds of people, perhaps 125,000 to 150,000, lined the streets and rooftops to view the parade along the avenues of Richmond. In Mosby's absence, it was Chapman who led the rangers. He "looked happy and very natural at the head of his old command," thought Josie. The parade brought a massive outpouring of nostalgia, camaraderie, and Southern pride. The crowd cheered the veterans marching with "old battle flags, torn with bullets, and eaten by moths." Women offered the veterans water, provided "sweet words of praise for what they had endured thirty years ago," and serenaded the aged soldiers with wartime songs. "I do not think I ever enjoyed myself more," Josie told her daughter.[39]

Chapman attended annual reunions during the period 1909–14 while working in Richmond and served as commander from 1908 until 1913. The 1913 reunion, Confederate Day, 2 October, featured a parade of over 400 veterans through the streets of Fredericksburg, but by then the number of rangers had dwindled to 63. Chapman was still active in ranger reunions in the summer of 1924, when he and Josie traveled to Remington, the former Rappahannock Station where his Dixie Artillery had dueled Federal guns sixty-two years earlier, and paid tribute to his remaining ranger comrades and their families. Chapman received his own bittersweet remembrance in 1904 when a wartime Colt revolver found its way from a shop in Buffalo back to his hands.[40]

One of Chapman's proudest moments came at the University of Virginia. He, like so many other students, had abandoned his studies in April 1861 to fight for the fledgling Confederacy. Fifty-one years later, university officials hosted 118 surviving student warriors as honored guests for the annual commencement exercises, 10–12 June 1912. Chapman attended with Josie and son James. Over the three days, the university feted the veterans with a dinner banquet, alumni luncheon, and procession on the Lawn. Everyone they met acclaimed the veterans as heroes. University administrators presented each soldier with a medal honoring their sacrifices. Chapman enjoyed his medal very much.[41]

Chapman returned to Charlottesville three years later, on 1 May 1915, for a ceremony honoring another former student. This time, the guest of honor was John Mosby. While attending the University of Virginia many years earlier, Mosby had shot a fellow student in self-defense. For this he was unceremoniously expelled and wrongly imprisoned. The faculty had previously tried to atone for this transgression, but Mosby had declined that invitation. Now, Mosby was again suspicious of the invitation: "I shed my blood for her people and you know what I got in return. It is too late for them to atone for it now." Instead, he went because it was "very gratifying for my old men to go there to meet me." He sat on the stage at Cabell Hall before a packed room, surrounded by several rangers, including the Chapman brothers, Dolly Richards, William Dunn, Ben Palmer, and others. Mosby graciously accepted the heartfelt cheers, and though his speech warmed the crowd, he did not indulge the students and faculty with war stories. Afterwards, he acknowledged he had had a pleasant time and said that "for the first time in my life I felt that I was a rich man—that the kindness and consideration shown me where I was raised and educated convinced me that I possessed something that gold could not buy and that I have not lived in vein."[42]

One of the more poignant reunions concerned Chapman's own family. Four years of civil war had led to a breach between the Ohio and Virginia branches of the Forrer family. Chapman and his brothers Samuel and Edmund, grandsons of Samuel Forrer, had fought for Southern independence. Their cousins, grandchildren of Samuel Forrer's older brother Christian, were equally tested by their resolve to preserve the Union—a determination that left a 31-year-old mother widowed, her 7-year-old son fatherless, and her 22-year-old brother dead. Augusta Forrer Bruen's husband, Maj. Luther Bruen, was mortally wounded when a shell exploded near him and shattered his knee at Spotsylvania Court House during the Wilderness campaign. Surgeons amputated his leg, and Augusta was at his side when he died after a month of intense suffering. Tragedy struck again one month later when a bullet to the neck killed her brother in battle at Decatur, Georgia. It took the research of Frank Bruen, who barely knew his father but knew the oral history and tales of the Forrer clan, to reunite the Ohio and Virginia relatives—a breach reconciled in part by the kindness of Chapman and Josie.[43]

On the morning of 18 June 1908, Chapman boarded a train at Manassas bound for Front Royal to meet a group of Confederate veterans. He chose a seat by the window, and as the train slowly climbed through the Bull Run Mountains at Thoroughfare Gap and crossed out into upper Fauquier County, past the small towns of The Plains, Salem (now Marshall), and Piedmont (now Delaplane), he watched the countryside closely, searching for familiar faces and places of his youth. A generation had passed away and a new generation had been born since those days long ago, and Chapman saw few familiar faces to greet him at the train stations. But the scenes that flowed past his window "called up so many memories that I could easily feel myself back 44 and 45 years ago." He saw the walnut tree near Goose Creek where he had first laid eyes upon the 17-year-old Josie. More visions of past events, memories of youth, love, and adventure flooded his mind as he saw the familiar fields that he and Josie had walked over, and he recalled how they would gather at a big rock, their private Eden for lovers' bliss. "That section of country," he told Josie, "and particularly that old home of your Uncle John's will always be very dear to me. I wish we could go over the fields together once more. I hope the present occupants are as happy as we were then."[44]

Chapman was sixty-eight years old. The memories of his youth were vivid, but the people he saw were mostly strangers; a new generation had arisen. He had spent the past thirty years enforcing federal law throughout the South. He had been wounded not in defense of his beloved South, but in defense of the United States government. His job had kept him away from the one true joy in his life, Josie and their children, but had also provided a better future for them and the South. Entering the twilight of his life, images from his youth came alive once more outside his window, and perhaps he could not help but wonder how history would remember him. His sense of duty to family and country had led him to four years of rebel warfare as a youth, but also to tribute, remembrance, and reconciliation as an adult.

Josie died at home in Greensboro on 31 December 1927, at the age of 81. Chapman, nearly blind in his latter years, survived her by 20 months and died on 6 September 1929, at the age of eighty-nine. The turmoil of armed conflict, the poverty and privation of defeat, and the prosperity and progress of the new South marked his passage through life. For more than 60 years, Chapman devoted himself to healing the wounds of war, reuniting the country, and rebuilding the shattered South that he loved. A recount of the role of the Dixie Artillery at Second Manassas figured prominently in Chapman's obituary in the Greensboro newspaper. So, too, did his adventures with Mosby. But equally noted were his years of service as a government agent and the military and civic contributions of his eight children.[45]

A eulogist wrote that "with Col. and Mrs. Chapman, as with their immortal leader, the war between the states was over when the sun went down on Appomattox. Holding in tender memory a sacred and noble past, enshrining with hallowed affection the heroes of the 'Lost Cause,' they yet lifted their eyes over to the sunrise and looked and prayed for a better world to rise from the sorrows of the past, purified by sacrifice, knit together in brotherhood, moulded and fashioned by love." For Chapman, the war was indeed finally over; for the generations to come, the search for a legacy had only just begun.[46]

Notes | Bibliography | Index

NOTES

ABBREVIATIONS

BWAC-TU Battalion Washington Artillery Collection, Tulane University
CSR-VA Compiled Service Records (Virginia), National Archives
CSR-LA Compiled Services Records (Louisiana), National Archives
FC Ned Fanfani Collection
HC Archer Ellis Hansen Collection
JBW James B. Walton
JBW-TU James B. Walton Papers, Tulane University
JJC Josephine Jeffries Chapman
JSM John S. Mosby
JSM-DU John Singleton Mosby Papers, Duke University
JSMSB-UVA John S. Mosby Scrapbooks, University of Virginia
NA-CP National Archives at College Park, Md.
OR U.S. War Department, *The War of the Rebellion*
RC Carolyn and Chris Russell Collection
SFC Samuel Forrer Chapman
UVA Special Collections, University of Virginia Library
VHS Virginia Historical Society
WAP-TU Washington Artillery Papers, Tulane University
WHC William Henry Chapman
WHCLA Capt. W. H. Chapman's Company, Light Artillery, Compiled Service Records (Virginia), National Archives
WHCLB William H. Chapman ledger book, Russell Collection

1. A MAN'S COURAGE

1. Ramage, *Gray Ghost,* 344–47. Wert, *Mosby's Rangers,* 74, claimed a cumulative total of 1,902 men served with Mosby. Keen and Mewborn, *43rd Battalion,* 287, stated at least 1,881 men enlisted. Ramage, *Gray Ghost,* 344, reported 1,570 enlistees.

2. Scott, *Partisan Life;* Crawford, *Mosby and His Men;* Monteiro, *War Reminiscences;* Williamson, *Mosby's Rangers;* Munson, *Reminiscences;* J. H. Alexander, *Mosby's Men;* Williamson, *Mosby's Rangers,* 2d ed.

3. Krick, *Lee's Colonels,* 78; Keen and Mewborn, *43rd Battalion,* 305–6; Moore, *Danville,* 100; Sifakis, *Who Was Who,* 116; Evans and Bridgers, *Confederate Military History,* 4:801; Spratt, *Page County,* 49.

4. CSR-VA, Mosby's Regiment; Monteiro, *War Reminiscences,* 155, 177, 188, 191, 194; unidentified newspaper clipping, JSMSB-UVA, 1:50–53; Munson, *Reminiscences,* 59.

5. *OR,* 46(3): 897.

6. Krick, *Lee's Colonels,* xi-xix, from a biographical study of 1,954 men who attained the rank of major, lieutenant colonel, or colonel.

7. Mosby, *Mosby's War Reminiscences,* 211.

8. Wert, *Mosby's Rangers,* 292; Ramage, *Gray Ghost,* 344; Keen and Mewborn, *43rd Battalion,* 305, 320, 350, 351, 370, 377.

9. McPherson, *For Cause and Comrades;* McPherson, *What They Fought For.*

10. JSM to SFC, 30 September 1909, JSM-DU; Coski, *Confederate Battle Flag.*

2. LIBERTY AND UNION

1. Bruen, *Christian Forrer,* 1–45, 47, 72, 87, 171; Brown, *Mosby's Fighting Parson,* 24–25.

2. Strickler, *Short History,* 2–5, 48–49, 58–59.

3. Bruen, *Christian Forrer,* 87–90, 96–100, 166; Strickler, *Short History,* 97, 114; Kerkhoff, *Old Homes,* 77, 106–7; Brown, *Mosby's Fighting Parson,* 25.

4. Bruen, *Christian Forrer,* 96, 166, 171, 193; Strickler, *Short History,* 308; Kerkhoff, *Old Homes,* 107; Brown, *Mosby's Fighting Parson,* 25–26.

5. Strickler, *Short History,* 1, 4, 120, 207–8.

6. Kerkhoff, *Old Homes,* 105, 108; Bruen, *Christian Forrer,* 168; Brown, *Mosby's Fighting Parson,* 23.

7. Strickler, *Short History,* 98–99, 225–27, 327; Bruen, *Christian Forrer,* 174, 179, 180, 182; Kerkhoff, *Old Homes,* 169–70; Brown, *Mosby's Fighting Parson,* 29–30, 47–48; Eighth U.S. Census (1860), Population Schedules, Page County, Va., 732. The Mossy Creek Ironworks is marked on a Library of Congress map of the Shenandoah Valley prepared by Jedediah Hotchkiss in 1862. See map H89, Stephenson, *Civil War Maps,* 313.

8. Edmonds, *John Chapman,* 3, 5, 12; Brown, *Mosby's Fighting Parson,* 26.

9. Edmonds, *John Chapman,* 5, 12, 13; Dove, *Madison County Homes,* 298–99; Yowell, *History of Madison County,* 56, 160; Brown, *Mosby's Fighting Parson,* 26.

10. Bruen, *Christian Forrer,* 193; Blackwell, *Blackwell Genealogy,* 52; Dove, *Madison County Homes,* 228, 298; Third U.S. Census (1810), Population Schedules, Madison County, Va., 682; Fourth U.S. Census (1820), Population Schedules, Madison County, Va., 105; Fifth U.S. Census (1830), Population Schedules, Madison County, Va., 5. Catherine Gaines was the daughter of Edmund Pendleton Gaines and Tabitha Rucker. Her father was not the Gen. Edmund Pendleton Gaines claimed by Edmonds, *John Chapman,* 14. See Armstrong, *Notable Southern Families,* 1:78, for the correct lineage, confirmed also in A. W. Gaines to WHC, 8 December 1896, WHCLB-RC, 254–55. In exception, Dove, *Madison County Homes,* 298, says William Allen Chapman married Hattie Gains on 29 April 1799. This name and date are shown in the handwritten *Madison County Marriage Register,* 249, microfilm copy, Library of Virginia.

11. Bruen, *Christian Forrer,* 171, 193, 196, 197, 208; Edmonds, *John Chapman,* 14; Vogt and Kethley, *Page County Marriage Bonds,* 14; Sixth U.S. Census (1840), Population Schedules, Madison County, Va., 308, 328.

12. Bruen, *Christian Forrer,* 197, 205–8, 210–12; Strickler, *Short History,* 378; "Col. William Henry Chapman Passes at His Home in City," *Greensboro Daily News,* 7 September 1929; "One of Mosby's Officers Dies at Greensboro," *Richmond Times-Dispatch,* 17 September 1929.

13. Bruen, *Christian Forrer,* 197, 208, 211; Kerkhoff, *Old Homes,* 26–27; Edmonds, *John Chapman,* 14; Brown, *Mosby's Fighting Parson,* 27; Seventh U.S. Census (1850), Population Schedules, Page County, Va., 319, Slave Schedules, Page County, Va., 415; Nonpopulation Census Schedules, Page County, Va., Roll 3, 351–52. The house is marked on map H89, in Stephenson, *Civil War Maps,* 313.

14. Eighth U.S. Census (1860), Population Schedules, Page County, Va., 822, Slave Schedules, Page County, Va., 426–27; Nonpopulation Census Schedules, Page County, Roll 7, 304–5; Luray (Main Street) Baptist Church Minutes, 53, 83, Library of Virginia;

Daniel Hite to Isaac Hite, 17 August 1862, in Jessup, *Painful News,* 108–10; Brown, *Mosby's Fighting Parson,* 34, 297.

15. Sixth U.S. Census (1840), Population Schedules, Page County, Va., 156–87; Seventh U.S. Census (1850), Population Schedules, Page County, Va., 347, Slave Schedules, Page County, Va., 411–22; Eighth U.S. Census (1860), Population Schedules, Page County, Va., 687–870, Slave Schedules, Page County, Va., 423–28.

16. Hotchkiss Papers, reel 60, 691–741, 769–852, Library of Virginia; Booker, "History of the Academies," 79–90; "Life at Mossy Creek Academy"; W. J. Miller, *Mapping for Stonewall,* 15–17; Brown, *Mosby's Fighting Parson,* 31–32.

17. Papers of the Mossy Creek Academy are found in Hotchkiss Papers, reel 60, Library of Virginia. Newspaper reports claim Hotchkiss resigned following the 1855–56 session (ibid., 722, 812, 813), yet he and his wife remained with the school for the 1856–57 session (ibid., 728–39, 817–29). T. J. White became principal for the 1857–58 session. The first session of the Loch Willow school was not held until 1859–60 (ibid., 742–67). W. J. Miller, *Mapping for Stonewall,* 17, states that Hotchkiss resigned from the school in 1858.

18. "Catalogue of the Officers and Students of Mossy Creek Academy, Mossy Creek, Augusta County, Virginia," 1853–58, Hotchkiss Papers, reel 60, 691–741, 769–852, Library of Virginia.

19. Hotchkiss Papers, reel 60, 726–27, 815–17; Brown, *Mosby's Fighting Parson,* 32; Webster, *Writings and Speeches,* 6:3–75.

20. Ford, *Origins of Southern Radicalism,* 120–44.

21. Brown, *Mosby's Fighting Parson,* 34–36.

22. Catalogues, University of Virginia, 1859–60, 1860–61, UVA.

23. Clemons, "University of Virginia Library," 27, 24n 117, UVA; Bruce, *History,* 3:21; WHC to W. Sam Burnley, 18 November 1911, Burnley Papers, UVA.

24. WHC to W. Sam Burnley, 18 November 1911, Burnley Papers, UVA.

25. Clemons, "University of Virginia Library," 24n 117, UVA; Bruce, *History,* 3:21.

26. Shanks, *Secession Movement,* 85–102, 237n 39; Bruce, *History,* 3:261; Jordan, *Charlottesville,* 15; "Letter from the University," *Richmond Daily Whig,* 25 November 1859.

27. Patton, *Jefferson,* 199, 202; Bruce, *History,* 3:262; Shanks, *Secession Movement,* 78.

28. Bledsoe, *Essay,* 8; Elliott, *Cotton,* 273, 416–17; McKim, *Soldier's Recollections,* 3; Bruce, *History,* 3:262; Shanks, *Secession Movement,* 71, 78, 234n 85.

29. Holcombe, *Address,* 11, 19, 20; Patton, *Jefferson,* 199; Bruce, *History,* 3:71–73, 262; Shanks, *Secession Movement,* 71, 78, 234n 85.

30. Holcombe, *Election,* 15.

31. Bruce, *History,* 3:262; William Pegram to "Jennie," 10 November 1860, Pegram-Johnson-McIntosh Papers, VHS.

32. McPherson, *Battle Cry,* 223, 232, 236.

33. Burnham, *Presidential Ballots,* 816, 818, 832.

34. McPherson, *Battle Cry,* 234–35, 257–59, 265.

35. Reese, *Proceedings,* 1:795, 3:163; Gaines, *Biographical Register,* 18, 44–45, 70; Eighth U.S. Census (1860), Population Schedules, Page County, Va., 791, Slave Schedules, Page County, Va., 426.

36. Reese, *Proceedings,* 4:115, 144; McPherson, *For Cause and Comrades,* 17.

37. Shanks, *Secession Movement,* 5, 10, 12, 205–8; Wooster, *Secession Conventions,* 145, 153; McPherson, *Battle Cry,* 283.

38. Shanks, *Secession Movement,* 10; Reese, *Proceedings,* 3:163, 4:144; Gaines, *Biographical Register.* This is the same geographic definition of the valley used by Shanks, in *Secession Movement,* 117, 205.

39. Burnham, *Presidential Ballots,* 816–43, 852–65; Shanks, *Secession Movement,* 116–17; Wooster, *Secession Conventions,* 152.

40. Shanks, *Secession Movement,* 31, 123.

41. See note 15; and Ballard, *Dismissing the Peculiar Institution.*

42. McPherson, *For Cause and Comrades;* McPherson, *What They Fought For;* "Bravery of Mosby's Daring Rebel Band Was Unrivaled," *Greensboro Daily Record,* 10 June 1923; Wall, "Students," 284; Jordan, *Charlottesville,* 23.

3. A MUCH PLEASANTER SERVICE

1. A primary source of information is Maupin's "Faculty Chairman's Journal," 17 and 22 April 1861, in UVA. See also Jordan, *Charlottesville,* 24–26, 133–37; Patton, *Jefferson,* 198, 203–12; Bruce, *History,* 3:265–67, 270, 275–80; Wall, "Students," 282–83; Wallace, *Guide,* 143, 147, 148; Field and Smith, *Uniforms,* 226. Recollections of four student members are given in Robertson, "Sons of Liberty"; Payne, "University of Virginia Companies"; Smythe, "Englishman's Visit"; and Garnett, "Personal Recollections." Randolph McKim, in *Soldier's Recollections,* 7–8, briefly mentioned the Southern Guard, of which he was a member. Chapman's recollections of the Southern Guard are sparse. See WHC to SFC, 18 November 1904, Daniel Papers, UVA; "Bravery of Mosby's Daring Rebel Band Was Unrivaled," *Greensboro Daily Record,* 10 June 1923; and WHC, "War Record of Colonel W. H. Chapman, from 1861 to 1864," 2 pages, HC. There is some question as to when these student companies formed. Wallace, *Guide,* 147, 148, stated the Sons of Liberty organized first, early in 1860, followed by the Southern Guard in January 1861. See also, Jordan, *Charlottesville,* 24. Garnett, "Personal Recollections," 332, claimed the two companies formed after 1 January. Patton, *Jefferson,* 205, stated the student companies organized immediately after the presidential election and the Southern Guard formed first. Bruce, *History,* 3:265, said they formed shortly after South Carolina seceded, which is repeated by Wall, "Students," 282. McKim, *Soldier's Recollections,* 7, said both companies organized in the fall of 1860, as did Payne, "University of Virginia Companies," 256. A tribute to William Pegram, a member of the Southern Guard, reprinted in Wise, *Long Arm,* 1:251, said the two companies formed in the fall of 1860 and the Southern Guard organized first. For Robert E. Lee's view, see Jordan, *Charlottesville,* 25–26; Freeman, *R. E. Lee,* 1:511.

2. Dunaway, *Reminiscences,* 7–11; McKim, *Soldier's Recollections,* 1–3; Patton, *Jefferson,* 200–203; Bruce, *History,* 3:267–69; Garnett, "Personal Recollections," 332–33; Jordan, *Charlottesville,* 17.

3. Patton, *Jefferson,* 207; Bruce, *History,* 3:270; Wall, "Students," 283.

4. See note 1; Evans, *Confederate Military History,* 3:63–65.

5. See note 1. There is some uncertainty about when the students left Harpers Ferry. Maupin wrote that Letcher ordered the students to return on 23 April and that they arrived in Charlottesville the evening of the twenty-fourth ("Faculty Chairman's Journal," 22 April 1861, UVA). Bruce, *History,* 3:278, and Wallace, *Guide,* 143, 147, 148, also claimed the students departed on 23 April. John Payne of the Southern Guard said they left on the twenty-first and reached Charlottesville the next day (Payne, "University of Virginia Companies," 257). Jordan, *Charlottesville,* 25, stated they departed on the twenty-first and returned by the evening of the twenty-fourth. Frank Robertson of the Sons of Liberty remembered being gone for ten days (Robertson, "Sons of Liberty," 399). Chapman's remembrances are conflicting, saying he remained there one week ("Bravery of Mosby's Daring Rebel Band Was Unrivaled," *Greensboro Daily Record,* 10 June 1923), ten days (WHC, "War Record," HC), or two weeks (WHC to SFC, 18 November 1904, Daniel Papers, UVA). The longest estimate is that they remained at Harpers Ferry for

three weeks (Wall, "Students," 283). McKim, *Soldier's Recollections*, 8, also said they remained for several weeks. James Garnett, Southern Guard, stated most emphatically that the students stayed at Harpers Ferry for only four days, from Friday, 19 April, to Monday, 22 April (Garnett, "Personal Recollections," 337n 4).

6. *OR*, 2:802; Strickler, *Short History*, 169, 393; Wallace, *Guide*, 48, 95, 117.

7. Brown, *Mosby's Fighting Parson*, 47, 71; Strickler, *Short History*, 400; Bruen, *Christian Forrer*, 174; Wallace, *Guide*, 132.

8. Brown, *Mosby's Fighting Parson*, 41–45.

9. The most important records relating to the Dixie Artillery are a 7½-page typed letter from William H. Chapman to Samuel F. Chapman and a subsequent 4-page typed letter from Samuel to John Warwick Daniel, both in response to Daniel's research regarding Confederate artillery. See WHC to SFC, 18 November 1904, and SFC to John W. Daniel, 25 November 1904, Daniel Papers, UVA. Strickler, *Short History*, 401, provides a brief account from Booton's son. Another very brief record of events for July–September 1861 is found in WCHLA (reproduced in Strickler, *Short History*, 401; and Hewett et al., *Supplement*, Pt. 2, 70:403–4). The WHCLA has a muster roll dated 31 October 1861 (see also Strickler, *Short History*, 400–401) and other records such as payroll vouchers, requisitions, discharge papers, and medical forms. These records form much of the basis for histories of the Dixie Artillery by Moore, *Danville*, 85–106, and Brown, *Mosby's Fighting Parson*, 46–47, 49–82. An additional brief supporting account is given in WHC, "War Record," HC. The Dixie Artillery was associated with the Battalion Washington Artillery of New Orleans in the spring of 1862. Scattered documents can be found in the WAP-TU, JBW-TU, and BWAC-TU.

10. E. P. Alexander, *Fighting for the Confederacy*, 62; Wise, *Long Arm*, 1:53; Wallace, *Guide*, 147; WHC, "War Record," HC. For artillery strength in 1862, see *OR*, 5:1086; Allan, "Relative Strength at Second Manassas"; Wise, *Long Arm*, 1:259.

11. WHC to SFC, 18 November 1904, Daniel Papers, UVA; Strickler, *Short History*, 401. Chapman called the cannons "iron guns." However, Booton's son stated the company had "two small brass [bronze] cannon about a yard long when they entered the service" and later received two iron guns. Bronze field cannons prior to the war included: the 6-pounder field gun with a nominal length of 54 inches (Models 1838, 1840) or 60 inches (Models 1835, 1841); the 12-pounder field howitzer with a nominal length of 49 inches (Model 1838) or 53 inches (Models 1835, 1841); and the Model 1835 12-pounder mountain howitzer with a total length of 37 inches (Hazlett, Olmstead, and Parks, *Field Artillery*, 33, 71, 134–37). Although designed for mountain service, the 12-pounder mountain howitzer was merely a small, lightweight field cannon. Mountain howitzers saw action in several battles in the Virginia theatre. Federal infantry used them around Big Bethel, in June 1861 (*OR*, 2:83); in an ill-fated crossing of the Potomac River near Leesburg (Ball's Bluff), in October 1861 (*OR*, 5:294, 321, 365); and at Second Manassas (*OR*, 12[2]:284, 299). Confederates used mountain howitzers at Fredericksburg, in May 1863 (*OR*, 25[1]:610). The Washington Artillery of New Orleans received four mountain howitzers in the spring of 1862 (T. L. Rosser to W. M. Owen, 22 May 1862, BWAC-TU).

12. WHCLA gives a muster roll for 1 July–1 November 1861, dated 31 October 1861. See also CSR-VA, Capt. Cayce's Co., Light Artillery (Purcell Artillery) for men transferred to the Purcell Artillery. This 80-man roster agrees with an original muster roll of Booton's son (reproduced in Strickler, *Short History*, 400–401) except that it shows J. G. Booton enlisted 21 June while Strickler does not. This discrepancy is explained in that John G. Booton resigned on 21 August 1861 at Winchester (a pay voucher for J. G. Booton, filed in WHCLA with records for John K. Booton, shows he was paid as a

second lieutenant for 1 July to 21 August). The CSR-VA muster roll shows sixty-six men enlisted on 21 June, 13 men joined at Winchester, and 1 joined at Manassas. Eight other men are included in WHCLA, but enlistment dates are either not shown or occurred at a later date. Seven additional men transferred from the Dixie Artillery to the Purcell Artillery, but all enlisted in 1862. Confederate Rosters, 18:67–71, in Library of Virginia, lists nine other men associated with the Dixie Artillery, but enlistment dates are missing. For payroll, see Wise, *Long Arm,* 1:108. See also payroll vouchers in WHCLA.

13. WHC to SFC, 18 November 1904, Daniel Papers, UVA; Strickler, *Short History,* 401; WHCLA, record of events. Chapman erroneously wrote that the company left on 21 July. Records in WHCLA show that John K. Booton was reimbursed by the quartermaster in Winchester to pay for transporting a caisson from Luray. For troop strength, see *OR,* 2:187, 470.

14. WHC to SFC, 18 November 1904, Daniel Papers, UVA. Manual artillery drill is mentioned in *OR,* 2:868, and Gilham, *Manual,* 380, described a specific drill to maneuver cannons by hand while limbered.

15. WHCLA, record of events; WHC to SFC, 18 November 1904, Daniel Papers, UVA. Records in WHCLA show that John K. Booton requisitioned coal from the quartermaster at Winchester to use in a traveling forge to shoe horses.

16. Owen, *In Camp,* 7–17, 24–69; *OR,* 2:462; "The Washington Artillery," *Richmond Daily Whig,* 5, 6 June 1861. See also CSR-LA, Washington Battalion, Artillery, record of events (reproduced in Hewett et al., *Supplement,* Pt. 2, 23:605–28).

17. Gibbon, *Artillerist's Manual,* appendix, 1–2, 40–42; Hazlett, Olmstead, and Parks, *Field Artillery,* 40–41, 74–75, 135–36; Thomas, *Cannons,* 27, 31, 32. For armament, see *OR,* 19(1):836–37; Wise, *Long Arm,* 1:284–86.

18. Hazlett, Olmstead, and Parks, *Field Artillery,* 90, 111, 122; Thomas, *Cannons,* 28, 33, 39.

19. WHCLA; Wise, *Long Arm,* 1:110–11, 135.

20. See Assistant Surgeon E. M. Crew's report of sick and wounded for November, filed with William Harvey's records, WHCLA.

21. Billings, *Hardtack,* 180, mentioned the terrible toll placed on horses in the Federal army. Details regarding the horses of the Dixie Artillery are found in forage requisitions by WHC and Francis Conrad, in WHCLA. Four horses died in February (WHC to JBW, 22 May 1862, item 152, Folder 10, JBW-TU; and Army of Northern Virginia Papers, item 153, Folder 4, Tulane University). For Washington Artillery losses, see JBW to P. G. T. Beauregard, 26 November 1861, C. W. Squires to JBW, 20 May 1862, and M. B. Miller to JBW, 20, 21 May 1862, JBW-TU. Lack of suitable forage in January is mentioned by Johnston in *OR,* 5:1028. Forage requisitions by Conrad and WHC confirm the short supply. Forage requisitions by Charles W. Squires, Merritt B. Miller, and Benjamin F. Eshleman (First, Third, and Fourth Companies) dated 28 February in CSR-LA, Washington Battalion, Artillery, show the Washington Artillery also had insufficient forage from 14 to 28 February. Owen, *In Camp,* 69, described the horse shelters. Additional details are in Chapman's requisitions for lumber to construct horse shelters dated 28 January and 1 February, in WHCLA.

22. SFC records in CSR-VA, 17th Virginia Infantry, and WHCLA; Judah Forrer records, in WHCLA; Brown, *Mosby's Fighting Parson,* 46–47.

23. Elections were held on 23 May 1861 (see Page County results in "The Election," *Richmond Dispatch,* 30 May 1861). Booton's resignation is mentioned in WHCLA. See also Virginia General Assembly, *Journal of the House of Delegates.* Other evidence in WHCLA support this date. Notes specifically refer to Chapman's promotion to captain on 8 December. This is supported by his payroll receipt for the month of December.

WHC's earnings of $133 were as second lieutenant for 1–7 December and as captain for 8–31 December ($90 per 30 days for 7 days and $140 per 30 days for 24 days). Conrad was paid as second lieutenant for 8–31 December. A note refers to a report from Edward Porter Alexander dated 9 December acknowledging the election of Conrad as lieutenant. Brent's records give a commission as second lieutenant dated 8 December. Crisp was granted leave on 9 January 1862 and extended on 30 January. He resigned 6 May 1862 (Adjutant and Inspector General's Office Special Orders No. 104, JBW-TU; see also payroll receipts in WHCLA). He listed his residence as New Orleans on 17 May. WHC stated that SFC was elected first lieutenant, with Conrad and Brent the other lieutenants (WHC to SFC, 18 November 1904, Daniel Papers, UVA). Chapman's recollections referred to later in 1862, not December 1861 (see chapter 4, note 13).

24. Camp locations in September are from a record of events in WHCLA. Camp locations in October and November are found in WHCLA records for James Abbott, Townsend Conrad, and William Harvey (Assistant Surgeon E. M. Crew's report of sick and wounded). A map of Centreville encampments drawn 18 December 1861 (National Park Service, Manassas National Battlefield Park) shows the Dixie Artillery as a separate and distinct camp located close to the Washington Artillery and near Beauregard's headquarters. Owen, *In Camp,* 68–69, mentioned the Dixie Artillery was near the Washington Artillery's winter encampment.

25. *OR,* 5:1028–32; Lee, *Memoirs,* 165, 169; Wise, *Long Arm,* 1:142–43. Organizational records of the army for January 1862 show the separate commands of Pendleton and Walton in the reserve artillery, but do not list the Dixie Artillery. However, evidence suggests the Dixie Artillery was under Walton's command as early as January 1862. Francis Conrad's requisition of 12 January for lumber to construct winter quarters and Chapman's requisition of 28 January for additional lumber were both signed by Walton (WHCLA). See also chapter 4, note 2.

26. *OR,* 2:977, 5:1049; *OR,* ser. 4, 1:761, 867; Wise, *Long Arm,* 1:127, 130, 146, 2:848–50; Owen, *In Camp,* 53–54n 1. Assessments of Pendleton's capabilities are given in E. P. Alexander, *Military Memoirs,* 158–59; E. P. Alexander, *Fighting for the Confederacy,* 112, 336; Sorrel, *Recollections,* 121; Gallagher, "Introduction," 6–7. Walton was promoted to colonel 26 March 1862 (CSR-LA, Washington Battalion, Artillery; Krick, *Lee's Colonels,* 360). Walton's views are clear from a letter he wrote to his Washington Artillery comrades (Owen, *In Camp,* 338–44n 1).

27. John Hite diary in Jessup, *Painful News,* 32, 33, 35, 36, 38, 43; Owen, *In Camp,* 64–67; Lee, *Memoirs,* 160–61, 163–65.

28. Owen, *In Camp,* 68–69, 71–73; CSR-LA, Washington Battalion, Artillery, record of events; JBW to P. G. T. Beauregard, 26 November 1861, JBW-TU. Requisitions by Francis Conrad on 12 January and by WHC on 28 January and 1 February, in WHCLA, provide details of the Dixie Artillery cabins and horse sheds. Forage requisitions dated 3, 7–9 January were signed by Francis Conrad and identified him as lieutenant commanding the Dixie Artillery. Conrad also signed the initial requisition for lumber dated 12 January. Chapman was back in camp by 19 January, when he began requisitioning forage. Mary Ellen Modesitt mentioned a party at the Chapman's Luray house on 31 December (Mary Ellen Modesitt to John Hite, 31 December 1861, in Jessup, *Painful News,* 71–72).

4. WE SUFFERED CONSIDERABLY

1. Sears, *To the Gates,* 4–9, 12–14.

2. In his history of the Washington Artillery, battalion adjutant William Miller Owen made no mention of the Dixie Artillery after leaving winter quarters except to say that the battalion passed by the Dixies on 1 July (Owen, *In Camp,* 92). However,

Chapman wrote that the Dixie Artillery was attached to Walton's battalion (WHC to SFC, 18 November 1904, Daniel Papers, UVA). Much evidence supports this claim. A transportation voucher for John Stanley dated 26 March 1862 and the discharge paper of Townsend Conrad dated 10 July 1862 identified the Dixie Artillery as attached to the Washington Artillery (WHCLA). Requisitions by Chapman in WHCLA show that his battery marched south to Richmond with the Washington Artillery and that Chapman requisitioned supplies from Capt. C. McRae Selph, battalion quartermaster, throughout March and into April. The 31 March requisition at "Camp Washington Artillery" was for forage on the march to Orange Court House, which was not supplied in full. Records in CSR-LA, Washington Battalion, Artillery, show John Richardson (Second Company), Merritt Miller (Third Company), and Benjamin Eshleman (Fourth Company) made similar forage requisitions, also not supplied in full, to Selph at "Camp Washington Artillery" on 31 March. That the Dixie Artillery was in camp with the Washington Artillery is substantiated by an order from Longstreet to Eshleman, acting commander in Walton's absence, to arrest a man at the camp of the Dixie Artillery (G. M. Sorrel to B. F. Eshleman, 24 March 1862, BWAC-TU). For details of the march, see Owen, *In Camp*, 49, 74; Bartlett, *Soldier's Story*, 78–79; *OR*, 5:526–27, 1091; CSR-LA, Washington Battalion, Artillery, record of events (reproduced in Hewett et al., *Supplement*, Pt. 2, 23:605–28); General Orders No. 31 (J. E. Johnston), 6 March 1862, and G. M. Sorrel to B. F. Eshleman, 7 March 1862, BWAC-TU; Lee, *Memoirs*, 172–74. For horse losses, see WHC to JBW, 22 May 1862, item 152, Folder 10, JBW-TU, and Army of Northern Virginia Papers, item 153, Folder 4, Tulane University; C. W. Squires to JBW, 20 May 1862, and M. B. Miller to JBW, 20, 21 May 1862, JBW-TU.

3. Owen, *In Camp*, 75–76; Bartlett, *Soldier's Story*, 79; Special Orders No. 39 (Longstreet), 22 March 1862, in BWAC-TU. Various records place the Washington Artillery at Camp Taylor. See Morning Reports: 1861–62, WAP-TU; CSR-LA, Washington Battalion, Artillery, record of events. The encampment of Longstreet's division was known as "Camp Taylor," with headquarters at "Taylor's house on the old Fredericksburg Road" (G. M. Sorrel, 21, 22 March 1862, BWAC-TU). Wert, *General James Longstreet*, 99, identified Camp Taylor as Longstreet's headquarters at the farm of Erasmus Taylor near Orange Court House.

4. Owen, *In Camp*, 76–77; Squires, "Autobiography," Library of Congress; Lee, *Memoirs*, 176–77; CSR-LA, Washington Battalion, Artillery, record of events; Muster Rolls, WAP-TU; G. M. Sorrel to B. F. Eshleman, 6, 7 April 1862, and P. T. Manning to B. F. Eshleman, 6 April 1862, BWAC-TU; *OR*, 51(2):533–34; Casey, *Outline*, 8; Andrus, *Brooke*, 48. Records at the Naval Observatory show similar weather prevailed in Washington, D.C. ("Journals," Records of the Weather Bureau, vol. 23, NA-CP).

5. Sears, *To the Gates*, 25–26, 35–39, 44–45, 61.

6. Ibid., 68–70, 82, 89, 95, 98, 109–10.

7. The Dixie Artillery was not listed in an organization of the army on the Peninsula at the end of April (*OR*, 11[3]:479–84). However, that organization showed Walton commanded the "Washington Artillery" with twenty guns. The Washington Artillery had sixteen guns during the Seven Days' battle, and the Dixie Artillery had four (Owen, *In Camp*, 91; *OR*, 51[2]:559). Numerous records suggest that the Dixie Artillery continued to be attached to Walton's battalion during this period. The earliest association in the official records is 15 May, when Walton mentioned the Dixie Artillery as part of his command (*OR*, 51[2]:558–59). From 4 May to 25 June, the morning reports of the Dixie Artillery were added to those of the Washington Artillery (Morning Reports: 1862–63, WAP-TU). Requisition requests to Capt. C. McRae Selph, battalion quartermaster, indicate attachment throughout March–June. Selph transferred horses to the

Dixie Artillery on three occasions during this period (C. McRae Selph, 19 May 1862, in BWAC-TU). Chapman drew supplies from Selph on numerous dates (WHCLA). Several requisitions were made at "Camp Washington Artillery." For details of events, see Owen, *In Camp,* 77–81; Bartlett, *Soldier's Story,* 85–86, 93; CSR-LA, Washington Battalion, Artillery, record of events; *OR,* 51(2):546–47, 552–53, 555–56; Morning Reports: 1862–63 and Muster Rolls, WAP-TU; Kensey Johns to JBW, 19 April 1862, and G. M. Sorrel to JBW, 24 April 1862, JBW-TU; Casey, *Outline,* 8–9. See also Andrus, *Brooke,* 48; Stribling, "From Markham to Appomattox," 185; Moore, *Richmond Fayette,* 56.

8. *OR,* 51(2):557–59, 11(3):516.

9. Sears, *To the Gates,* 117–47.

10. Isaac Hite letter, 2 June 1862, in Jessup, *Painful News,* 104–5. For other batteries, see Owen, *In Camp,* 82–83; Andrus, *Brooke,* 49, 64–66; Wallace, *Richmond Howitzers,* 83; Bergeron, *Guide,* 29–30; Moore, *Richmond Fayette,* 57–62; Stribling, "From Markham to Appomattox," 185–87; Wise, *Long Arm,* 1:193–94.

11. Sears, *To the Gates,* 167–77; Owen, *In Camp,* 79, 85; Andrus, *Brooke,* 49. Robert Krick (Richmond National Battlefield Park) provided information about Blakey's Millpond, Oakwood Cemetery, and their use as artillery encampments. See also Wallace, *Richmond Howitzers,* 56.

12. WHC to JBW, 22 May 1862, item 152, Folder 10, JBW-TU; and Army of Northern Virginia Papers, item 153, Folder 4, Tulane University; C. W. Squires to JBW, 20 May 1862, M. B. Miller to JBW, 20, 21 May 1862, B. F. Eshleman to JBW, 22 May 1862, and JBW to Col. Arch Cole, 22 May 1862, JBW-TU.

13. Morning reports of the Dixie Artillery for 4 May–25 June are found in Morning Reports: 1862–63, WAP-TU. These reports show the Dixie Artillery carried three lieutenants during this period. One lieutenant, presumably Crisp, was absent and dropped from the reports on 17 May with the note that Crisp resigned (see chapter 3, note 23). Crisp's resignation left the battery without a first lieutenant and with just two lieutenants on the muster rolls, both present in camp. Conrad was promoted to first lieutenant 24 May 1862 (a 10 July 1862 payroll receipt in WHCLA shows Conrad was paid as second lieutenant for 30 April–24 May and as first lieutenant for 24 May–30 June). That the other lieutenant was Brent is likely in that he remained with the battery until it was disbanded (WHCLA). Crisp's resignation left the battery short one lieutenant. The 29 May report contains the note "Sergt Chapman promoted to Jr. 1st lieutenant." Thereafter, three lieutenants were listed as present in the morning reports. For Edmund Chapman, see CSR-VA, Capt. Cayce's Co., Light Artillery (Purcell Artillery); CSR-VA, 10th Virginia Infantry. On 23 June the seventeen Virginia batteries in Longstreet's right wing (including the Dixie Artillery with 75 men present) ranged in strength from 50 to 130 men present for duty with an average of 77 men (*OR,* 11[3]:614–15).

14. *OR,* 51(2):572–73, 576, 11(3):609, 687; Owen, *In Camp,* 85; Wise, *Long Arm,* 1:204. In the official records, only the Washington Artillery was identified as Longstreet's reserve; the Dixie Artillery and Dearing's Lynchburg Artillery were listed as miscellaneous batteries (*OR,* 11[2]:483–89). However, Longstreet included both batteries as part of his command in a report dated 23 June (*OR,* 11[3]:614–15), and Wise, *Long Arm,* 1:204, listed both as part of Longstreet's reserve artillery under Walton's command. The morning reports of the Dixie Artillery show it camped with the Washington Artillery until 25 June (Morning Reports: 1862–63, WAP-TU). Three requisitions during June filed with Chapman's records in WCHLA, which indicate Chapman was in a different camp, were in fact filed by Captain W. H. Chapman of the Clayton Dragoons, Company F, 2d Georgia Cavalry stationed at Camp McDonald, Georgia (Poole, *Cracker Cavaliers,* 5–7).

15. *OR,* 11(3):605–6.

16. Sears, *To the Gates,* 183–89, 193–209.

17. Ibid., 210–49.

18. WHC to SFC, 18 November 1904, Daniel Papers, UVA; Isaac Hite letter, 8 July 1862, in Jessup, *Painful News,* 107–8; "How the Seven Days' Battle around Richmond Began," 95; Andrus, *Brooke,* 50. Chapman was close enough to the action to see Wayland Fuller Dunaway, 47th Virginia, form in line of battle (handwritten note in WHC's copy of Dunaway, *Reminiscences,* 29, RC).

19. Sears, *To the Gates,* 255–56, 261–62, 265–74.

20. *OR,* 11(2):775; Longstreet, *From Manassas,* 131; Longstreet, "'The Seven Days,'" 399; Owen, *In Camp,* 89.

21. Sears, *To the Gates,* 278–79, 284–89, 291–93; Burton, *Extraordinary Circumstances,* 231–35, 251–75.

22. Burton, *Extraordinary Circumstances,* 251, 277; Sears, *To the Gates,* 293.

23. Burton, *Extraordinary Circumstances,* 236–39, 249–50, 277; Sears, *To the Gates,* 282, 293–94, 296.

24. *OR,* 11(2):171–72, 255, 384, 390, 402–3, 51(1):116.

25. *OR,* 11(2):759; Hewett et al., *Supplement,* Pt. 1, 2:442; WHC to SFC, 18 November 1904, Daniel Papers, UVA; Longstreet, *From Manassas,* 134–35; Longstreet, "'The Seven Days,'" 400–401; Burton, *Extraordinary Circumstances,* 251, 267.

26. Sears, *To the Gates,* 132–33; Fox, *Regimental Losses,* 557, 561.

27. Gilham, *Manual,* 42, 387–432; Billings, *Hardtack,* 184–85.

28. Gilham, *Manual,* 368–86; Thomas, *Cannons,* 3–4; Billings, *Hardtack,* 182–83; Gibbon, *Artillerist's Manual,* 271, 404.

29. *OR,* 11(2):255, 410; Hewett et al., *Supplement,* Pt. 1, 2:444; WHC to SFC, 18 November 1904, Daniel Papers, UVA; Owen, *In Camp,* 92; E. P. Alexander, "Records of Longstreet's Corps," 68; Burton, *Extraordinary Circumstances,* 276–77.

30. Isaac Hite letter, 8 July 1862, in Jessup, *Painful News,* 107–8; Brubaker records in WCHLA; Brown, *Mosby's Fighting Parson,* 59. A requisition by WHC dated 12 August was for seven horses to replace losses incurred 30 June (WCHLA).

31. Burton, *Extraordinary Circumstances,* 277–80; Sears, *To the Gates,* 295–96; Hewett et al., *Supplement,* Pt. 1, 2:441–44; Thomas, *Career,* 17; Baldwin, *Struck Eagle,* 138, 140; Swisher, *Prince of Edisto,* 75; Fox, *Regimental Losses,* 430; Longstreet, *From Manassas,* 135.

32. Burton, *Extraordinary Circumstances,* 280–89; *OR,* 11(2):421, 762, 766, 770, 777–78, 979–80; Fox, *Regimental Losses,* 557, 563.

33. Burton, *Extraordinary Circumstances,* 290–93; Sears, *To the Gates,* 299, 302–3; *OR,* 11(2):32.

34. Burton, *Extraordinary Circumstances,* 293–98; Sears, *To the Gates,* 303–6; handwritten note in WHC's copy of Dunaway, *Reminiscences,* 32, RC.

35. Burton, *Extraordinary Circumstances,* 282–88, 294–97; Sears, *To the Gates,* 299–306.

36. Sears, *To the Gates,* 307; Burton, *Extraordinary Circumstances,* 298, 304; *OR,* 11(2):112.

37. Sears, *To the Gates,* 308–36; Burton, *Extraordinary Circumstances,* 308–9; Bohannon, "One Solid Unbroken Roar."

38. Sears, *To the Gates,* 337–42. For rainfall, see E. P. Alexander, *Military Memoirs,* 50, 358; Owen, *In Camp,* 93, 126; Sneden, *Eye of the Storm,* 47.

39. For overall losses, see Sears, *To the Gates,* 343–45. See also Burton, *Extraordinary Circumstances,* 386–87, 401–3. Burton estimated Lee's effective army to have been about 90,000 men. Longstreet's effective strength is thought to have been about

9,000 men. For Longstreet's casualties, see *OR*, 11(2):761; E. P. Alexander, "Records of Longstreet's Corps," 76.

40. *OR*, 11(2):762–63, 769, 771–72, 780–83, 785, 980–81, 11(3):689–90, 51(2):580, 585–86; Wallace, *Richmond Howitzers*, 83–84; Sifakis, *Compendium*, 20–21; Bergeron, *Guide*, 29–30; Moore, *Richmond Fayette*, 41, 63; Andrus, *Brooke*, 50, 51, 68; Stribling, "From Markham to Appomattox," 188; Owen, *In Camp*, 86–93; Bartlett, *Soldier's Story*, 95.

41. An army organization dated 23 July 1862 shows the Washington Artillery and Dixie Artillery comprised the artillery brigade for Longstreet's division (*OR*, 11[3]:648–52). For excursions to the James River, see *OR*, 11(2):924–27, 51(2):599–600; Owen, *In Camp*, 95; Andrus, *Brooke*, 51–52; Stribling, "From Markham to Appomattox," 188; WHC to SFC, 18 November 1904, Daniel Papers, UVA. Garnett commanded the artillery in David R. Jones's division, which included Toombs's brigade (*OR*, 11[2]:485, 51(2):579).

42. *OR*, 11(2):533–37, 11(3):612–13, 51(2):577–78; Wise, *Long Arm*, 1:155–58, 199–200, 236–40; E. P. Alexander, *Military Memoirs*, 90, 158–59; E. P. Alexander, *Fighting for the Confederacy*, 104–5, 112. For casualties, see *OR*, 11(2):973–84.

5. OPPORTUNELY DELIVERED FIRE

1. Hennessy, *Return to Bull Run*, 5–10.

2. Ibid.,, 22–31.

3. *OR*, 11(3):649; see records of Townsend Conrad, John Corbin, Ephraim Keyser, Isaac Kibler, Samuel Smith, and James Young, in WCHLA.

4. *OR*, 51(2):606; Morning Reports: 1862–63, WAP-TU; Alex C. Jones diary, 9–13 August 1862, and Frank Lobrano diary, 9–13 August 1862, in Civil War diaries, Tulane University; Owen, *In Camp*, 99; Bartlett, *Soldier's Story*, 109–10; CSR-LA, Washington Battalion, Artillery, record of events; Casey, *Outline*, 13; "Journals," Records of the Weather Bureau, vol. 23, NA-CP.

5. Hennessy, *Return to Bull Run*, 33–37.

6. Owen, *In Camp*, 100; G. M. Sorrel to JBW, 31 August and 5 September 1862, JBW-TU; *OR*, 12(2):546–51; Wise, *Long Arm*, 1:255, 257–59. The *OR* and Wise, *Long Arm*, list twenty-two batteries in Longstreet's command. The records of the Washington Artillery show an additional battery, Brown's Wise Artillery, which had been attached to G. T. Anderson's brigade of David R. Jones's division during the Peninsula campaign and remained with the brigade for the Manassas campaign (Moore, *Miscellaneous*, 35, 38–39). Two batteries listed in the *OR* and Wise, *Long Arm*, as miscellaneous (Huger's Norfolk and Moorman's Lynchburg) were attached to Anderson's division (Crew and Trask, *Grimes' Battery*, 55–56; Moore, *Chew's Ashby*, 68–69). See also Moore, *Richmond Fayette;* Moore, *Danville;* Andrus, *Brooke;* Weaver, *Goochland Light.*

7. Owen, *In Camp*, 99–100; *OR*, 51(2):608; G. M. Sorrel, General Orders No. 32, 15 August 1862, and G. M. Sorrel to JBW, 15, 16 August 1862, JBW-TU; Alex C. Jones diary, 16–18 August 1862 and Frank Lobrano diary, 15–18 August 1862, Civil War diaries, Tulane University; Casey, *Outline*, 13; Hennessy, *Return to Bull Run*, 42.

8. Hennessy, *Return to Bull Run*, 42–59; *OR*, 12(2):729, 51(2):608; Alex C. Jones diary, 19–20 August 1862, and Frank Lobrano diary, 19–20 August 1862, in Civil War diaries, Tulane University.

9. Hennessy, *Return to Bull Run*, 60–74.

10. *OR*, 12(2):553, 563–64, 569–70, 573–76, 51(2):610; Owen, *In Camp*, 103–10; Squires, "Autobiography," Library of Congress; G. M. Sorrel to JBW, 23 August 1862, JBW-TU; Longstreet, "Our March against Pope," 516; Hennessy, "On the Rappahannock," 169–77, Manassas National Battlefield Park; Hennessy, *Return to Bull Run*, 85; Andrus, *Brooke*, 53–54, 70–71.

11. Bartlett, *Soldier's Story,* 111.

12. For Dixie Artillery wounded, see Owen, *In Camp,* 109; Squires, "Autobiography," Library of Congress; CSR-VA, Capt. Cayce's Co., Light Artillery (Purcell Artillery); Confederate Rosters 18:67–71, Library of Virginia. For Squires's company, see also Alex C. Jones diary, 23 August 1862 and Frank Lobrano diary, 23 August 1862, Civil War diaries, Tulane University.

13. Hennessy, *Return to Bull Run,* 85–86; *OR,* 12(2):639–40.

14. Hennessy, *Return to Bull Run,* 81–92; Owen, *In Camp,* 107–9.

15. Hennessy, *Return to Bull Run,* 92–95, 103, 107; Wise, *Long Arm,* 1:260–61.

16. Hennessy, *Return to Bull Run,* 96–101, 106–7, 111–47.

17. Ibid., 108, 153–61; Owen, *In Camp,* 110–12; Frank Lobrano diary, 26–29 August 1862, Civil War diaries, Tulane University.

18. Hennessy, *Return to Bull Run,* 168–93, 200–223.

19. Ibid., 224–30; Hennessy, *Second Manassas,* 76, 110–14; *OR,* 12(2):556, 564–65, 607; Owen, *In Camp,* 113–15; Andrus, *Brooke,* 55, 72; Longstreet, "Our March against Pope," 518; Longstreet, *From Manassas,* 180; Alex C. Jones diary, 29 August 1862, in Civil War diaries, Tulane University.

20. Owen, *In Camp,* 116–18; *OR,* 12(2):570–71, 607; Squires, "Autobiography," Library of Congress; M. B. Miller to JBW, 29 August 1862, JBW-TU; W. M. Owen to G. M. Sorrel, 26 November 1862, BWAC-TU; Hennessy, *Return to Bull Run,* 229; Hennessy, *Second Manassas,* 134–37, 162–64.

21. "Letter of Captain W. K. Bachman," *Charleston (S.C.) Daily Courier,* 17 September 1862.

22. Hennessy, *Return to Bull Run,* 243–86.

23. Ibid., 309–24.

24. Ibid., 333–38; *OR,* 12(2): 368.

25. *OR,* 12(2):472–73; Hennessy, *Return to Bull Run,* 338.

26. *OR,* 12(2): 368, 471–81; Hennessy, *Second Manassas,* 286–91, 294–98; Hennessy, *Return to Bull Run,* 341, 354.

27. Hennessy, *Return to Bull Run,* 339–61; *OR,* 12(2): 577–78.

28. The primary source of information on the Dixie Artillery at Manassas is a 27 August 1887 letter from Chapman to Longstreet and Longstreet's reply the next day. Chapman published these letters shortly thereafter ("The Three Guns Which Turned the Tide of Battle at Bull Run," *Atlanta Constitution,* 11 September 1887). These letters were published again in 1904 ("Noted Guns at Manassas," *Richmond Times-Dispatch,* 4 September 1904) and in the *Southern Historical Society Papers* in 1914 (Chapman, "Dixie Battery at the Second Battle of Manassas"). Some of this material is repeated in WHC to SFC, 18 November 1904, and SFC to John W. Daniel, 25 November 1904, Daniel Papers, UVA. Longstreet wrote that the battery had four guns (Longstreet, "Our March against Pope," 521). It is more likely that Chapman had three guns. An inspection of batteries on 5 September found the Dixie Artillery with three guns (G. M. Sorrel to JBW, 5 September 1862, JBW-TU). The 1887 newspaper article, written with Chapman's influence, claimed the battery had three guns. That two of these were a Napoleon and a 3-inch rifle is certain in that these guns saw action on 23 August at Rappahannock Station and on 19 September at Boteler's Ford (*OR,* 12[2]:569, 573, 19[1]:831). That the third gun was a 6-pounder is speculative, but the Dixie Artillery had four 6-pounders in May (*OR,* 51[2]:559), and these guns were still the most common artillery piece in September (*OR,* 19[1]:836–37). See also Hennessy, *Second Manassas,* 251, 305; Hennessy, *Return to Bull Run,* 350.

29. SFC to John W. Daniel, 25 November 1904, Daniel Papers, UVA.

30. *OR*, 12(2):476–77, 599; WHC to A. L. Henry, 26 March 1923, RC (the Manassas National Battlefield Library has a copy of this letter).

31. WHC to A. L. Henry, 26 March 1923, RC; *OR*, 12(2):479; Hennessy, *Return to Bull Run*, 337, 351–52.

32. S. D. Lee, "Second Battle of Manassas," 69.

33. Longstreet, *From Manassas*, 188; *OR*, 12(2):259, 471–81. Casualties were reported for the entire campaign, but Porter's men were engaged only on the afternoon of 30 August, and regimental reports indicated the casualties occurred during the assault.

34. Hennessy, *Return to Bull Run*, 362–438.

35. Ibid., 365, 383, 391, 400, 402, 404, 415, 420; Hennessy, *Second Manassas*, 337–39, 367, 371–72, 396–99, 433–35. See also *OR*, 12(2):570–73, 575–76, 607–8, 640, 750–51; Andrus, *Brooke*, 55–57, 72–73; Stribling, "From Markham to Appomattox," 190–91; "Letter of Captain W. K. Bachman," *Charleston (S.C.) Daily Courier*, 17 September 1862. For Dixie Artillery, see Chapman, "Dixie Battery at the Second Battle of Manassas," 193; WHC to A. L. Henry, 26 March 1923, RC; Hennessy, *Second Manassas*, 334, 362, 394, 433; *OR*, 12(2):604.

36. Hennessy, *Return to Bull Run*, 441; Livermore, *Numbers and Losses*, 88–89; *OR*, 12(2):249–62, 560–62, 568, 810–14; CSR-VA, 33rd Virginia Infantry. For cannon fire and rainfall, see chapter 4, note 38.

37. *OR*, 12(2):557, 565, 599, 604; Longstreet, *From Manassas*, 186–88; Longstreet, "Our March against Pope," 520–21; Longstreet, "General Longstreet's Second Paper on Gettysburg," 267; S. D. Lee, "The Second Battle of Manassas: A Reply to General Longstreet"; Longstreet, "The Artillery at Second Manassas: General Longstreet's Reply"; S. D. Lee, "The Artillery at Second Manassas: Rejoinder."

38. Wise, *Long Arm*, 1:278–79; Moore, *Richmond Fayette*, 43; Andrus, *Brooke*, 58, 73; Stribling, "From Markham to Appomattox," 191.

39. *OR*, 19(1):803–10; WHC to SFC, 18 November 1904, Daniel Papers, UVA. For the armament, see *OR*, 19(1):831, 836–37; Wise, *Long Arm*, 1:284–86.

40. Sears, *Landscape Turned Red*, 294, 296; *OR*, 19(1):843–51; Wise, *Long Arm*, 1:296–312, 321–26. Chapman's description of the march is similar to that of McLaw's. See WHC to SFC, 18 November 1904, Daniel Papers, UVA; *OR*, 19(1):857.

41. *OR*, 19(1):830–35; Wise, *Long Arm*, 1:318–20; Lee, *Memoirs*, 213–15.

42. WHC to SFC, 18 November 1904, and SFC to John W. Daniel, 25 November 1904, Daniel Papers, UVA.

43. *OR*, 19(1):830–35.

44. WHC to SFC, 18 November 1904, Daniel Papers, UVA; *OR*, 19(2):649.

45. Wise, *Long Arm*, 1:110, 327–32; *OR*, ser. 4, 2:153; *OR*, 19(2):642–43.

46. E. P. Alexander, "Confederate Artillery Service." For another reorganization proposed by Pendleton in February 1863 and enacted shortly thereafter, see *OR*, 25(2):614–19, 625–26, 728–30.

47. *OR*, 19(2):646–54; Wise, *Long Arm*, 1:332–39.

48. WHC to SFC, 18 November 1904, Daniel Papers, UVA; Stribling, "From Markham to Appomattox," 191.

49. William Pegram to "Jennie," 7, 24 October 1862, Pegram-Johnson-McIntosh family papers, VHS; Carmichael, *Purcell*, 31–32; Carmichael, *Lee's Young Artillerist*, 69–71.

50. WHC to SFC, 18 November 1904, Daniel Papers, UVA. For Walton's conflict with Pendleton during the Peninsula campaign, see *OR*, 51(2):546–47, 572–73, 576; 11(3):609, 687; Wise, *Long Arm*, 1:146. For an overview of events leading to Walton's dismissal, see Wise, *Long Arm*, 2:704, 754–56, 848–54. Pendleton's views were expressed

in a reorganization of the artillery proposed on 11 February 1863 (*OR*, 25[2]:616) and a 20 November 1863 reorganization (*OR*, 29[2]:840–41; Wise, *Long Arm*, 2:719–25). For Alexander's perspective, see E. P. Alexander, *Fighting for the Confederacy*, 167–69, 235–66; E. P. Alexander to James Longstreet, 5 February 1878, in Hewett et al., *Supplement*, Pt. 1, 5:363–64. For Walton, see Walton, "Letter from Colonel J. B. Walton" (see also Longstreet, "Letter from General Longstreet," and Longstreet, "General Longstreet's Second Paper on Gettysburg," 269); Owen, *In Camp*, 338–44; Wise, *Long Arm*, 2:848, 853–54; *OR*, 29(2):699. Walton's position in the army was a concern of Lee throughout the first half of 1864 (*OR*, 32(2):567, 32(3):595, 36(3):828). Walton was fifty years old when he resigned on 8 July 1864 (Adjutant and Inspector General's Office Special Orders No. 159, JBW-TU; see also Krick, *Lee's Colonels*, 360; CSR-LA, Washington Battalion, Artillery).

51. Livermore, *Numbers and Losses*, 80–93.

6. A THRILLING SENSATION

1. See WHC, SFC, and Daniel Brubaker records in WCHLA. Payroll receipts dated 20 December 1862 stated that WHC and SFC were late of the Dixie Artillery and on duty in Richmond with Col. Shields. Other records place WHC in Warrenton during January and February. WHC signed Brubaker's discharge paper at Luray on 15 January 1863. See also Scott, *Partisan Life*, 159, 185; SFC, "Memories of 'Mosby's Men,'" *Religious Herald*, 9, 16 January 1902; Brown, *Mosby's Fighting Parson*, 89–90.

2. *OR*, ser. 4, 1:1081, 1095, 1099, 1152, 2:5–6, 160, 171–72; Wallace, *Richmond Howitzers*, 4, 13, 14, 133; Shields, "Old Camp Lee."

3. *OR*, ser. 4, 2:171; *OR*, 19(1):142–43, 19(2):589–90.

4. Mosby, *Mosby's War Reminiscences*, 27–31; Scott, *Partisan Life*, 19–24; Ramage, *Gray Ghost*, 36–59.

5. *OR*, 25(1):5–6; Scott, *Partisan Life*, 24–29; Ramage, *Gray Ghost*, 58–61.

6. *OR*, 25(1):37–38, 25(2):649; Scott, *Partisan Life*, 34–36; Ramage, *Gray Ghost*, 61–62.

7. *OR*, 25(1):41–42, 1121; Scott, *Partisan Life*, 40–42; Mosby, *Mosby's War Reminiscences*, 47–61; Ramage, *Gray Ghost*, 62–63.

8. *OR*, 25(1):43–44, 1121–22, 25(2):856; Scott, *Partisan Life*, 43–50; Williamson, *Mosby's Rangers*, 2d ed., 33–46; Ramage, *Gray Ghost*, 63–74.

9. *OR*, 25(1):65–66, 25(2):667; Scott, *Partisan Life*, 54–57; Mosby, *Mosby's War Reminiscences*, 69–77; Williamson, *Mosby's Rangers*, 2d ed., 48–49; Ramage, *Gray Ghost*, 74–75.

10. Mosby, *Mosby's War Reminiscences*, 41–45, 79.

11. *OR*, 25(2):149–50, 183, 588; Ramage, *Gray Ghost*, 72–73; Jones, *Ranger Mosby*, 89.

12. *OR*, 25(2):664, 667, 678–79, 856–58, 51(2):688; Ramage, *Gray Ghost*, 60, 73; Scott, *Partisan Life*, 27; Mitchell, *Letters*, 29; Jones, *Ranger Mosby*, 78.

13. SFC, "Memories of 'Mosby's Men,'" *Religious Herald*, 9 January, 6 February 1902; Scott, *Partisan Life*, 159, 185; Brown, *Mosby's Fighting Parson*, 92–93; Wert, *Mosby's Rangers*, 32; Ramage, *Gray Ghost*, 1.

14. *OR*, 25(1):70–72; Scott, *Partisan Life*, 60–62; Mosby, *Mosby's War Reminiscences*, 84–94; Williamson, *Mosby's Rangers*, 2d ed., 50–51; Ramage, *Gray Ghost*, 75–76. For the Chapmans, see SFC, "Memories of 'Mosby's Men'" *Religious Herald*, 9, 16 January 1902; WHC to W. Sam Burnley, 18 November 1911, Burnley Papers, UVA; JSM to WHC, 6 November 1887, JSM-DU; Brown, *Mosby's Fighting Parson*, 102–4.

15. SFC, "Memories of 'Mosby's Men,'" *Religious Herald*, 9 January 1902.

16. Ibid.

17. Scott, *Partisan Life,* 59, 62; Mosby, *Mosby's War Reminiscences,* 30, 32, 54, 62–63, 68, 75, 78, 83–84, 86–87, 98–100, 102; Ramage, *Gray Ghost,* 77–78; Keen and Mewborn, *43rd Battalion,* 291, 330, 332, 337, 350, 377; SFC, "Memories of 'Mosby's Men,'" *Religious Herald,* 9 January 1902.

18. Scott, *Partisan Life,* 63–64; Mosby, *Mosby's War Reminiscences,* 102–4; Williamson, *Mosby's Rangers,* 2d ed., 52; SFC, "Memories of 'Mosby's Men,'" *Religious Herald,* 16 January 1902; WHC to Mrs. A. M. Crane, 25 June 1910, RC; Ramage, *Gray Ghost,* 78.

19. Scott, *Partisan Life,* 64–65; Mosby, *Mosby's War Reminiscences,* 104; Williamson, *Mosby's Rangers,* 2d ed., 52; Ramage, *Gray Ghost,* 80.

20. Scott, *Partisan Life,* 64–66; Mosby, *Mosby's War Reminiscences,* 104–5; Ramage, *Gray Ghost,* 78–81.

21. WHC to Mrs. A. M. Crane, 25 June 1910, RC; SFC, "Memories of 'Mosby's Men,'" *Religious Herald,* 16 January 1902; Munson, *Reminiscences,* 59; "Journals," Records of the Weather Bureau, vol. 24, NA-CP.

22. WHC to Mrs. A. M. Crane, 25 June 1910, RC; Scott, *Partisan Life,* 66–67; Mosby, *Mosby's War Reminiscences,* 106–7; Williamson, *Mosby's Rangers,* 2d ed., 54, 463; Munson, *Reminiscences,* 59; Ramage, *Gray Ghost,* 81.

23. Scott, *Partisan Life,* 67–68; Mosby, *Mosby's War Reminiscences,* 107–10; Williamson, *Mosby's Rangers,* 2d ed., 54; Ramage, *Gray Ghost,* 82.

24. Scott, *Partisan Life,* 68; WHC to Mrs. A. M. Crane, 25 June 1910, RC; SFC, "Memories of 'Mosby's Men'" *Religious Herald,* 16 January 1902.

25. *OR,* 25(1):72–73; Mosby, *Mosby's War Reminiscences,* 110; Ramage, *Gray Ghost,* 81–83; SFC, "Memories of 'Mosby's Men,'" *Religious Herald,* 16 January 1902.

26. *OR,* 25(1):77–78; Mosby, *Mosby's War Reminiscences,* 107; Ramage, *Gray Ghost,* 83.

27. WHC to Mrs. A. M. Crane, 25 June 1910, RC.

28. Ibid.; Munson, *Reminiscences,* 59.

29. *OR,* 25(1):80, 25(2):183; Wert, *Mosby's Rangers,* 55.

30. McPherson, *Battle Cry,* 639.

31. *OR,* 25(2):860; Scott, *Partisan Life,* 77–83; Mosby, *Mosby's War Reminiscences,* 117–26; Ramage, *Gray Ghost,* 167–69.

32. Scott, *Partisan Life,* 84; Mosby, *Mosby's War Reminiscences,* 130–31, 135; SFC, "Memories of 'Mosby's Men,'" *Religious Herald,* 23 January 1902; Williamson, *Mosby's Rangers,* 2d ed., 56.

33. *OR,* 25(1):1104–7, 25(2):861; Scott, *Partisan Life,* 85–86; Mosby, *Mosby's War Reminiscences,* 132–33; Williamson, *Mosby's Rangers,* 2d ed., 56–57.

34. Scott, *Partisan Life,* 85–86; Mosby, *Mosby's War Reminiscences,* 132–33; Williamson, *Mosby's Rangers,* 2d ed., 57; SFC, "Memories of 'Mosby's Men,'" *Religious Herald,* 23 January 1902; JSM to WHC, 6 November 1887, JSM-DU.

35. *OR,* 25(1):1104–7, 25(2):861; Scott, *Partisan Life,* 86–88; Mosby, *Mosby's War Reminiscences,* 133–35; Williamson, *Mosby's Rangers,* 2d ed., 57–58; SFC, "Memories of 'Mosby's Men'" *Religious Herald,* 23 January 1902; Munson, *Reminiscences,* 66–67.

36. *OR,* 25(1):1104–7.

37. *OR,* 25(2):862; Scott, *Partisan Life,* 92; Mosby, *Mosby's War Reminiscences,* 139, 142–43; Williamson, *Mosby's Rangers,* 2d ed., 63–64; Munson, *Reminiscences,* 68; Ramage, *Gray Ghost,* 85–86. WHC's presence for this raid cannot be confirmed.

38. Scott, *Partisan Life,* 92; Mosby, *Mosby's War Reminiscences,* 144; Williamson, *Mosby's Rangers,* 2d ed., 64–65; SFC, "Memories of 'Mosby's Men'" *Religious Herald,* 6 February 1902; Ramage, *Gray Ghost,* 86.

39. *OR,* 25(1):1117–19, 51(1):1042; Scott, *Partisan Life,* 94; Mosby, *Mosby's War Reminiscences,* 146–48; Williamson, *Mosby's Rangers,* 2d ed., 65; Munson, *Reminiscences,* 71–73; Ramage, *Gray Ghost,* 86–87.

40. Scott, *Partisan Life,* 95; Mosby, *Mosby's War Reminiscences,* 146, 148; Williamson, *Mosby's Rangers,* 2d ed., 65; SFC, "Memories of 'Mosby's Men'" *Religious Herald,* 6 February 1902; Ramage, *Gray Ghost,* 87–88.

41. *OR,* 25(1):1117–19; Scott, *Partisan Life,* 95; Mosby, *Mosby's War Reminiscences,* 148–51, 153; Williamson, *Mosby's Rangers,* 2d ed., 65–67; SFC, "Memories of 'Mosby's Men'" *Religious Herald,* 6 February 1902; Munson, *Reminiscences,* 73–74; Ramage, *Gray Ghost,* 88–89.

42. *OR,* 18:334–35; SFC, "Memories of 'Mosby's Men'" *Religious Herald,* 6, 27 February 1902; Brown, *Mosby's Fighting Parson,* 114, 132–35.

7. A FASCINATING LIFE

1. WHC, "Talk Made at Meeting of Men's Bible Class at Grace Church, Richmond," 20 February 1912, RC.

2. Jones, *Ranger Mosby,* viii–ix; Wert, *Mosby's Rangers,* 37–39, 116. Several towns have changed names. Salem is now called Marshall; Piedmont is Delaplane; Rector's Cross Roads is Atoka; Snickersville is Bluemont.

3. Mosby, *Mosby's War Reminiscences,* 43–44, 79.

4. Munson, *Reminiscences,* 8–9; J. H. Alexander, *Mosby's Men,* 20, 24; Wert, *Mosby's Rangers,* 75; Ramage, *Gray Ghost,* 97.

5. *OR,* ser. 4, 1:1094–95, 2:498–99; *OR,* 33:1081–82; Williamson, *Mosby's Rangers,* 2d ed., 19–20; J. H. Alexander, *Mosby's Men,* 29; Wert, *Mosby's Rangers,* 69–71.

6. *OR,* ser. 4, 3:194; *OR,* 25(2):857–58, 33:1113, 1252–53; Ramage, *Gray Ghost,* 73, 132–36.

7. Mosby, *Mosby's War Reminiscences,* 45, 139; Wert, *Mosby's Rangers,* 75.

8. Mosby, *Mosby's War Reminiscences,* 49, 64–65; Scott, *Partisan Life,* 30.

9. Williamson, *Mosby's Rangers,* 2d ed., 25; Munson, *Reminiscences,* 4, 21, 39; Crawford, *Mosby and His Men,* 14; Monteiro, *War Reminiscences,* 20, 33; Richards, "Mosby's 'Partizan Rangers,'"104.

10. Scott, *Partisan Life,* 59, 392–93; Williamson, *Mosby's Rangers,* 2d ed., 22–23; Richards, "Mosby's 'Partizan Rangers,'" 113; Munson, *Reminiscences,* 37, 227; Wert, *Mosby's Rangers,* 84; Ramage, *Gray Ghost,* 105–8.

11. Munson, *Reminiscences,* 208; Williamson, *Mosby's Rangers,* 2d ed., 95, 107.

12. Munson, *Reminiscences,* 25–27, 111; Monteiro, *War Reminiscences,* 67–70; Wert, *Mosby's Rangers,* 76, 110.

13. *OR,* 27(2):992, 29(2):652–53; Crawford, *Mosby and His Men,* 154–55; Ramage, *Gray Ghost,* 105, 111–12.

14. Scott, *Partisan Life,* 395; Williamson, *Mosby's Rangers,* 2d ed., 97; Munson, *Reminiscences,* 10, 22, 37; Richards, "Mosby's 'Partizan Rangers,'" 104, 108; J. H. Alexander, *Mosby's Men,* 27, 44–45; Monteiro, *War Reminiscences,* 95–96; Wert, *Mosby's Rangers,* 82; Ramage, *Gray Ghost,* 97, 98, 104.

15. Munson, *Reminiscences,* 15–17; Williamson, *Mosby's Rangers,* 2d ed., 14–15, 96–97; Grant, *Personal Memoirs,* 2:142; Wert, *Mosby's Rangers,* 31–32, 77.

16. Mosby, *Mosby's War Reminiscences,* 157; Monteiro, *War Reminiscences,* 94–95.

17. Richards, "Mosby's 'Partizan Rangers,'" 114; Williamson, *Mosby's Rangers,* 2d ed., 21; Munson, *Reminiscences,* 30; Mosby, *Mosby's War Reminiscences,* 45.

18. Mosby, *Mosby's War Reminiscences,* 92, 107, 138; Mosby, *Memoirs,* 284–86; Richards, "Mosby's 'Partizan Rangers,'" 113–14; Munson, *Reminiscences,* 22–25; Williamson,

Mosby's Rangers, 2d ed., 21; J. H. Alexander, *Mosby's Men,* 21; Wert, *Mosby's Rangers,* 81; Ramage, *Gray Ghost,* 102–3.

19. Mosby, *Mosby's War Reminiscences,* 163; Richards, "Mosby's 'Partizan Rangers,'" 113, 115; Munson, *Reminiscences,* 31, 34; J. H. Alexander, *Mosby's Men,* 15; Monteiro, *War Reminiscences,* 45, 48; Wert, *Mosby's Rangers,* 80.

20. Mosby, *Mosby's War Reminiscences,* 89–90; Munson, *Reminiscences,* 23; Monteiro, *War Reminiscences,* 123; J. H. Alexander, *Mosby's Men,* 17–19; Wert, *Mosby's Rangers,* 83–84; Ramage, *Gray Ghost,* 102–3.

21. Munson, *Reminiscences,* 79–80, 158.

22. Mosby, *Mosby's War Reminiscences,* 44–45; Scott, *Partisan Life,* 394–95; Williamson, *Mosby's Rangers,* 2d ed., 18–19, 60; Munson, *Reminiscences,* 30; Richards, "Mosby's 'Partizan Rangers,'" 106–7; Monteiro, *War Reminiscences,* 67; J. H. Alexander, *Mosby's Men,* 29; Crawford, *Mosby and His Men,* 179; Hunter, *Women,* 62–63, 199–205; Wert, *Mosby's Rangers,* 79, 121; Ramage, *Gray Ghost,* 99, 101–2.

23. Cochran recollections, 4 April 1863, in VHS; Dulany diary, 1, 7, 11 May 1863, VHS; Wert, *Mosby's Rangers,* 125–26.

24. *OR,* 33:365; Hunter, *Women,* 102–3.

25. Mosby, *Mosby's War Reminiscences,* 41–42; Cochran recollections, 26 September 1864, VHS; Richards, "Mosby's 'Partizan Rangers,'" 106; Monteiro, *War Reminiscences,* 100; Wert, *Mosby's Rangers,* 116–17; Ramage, *Gray Ghost,* 100–101.

26. Scott, *Partisan Life,* 398–99; Williamson, *Mosby's Rangers,* 2d ed., 105; Richards, "Mosby's 'Partizan Rangers,'" 107; Munson, *Reminiscences,* 21–22, 28; Monteiro, *War Reminiscences,* 93–94; Wert, *Mosby's Rangers,* 124–25; Ramage, *Gray Ghost,* 100; *OR,* 33:9, 1252.

27. Third Pennsylvania Cavalry Association, *History,* 330; Newhall, *Memoir,* 124–25; Hoadley, *Memorial,* 149–50; Ramage, *Gray Ghost,* 165–67, 175–77.

28. Newhall, *Memoir,* 131; Taylor, *With Sheridan up the Valley,* 77.

29. Melville, *Battle-Pieces,* 187; Ramage, *Gray Ghost,* 174–75.

30. Melville, *Battle-Pieces,* 188.

31. Humphreys, *Field, Camp, Hospital,* 29; Melville, *Battle-Pieces,* 197.

32. Melville, *Battle-Pieces,* 198.

33. Humphreys, *Field, Camp, Hospital,* 33; Melville, *Battle-Pieces,* 222.

34. *OR,* 29(2):397.

35. Third Pennsylvania Cavalry Association, *History,* 339; *OR,* 43(1):672.

36. *OR,* 37(2):387–90.

37. Emerson, *Life and Letters,* 35, 313, 353.

8. EFFICIENT SERVICES

1. Scott, *Partisan Life,* 97, 141–42; Williamson, *Mosby's Rangers,* 2d ed., 69, 94; Keen and Mewborn, *43rd Battalion,* 369–70.

2. Scott, *Partisan Life,* 152; Keen and Mewborn, *43rd Battalion,* 84.

3. Scott, *Partisan Life,* 152–53; Wert, *Mosby's Rangers,* 101–2; Keen and Mewborn, *43rd Battalion,* 84–85.

4. *OR,* 29(1):492–93, 29(2):344–45, 350, 931; Williamson, *Mosby's Rangers,* 2d ed., 94–103; Ramage, *Gray Ghost,* 120–21. Freeman, *R. E. Lee,* 3:169–94, provides an overview of the campaign.

5. *OR,* 29(1):495, 29(2):392; Scott, *Partisan Life,* 150; Williamson, *Mosby's Rangers,* 2d ed., 103–4; Ramage, *Gray Ghost,* 121–22.

6. Williamson, *Mosby's Rangers,* 2d ed., 105; Scott, *Partisan Life,* 159–60.

7. Freeman, *R. E. Lee,* 3:194–202.

8. *OR,* 29(1):552; Ramage, *Gray Ghost,* 122–23.

9. *OR,* 29(1):652, 658, 659–60; Williamson, *Mosby's Rangers,* 2d ed., 107–11; Ramage, *Gray Ghost,* 221. WHC's participation in a raid at Bealeton Station is mentioned in JJC, n.d., "Membership Application, United Daughters of the Confederacy," HC.

10. *OR,* 29(1):826; Scott, *Partisan Life,* 157–58; Williamson, *Mosby's Rangers,* 2d ed., 111–14; Ramage, *Gray Ghost,* 123–24; "Journals," Records of the Weather Bureau, vol. 24, NA-CP.

11. Scott, *Partisan Life,* 159–60; Wert, *Mosby's Rangers,* 109–10; Keen and Mewborn, *43rd Battalion,* 360. For relations with Richards, see JSM to SFC, 4 February 1915, in Brown, *Take Sides,* 139.

12. SFC, "Memories of 'Mosby's Men'" *Religious Herald,* 27 February 1902; Robert von Massow to WHC, 21 March 1910, RC.

13. I am indebted to Max Roha and Mary Chapman Roha (a granddaughter of William H. and Josephine Jeffries Chapman) for providing their genealogy of Josie. The documentation of their genealogy is the source of the published material referenced here. Additional genealogy is from Archer Ellis Hansen and her mother, Esther Foote Brooking Ellis (another granddaughter of the Chapmans). That genealogy was prepared in part by Josie, who was researching her father's family for membership in the Daughters of the American Revolution and Society of Colonial Dames (Blackwell, *Blackwell Genealogy,* 55–58). The Roha genealogy also uses the Ellis Hansen genealogy. The primary published sources are Blackwell, *Blackwell Genealogy;* Hardy, *Colonial Families;* and Hayden, *Virginia Genealogies.* Some family genealogies spell the name *McCray.* John Gott, a Fauquier County historian, stated the correct spelling is *Macrae* (John K. Gott to Archer Ellis Hansen, 30 June 1992, HC). For a description of Edge Hill, see Writers' Program (U.S.), *Old Homes,* 337–38; Evans and Moyer, *Mosby's Confederacy,* 17–18.

14. Seventh U.S. Census (1850), Population Schedules, Fauquier County, Va., 297, Slave Schedules, Fauquier County, Va., 446–47; Writers' Program (U.S.), *Old Homes,* 269, 421, 423–24; Blackwell, *Blackwell Genealogy,* 86–87.

15. Eighth U.S. Census (1860), Population Schedules, Fauquier County, Va., 14, Slave Schedules, Fauquier County, Va., 4; Wert, *Mosby's Rangers,* 119.

16. For Joseph and Eustace Jeffries, see Eighth U.S. Census (1860), Nonpopulation Census Schedules, Fauquier County, Va., roll 6, 292–93; Writers' Program (U.S.), *Old Homes,* 335–36, 589; Evans and Moyer, *Mosby's Confederacy,* 17; Blackwell, *Blackwell Genealogy,* 85–87. For Enoch Jeffries, see Seventh U.S. Census (1850), Population Schedules, Fauquier County, Va., 238, Slave Schedules, Fauquier County, Va., 386; Eighth U.S. Census (1860), Population Schedules, Fauquier County, Va., 196; Writers' Program (U.S.), *Old Homes,* 589.

17. Seventh U.S. Census (1850), Population Schedules, Fauquier County, Va., 322, Slave Schedules, Fauquier County, Va., 476–77; Nonpopulation Census Schedules, Fauquier County, Va., roll 2, 231–32. For information on the Macrae family, see John K. Gott to Archer Ellis Hansen, 30 June 1992, HC.

18. Eighth U.S. Census (1860), Population Schedules, Fauquier County, Va., 14, Slave Schedules, Fauquier County, Va., 4; Nonpopulation Census Schedules, Fauquier County, Va., roll 6, 282–83; Mosby Heritage Area Map, by Eugene M. Scheel, John Singleton Mosby Heritage Area, Inc. Lack of an arm is mentioned in Robert von Massow to WHC, 21 March 1910, RC.

19. Eighth U.S. Census (1860), Population Schedules, Fauquier County, Va., 14, Slave Schedules, Fauquier County, Va., 4.

20. WHC to JJC, 18 June 1908, FC.

21. Scott, *Partisan Life,* 154–55; Munson, *Reminiscences,* 87; newspaper clipping, JSMSB-UVA, 2:88.

22. Baird, *Journals,* 173–74; Wert, *Mosby's Rangers,* 123–24.

23. Genealogy was featured prominently in her obituaries. See "Funeral Service for Mrs. Chapman Is Held," *Greensboro Daily News,* 3 January 1928; "In Memoriam: Mrs. William Henry Chapman," *Southern Churchman,* 17 March 1928.

9. MUCH OBLIGED TO YOU

1. "Journals," Records of the Weather Bureau, vols. 24 and 25, NA-CP; Ramage, *Gray Ghost,* 124.

2. *OR,* 33:9, 12–15; Scott, *Partisan Life,* 177–78; Williamson, *Mosby's Rangers,* 2d ed., 118–23; Ramage, *Gray Ghost,* 170.

3. *OR,* 33:15; Scott, *Partisan Life,* 178; Ramage, *Gray Ghost,* 125–26.

4. *OR,* 33:15; Scott, *Partisan Life,* 179; Williamson, *Mosby's Rangers,* 2d ed., 125–26, 485–87 (for the original manuscript, see WHC, "Account of the Attack on Cole's Camp," in RC,); Ramage, *Gray Ghost,* 126; Brown, *Mosby's Fighting Parson,* 142.

5. *OR,* 33:15, 17; Scott, *Partisan Life,* 179–80; Williamson, *Mosby's Rangers,* 2d ed., 126, 127, 131, 485–87; Ramage, *Gray Ghost,* 126–27.

6. *OR,* 33:16–18; Scott, *Partisan Life,* 180; Williamson, *Mosby's Rangers,* 2d ed., 126; Ramage, *Gray Ghost,* 127.

7. *OR,* 33:16; Williamson, *Mosby's Rangers,* 2d ed., 126–28; Ramage, *Gray Ghost,* 127–28.

8. Williamson, *Mosby's Rangers,* 2d ed., 127, 485–87 (and also WHC, "Account of the Attack on Cole's Camp," RC); newspaper clipping, JSMSB-UVA, 2:89; Brown, *Mosby's Fighting Parson,* 143–44; Scott, *Partisan Life,* 180; Jones, *Ranger Mosby,* 169–70; Wert, *Mosby's Rangers,* 135.

9. WHC, "Account of the Attack on Cole's Camp," RC.

10. *OR,* 33:16–18, 1113; Ramage, *Gray Ghost,* 128–29. Horace Mewborn, in a personal communication, mentioned that he believes three rangers were mortally wounded and four were wounded.

11. *OR,* 33:16; Williamson, *Mosby's Rangers,* 2d ed., 129.

12. Williamson, *Mosby's Rangers,* 2d ed., 132, 487; Crawford, *Mosby and His Men,* 164; Scott, *Partisan Life,* 182; Wert, *Mosby's Rangers,* 136–37.

13. Scott, *Partisan Life,* 182–83; newspaper clipping, JSMSB-UVA, 2:88; *OR,* 33:16.

14. Scott, *Partisan Life,* 183; newspaper clipping, JSMSB-UVA, 2:88.

15. Scott, *Partisan Life,* 183–84; Williamson, *Mosby's Rangers,* 2d ed., 133; Jones, *Ranger Mosby,* 175; Wert, *Mosby's Rangers,* 138.

16. WHC to SFC, 5 February 1864, in RC; Brown, *Mosby's Fighting Parson,* 146.

17. *OR,* 33:155–56, 411, 568, 571; Williamson, *Mosby's Rangers,* 2d ed., 136; Wert, *Mosby's Rangers,* 140–41; Ramage, *Gray Ghost,* 222.

18. *OR,* 33:155–56, 570; Wert, *Mosby's Rangers,* 141–42; Ramage, *Gray Ghost,* 223; "Journals," Records of the Weather Bureau, vol. 25, NA-CP.

19. SFC, "Memories of 'Mosby's Men'" *Religious Herald,* 27 February 1902; Brown, *Mosby's Fighting Parson,* 146; Williamson, *Mosby's Rangers,* 2d ed., 134–35; Scott, *Partisan Life,* 185.

20. *OR,* 33:156; Williamson, *Mosby's Rangers,* 2d ed., 135–37; Scott, *Partisan Life,* 184.

21. *OR,* 33:157; Scott, *Partisan Life,* 197–98; Williamson, *Mosby's Rangers,* 2d ed., 137–38; Munson, *Reminiscences,* 80–82.

22. *OR,* 33:157; Scott, *Partisan Life,* 198–99; Williamson, *Mosby's Rangers,* 2d ed., 138–39; SFC, "Memories of 'Mosby's Men'" *Religious Herald,* 27 February 1902.

23. *OR,* 33:157; Scott, *Partisan Life,* 199; Williamson, *Mosby's Rangers,* 2d ed., 139; SFC, "Memories of 'Mosby's Men'" *Religious Herald,* 27 February 1902.

24. *OR,* 33:157; Williamson, *Mosby's Rangers,* 2d ed., 140; Munson, *Reminiscences,* 83; Keen and Mewborn, *43rd Battalion,* 344.

25. *OR,* 33:159; Scott, *Partisan Life,* 199–200, 203; Williamson, *Mosby's Rangers,* 2d ed., 141, 145.

26. *OR,* 33:159; Scott, *Partisan Life,* 200–201; Munson, *Reminiscences,* 84.

27. *OR,* 33:159–60; Scott, *Partisan Life,* 201; Williamson, *Mosby's Rangers,* 2d ed., 141–42; Ramage, *Gray Ghost,* 138.

28. Scott, *Partisan Life,* 201–2; Williamson, *Mosby's Rangers,* 2d ed., 142–43; Munson, *Reminiscences,* 84–85; SFC, "Memories of 'Mosby's Men'" *Religious Herald,* 20 March 1902; Ramage, *Gray Ghost,* 138.

29. Scott, *Partisan Life,* 202; Williamson, *Mosby's Rangers,* 2d ed., 143–44; Munson, *Reminiscences,* 85; Ramage, *Gray Ghost,* 138–39.

30. *OR,* 33:160; Scott, *Partisan Life,* 202; Williamson, *Mosby's Rangers,* 2d ed., 144, 145; Munson, *Reminiscences,* 85–87; Ramage, *Gray Ghost,* 139.

31. Keen and Mewborn, *43rd Battalion,* 114; Munson, *Reminiscences,* 88–91; SFC, "Memories of 'Mosby's Men'" *Religious Herald,* 20 March 1902; Brown, *Mosby's Fighting Parson,* 152.

32. Scott, *Partisan Life,* 203; Munson, *Reminiscences,* 87–88; Williamson, *Mosby's Rangers,* 2d ed., 145; newspaper clipping, JSMSB-UVA, 2:89; "Bravery of Mosby's Daring Rebel Band Was Unrivaled," *Greensboro Daily Record,* 10 June 1923.

33. *OR,* 33:159, 160, 587.

34. "Married," *Richmond Sentinel,* 19 April 1864; "Bravery of Mosby's Daring Rebel Band Was Unrivaled," *Greensboro Daily Record,* 10 June 1923; "Col. William Henry Chapman Passes at His Home in City," *Greensboro Daily News,* 7 September 1929; "One of Mosby's Officers Dies at Greensboro," *Richmond Times-Dispatch,* 17 September 1929; "Funeral Service for Mrs. Chapman Is Held," *Greensboro Daily News,* 3 January 1928; "Death of Noted Southern Woman," in RC. George Harris performed the ceremony (Marriage Register Book 7:41, Fauquier County Circuit Court Clerk). Scott, *Partisan Life,* 193, described an earlier ranger wedding attended by Mosby and other rangers, entertained by Buckner and his band.

35. Protection by loyal servants is mentioned in "One of Mosby's Officers Dies at Greensboro," *Richmond Times-Dispatch,* 17 September 1929; "Death of Noted Southern Woman," RC. Family recollections are from Esther Foote Brooking Ellis, daughter of Esther Foote Chapman Brooking and granddaughter of William and Josephine Chapman, 18 June 1975, HC.

36. That the Chapmans did not live at Edge Hill until after the war is mentioned in "Death of Noted Southern Woman," RC. Family letters written while Chapman was stationed on the Northern Neck, January–March 1865, further corroborate residence at Highlands. See WHC to William Allen Chapman, 3 January 1865, and WHC to JJC, 9, 11 January, 22 March 1865, RC. Some accounts state that Massow recuperated at the Jeffries' house under Josie's care. See "One of Mosby's Officers Dies at Greensboro," *Richmond Times-Dispatch,* 17 September 1929; "Col. William H. Chapman," *Confederate Veteran* 37, no. 11 (1929):426; "Death of Noted Southern Woman," RC. However, Scott, *Partisan Life,* 203, wrote that Massow recovered at another residence. See also Robert von Massow to WHC, 21 March 1910, RC (reprinted in newspaper clipping, JSMSB-UVA, 6:33.

37. WHC to William Allen Chapman, 3 January 1865, RC.

38. JJC to WHC, 12 January 1865, and WHC to JJC, 25 January 1865, RC.

39. *OR*, 33:249, 306, 847, 1275; Scott, *Partisan Life*, 207; Williamson, *Mosby's Rangers*, 2d ed., 158; Ramage, *Gray Ghost*, 140–45.

40. *OR*, 33:256, 259–60, 306, 315–16; Williamson, *Mosby's Rangers*, 2d ed., 156, 158–61.

41. Scott, *Partisan Life*, 209, 213; Williamson, *Mosby's Rangers*, 2d ed., 154, 158.

10. CATCH THOSE FELLOWS

1. McPherson, *Battle Cry*, 724.

2. *OR*, 37(1):2–3; Scott, *Partisan Life*, 219–23; Williamson, *Mosby's Rangers*, 2d ed., 162–67.

3. Scott, *Partisan Life*, 223–25; Williamson, *Mosby's Rangers*, 2d ed., 167; Brown, *Mosby's Fighting Parson*, 163–64.

4. Scott, *Partisan Life*, 215.

5. *OR*, 37(1):3; Scott, *Partisan Life*, 215–16; Keen and Mewborn, *43rd Battalion*, 125.

6. *OR*, 37(1):507–8, 512, 527; Scott, *Partisan Life*, 216–17; Williamson, *Mosby's Rangers*, 2d ed., 168; J. H. Alexander, *Mosby's Men*, 56–59; Ramage, *Gray Ghost*, 150–51.

7. *OR*, 37(1):527, 532; Scott, *Partisan Life*, 217–18; Williamson, *Mosby's Rangers*, 2d ed., 169–70; J. H. Alexander, *Mosby's Men*, 59–62; Ramage, *Gray Ghost*, 151.

8. Scott, *Partisan Life*, 226–27; Williamson, *Mosby's Rangers*, 2d ed., 171–72.

9. *OR*, 37(1):3; Williamson, *Mosby's Rangers*, 2d ed., 174–75. Scott, *Partisan Life*, 227, described a similar encounter but wrote that "Lt. Chapman" directed the attack.

10. *OR*, 37(1):528, 557; Scott, *Partisan Life*, 227–29; Wert, *Mosby's Rangers*, 164; Ramage, *Gray Ghost*, 152.

11. McPherson, *Battle Cry*, 737–39; Ramage, *Gray Ghost*, 152–53.

12. *OR*, 37(1):167–68; Williamson, *Mosby's Rangers*, 2d ed., 175–77.

13. *OR*, 37(1):168–69.

14. Ibid., 3; Williamson, *Mosby's Rangers*, 2d ed., 177, 464.

15. Williamson, *Mosby's Rangers*, 2d ed., 465.

16. *OR*, 37(1):3; Scott, *Partisan Life*, 232, 233–35; Williamson, *Mosby's Rangers*, 2d ed., 178; Ramage, *Gray Ghost*, 154.

17. *OR*, 37(1):357; Scott, *Partisan Life*, 235–36; Williamson, *Mosby's Rangers*, 2d ed., 178, 182; Ramage, *Gray Ghost*, 154–55.

18. *OR*, 37(1):357–58, 694–95; Scott, *Partisan Life*, 236–38; Williamson, *Mosby's Rangers*, 2d ed., 182; Ramage, *Gray Ghost*, 155.

19. McPherson, *Battle Cry*, 756.

20. *OR*, 37(1):3–4; Scott, *Partisan Life*, 238–40; Williamson, *Mosby's Rangers*, 2d ed., 184; Ramage, *Gray Ghost*, 155.

21. *OR*, 37(1):4; Scott, *Partisan Life*, 239–41; Williamson, *Mosby's Rangers*, 2d ed., 184–85; J. H. Alexander, *Mosby's Men*, 77–79.

22. Scott, *Partisan Life*, 239, 241–42; Williamson, *Mosby's Rangers*, 2d ed., 186; J. H. Alexander, *Mosby's Men*, 79–80, 83; Ramage, *Gray Ghost*, 156–58.

23. *OR*, 37(1):219, 358–59; Scott, *Partisan Life*, 246–47; Williamson, *Mosby's Rangers*, 2d ed., 186–87; Ramage, *Gray Ghost*, 158.

24. *OR*, 37(1):359; Scott, *Partisan Life*, 247; Williamson, *Mosby's Rangers*, 2d ed., 187; J. H. Alexander, *Mosby's Men*, 92; Humphreys, *Field, Camp, Hospital*, 96; Ramage, *Gray Ghost*, 158–59.

25. *OR*, 37(1):359; Scott, *Partisan Life*, 247–48; Williamson, *Mosby's Rangers*, 2d ed., 187; Humphreys, *Field, Camp, Hospital*, 96; Ramage, *Gray Ghost*, 159.

26. *OR*, 37(1):4, 359–60; Munson, *Reminiscences*, 97; Ramage, *Gray Ghost*, 159–60.

27. Williamson, *Mosby's Rangers,* 2d ed.,188; Munson, *Reminiscences,* 98; J. H. Alexander, *Mosby's Men,* 95.

28. *OR,* 37(1):4–5; Scott, *Partisan Life,* 253; Williamson, *Mosby's Rangers,* 2d ed., 192; Ramage, *Gray Ghost,* 164.

29. *OR,* 37(1):321–22.

30. Ibid., 322; Scott, *Partisan Life,* 254–55; Williamson, *Mosby's Rangers,* 2d ed., 192–94.

31. Wert, *From Winchester,* 8; Williamson, *Mosby's Rangers,* 2d ed., 194–96; Ramage, *Gray Ghost,* 164.

32. *OR,* 37(1):5; Scott, *Partisan Life,* 293–97; Williamson, *Mosby's Rangers,* 2d ed.,197–202; Ramage, *Gray Ghost,* 164, 179–81; Brown, *Mosby's Fighting Parson,* 191–93.

33. *OR,* 37(2):558.

11. NO QUARTER

1. Wert, *From Winchester,* 18–22, 26, 33–34.

2. *OR,* 43(1):623; Ramage, *Gray Ghost,* 186.

3. *OR,* 43(1):620, 623, 628, 631; Ramage, *Gray Ghost,* 187–88.

4. *OR,* 43(1):621–27, 629–31, 786; Ramage, *Gray Ghost,* 187–90.

5. *OR,* 43(1):18, 629, 776; Ramage, *Gray Ghost,* 187.

6. Williamson, *Mosby's Rangers,* 2d ed., 206; Munson, *Reminiscences,* 102–4; Ramage, *Gray Ghost,* 190–91.

7. *OR,* 43(1):634; Williamson, *Mosby's Rangers,* 2d ed., 206–7; Munson, *Reminiscences,* 104; Mosby, *Memoirs,* 291, 366–67; newspaper clipping, JSMSB-UVA, 1:68; Keen and Mewborn, *43rd Battalion,* 157.

8. *OR,* 43(1):621, 629; Scott, *Partisan Life,* 276–78; Williamson, *Mosby's Rangers,* 2d ed., 207–9; Perkins, *Summer,* 34; Ramage, *Gray Ghost,* 191.

9. *OR,* 43(1):623; Williamson, *Mosby's Rangers,* 2d ed., 209–10; Munson, *Reminiscences,* 105–6.

10. *OR,* 43(1): 484–85, 621, 633, 634; Scott, *Partisan Life,* 278–79; Williamson, *Mosby's Rangers,* 2d ed., 210; Munson, *Reminiscences,* 107–9; Ramage, *Gray Ghost,* 191. Chapman's quote is from a small reproduction of the painting at the VHS.

11. *OR,* 43(1):619–32, 783, 842; Ramage, *Gray Ghost,* 192.

12. *OR,* 43(1):811, 822, 831–32, 841, 843–44, 880; Ramage, *Gray Ghost,* 193–94.

13. *OR,* 43(1):698, 792, 822, 841; Jones, *Gray Ghosts,* 280; Wert, *Mosby's Rangers,* 195.

14. Williamson, *Mosby's Rangers,* 2d ed., 213, 449; Ramage, *Gray Ghost,* 194. Scott, *Partisan Life,* 279–80, and Williamson, *Mosby's Rangers,* 2d ed., 212, wrote that the raid occurred on 19 August, but the *New York Times* reported the events occurred on 18 August.

15. "More about the Massacre by Mosby," and "The Guerrillas and Bushwackers," *New York Times,* 25 August 1864; Ramage, *Gray Ghost,* 194.

16. Scott, *Partisan Life,* 281; Williamson, *Mosby's Rangers,* 2d ed., 450–51.

17. Scott, *Partisan Life,* 281; Williamson, *Mosby's Rangers,* 2d ed., 213, 451.

18. Munson, *Reminiscences,* 147; Williamson, *Mosby's Rangers,* 2d ed., 213, 451; Scott, *Partisan Life,* 281.

19. Scott, *Partisan Life,* 281; Jones, *Gray Ghosts,* 281.

20. Scott, *Partisan Life,* 282; Williamson, *Mosby's Rangers,* 2d ed., 451; Patteson, "Swift Retribution for House-Burning."

21. "More about the Massacre by Mosby," *New York Times,* 25 August 1864.

22. Ibid.

23. Ibid.

24. *OR,* 43(1):634; Jones, *Gray Ghosts,* 281; Scott, *Partisan Life,* 282; Munson, *Reminiscences,* 147.

25. Scott, *Partisan Life,* 281–82; Williamson, *Mosby's Rangers,* 2d ed., 214; Munson, *Reminiscences,* 147; Patteson, "Swift Retribution for House-Burning."

26. McPherson, *For Cause and Comrades,* 148–62; "More about the Massacre by Mosby," *New York Times,* 25 August 1864.

27. *OR,* 43(1):634; Scott, *Partisan Life,* 286; Williamson, *Mosby's Rangers,* 2d ed., 223–24. Accounts differ about who led the squadron. Williamson wrote that WHC was in command. Mosby said SFC commanded, as did Scott. J. H. Alexander, *Mosby's Men,* 169, and Gold, *History of Clarke County,* 125–27, reported that WHC left prior to the attack to give captured dispatches to Fitzhugh Lee, whose cavalry was in the area west of Berryville.

28. *OR,* 43(1):634; Scott, *Partisan Life,* 287–88; Williamson, *Mosby's Rangers,* 2d ed., 224–25.

29. Hall, *History,* 352–53, 357.

30. Scott, *Partisan Life,* 304–5; Williamson, *Mosby's Rangers,* 2d ed., 231–33; Ramage, *Gray Ghost,* 196–97.

31. *OR,* 43(1):542–43, 43(2):74; Scott, *Partisan Life,* 292; Williamson, *Mosby's Rangers,* 2d ed., 234.

32. *OR,* 43(1):543; Scott, *Partisan Life,* 292–93; Williamson, *Mosby's Rangers,* 2d ed., 235–36; Mosby, *Memoirs,* 299.

33. Mosby, *Memoirs,* 298; JSM to Arthur B. Clarke, 16 September 1914, Mosby Papers, VHS.

34. Wert, *From Winchester,* 130–31; Wert, *Mosby's Rangers,* 210–11; Ramage, *Gray Ghost,* 198.

35. Newspaper clipping, JSMSB-UVA, 1:3; Scott, *Partisan Life,* 315–16; Williamson, *Mosby's Rangers,* 2d ed., 237.

36. Newspaper clipping, JSMSB-UVA, 1:3.

37. *OR,* 43(2):149, 177–78; newspaper clipping, JSMSB-UVA, 1:3; Scott, *Partisan Life,* 316–17; Williamson, *Mosby's Rangers,* 2d ed., 237.

38. Newspaper clipping, JSMSB-UVA, 1:3.

39. Ibid. The newspaper describes the capture of twenty-three men, though it ended with a claim of twenty-four prisoners. Scott, *Partisan Life,* 317, reported nineteen prisoners. Williamson, *Mosby's Rangers,* 2d ed., 238, claimed eighteen prisoners.

40. Scott, *Partisan Life,* 317–18; Williamson, *Mosby's Rangers,* 2d ed., 239; Ramage, *Gray Ghost,* 198.

41. *OR,* 43(1):428, 441; Scott, *Partisan Life,* 318–19; Williamson, *Mosby's Rangers,* 2d ed., 239–40; Baird, *Journals,* 206; Brown, *Mosby's Fighting Parson,* 228; Ramage, *Gray Ghost,* 198–99.

42. Scott, *Partisan Life,* 320; Williamson, *Mosby's Rangers,* 2d ed., 240–41, 502–3; Ramage, *Gray Ghost,* 199–200.

43. *OR,* 43(1):183, 43(2):179; Williamson, *Mosby's Rangers,* 2d ed., 242, 244; Moyer, *History,* 128–29, 159–65; Keen and Mewborn, *43rd Battalion,* 179.

44. Cochran recollections, 26 September 1864, VHS; Scott, *Partisan Life,* 273–74; WHC to Captain Martin, 23 November 1864, JSM-DU.

12. NOTHING BUT YANKEES

1. JSM to Bob Walker, 12 December 1899, in Mitchell, *Letters,* 96–101; Scott, *Partisan Life,* 321; Wert, *Mosby's Rangers,* 222.

2. JSM to Bob Walker, 12 December 1899, in Mitchell, *Letters,* 96–101; Baird, *Journals,* 207.

3. *OR,* 43(1):618, 943, 43(2):151, 166–67; Williamson, *Mosby's Rangers,* 2d ed., 245.

4. *OR,* 43(2):141, 187, 196, 257–60, 265–67, 268, 276, 290; Ramage, *Gray Ghost,* 201–3.

5. *OR,* 43(2):273.

6. *OR,* 43(1):633, 43(2):298–99, 301, 310; Scott, *Partisan Life,* 324–25; Williamson, *Mosby's Rangers,* 2d ed., 250–51; Ramage, *Gray Ghost,* 203.

7. Scott, *Partisan Life,* 325–26; Williamson, *Mosby's Rangers,* 2d ed., 253–54; Ramage, *Gray Ghost,* 203–4.

8. *OR,* 43(2):298–301, 311–12, 319, 334, 364, 378, 910; Scott, *Partisan Life,* 327; Williamson, *Mosby's Rangers,* 2d ed., 255, 257; Baird, *Journals,* 207; Ramage, *Gray Ghost,* 204.

9. *OR,* 43(2):334–35, 341, 347–48, 388–89, 405, 909; Scott, *Partisan Life,* 327; Williamson, *Mosby's Rangers,* 2d ed., 267, 272–75; Ramage, *Gray Ghost,* 204–5.

10. Scott, *Partisan Life,* 327; Williamson, *Mosby's Rangers,* 2d ed., 275; Mosby, *Memoirs,* 373; JSM to Bob Walker, 12 December 1899, in Mitchell, *Letters,* 96–101.

11. Keen and Mewborn, *43rd Battalion,* 188–89; Williamson, *Mosby's Rangers,* 2d ed., 255.

12. *OR,* 43(2):339, 351; Williamson, *Mosby's Rangers,* 2d ed., 259; Ramage, *Gray Ghost,* 210–11; Keen and Mewborn, *43rd Battalion,* 191.

13. *OR,* 43(1):508–9; Ramage, *Gray Ghost,* 211–12.

14. *OR,* 43(1):509; Williamson, *Mosby's Rangers,* 2d ed., 289–90n 2; J. H. Alexander, *Mosby's Men,* 142; Ramage, *Gray Ghost,* 211–12.

15. *OR,* 43(1):633, 43(2):368; Scott, *Partisan Life,* 334–39; Williamson, *Mosby's Rangers,* 2d ed., 260–63; Ramage, *Gray Ghost,* 207–8.

16. *OR,* 43(2):369–72; Scott, *Partisan Life,* 339–41; Williamson, *Mosby's Rangers,* 2d ed., 264–65; Ramage, *Gray Ghost,* 207–8.

17. Scott, *Partisan Life,* 341–42; Williamson, *Mosby's Rangers,* 2d ed., 264–65; Keen and Mewborn, *43rd Battalion,* 199.

18. *OR,* 43(1):618–19, 635; Scott, *Partisan Life,* 339; Williamson, *Mosby's Rangers,* 2d ed., 266; Ramage, *Gray Ghost,* 208–9.

19. *OR,* 43(2):412, 414–15; Scott, *Partisan Life,* 349; Williamson, *Mosby's Rangers,* 2d ed., 269–71; Ramage, *Gray Ghost,* 212.

20. Scott, *Partisan Life,* 348; Williamson, *Mosby's Rangers,* 2d ed., 277.

21. Scott, *Partisan Life,* 348–49; Williamson, *Mosby's Rangers,* 2d ed., 277–78.

22. *OR,* 43(1):186; Williamson, *Mosby's Rangers,* 2d ed., 280–81.

23. *OR,* 43(1):35; Scott, *Partisan Life,* 350; Williamson, *Mosby's Rangers,* 2d ed., 281.

24. Scott, *Partisan Life,* 350–52; Williamson, *Mosby's Rangers,* 2d ed., 283–84.

25. Ramage, *Gray Ghost,* 202, 205–6; *OR,* 43(1):553, 635, 43(2):466, 475, 528, 537, 909, 918.

26. Cochran recollections, 1 November 1864, VHS.

27. *OR,* 43(2):909–10, 922.

28. Scott, *Partisan Life,* 357–59; Williamson, *Mosby's Rangers,* 2d ed., 288–92; J. H. Alexander, *Mosby's Men,* 144–47; Ramage, *Gray Ghost,* 213.

29. *OR,* 43(2):566; Scott, *Partisan Life,* 359–61; Williamson, *Mosby's Rangers,* 2d ed., 292–95, 455–57; Ramage, *Gray Ghost,* 213–15. Keen and Mewborn, *43rd Battalion,* 211, wrote that only one man was exchanged. Other accounts reported two Masons were exchanged.

30. *OR,* 43(1):615–16, 860, 43(2):648, 654; Scott, *Partisan Life,* 363–71; Williamson, *Mosby's Rangers,* 2d ed., 299–306; Ramage, *Gray Ghost,* 225–27.

31. Scott, *Partisan Life,* 371–72; Williamson, *Mosby's Rangers,* 2d ed., 310, 458.

32. Scott, *Partisan Life,* 372–73; Williamson, *Mosby's Rangers,* 2d ed., 310–11, 458–59.

33. *OR,* 43(1):670, 43(2):689; Scott, *Partisan Life,* 374–75; Williamson, *Mosby's Rangers,* 2d ed., 311–12.

34. *OR,* 43(1):671–73, 43(2):581, 671–72, 679, 687.

35. Baird, *Journals,* 209; Broun diary, 29 November, 1 December 1864, UVA; *OR,* 43(2):712; Williamson, *Mosby's Rangers,* 2d ed., 317.

36. *OR,* 43(1):673, 43(2):730; Scott, *Partisan Life,* 376–78; Williamson, *Mosby's Rangers,* 2d ed., 319–23; Denison, *Sabres and Spurs,* 381; Ramage, *Gray Ghost,* 228–30.

37. Humphreys, *Field, Camp, Hospital,* 192; *OR,* 43(2):730; Broun diary, 28 December 1864, UVA; Cochran recollections, 15 January 1865, VHS.

38. *OR,* 43(2):937; Scott, *Partisan Life,* 397–98; Williamson, *Mosby's Rangers,* 2d ed., 325, 327; Ramage, *Gray Ghost,* 232; CSR-VA, Mosby's Regiment.

39. Scott, *Partisan Life,* 381; Williamson, *Mosby's Rangers,* 2d ed., 325; Keen and Mewborn, *43rd Battalion,* 232–33; Gold, *History of Clarke County,* 130.

40. *OR,* 43(2):798; Scott, *Partisan Life,* 381–83; Williamson, *Mosby's Rangers,* 2d ed., 325–26; Keen and Mewborn, *43rd Battalion,* 233–34; Gold, *History of Clarke County,* 130.

41. *OR,* 43(2):806–7, 811, 821–22; Ramage, *Gray Ghost,* 233.

42. *OR,* 43(2):831–32, 834, 838–40, 843–44; Scott, *Partisan Life,* 387–90; Williamson, *Mosby's Rangers,* 2d ed., 328–37; Ramage, *Gray Ghost,* 233–37.

13. ALL WILL BE RIGHT

1. WHC to William Allen Chapman, 3 January 1865, RC; Williamson, *Mosby's Rangers,* 2d ed., 339–40.

2. *OR,* 40(2):684, 689, 43(1):990–91; newspaper clipping, JSMSB-UVA, 6:23; Scott, *Partisan Life,* 390–91; Williamson, *Mosby's Rangers,* 2d ed., 313–15, 339–40; Ramage, *Gray Ghost,* 232.

3. WHC to Elizabeth Forrer Chapman, 11 January 1865, RC.

4. Williamson, *Mosby's Rangers,* 2d ed., 490.

5. Ibid., 489–93; and for the original manuscript, see also WHC, "Account of Operations of a Portion of Mosby's Command in Northern Neck of Virginia in 1865," RC.

6. Ward, *Children of Bladensfield,* 97–109.

7. WHC to William Allen Chapman, 3 January 1865, WHC to Elizabeth Forrer Chapman, 11 January 1865, JJC to WHC, 12, 15 January 1865, and WHC to JJC, 25, 28 January, 22 March 1865, RC.

8. *OR,* 46(2):576, 650, 665–66, 683, 713, 790, 832; Williamson, *Mosby's Rangers,* 2d ed., 490; Brown, *Mosby's Fighting Parson,* 276.

9. *OR,* 46(1):542–45, 46(2):832, 901, 914, 940; Scott, *Partisan Life,* 464; Williamson, *Mosby's Rangers,* 2d ed., 491; Brown, *Mosby's Fighting Parson,* 277–78.

10. *OR,* 46(1):549, 46(2):891, 900, 903, 907–8, 940; Scott, *Partisan Life,* 465; Brown, *Mosby's Fighting Parson,* 278–79.

11. Williamson, *Mosby's Rangers,* 2d ed., 491 (and also WHC, "Account of Operations of a Portion of Mosby's Command in Northern Neck of Virginia in 1865," RC); *OR,* 46(1):549.

12. Williamson, *Mosby's Rangers,* 2d ed., 491; Brown, *Mosby's Fighting Parson,* 279.

13. Williamson, *Mosby's Rangers,* 2d ed., 491–92; Brown, *Mosby's Fighting Parson,* 279–80.

14. *OR,* 46(1):549; Williamson, *Mosby's Rangers,* 2d ed., 492.

15. *OR,* 46(1):549; Williamson, *Mosby's Rangers,* 2d ed., 493.

16. *OR,* 46(1):550, 46(2):891, 954.

17. Williamson, *Mosby's Rangers,* 2d ed., 492–93; Ward, *Children of Bladensfield,* 108; newspaper clipping, JSMSB-UVA, 2:88; Brown, *Mosby's Fighting Parson,* 280–81.

18. *OR,* 46(3):16–17, 25, 84, 618, 681–82; WHC to JJC, 22 March 1865, RC; Williamson, *Mosby's Rangers,* 2d ed., 493; Brown, *Mosby's Fighting Parson,* 283–84.

19. *OR,* 46(3):715, 741, 1359; Williamson, *Mosby's Rangers,* 2d ed., 493.

20. *OR,* 46(3):675, 692; Williamson, *Mosby's Rangers,* 2d ed., 365–67.

21. *OR,* 46(3):684–85, 697, 699.

22. *OR,* 46(3):714; Scott, *Partisan Life,* 470; Williamson, *Mosby's Rangers,* 2d ed., 376; Ramage, *Gray Ghost,* 262.

23. *OR,* 46(1):526–27, 46(3):725, 742–43, 750, 752; Ramage, *Gray Ghost,* 263.

24. *OR,* 46(3):765–66; Monteiro, *War Reminiscences,* 126–29, 143; Ramage, *Gray Ghost,* 263.

25. Monteiro, *War Reminiscences,* 147–49; Williamson, *Mosby's Rangers,* 2d ed., 377.

26. Ibid., 149–50, 153–55.

27. Ibid., 155–57, 190.

28. Ibid., 157–58.

29. Ibid., 159–60, 166–67, 190.

30. Ibid., 168–69; Scott, *Partisan Life,* 471–72; Williamson, *Mosby's Rangers,* 2d ed., 380–81.

31. Monteiro, *War Reminiscences,* 176–82, 186–92.

32. Ibid., 177–78, 188, 191, 194.

33. *OR,* 46(3):799–800, 804, 817; Ramage, *Gray Ghost,* 264.

34. *OR,* 46(3):828, 830–31, 839; Scott, *Partisan Life,* 472–73; Williamson, *Mosby's Rangers,* 2d ed., 384–86; Monteiro, *War Reminiscences,* 202–3; Ramage, *Gray Ghost,* 264.

35. *OR,* 46(3):830–31, 838–40; Ramage, *Gray Ghost,* 264–65.

36. *OR,* 46(3):868–70; Monteiro, *War Reminiscences,* 204, 206–7; Ramage, *Gray Ghost,* 265.

37. Scott, *Partisan Life,* 474–77; Williamson, *Mosby's Rangers,* 2d ed., 392–94; Munson, *Reminiscences,* 270–71; Ramage, *Gray Ghost,* 265–66. Munson, *Reminiscences,* 269, said that the farewell letter was penned at "Glen Welby," the estate of Richard Carter. Chapman claimed Mosby wrote the address at a table in Chapman's home at Highlands. See, "Bravery of Mosby's Daring Rebel Band Was Unrivaled," *Greensboro Daily Record,* 10 June 1923.

38. "Bravery of Mosby's Daring Rebel Band Was Unrivaled," *Greensboro Daily Record,* 10 June 1923; Broun diary, 2 May 1865, UVA.

39. Williamson, *Mosby's Rangers,* 2d ed., 394–95; CSR-VA, Mosby's Regiment; *OR,* 46(3):897.

14. A SENSE OF DUTY

1. Brown, *Mosby's Fighting Parson,* 295–96.

2. JJC to Hannah "Kate" Chapman, 15 April 1867, in Sampson Collection; Bruen, *Christian Forrer,* 202; Blackwell, *Blackwell Genealogy,* 54.

3. Ninth U.S. Census (1870), Population Schedules, Fauquier County, Va., 596, 602; Nonpopulation Census Schedules, Scott Township, Fauquier County, Va., roll 12, 1–2; Bruen, *Christian Forrer,* 203; Blackwell, *Blackwell Genealogy,* 54–55; Brown, *Mosby's*

Fighting Parson, 296–97. Blackwell stated that two children died in infancy. JJC mentioned the loss of a young child in JJC to WHC, 21 November 1892, FC. Family history maintains that Chapman taught military tactics at Bethel Academy after the war (Carolyn and Chris Russell as related by William Brooking, Chapman's grandson). The Bethel Military Academy, founded in 1867, was located four miles from Warrenton in Fauquier County, near Edge Hill. Though military tactics were studied, Smith, "History," says nothing about Chapman as a faculty member or instructor. However, Mosby was affiliated with the school, and it is not inconceivable that Chapman, when he lived nearby in Fauquier County, offered his views on military tactics to the cadets.

4. Ramage, *Gray Ghost*, 267–99; Evans and Moyer, *Mosby's Confederacy*, 17; Writers' Program (U.S.), *Old Homes*, 335–36.

5. "Virginia News," *Alexandria Gazette*, 9 June 1873; U.S. Dept. of the Interior, *Register of Officers and Agents*, 1873:420, 1875:510, 1877:410; Fauquier County, Va., Circuit Court Clerk, Deed Book 66:123–25; Alexandria, Va., Circuit Court Clerk, Deed Book 4:263–64, 333–34; Tenth U.S. Census (1880), Population Schedules, Alexandria, Va., 276, 346–47; Brown, *Mosby's Fighting Parson*, 298. Genealogy from Bruen, *Christian Forrer*, 204–5; Blackwell, *Blackwell Genealogy*, 55; Katharine Neal, from Green Hill Cemetery, Greensboro, N.C., section 33, lot 109.

6. Alexandria, Va., Deed Book 4:506–9, 516–18, 6:109–10, 8:65–67; "Gadsby's Tavern Historic Structures Report," 65, 98, Gadsby's Tavern Museum, Alexandria.

7. WHC to JJC, 3 September 1876, FC; J. D. Brady to Secretary of State [William Maxwell Evarts], 13 March 1877, JSM-DU.

8. "Letters Sent," 1:285–90, Records of the Internal Revenue Service, NA-CP; U.S. Internal Revenue Service, *History*, 6.

9. Newspaper clipping, JSMSB-UVA, 1:31; "Letters Sent," 1:457–58, Records of the Internal Revenue Service, NA-CP; U.S. Dept. of the Interior, *Official Register*, 1879:79; U.S. Internal Revenue Service, *History*, 5; Siepel, *Rebel*, 201; Brown, *Mosby's Fighting Parson*, 298.

10. JJC to WHC, 22 August 1878 and WHC to JJC, 23 May 1880, FC. Correspondence of JJC and WHC, 1875–1919, FC, shows he was stationed in Statesville (September 1878–March 1879), Atlanta (May 1880), and New York City (February–March 1881).

11. WHC to JJC, 22 September 1878, FC.

12. Ramage, *Gray Ghost*, 271–84; Wert, *General James Longstreet*, 410–27.

13. JJC to Esther Jeffries, 28 February 1881, and JJC to WHC, 22 September 1878, FC; "Hettie" [Ester Foote] and Elizabeth Chapman et al. to James A. Garfield, 5 November 1880, and James A. Garfield to Hettie and Elizabeth Chapman et al., 20 November 1880, HC. Hayes was acquainted with both Chapman brothers and at some point told Sam Chapman of the great debt Ohioans owed Samuel Forrer for his engineering (Bruen, *Christian Forrer*, 104). Sam Chapman joined Mosby and traveled with Hayes to visit Montpelier, the former residence of James Madison near Orange, Va., on 9 October 1878 (Hayes, *Diary*, 3:503). Chapman acknowledged his support by Grant and Hayes when seeking a more senior appointment (WHC to John W. Daniel [U.S. senator, Va.], 4 February 1899, and WHC to James E. Boyd [assistant attorney general], 11 February 1899, WHCLB, 306–7, 326–27). He remained a lifelong Republican and supported Republican congressional and presidential elections (J. E. Hetherington to S. A. Whitfield [assistant postmaster general], 14 October 1890, and WHC to Park Agnew [revenue collector, 6th district Va.], 20 September 1900, WHCLB, 120–23, 371–72). He was not above using his own influence in the Republican Party to secure appointments for friends (WHC to JSM, 24 March 1889, and WHC to S. A. Whitfield, 11 June 1889, WHCLB, 110–14, 115–17).

14. The register of government employees gives the dates of Chapman's service (U.S. Dept. of the Interior, *Official Register,* 1881:85, 1883:89, 1885:87, 1887:88, 1889:93, 1891:177, 1893:199, 1895:83, 1897:271, 1899:286, 1901:300, 1905:80; U.S. Bureau of the Census, *Official Register,* 1907:196, 1909:219, 1911:215, 1913:227, 1915:233). Locations of service are from Internal Revenue records and personal correspondence ("Letters Sent," vols. 1–11, 14–18, Records of the Internal Revenue Service, NA-CP; Chapman ledger book, 1886–1905, RC; correspondence of JJC and WHC, 1875–1919, FC). Personal letters show that he continued on Internal Revenue business in Richmond until 1915 (WHC to Eleanor R. Walker, 17 March 1924, Palmer file, Museum of the Confederacy); Greensboro in 1915, San Francisco and Salt Lake City in 1917, and Philadelphia in 1918 (JJC to WHC, 6, 8 June 1915, WHC to JJC, 1 May 1917, and JJC to WHC, 2 June 1918, FC); and was in Richmond in 1919 (WHC to JJC, 11 January 1919, RC). A tribute to Chapman stated that he was active until forced to retire in 1920 ("Bravery of Mosby's Daring Rebel Band Was Unrivaled," *Greensboro Daily Record,* 10 June 1923). Chapman was stationed in San Francisco in 1916 (Bruen, *Christian Forrer,* 193, 205).

15. JJC to Ester Foote Chapman, 11 October 1884, JJC to "my dear little children" [James, John, Katie, Sam], 26 October 1884, Joseph S. Miller [commissioner of Internal Revenue] to JJC, 8 April 1885, Frank Hereford to JJC, 15 April 1885, WHC to JJC, 17 May, 14 June, 22 November 1885, and JJC to WHC, 13 February 1889, FC.

16. For dates of appointment, see WHC to Joseph S. Miller [commissioner of Internal Revenue], 22 February 1887, WHC to S. A. Whitfield [assistant postmaster general], 11 June 1889, and WHC to W. W. Colquitt [chief revenue agent], 22 June 1895, WHCLB, 55–80, 115–17, 497–99.

17. WHC to JJC, 9 April 1888, WHC to "Willie" [William Allen Chapman], 10 April 1888, and "Willie" to JJC, 10, 11 April 1888, FC.

18. WHC to John W. Mason [commissioner of Internal Revenue], 11 March 1893, WHCLB, 139–60.

19. WHC to Joseph S. Miller [commissioner of Internal Revenue], 15, 17, 22 February, 24 April, 1887, WHCLB, 44–50, 51, 55–80, 89–91.

20. WHC to Joseph S. Miller, 22 April 1893, 6 June 1895, WHCLB, 162–63, 203–8.

21. WHC to W. W. Colquitt [chief revenue agent], 27 September, 12, 27 October 1894, 22 June 1895, 9 September 1896, WHCLB, 171–72, 173–76, 177–80, 497–99, 245–46; WHC to Joseph S. Miller, 27 October, 17 November 1894, 28 May, 6, 8 June 1895, WHCLB, 181–84, 185–95, 199–202, 203–8, 209–15; James Hetherington to Joseph S. Miller, July 1895, WHCLB, 216–32.

22. James Hetherington to Joseph S. Miller, July 1895, WHCLB, 216–32.

23. WHC to John W. Yerkes [commissioner of Internal Revenue], 26 August, 4 September 1905, WHCLB, 471–74, 475–77. These letters describe charges of corruption that Chapman leveled against a district attorney.

24. "Letters Sent," 1:451, 451½, Records of the Internal Revenue Service, NA-CP.

25. WHCLB, 295–98, 302–46; L. J. Bryan to William McKinley, 6 February 1899, Emory Speer to William McKinley, 11 February 1899, Tinsley W. Rucker to William McKinley, 14 February 1899, J. C. Pritchard [U.S. senator, N.C.] to William McKinley, 14 February 1899, and WHC to Lyman Gage [secretary of Treasury], 23 February 1899, RC.

26. WHC to Lyman Gage, 23 February 1899, RC. Brown, *Take Sides,* 82–83, mentions that a political complaint against Chapman was lodged in 1907 because of his part in the killings.

27. WHC to JJC, 12 May 1883, FC.

28. Bruen, *Christian Forrer,* 202–5; "Funeral Service for Mrs. Chapman Is Held," *Greensboro Daily News,* 3 January 1928; "Death of Noted Southern Woman," RC; "Col.

William Henry Chapman Passes at His Home in City," *Greensboro Daily News,* 7 September 1929; U.S. Bureau of the Census, *Official Register,* 1913:227, 1915:233, 1917:235, 1921:291.

29. Orange County, Va., Deed Book 52:534–35, 59:351–55, 70:576–77; WHCLB, 4–11, 18, 35–38, 362–65, 397–98, 478–79; A. L. Miller, *Antebellum Orange,* 37; Twelfth U.S. Census (1900), Population Schedules, Orange County, Va., 68. Chapman sold part of the Patrick Street property in 1889 for $1,200 and the remaining property two years later for $5,000. See Alexandria, Va., Deed Book, 21:512–13, 26:135–37. Correspondence of JJC and WHC, 1875–1919, FC, shows they lived in Richmond (1908–15) and in Greensboro with Katie by 1918. For the Milton farm, see Bruen, *Christian Forrer,* 197; WHCLB, 466–67, 480–81; JJC to WHC, 2 June 1918, FC.

30. WHCLB, 290–91, 388–89, 401–4, 408–14, 417–19, 422–23, 425–32, 437–44, 468–70.

31. Ramage, *Gray Ghost,* 307–17.

32. WHC to JJC, 18 November 1885, FC; WHC to James Longstreet, 8 April 1886, and WHC to Joseph Bryan, 19 August 1904, WHCLB, 13, 459–61; *OR,* 12(2):565, 599.

33. "The Three Guns Which Turned the Tide of Battle at Bull Run," *Atlanta Constitution,* 11 September 1887; "To Fight Over Again the Famous Battles of Manassas," *Richmond Times-Dispatch,* 14 August 1904; "Noted Guns at Manassas," *Richmond Times-Dispatch,* 4 September 1904; WHC to Joseph Bryan, 19 August 1904, WHCLB, 459–61; WHC to SFC, 18 November 1904, and SFC to John W. Daniel, 25 November 1904, Daniel Papers, UVA.

34. Chapman, "Dixie Battery at the Second Battle of Manassas"; WHC to Walton Moore, 21 November 1922, Manassas National Battlefield Library; A. L. Henry to WHC, 11 December 1922, RC; WHC to A. L. Henry, 26 March 1923, RC (the Manassas National Battlefield Library has a copy of this letter); "Bravery of Mosby's Daring Rebel Band Was Unrivaled," *Greensboro Daily Record,* 10 June 1923; "Col. William Henry Chapman Passes at His Home in City," *Greensboro Daily News,* 7 September 1929. Freeman, *R. E. Lee,* 2:332, acknowledged Chapman's battery as first to arrive but misidentified it as "Samuel Chapman's company." Hennessy, *Historical Report,* correctly identified and placed the Dixie Artillery. For Longstreet's debate with Stephen D. Lee, see Longstreet, "General Longstreet's Second Paper on Gettysburg," 267; S. D. Lee, "The Second Battle of Manassas: A Reply to General Longstreet"; Longstreet, "The Artillery at Second Manassas: General Longstreet's Reply"; S. D. Lee, "The Artillery at Second Manassas: Rejoinder."

35. JSM to WHC, 6 November 1887, JSM-DU. SFC's exploits are in Mosby, *Mosby's War Reminiscences,* 108–9, 133, 143–51. WHC is mentioned on page 149. For relations, see JJC to WHC, 22 August 1878 and 27 November 1886, FC; JSM to WHC, 19 January, 12 February, and 27 July 1894, JSM-DU; WHC to JSM, 4 December 1913, Stuart-Mosby Historical Society Papers, VHS. For relations with SFC, see Brown, *Mosby's Fighting Parson,* 321–22, 324, 336, 338–39, 341, 345.

36. JSM to WHC, 29 April, 20 May 1891, 19 January 1894, 29 January, 12 February 1895, JSM-DU. For Longstreet, see JSM to WHC, 5 September 1889, 29 April, 20 May, 17 September 1891, 30 July, 10, 26 October 1892, 24 March, 27 November 1894, JSM-DU.

37. Newspaper clipping, JSMSB-UVA, 1:12, 50–53; Williamson, *Mosby's Rangers,* 2d ed., 520–22; Brown, *Mosby's Fighting Parson,* 323.

38. JSM to H. C. Jordan, 23 August 1909, and JSM to SFC, 30 September 1909, JSM-DU; Siepel, *Rebel,* 281–83.

39. JJC to Elizabeth Forrer Chapman, 5 July 1896, HC; Brown, *Mosby's Fighting Parson,* 343.

40. Mosby Reunion Rolls, 40, 58, 66, 70, 74, 78, Museum of the Confederacy; "Fourteenth Reunion of the 43rd battalion of Virginia Cavalry," RC; "Mosby's Men Holding Annual Meeting Here," *Fredericksburg (Va.) Daily Star*, 2 October 1913; Bruen, *Christian Forrer*, 200–201. Chapman had given the revolver to Abraham S. Wilson, a private in Company C, during the war. Engraved on the handle was "A. S. W. from W. H. C., Lieut. Col. Mosby's Command." See WHC to J. W. Dwyer, 21 October 1904, WHCLB, 462–63.

41. *Alumni Bulletin of the University of Virginia*, 3rd ser., 5, no. 3 (July 1912) gives an account of the reunion. See also JJC to Samuel Forrer Chapman [son], 19 June 1912, Roha Collection; Jordan, *Charlottesville*, 104.

42. JSM to Mosby Campbell, 16 April and 5 May 1915, Mosby Papers, UVA (see also Mitchell, *Letters*, 214–16); JSM to Arthur B. Clarke, 7 May 1915, Mosby Papers, VHS; "Colonel Mosby Wins Hearts of Audience," *College Topics* (University of Virginia), 5 May 1915; Ramage, *Gray Ghost*, 331–32.

43. Bruen, *Christian Forrer*, 104, 129, 132–33, 140–42, 164, 202; Frank Bruen to WHC and JJC, 26 August 1923, and Frank Bruen to JJC, 8 October 1923, HC.

44. WHC to JJC, 18 June 1908, FC.

45. "Funeral Service for Mrs. Chapman Is Held," *Greensboro Daily News*, 3 January 1928; "In Memoriam: Mrs. William Henry Chapman," *Southern Churchman*, 17 March 1928; "Col. William Henry Chapman Passes at His Home in City," *Greensboro Daily News*, 7 September 1929; "One of Mosby's Officers Dies at Greensboro," *Richmond Times-Dispatch*, 17 September 1929; Bruen, *Christian Forrer*, 196–99; Standard Certificate of Death, Office of Register of Deeds, Guilford County, N.C., vol. 18, 731 (JJC), and vol. 34, 532 (WHC). The Chapmans are buried at Green Hill Cemetery, Greensboro, N.C., section 33, lot 109. "Col. William H. Chapman," *Confederate Veteran* 37, no. 11 (1929):426, and Bruen, *Christian Forrer*, 196, erroneously reported that Chapman died on 13 September 1929, an error that is repeated by Blackwell, *Blackwell Genealogy*, 53, Moore, *Danville*, 100, and Krick, *Lee's Colonels*, 78.

46. "Death of Noted Southern Woman," RC.

Bibliography

MANUSCRIPT SOURCES

City of Alexandria, Va., Circuit Court Clerk
  Deed Books, Corporation Court
Duke University, Special Collections Library, Durham, N.C.
  John Singleton Mosby Papers, 1862–1912
Ned Fanfani, Middleburg, Va.
  Chapman correspondence, 1875–1919
Fauquier County Circuit Court Clerk, Warrenton, Va.
  Deed Books
  Marriage Register Books
Gadsby's Tavern Museum, Alexandria, Va.
  "Gadsby's Tavern Historic Structures Report," vol. 1, 1 February 2001
Guilford County Office of Register of Deeds, Greensboro, N.C.
  Standard Certificate of Death
Archer Ellis Hansen, Winchester, Va.
  Chapman letters and memorabilia
Library of Congress, Washington, D.C.
  Jedediah Hotchkiss, "Map of the Shenandoah Valley, 1862"
  "Preliminary Map of Northern Virginia Embracing Portions of Loudoun, Fauquier, Prince William, and Culpeper Counties. 186_"
  Charles W. Squires, "Autobiography of Charles W. Squires: The Last of Lee's Battle-line."
Library of Virginia, Richmond, Va.
  Confederate Rosters, Captain John K. Booton's Dixie Battery
  Jedediah Hotchkiss Papers, 1845–1908
  Luray (Main Street) Baptist Church, Page County, Va., Minutes, 1844–76
  Madison County Marriage Register Number 1 (1793–1905), Madison County, Va.
John Singleton Mosby Heritage Area, Inc., Middleburg, Va.
  Eugene M. Scheel map
Museum of the Confederacy, Eleanor S. Brockenbrough Library, Richmond, Va.
  Mosby Reunion Rolls, 1904, 1905, 1909–14, Confederate Veterans Collection
  W. Ben Palmer file P-673a, MC-3 Collection Series
National Archives at College Park, Md.
  "Journals of Daily Observations Made at the Naval Observatory, Washington, D.C., 1842–1913," vols. 22–26 (1861–65), Records of Surface Land Observations, Records of the Weather Bureau, Record Group 27
  "Letters Sent to Internal Revenue Agents (1874–1909)," vols. 1–11, 14–18, Correspondence of the Office of the Commissioner of Internal Revenue, Records of the Internal Revenue Service, Record Group 58
National Archives and Records Administration, Washington, D.C.

Census of the United States, 1810–80, 1900, Record Group 29
Compiled Service Records of Confederate Soldiers Who Served in Organizations from the State of Louisiana, Record Group 109
Compiled Service Records of Confederate Soldiers Who Served in Organizations from the State of Virginia, Record Group 109
Nonpopulation Census Schedules for Virginia (1850–80), Record Group 29
National Park Service, Manassas National Battlefield Park, Manassas, Va.
Chapman correspondence
John J. Hennessy, "On the Rappahannock—Unedited and Fully Footnoted Copy of Chapter on the Actions along the Rappahannock, August 20–24, 1862, from Hennessy's Return to Bull Run"
Map of Centreville encampments, 18 December 1861
Orange County Circuit Court Clerk, Orange, Va.
Deed Books
Max and Mary Eustace Chapman Roha, Brecksville, Ohio
Chapman genealogy and correspondence
Carolyn and Chris Russell, Millersville, Md.
Chapman correspondence, ledger book (1886–1905), and wartime recollections
T. Ritchie Sampson, San Antonio, Tex.
Chapman correspondence
Tulane University, Manuscripts Department, Special Collections, New Orleans, La.
Civil War Papers (55-B)
Army of Northern Virginia Papers
Battalion Washington Artillery Collection
Civil War diaries
J. B. Walton Papers, 1861–78 (55-G)
Washington Artillery Papers (55-W)
Morning Reports: 1861–62, 1862–63
Muster Rolls: Battalion Washington Artillery, 1861–65
University of Virginia, Special Collections Library, Charlottesville, Va.
Alumni Bulletin of the University of Virginia
Catherine Broun, Diary, 1862–69, 1885
William Sam Burnley Papers
Catalogues, University of Virginia, 1859–60, 1860–61
Harry Clemons, "The University of Virginia Library, 1825–1950: Story of a Jeffersonian Foundation," typescript and notes
John Warwick Daniel Papers
Faculty Chairman's Journal, University of Virginia, 1851–61
John S. Mosby Papers, 1881–1916
John S. Mosby Scrapbooks, 1869–1915
Virginia Historical Society, Richmond, Va.
Catherine Cochran, "Recollections, 1861–65, of Experiences in Middleburg, Loudoun County, Va., and Richmond, Va."
Mary Eliza Powell Dulany, "Diary, 6 June 1862–18 July 1863"
John S. Mosby Papers, 1908–16
Pegram-Johnson-McIntosh family papers, 1825–1941
Stuart-Mosby Historical Society Papers, 1858–1929
West and Johnston, "Map of Virginia, 1862" (Map F221 1862:2, copy 6; Mss6:1 C366:1)

BOOKS AND ARTICLES

Alexander, Edward Porter. "Confederate Artillery Service." *Southern Historical Society Papers* 11 (1883): 98–113.

———. *Fighting for the Confederacy: The Personal Recollections of General Edward Porter Alexander.* Edited by Gary W. Gallagher. Chapel Hill: University of North Carolina Press, 1989.

———. *Military Memoirs of a Confederate: A Critical Narrative.* New York: Charles Scribner's Sons, 1907.

———. "Records of Longstreet's Corps, A.N.V.: 'The Seven Days' Battles.'" *Southern Historical Society Papers* 1 (1876): 61–76.

Alexander, John H. *Mosby's Men.* New York: Neale Publishing Co., 1907.

Allan, William. "Relative Strength at Second Manassas." *Southern Historical Society Papers* 8 (1880): 217–21.

Andrus, Michael J. *The Brooke, Fauquier, Loudoun and Alexandria Artillery.* Lynchburg, Va.: H. E. Howard, 1990.

Armstrong, Zella. *Notable Southern Families.* 6 vols. Chattanooga: Lookout Publishing Co., 1918–33.

Baird, Nancy Chappelear, ed. *Journals of Amanda Virginia Edmonds: Lass of the Mosby Confederacy, 1859–1867.* Stephens City, Va.: Commercial Press, 1984.

Baldwin, James J., III. *The Struck Eagle: A Biography of Brigadier General Micah Jenkins, and a History of the Fifth South Carolina Volunteers and the Palmetto Sharpshooters.* Shippensburg, Pa.: Burd Street Press, 1996.

Ballard, Charles C. *Dismissing the Peculiar Institution: Assessing Slavery in Page and Rockingham Counties, Virginia.* Luray, Va.: Page County Heritage Association, 1998.

Bartlett, Napier. *A Soldier's Story of the War; Including the Marches and Battles of the Washington Artillery, and of Other Louisiana Troops.* New Orleans: Clark and Hofeline, 1874.

Bergeron, Arthur W., Jr. *Guide to Louisiana Confederate Military Units, 1861–1865.* Baton Rouge: Louisiana State University Press, 1989.

Billings, John D. *Hardtack and Coffee; or, The Unwritten Story of Army Life, Including Chapters on Enlisting, Life in Tents and Log Huts, Jonahs and Beats, Offences and Punishments, Raw Recruits, Foraging, Corps and Corps Badges, the Wagon Trains, the Army Mule, the Engineer Corps, the Signal Corps, etc.*. Boston: George M. Smith and Co., 1888.

Blackwell, Edward Maurice. *Blackwell Genealogy.* Richmond: Old Dominion Press, 1948.

Bledsoe, Albert Taylor. *An Essay on Liberty and Slavery.* Philadelphia: J. B. Lippincott and Co., 1856.

Bohannon, Keith S. "One Solid Unbroken Roar of Thunder: Union and Confederate Artillery at the Battle of Malvern Hill." In *The Richmond Campaign of 1862: The Peninsula and the Seven Days,* edited by Gary W. Gallagher, 217–49. Chapel Hill: University of North Carolina Press, 2000.

Booker, Andrew Brooks. "History of the Academies of Augusta County, Virginia." Master's thesis, University of Virginia, 1949.

Brown, Peter A. *Mosby's Fighting Parson: The Life and Times of Sam Chapman.* Westminster, Md.: Willow Bend Books, 2001.

———, ed. *Take Sides with the Truth: The Postwar Letters of John Singleton Mosby to Samuel F. Chapman.* Lexington: University Press of Kentucky, 2007.

Bruce, Philip Alexander. *History of the University of Virginia, 1819–1919: The Lengthened Shadow of One Man.* 5 vols. New York: Macmillan, 1920–22.

Bruen, Frank. *Christian Forrer, the Clockmaker, and His Descendants.* Rutland, Vt.: Tuttle Publishing Co., 1939.

Burnham, W. Dean. *Presidential Ballots, 1836–1892.* Baltimore: Johns Hopkins University Press, 1955.

Burton, Brian K. *Extraordinary Circumstances: The Seven Days' Battles.* Bloomington: Indiana University Press, 2001.

Carmichael, Peter S. *Lee's Young Artillerist: William R. J. Pegram.* Charlottesville: University Press of Virginia, 1995.

———. *The Purcell, Crenshaw and Letcher Artillery.* Lynchburg, Va.: H. E. Howard, 1990.

Casey, Powell A. *An Outline of the Civil War Campaigns and Engagements of the Washington Artillery of New Orleans.* Baton Rouge: Claitor's Publishing, 1986.

Chapman, William H. "Dixie Battery at the Second Battle of Manassas." *Southern Historical Society Papers* 39 (1914): 190–94.

Clemons, Harry. *The University of Virginia Library, 1825–1950: Story of a Jeffersonian Foundation.* Charlottesville: University of Virginia Library, 1954.

"Col. William H. Chapman." *Confederate Veteran* 37, no. 11 (1929): 426.

Coski, John M. *The Confederate Battle Flag: America's Most Embattled Emblem.* Cambridge: Belknap Press of Harvard University Press, 2005.

Crawford, J. Marshall. *Mosby and His Men: A Record of the Adventures of That Renowned Partisan Ranger.* New York: G. W. Carleton, 1867.

Crew, Roger Thomas, Jr., and Benjamin H. Trask. *Grimes' Battery, Grandy's Battery and Huger's Battery, Virginia Artillery.* Lynchburg, Va.: H. E. Howard, 1995.

Denison, Frederic. *Sabres and Spurs: The First Regiment Rhode Island Cavalry in the Civil War, 1861–1865.* Central Falls, R.I.: E. L. Freeman and Co., 1876.

Dove, Vee. *Madison County Homes: A Collection of Pre-Civil War Homes and Family Heritages.* Madison County, Va.: Vee Dove, 1975.

Dunaway, Wayland Fuller. *Reminiscences of a Rebel.* New York: Neale Publishing Co., 1913.

Edmonds, Elsie Chapman. *John Chapman of Spotsylvania County, Virginia, Thomas Powe of Cheraw, South Carolina, and Related Families.* Newton, Miss.: Elsie Chapman Edmonds, 1971.

Elliott, E. N., ed. *Cotton Is King, and Pro-Slavery Arguments: Comprising the Writings of Hammond, Harper, Christy, Stringfellow, Hodge, Bledsoe, and Cartwright, on This Important Subject.* Augusta, Ga.: Pritchard, Abbott, and Loomis, 1860.

Emerson, Edward Waldo. *Life and Letters of Charles Russell Lowell.* Boston: Houghton Mifflin, 1907.

Evans, Clement A. *Confederate Military History: A Library of Confederate States History.* 12 vols. Atlanta: Confederate Publishing Co., 1899.

Evans, Clement A., and Robert S. Bridgers. *Confederate Military History: A Library of Confederate States History.* 17 vols. Wilmington, N.C.: Broadfoot Publishing Co., 1987.

Evans, Thomas J., and James M. Moyer. *Mosby's Confederacy: A Guide to the Roads and Sites of Colonel John Singleton Mosby.* Shippensburg, Pa.: White Mane Publishing Co., 1991.

Field, Ron, and Robin Smith. *Uniforms of the Civil War.* Guilford, Conn.: Lyons Press, 2001.

Ford, Lacy K., Jr. *Origins of Southern Radicalism: The South Carolina Upcountry, 1800–1860.* New York: Oxford University Press, 1988.

Fox, William F. *Regimental Losses in the American Civil War, 1861–1865: A Treatise on the Extent and Nature of the Mortuary Losses in the Union Regiments, with Full and Exhaustive Statistics Compiled from the Official Records on File in the State Military Bureaus and at Washington.* Albany: Albany Publishing Co., 1889.

Freeman, Douglas Southall. *R. E. Lee: A Biography.* 4 vols. New York: Charles Scribner's Sons, 1934–35.

Gaines, William H., Jr. *Biographical Register of Members: Virginia State Convention of 1861, First Session.* Richmond: Virginia State Library, 1969.

Gallagher, Gary W. Introduction to *The Long Arm of Lee; or, The History of the Artillery of the Army of Northern Virginia,* by Jennings Cropper Wise, 1:1–13. Lincoln: University of Nebraska Press, 1991.

Garnett, James M. "Personal Recollections of the University of Virginia at the Outbreak of the War of 1861–65." *Alumni Bulletin of the University of Virginia,* 3rd ser., 5, no. 3 (July 1912): 331–39.

Gibbon, John. *The Artillerist's Manual, Compiled from Various Sources, and Adapted to the Service of the United States.* New York: Van Nostrand, 1860.

Gilham, William. *Manual of Instruction for the Volunteers and Militia of the Confederate States.* Richmond: West and Johnston, 1862.

Gold, Thomas Daniel. *History of Clarke County, Virginia, and Its Connection with the War between the States.* Berryville, Va.: C. R. Hughes, 1914.

Grant, Ulysses S. *Personal Memoirs of U.S. Grant.* 2 vols. New York: Charles L. Webster, 1885–86.

Hall, Hillman A. *History of the Sixth New York Cavalry (Second Ira Harris Guard) Second Brigade—First Division—Cavalry Corps, Army of the Potomac, 1861–1865.* Worcester: Blanchard Press, 1908.

Hardy, Stella Pickett. *Colonial Families of the Southern States of America: A History and Genealogy of Colonial Families Who Settled in the Colonies prior to the Revolution.* 2d ed. Baltimore: Southern Book Co., 1958.

Hayden, Horace Edwin. *Virginia Genealogies: A Genealogy of the Glassell Family of Scotland and Virginia; Also of the Families of Ball, Brown, Bryan, Conway, Daniel, Ewell, Holladay, Lewis, Littlepage, Moncure, Peyton, Robinson, Scott, Taylor, Wallace, and Others, of Virginia and Maryland.* 1891. Reprint, Baltimore: Genealogical Publishing Co., 1979.

Hayes, Rutherford B. *Diary and Letters of Rutherford Birchard Hayes, Nineteenth President of the United States.* Edited by Charles Richard Williams. 5 vols. Columbus: Ohio State Archeological and Historical Society, 1922–26.

Hazlett, James C., Edwin Olmstead, and M. Hume Parks. *Field Artillery Weapons of the Civil War.* 2d ed. Newark: University of Delaware Press, 1988.

Hennessy, John J. *Historical Report on the Troop Movements for the Second Battle of Manassas, August 28 through August 30, 1862.* Denver: U.S. Dept. of the Interior, National Park Service, 1985.

———. *Return to Bull Run: The Campaign and Battle of Second Manassas.* New York: Simon and Schuster, 1993.

———. *Second Manassas Battlefield Map Study.* Lynchburg, Va.: H. E. Howard, 1991.

Hewett, Janet B., et al., eds. *Supplement to the Official Records of the Union and Confederate Armies.* Part 1: Reports, 12 vols. Part 2: Record of Events, 80 vols. Part 3: Correspondence. Wilmington, N.C.: Broadfoot Publishing Co., 1994–.

Hoadley, J. C. *Memorial of Henry Sanford Gansevoort.* Boston: Rand, Avery and Co., 1875.

Holcombe, James P. *An Address Delivered before the Seventh Annual Meeting of the Virginia State Agricultural Society, November 4th, 1858.* Richmond: Macfarlane and Fergusson, 1858.

———. *The Election of a Black Republican President an Overt Act of Aggression on the Right of Property in Slaves: The South Urged to Adopt Concerted Action for Future Safety.* Richmond: Chas. H. Wynne, 1860.

"How the Seven Days' Battle around Richmond Began." *Southern Historical Society Papers* 28 (1900): 90–97.

Humphreys, Charles A. *Field, Camp, Hospital and Prison in the Civil War, 1863–1865.* Boston: George H. Ellis, 1918.

Hunter, Alexander. *The Women of the Debatable Land.* Washington, D.C.: Cobden Publishing Co., 1912.

Jessup, Harlan R. *The Painful News I Have to Write: Letters and Diaries of Four Hite Brothers of Page County in the Service of the Confederacy.* Baltimore: Butternut and Blue, 1998.

Jones, Virgil Carrington. *Gray Ghosts and Rebel Raiders.* New York: Henry Holt, 1956.

———. *Ranger Mosby.* Chapel Hill: University of North Carolina Press, 1944.

Jordan, Ervin L., Jr. *Charlottesville and the University of Virginia in the Civil War.* 2d ed. Lynchburg, Va.: H. E. Howard, 1988.

Keen, Hugh C., and Horace Mewborn. *43rd Battalion Virginia Cavalry: Mosby's Command.* 2d ed. Lynchburg, Va.: H. E. Howard, 1993.

Kerkhoff, Jennie Ann. *Old Homes of Page County, Virginia.* Luray, Va.: Lauck and Co., 1962.

Krick, Robert K. *Lee's Colonels: A Biographical Register of the Field Officers of the Army of Northern Virginia.* Dayton: Press of Morningside Bookshop, 1979.

Lee, Stephen D. "The Artillery at Second Manassas: Rejoinder of General S. D. Lee to General Longstreet." *Southern Historical Society Papers* 6 (1878): 250–54.

———. "The Second Battle of Manassas: A Reply to General Longstreet." *Southern Historical Society Papers* 6 (1878): 59–70.

Lee, Susan P. *Memoirs of William Nelson Pendleton, D.D., Rector of Latimer Parish, Lexington, Virginia; Brigadier-General C.S.A.; Chief of Artillery, Army of Northern Virginia.* Philadelphia: J. B. Lippincott Co., 1893.

"Life at Mossy Creek Academy." *Augusta Historical Bulletin* [Augusta County Historical Society, Staunton, Va.] 14, no. 2 (Fall 1978): 51–52.

Livermore, Thomas L. *Numbers and Losses in the Civil War in America: 1861–65.* 1900. Reprint, with an introduction by Edward E. Barthell Jr., Bloomington: Indiana University Press, 1957.

Longstreet, James. "The Artillery at Second Manassas: General Longstreet's Reply to General S. D. Lee." *Southern Historical Society Papers* 6 (1878): 215–17.

———. *From Manassas to Appomattox: Memoirs of the Civil War in America.* Philadelphia: J. B. Lippincott, 1896.

———. "General Longstreet's Second Paper on Gettysburg." *Southern Historical Society Papers* 5 (1878): 257–70.

———. "Letter from General Longstreet." *Southern Historical Society Papers* 5 (1878): 52–53.

———. "Our March against Pope." In *Battles and Leaders of the Civil War,* edited by Robert Underwood Johnson and Clarence Clough Buel, 2:512–26. New York: Century Co., 1888.

———. "'The Seven Days,' Including Frayser's Farm." In *Battles and Leaders of the Civil*

War, edited by Robert Underwood Johnson and Clarence Clough Buel, 2:396–405. New York: Century Co., 1888.

McKim, Randolph H. *A Soldier's Recollections: Leaves from the Diary of a Young Confederate, with an Oration on the Motives and Aims of the Soldiers of the South.* New York: Longmans, Green, and Co., 1910.

McPherson, James M. *Battle Cry of Freedom.* New York: Oxford University Press, 1988.

———. *For Cause and Comrades: Why Men Fought in the Civil War.* New York: Oxford University Press, 1997.

———. *What They Fought For, 1861–1865.* Baton Rouge: Louisiana State University Press, 1994.

Melville, Herman. *Battle-Pieces and Aspects of the War.* New York: Harper, 1866.

Miller, Ann L. *Antebellum Orange: The Pre–Civil War Homes, Public Buildings and Historic Sites of Orange County, Virginia.* Orange, Va.: Orange County Historical Society, 1988.

Miller, William J. *Mapping for Stonewall: The Civil War Service of Jed Hotchkiss.* Washington, D.C.: Elliott and Clark, 1993.

Mitchell, Adele. H., ed. *The Letters of John S. Mosby.* 2d ed. Richmond: Stuart-Mosby Historical Society, 1986.

Monteiro, Aristides. *War Reminiscences by the Surgeon of Mosby's Command.* Richmond, 1890.

Moore, Robert H., II. *Chew's Ashby, Shoemaker's Lynchburg and the Newtown Artillery.* Lynchburg, Va.: H. E. Howard, 1995.

———. *The Danville, Eighth Star New Market and Dixie Artillery.* Lynchburg, Va.: H. E. Howard, 1989.

———. *Miscellaneous Disbanded Virginia Light Artillery.* Lynchburg, Va.: H. E. Howard, 1997.

———. *The Richmond Fayette, Hampden, Thomas, and Blount's Lynchburg Artillery.* Lynchburg, Va.: H. E. Howard, 1991.

Mosby, John Singleton. *The Memoirs of Colonel John S. Mosby.* Edited by Charles Wells Russell. Boston: Little, Brown, and Co., 1917.

———. *Mosby's War Reminiscences and Stuart's Cavalry Campaigns.* New York: Dodd, Mead, and Co., 1887.

Moyer, Henry P. *History of the Seventeenth Regiment Pennsylvania Volunteer Cavalry; or, One Hundred and Sixty-Second in the Line of Pennsylvania Volunteer Regiments, War to Suppress the Rebellion, 1861–1865.* Lebanon, Pa.: Sowers Printing Co., 1911.

Munson, John W. *Reminiscences of a Mosby Guerrilla.* New York: Moffat, Yard, and Co., 1906.

Newhall, Walter Symonds. *A Memoir.* Philadelphia: Sanitary Commission, 1864.

Owen, William Miller. *In Camp and Battle with the Washington Artillery of New Orleans: A Narrative of Events during the Late Civil War from Bull Run to Appomattox and Spanish Fort.* Boston: Ticknor and Co., 1885.

Patteson, William W. "Swift Retribution for House-Burning." *Confederate Veteran* 12, no. 10 (1904): 472.

Patton, John S. *Jefferson, Cabell and the University of Virginia.* New York: Neale Publishing Co., 1906.

Payne, John M. "University of Virginia Companies." *Confederate Veteran* 40, no. 7 (1932): 256–58.

Perkins, George. *A Summer in Maryland and Virginia; or, Campaigning with the 149th Ohio Volunteer Infantry.* Chillicothe, Ohio: Scholl Printing Co., 1911.

Poole, John Randolph. *Cracker Cavaliers: The 2nd Georgia Cavalry under Wheeler and Forrest.* Macon, Ga.: Mercer University Press, 2000.

Ramage, James A. *Gray Ghost: The Life of Col. John Singleton Mosby.* Lexington: University Press of Kentucky, 1999.

Reese, George H., ed. *Proceedings of the Virginia State Convention of 1861, February 13–May 1.* 4 vols. Richmond: Virginia State Library, 1965.

Richards, A. E. "Mosby's 'Partizan Rangers.'" In *Famous Adventures and Prison Escapes of the Civil War,* 102–15. New York: Century Co., 1893.

Robertson, Frank S. "The Sons of Liberty." *Confederate Veteran* 22, no. 9 (1914): 399.

Scott, John. *Partisan Life with Col. John S. Mosby.* New York: Harper, 1867.

Sears, Stephen W. *Landscape Turned Red: The Battle of Antietam.* New York: Ticknor and Fields, 1983.

———. *To the Gates of Richmond: The Peninsula Campaign.* New York: Ticknor and Fields, 1992.

Shanks, Henry T. *The Secession Movement in Virginia, 1847–1861.* Richmond: Garrett and Massie, 1934.

Shields, John C. "The Old Camp Lee." *Southern Historical Society Papers* 26 (1898): 241–46.

Siepel, Kevin H. *Rebel: The Life and Times of John Singleton Mosby.* New York: St. Martin's Press, 1983.

Sifakis, Stewart. *Compendium of the Confederate Armies.* Vol. 9: *Louisiana.* New York: Facts on File Publications, 1995.

———. *Who Was Who in the Civil War.* New York: Facts on File Publications, 1988.

Smith, Peter Bartow, Jr. "The History of Bethel Military Academy, Warrenton, Virginia." Master's thesis, University of Virginia, 1945.

Smythe, Gerald. "An Englishman's Visit to Capt. R. E. Lee." *Confederate Veteran* 23, no. 6 (1915): 250–52.

Sneden, Robert Knox. *Eye of the Storm: A Civil War Odyssey.* Edited by Charles F. Bryan Jr. and Nelson D. Lankford. New York: Free Press, 2000.

Sorrel, G. Moxley. *Recollections of a Confederate Staff Officer.* New York: Neale Publishing Co., 1905.

Spratt, Thomas M. *Page County, Virginia, Men in Gray.* Athens, Ga.: Iberian Publishing Co., 1994.

Stephenson, Richard W. *Civil War Maps: An Annotated List of Maps and Atlases in the Library of Congress.* 2d ed. Washington, D.C.: Library of Congress, 1989.

Stribling, Robert M. "From Markham to Appomattox with the Fauquier Artillery." In *The Years of Anguish: Fauquier County, Virginia, 1861–1865,* edited by Emily G. Ramey and John K. Gott, 184–97. Bowie, Md.: Heritage Books, 1998.

Strickler, Harry M. *A Short History of Page County, Virginia.* Richmond: Dietz Press, 1952.

Swisher, James K. *Prince of Edisto: Brigadier General Micah Jenkins, C.S.A.* Berryville, Va.: Rockbridge Publishing Co., 1996.

Taylor, James E. *With Sheridan up the Shenandoah Valley in 1864: Leaves from a Special Artist's Sketchbook and Diary.* Cleveland: Western Reserve Historical Society, 1989.

Third Pennsylvania Cavalry Association. *History of the Third Pennsylvania Cavalry, Sixtieth Regiment Pennsylvania Volunteers, in the American Civil War, 1861–1865.* Philadelphia: Franklin Printing Co., 1905.

Thomas, Dean S. *Cannons: An Introduction to Civil War Artillery.* Gettysburg: Thomas Publications, 1985.

Thomas, John P. *Career and Character of General Micah Jenkins, C.S.A.* Columbia: State Company, 1903.

U.S. Bureau of the Census. *Official Register of the United States: Persons in the Civil, Military, and Naval Service, Exclusive of the Postal Service.* Vol. 1: *Directory.* Washington, D.C.: Government Printing Office, 1913.

———. *Official Register: Persons in the Civil, Military, and Naval Service of the United States.* Vol. 1: *Directory.* Washington, D.C.: Government Printing Office, 1907.

U.S. Department of the Interior. *Official Register of the Unites States, Containing a List of Officers and Employees in the Civil, Military, and Naval Service.* Vol. 1: *Legislative, Executive, Judicial.* Washington, D.C.: Government Printing Office, 1879.

———. *Register of Officers and Agents, Civil, Military, and Naval, in the Service of the United States.* 3 vols. Washington, D.C.: Government Printing Office, 1873–77.

U.S. Internal Revenue Service. *History of the Internal Revenue Service, 1791–1929.* Washington, D.C.: Government Printing Office, 1930.

U.S. War Department. *Atlas to Accompany the Official Records of the Union and Confederate Armies,* Washington, D.C.: Government Printing Office, 1891–95.

———. *The War of the Rebellion: A Compilation of the Official Records of the Union and Confederate Armies.* 70 vols. Washington, D.C.: Government Printing Office, 1880–1901.

Virginia General Assembly. House of Delegates. *Journal of the House of Delegates of the State of Virginia, for the Session of 1861–62.* Richmond: William F. Ritchie, 1861.

Vogt, John, and T. William Kethley Jr. *Page County Marriage Bonds, 1831–1850.* Athens, Ga.: Iberian Press, 1983.

Wall, Charles Coleman, Jr. "Students and Student Life at the University of Virginia, 1825 to 1861." Ph.D. diss., University of Virginia, 1978.

Wallace, Lee A., Jr. *A Guide to Virginia Military Organizations, 1861–1865.* 2d ed. Lynchburg, Va.: H. E. Howard, 1986.

———. *The Richmond Howitzers.* Lynchburg, Va.: H. E. Howard, 1993.

Walton, J. B. "Letter from Colonel J. B. Walton." *Southern Historical Society Papers* 5 (1878): 47–52.

Ward, Evelyn D. *The Children of Bladensfield.* New York: Viking Press, 1978.

Weaver, Jeffrey C. *Goochland Light, Goochland Turner and Mountain Artillery.* Lynchburg, Va.: H. E. Howard, 1994.

Webster, Daniel. *The Writings and Speeches of Daniel Webster.* 18 vols. Boston: Little, Brown, and Co., 1903.

Wert, Jeffry D. *From Winchester to Cedar Creek: The Shenandoah Campaign of 1864.* Carlisle, Pa.: South Mountain Press, 1987.

———. *General James Longstreet: The Confederacy's Most Controversial Soldier; A Biography.* New York: Simon and Schuster, 1993.

———. *Mosby's Rangers.* New York: Simon and Schuster, 1990.

Williamson, James J. *Mosby's Rangers: A Record of the Operations of the Forty-third Battalion of Virginia Cavalry, from Its Organization to the Surrender.* New York: Ralph B. Kenyon, 1896.

———. *Mosby's Rangers: A Record of the Operations of the Forty-third Battalion of Virginia Cavalry from Its Organization to the Surrender.* 2d ed. New York: Sturgis and Walton, 1909.

Wise, Jennings Cropper. *The Long Arm of Lee; or, The History of the Artillery of the Army of Northern Virginia with a Brief Account of the Confederate Bureau of Ordnance.* 2 vols. Lynchburg, Va.: J. P. Bell, 1915.

Wooster, Ralph A. *The Secession Conventions of the South.* Princeton: Princeton University Press, 1962.

Writers' Program (U.S.). *Old Homes and Families of Fauquier County, Virginia (The W.P.A. Records).* Berryville, Va.: Virginia Book Co., 1978.

Yowell, Claude Lindsay. *A History of Madison County, Virginia.* Strasburg, Va.: Shenandoah Publishing House, 1926.

INDEX

The initials WHC are used to refer to William Henry Chapman in subheadings. "*Gallery*" indicates illustrations in the gallery, following page 76.

Gordon B. Bonan is a senior scientist at the National Center for Atmospheric Research in Boulder, Colorado. He has published three books on ecology and climatology and more than one hundred scientific articles and papers on climate–vegetation interactions. He is a descendant of William H. Chapman.